SCHOLASTIC

GO MATHS

Ruchi Mehta

Course Book

Level 7

Cover design by Kavita C. Dikshit

Published by Scholastic India Pvt. Ltd.
A subsidiary of Scholastic Inc., New York, 10012 (USA)
Publishers since 1920, with international operations in Canada, Australia, New Zealand, the United Kingdom, India, and Hong Kong.

For information regarding permission, write to:
Scholastic India Pvt. Ltd.
A-27, Ground Floor, Bharti Sigma Centre
Infocity-1, Sector 34, Gurgaon (Haryana) - 122001
Email: education@scholastic.co.in

Typeset by: Access to Solutions

Series editor: Sonia Kapoor

First edition: 2010
Reprinted: 2011 (thrice), 2012 (twice), 2013 (twice), 2014 (thrice), 2015, 2016 (thrice),
2017, 2018 (twice), 2019 (twice), 2020, 2021, 2022, 2023, 2024, 2026

ISBN-13: 978-81-8477-495-5

Contents

Introduction

Go Maths is a graded series of middle school mathematics course books that have been authored by a highly respected and experienced mathematics educator. The series conforms to the NCERT syllabus and the books are provided with tools for Continuous and Comprehensive Evaluation (CCE). The objective of these books is to move away from the rote method of learning and associate the knowledge gained with everyday life experiences.

These books are designed to help students learn a wide range of mathematical concepts including the number system, algebra, geometry, mensuration, data handling and much more. Each topic has a set of challenging and imaginative activities.

The *Go Maths* series is comprehensive and rigorous. It has been created based on the following beliefs:

Learning through involvement

Students learn through involvement and substantive communication between teachers and students, as well as between students and students. This helps students internalise and acquire new skills

Learning through interaction

Students build their mathematical understanding by interacting with the world around them through a range of engaging learning experiences using real-life contexts to explore mathematical ideas. Quality teaching and learning is required for students to develop a rich conceptual understanding of mathematical ideas.

Learning through thinking critically

Learning should be as much 'minds on' as it is 'hands on'. Students should be encouraged to think critically.

Learning through practice

Skills should be practiced after they have developed from deep conceptual understanding.

Some of the unique features of this series are:

- ➢ Mathematical concepts introduced in a simple and concise manner and aid in developing sharp calculation skills and clear concepts.
- ➢ Summary **Highlights** at the end of each chapter and **Rewind** after every two chapters to recapitulate and reinforce concepts and formulae.
- ➢ Several practice exercises, **Test Yourself** and a **Model question paper** to assess mathematical proficiency with a focus on confidence, speed and accuracy.
- ➢ Enrichment material and **HOTS** questions for curious minds and fast finishers.
- ➢ Maths Lab Activity to strengthen basic mathematical concepts.
- ➢ **Alert**, a section emphasising the important points, and brainteasers/jokes in every chapter.

The *Go Maths* series provides an innovative and interactive approach to learning mathematics. The emphasis on critical thinking ensures that students learn concepts and basic operations with great thoroughness and clarity.

Ruchi Mehta is a post graduate in mathematics with 35 years of teaching experience. She started her career from St Joseph's College, Allahabad and has taught at Mount Saint Mary's, New Delhi, for 31 years. Post retirement she is a visiting faculty at DPS, Gurgaon and Mount Saint Mary's, New Delhi.

Integers

CHAPTER 1

The various types of numbers that we know of are as follows:

Natural numbers (N): The counting numbers such as 1, 2, 3, 4, 5, 6, 7, 8, 9 ... are called natural numbers.

Whole numbers (W): All natural numbers together with 0 (zero) are called whole numbers. Every natural number is a whole number but '0' is a whole number that is not a natural number.

Integers (Z or I): All natural numbers, 0 and the negatives of counting numbers are called integers. Thus, ... −5, −4, −3, −2, −1, 0, 1, 2, 3, 4, 5 ... are all integers.

Positive integers: The numbers 1, 2, 3, 4, 5 ... are positive integers.

Negative integers: The numbers −1, −2, −3, −4, −5 ... are negative integers.

Zero is an integer that is neither positive nor negative.

Alert!

1. The addition of a natural number to another natural number always results in a natural number.
2. The subtraction of any natural number from itself yields zero.
3. When a larger natural number is subtracted from a smaller natural number, we get a negative integer.

Addition and Subtraction of Integers

The properties of integers are mentioned in brief below.

Properties of Addition and Subtraction of Integers

1. Closure property

If we add or subtract two integers, the answer is always an integer.

2. Commutative property

If we add two integers, the result does not depend on the placement of the integers. Hence, addition of integers is commutative. If a and b are two integers, then

$$a + b = b + a$$

If we subtract two integers, the result depends on the placement and value of the integers. Hence, subtraction of integers is not commutative.

$$a - b \neq b - a$$

3. Associative property

When we add three or more integers, the result does not depend on their grouping. Hence, addition of integers is associative.

$$(a + b) + c = a + (b + c)$$

When we subtract three or more integers, the result depends on their grouping. Hence, subtraction of integers is not associative.

$$(a - b) - c \neq a - (b - c)$$

4. Additive identity

Zero is the additive identity. If we add 0 to any integer or any integer to 0, the answer is the same integer.

$$a + 0 = a = 0 + a$$

Practice Exercise 1.1

1. Write the additive inverse of the following numbers.
   a. (-87) b. 253 c. 0 d. (-2010) e. 18
2. Evaluate the following.
   a. $15 + (-7)$ b. $(-17) + 8$ c. $(-8) + (-24)$
   d. $(-96) + 45$ e. $(-61) + (-16)$
3. Find the sum of the following numbers.
   a. 151 and (-202) b. 1,001 and (-275) c. $(-3{,}031)$ and 942
   d. (-487) and (-683) e. (-146) and 146
4. Subtract the following.
   a. 28 from (-46) b. (-35) from 71 c. 219 from 0
   d. (-47) from (-57) e. (-66) from (-38)
5. Subtract the sum of (-32) and 78 from (-34).
6. Subtract (-24) from the sum of 38 and (-83).
7. The sum of two integers is (-18). If one of them is 53, find the other.
8. The sum of three integers is 65. If two of them are (-31) and 14, find the third integer.
9. Given that $a = (-10)$, $b = 7$ and $c = (-3)$, verify that addition is commutative and associative. Also show that subtraction is neither commutative nor associative.
10. For each of the following statements, indicate whether they are true (T) or false (F).
    a. The smallest integer is 0.
    b. The number (-15) is greater than (-10).
    c. Zero is larger than every negative integer.
    d. The sum of two negative integers is a negative integer.
    e. The sum of a negative integer and a positive integer is always a positive integer.

Multiplication of Integers

Multiplication is repeated addition. For instance, 4×3 means that the number 4 has to be added three times. Hence, 4×3 is the same as $4 + 4 + 4$.

$$4 \times 3 = 4 + 4 + 4 = 12$$

If we have a negative integer such as -2, then

$$(-2) \times 4 = (-2) + (-2) + (-2) + (-2) = (-8)$$

Let us observe a pattern

$$\left.\begin{aligned} 5 \times 4 &= 20 \\ 5 \times 3 &= 15 \\ 5 \times 2 &= 10 \\ 5 \times 1 &= 5 \\ 5 \times 0 &= 0 \end{aligned}\right\} \text{ Here the values are decreasing by 5.}$$

Let us proceed further below 0 to the negative integers.

$$\left.\begin{aligned} 5 \times (-1) &= (-5) \\ 5 \times (-2) &= (-10) \\ 5 \times (-3) &= (-15) \end{aligned}\right\} \text{ Here also the values are decreasing by 5.}$$

Hence, if we multiply a positive integer with a negative integer, the product is negative.

If we have

$$\left.\begin{aligned} (-5) \times 3 &= (-15) \\ (-5) \times 2 &= (-10) \\ (-5) \times 1 &= (-5) \\ (-5) \times 0 &= 0 \end{aligned}\right\} \text{ Here the answer is increasing by 5.}$$

Hence, if we multiply a negative integer with a positive integer, the answer is a negative integer, the exception being 0.

Let us proceed further.

$$\left.\begin{aligned} (-5) \times (-1) &= 5 \\ (-5) \times (-2) &= 10 \\ (-5) \times (-3) &= 15 \end{aligned}\right\} \text{ Here the answer is increasing by 5.}$$

Hence, we see that if we multiply a negative integer with a negative integer, the answer is a positive integer.

From the above pattern, we can formulate the following rules for multiplication of integers.

Rule 1: The product of two integers of the same sign (i.e. either both positive or both negative) is a positive integer.

Rule 2: The product of two integers of different signs (i.e. one positive and one negative) is a negative integer.

Alert!

positive × positive = positive negative × negative = positive	Rule 1
positive × negative = negative negative × positive = negative	Rule 2

Properties of Multiplication of Integers

1. Closure property

The product of two integers is always an integer. If a and b are two integers, then $a \times b = c$ is also an integer. This is the closure property of multiplication of integers.

Example 1 : $(-7) \times (-2) = 14$ (integer)

Example 2 : $(-3) \times 5 = (-15)$ (integer)

Example 3 : $5 \times (-7) = (-35)$ (integer)

Example 4 : $4 \times 8 = 32$ (integer)

2. Commutative property

According to the commutative property, if a and b are any two integers, then $a \times b = b \times a$. The product of two integers remains unchanged even if the order of the integers is changed.

Example 1 : $(-2) \times 7 = (-14) = 7 \times (-2)$

Example 2 : $3 \times 5 = 15 = 5 \times 3$

Example 3 : $(-4) \times (-8) = 32 = +(-8) \times (-4)$

3. Associative property

According to the associative property, the product of three numbers remains unchanged even if the grouping is changed. Thus, if a, b and c are three integers, then $(a \times b) \times c = a \times (b \times c)$.

This is the associative property of multiplication of integers.

Example 1 : $[(-2) \times (-3)] \times 4 = (-2) \times [(-3) \times 4]$

$$6 \times 4 = (-2) \times (-12)$$

$$24 = 24$$

Example 2 : $[5 \times (-4)] \times (-6) = 5 \times [(-4) \times (-6)]$

$$(-20) \times (-6) = 5 \times 24$$

$$120 = 120$$

4. Distributive property

If a, b and c are three integers, then a × (b + c) = a × b + a × c.

We say that multiplication distributes over addition.

This is the distributive property of multiplication over addition.

Example 1 : $3 \times [(-4) + (-5)] = 3 \times (-4) + 3 \times (-5)$

$$3 \times (-9) = (-12) + (-15)$$
$$(-27) = (-27)$$
$$(-5) \times [(-6) + (-7)] = (-5) \times (-6) + (-5) \times (-7)$$
$$(-5) \times (-13) = 30 + 35$$
$$65 = 65$$

5. Multiplicative identity

When we multiply any integer by the number 1 or 1 by any integer, its value does not change. Thus for every integer a, we have a × 1 = 1 × a = a. The integer 1 is the multiplicative identity for integers.

Example 1: $(-6) \times 1 = (-6)$ and $1 \times (-6) = (-6)$

Example 2: $5 \times 1 = 5$ and $1 \times 5 = 5$

6. Multiplication by 0

When any integer is multiplied by 0, the product is always 0. Hence, for every integer a, a × 0 = 0 × a = 0.

Example: $7 \times 0 = 0$ and $(-7) \times 0 = 0$

7. Multiplicative inverse

An integer multiplied by its multiplicative inverse is equal to 1 (the multiplicative identity). Hence, for every non-zero integer a, the number $\frac{1}{a}$ is the multiplicative inverse of a.

So, $$a \times \frac{1}{a} = \frac{1}{a} \times a = 1$$

Example 1: $6 \times \frac{1}{6} = 1$

Example 2: $\frac{1}{(-7)} \times (-7) = 1$

8. Product of three or more negative integers

If we multiply two negative integers, we know that the answer is a positive integer.

Example: $(-2) \times (-3) = 61$

Now let us multiply three negative integers.

The product obtained by multiplying three negative integers is a negative integer.

Example: $\underbrace{(-2) \times (-3)} \times (-4) = 6 \times (-4) = (-24)$

Now let us multiply four negative integers.

Here, $\underbrace{(-2) \times (-3)} \times (-4) \times (-5)$

$$= \underbrace{6 \times (-4)} \times (-5) = \underbrace{(-24) \times (-5)} = 120$$

Thus, from the pattern we observe that if we multiply an *even* number of negative integers, the product will be a positive integer. If we multiply an *odd* number of negative integers, the product will be a negative integer.

Alert!

A negative integer (-1) multiplied by itself an odd number of times $= (-1)$.
A negative integer (-1) multiplied by itself an even number of times $= 1$.

Example 1: Find the products of the following.

a. $(-7) \times (-8) = 56$

Both the integers have negative signs, therefore their product is a positive integer.

b. $8 \times (-5) = (-40)$

One integer is positive and the other is negative, so the product is a negative integer.

c. $14 \times 5 = 70$

Both integers are positive, so their product is also a positive integer.

d. $(-10) \times 11 = (-110)$

One integer is negative and the other is positive, so their product is a negative integer.

Example 2: Find the products of the following.

a. $(-12) \times (-6) = 72$

Here there are two negative integers, i.e. an even number of integers, therefore their product is a positive integer.

b. $(-8) \times (-4) \times (-2) = (-64)$

Here there are three negative integers, i.e. there are an odd number of integers, therefore their product is a negative integer.

c. $(-10) \times (-5) \times (-3) \times (-1) = 150$

Here there are four negative integers, i.e. there are an even number of integers, therefore their product is a positive integer.

d. $(-3) \times (-6) \times (-9) \times (-2) \times (-1) = (-324)$

Here there are five negative integers, i.e. there are an odd number of integers, therefore their product is a negative integer.

Example 3: Find the products of the following using the distributive property of multiplication.

a. $(-4025) \times 29 + (-4025) \times 71$
$= (-4025)[29 + 71]$
$= (-4025)(100) = (-402500)$

b. $(-425) \times 98 + (-425) \times 2$
$= (-425)[98 + 2]$
$= (-425)(100) = (-42500)$

c. $(-76) \times 4 + (-76) \times 5 + (-76)$
$= (-76)[4 + 5 + 1]$
$= (-76) \times 10 = (-760)$

Division of Integers

We know that division is the inverse operation of multiplication. So, when $4 \times 6 = 24$, we can say that $24 \div 4 = 6$, or $24 \div 6 = 4$. For each multiplication statement, there are two division statements.

Example 1: If $(-5) \times 6 = (-30)$,
then, $(-30) \div (-5) = 6$ and $(-30) \div 6 = (-5)$

Example 2: If $(-5) \times (-7) = 35$,
then, $(35) \div (-5) = (-7)$ and $(35) \div (-7) = (-5)$

By observing the above division patterns, we can formulate the following rules for division of integers.

Rule 1: When the dividend and the divisor have the same sign (i.e., either both are positive or both are negative), the quotient has a positive sign.

Rule 2: When the dividend and the divisor have different signs (i.e., one is negative and the other is positive), the quotient has a negative sign.

Alert!

positive ÷ positive = positive negative ÷ negative = positive	Rule 1
positive ÷ negative = negative negative ÷ positive = negative	Rule 2

Properties of Division of Integers

1. Closure property

If a and b are two integers, then their quotient may not always be an integer. Thus, the closure property is not always true for the division of integers.

Example 1: $(-30) \div (5) = (-6)$ (integer)

Example 2: $(-7) \div (-7) = 1$ (integer)

Example 3: But $(-7) \div (-8) = \frac{7}{8}$ (*not* an integer)

Example 4: $(25) \div (-3) = \left(-\frac{25}{3}\right)$ (*not* an integer)

2. Commutative property

If a and b are two integers, then their quotient may or may not be an integer. Thus, $a \div b = \frac{a}{b}$ is not equal to $b \div a = \frac{b}{a}$ since $\frac{a}{b} \neq \frac{b}{a}$. Hence the commutative property is not true for division of integers.

Example 1: $15 \div (-5) = (-3)$ but $(-5) \div 15 = \left(-\frac{1}{3}\right)$

Example 2: $(-18) \div 3 = (-6)$ but $3 \div (-18) = \frac{3}{(-18)}$

3. Associative property

If a, b and c are three integers, then $(a \div b) \div c \neq a \div (b \div c)$. Thus, the associative property is not true for division of integers.

Example: $[15 \div (-3)] \div 2 \neq 15 \div [(-3) \div 2]$

$$\left(\frac{15}{-3}\right) \div \frac{2}{1} \neq 15 \div \left[\frac{(-3)}{2}\right]$$

$$(-5) \div \frac{2}{1} \neq 15 \div \left(\frac{-3}{2}\right)$$

$$(-5) \times \frac{1}{2} \neq 15 \times \frac{2}{(-3)}$$

$$-\frac{5}{2} \neq \frac{30}{(-3)}$$

$$\left(-\frac{5}{2}\right) \neq (-10)$$

4. Division of an integer by itself

For any integer a, where a is not equal to 0, if it is divided by itself, the result will always be 1.

Thus, $(-4) \div (-4) = \frac{(-4)}{(-4)} = 1$ and $7 \div 7 = \frac{7}{7} = 1$

5. Division of an integer by 1

Any integer divided by 1, is the integer itself.

Thus, $7 \div 1 = \frac{7}{1} = 7$ and $(-8) \div 1 = \frac{(-8)}{1} = (-8)$

6. Division of 0 by an integer

When 0 is divided by any integer a, where a is not equal to 0, the result is 0.

Thus, $0 \div (-4) = \frac{0}{(-4)} = 0$ and $0 \div (5) = \frac{0}{5} = 0$

7. Division of an integer by 0

Integers cannot be divided by 0. Division is the inverse operation of multiplication. Let us assume that the answer to $\frac{a}{0} = x$. As division is the inverse operation of multiplication, $x \times 0$ should be a. But, we know that $x \times 0 = 0$.

Hence, $a \div 0 = \frac{a}{0}$, which is not possible.

Example 1: Divide the following.

a. $45 \div (-5) = (-9)$

Here the dividend is a positive integer and the quotient is a negative integer. Hence, the divisor will be a negative integer.

The dividend and the divisor have different signs.

b. $121 \div 11 = 11$

Here the dividend and the divisor are both positive. Hence, the quotient is also a positive integer. The dividend and divisor have the same sign.

c. $(-81) \div 9 = (-9)$

Here the dividend is a negative integer and the quotient is a negative integer. Hence, the divisor is a positive integer.

The dividend and divisor have different signs.

d. $(-200) \div (-10) = 20$

Here the dividend is a negative integer and the quotient is a positive integer. Hence, the divisor is a negative integer.

The dividend and divisor have the same sign.

Example 2: The product of two integers is (-54). If one of them is (-6), find the other.
The required integer will be $(-54) \div (-6) = 9$.

Example 3: Divide the product of (-3), (-5) and (-2) by the sum of (-7) and (-3).
Product of (-3), (-5) and (-2) will be

$$(-3) \times (-5) \times (-2) = (-30)$$

Here we have an odd number of negative integers, so their product will be a negative integer.

The sum of (-7) and (-3) will be $(-7) + (-3) = (-10)$

$$(-30) \div (-10) = 3$$

The dividend as well as the divisor have the same sign. Hence, the quotient will be positive.

Practice Exercise 1.2

1. Multiply the following.

a. $(-7) \times 12$
b. $14 \times (-6)$
c. $(-10) \times (-8)$
d. 16×5
e. $0 \times (-23)$
f. $(-18) \times (-1)$

g. $(-17) \times 1$ h. $(-20) \times (-5)$
i. $(-28) \times 2$ j. $24 \times (-4)$

2. Multiply the following using the associative property.
   a. $(-2) \times (-3) \times 5$ b. $(-7) \times 10 \times 11$ c. $(-4) \times 7 \times (-10)$
   d. $(-9) \times 7 \times (-5)$ e. $6 \times 7 \times (-8)$

3. Multiply the following using the associative property.
   a. $(-3) \times (-3) \times (-3)$
   b. $(-4) \times (-4) \times (-4) \times (-4)$
   c. $(-5) \times (-4) \times (-3) \times (-2) \times (-1)$
   d. $(-6) \times (-3) \times (-1) \times (-2) \times (-4) \times (-8)$
   e. $(-2) \times (-4) \times (-6) \times (-1) \times (-3) \times (-5) \times (-2)$

4. Find the value of the following using the distributive property.
   a. $19 \times (-13) + 19 \times (-7)$
   b. $(-517) \times 9 + (-517)$
   c. $(-700) \times 49 + (-700)$
   d. $(-2478) \times 96 + (-2478) \times 4$
   e. $(-3989) \times 8 + 3989 \times (-92)$

5. Which of the two is greater and by how much—the product of (-27) and 77 or the product of (-35) and 65?

6. Divide the following.
   a. 65 by (-5) b. (-72) by 12
   c. (-18) by (-3) d. 54 by 6
   e. (-91) by 7 f. 150 by (-25)
   g. (-105) by (-21) h. (-38) by (-1)
   i. (-48) by 1 j. (-73) by 73

7. Solve the following.
   a. $[(-5) \times (-8)] \div [(-2) \times (-10)]$
   b. $[(-7) \times (-6)] \div [3 \times (-7)]$
   c. $[9 \times (-8)] \div [(-2) \times (-6)]$
   d. $[(-18) \times 3] \div [(-6) \times (-9)]$
   e. $[(-100) \div 20] \div [25 \div (-5)]$

8. Divide the sum of (-23), (-62) and (-25) by the product of (-11) and 10.

9. Subtract (-40) from (-100) and then divide the difference by the product of (-6) and 5.

10. Divide (-125) by 25 and then add the quotient to the product of (-30) and (-3).

Order of Operations

We have studied four basic operations on integers—addition, subtraction, multiplication and division. When a mathematical expression consists of all the four operations, we follow a rule to simplify the expression. This is done so that we all come to the same result, otherwise it could differ.

Example: The expression $24 - 6 \div 2 + 5$ can be simplified as $18 \div 2 + 5 = 9 + 5 = 14$.

Here we first carry out subtraction, then division and finally addition. Another way of solving the expression is as follows:

$$24 - 6 \div 7 = 18 \div 7 = \frac{18}{7}$$

Here we first carry out addition, then subtraction and finally division. This is how we arrive at two different answers.

Hence, it is important to have a rule to simplify an expression. To simplify an expression involving all four operations, the order is "DMAS", which implies division (first), multiplication (second), addition (third) and subtraction (fourth).

Now we apply the rule to the given expression and solve it.

$24 - \underbrace{6 \div 2} + 5$	(division)
	(no multiplication)
$= \underbrace{24 - 3 + 5}$	(addition)
$= 29 - 3$	(subtraction)
$= 26$	

Example 1: Find the value of $(-7) + (-15) \div 3 + (-2) \times 5$ using the order DMAS.

$(-7) + \underbrace{(-15) \div 3} + (-2) \times 5$	(division)
$= (-7) + (-5) + \underbrace{(-2) \times 5}$	(multiplication)
$= (-7) + (-5) + (-10)$	
$= (-7) + (-5) + (-10)$	(addition)
Answer: (-22)	

Example 2: Find the value of, $19 - 18 \div 2 + 14 \times (-1)$ using the order DMAS.

$19 - \underbrace{18 \div 2} + 14 \times (-1)$	(division)
$= 19 - 9 + \underbrace{14 \times (-1)}$	(multiplication)
$= 19 - 9 + (-14)$	(addition)
$= \underbrace{19 + (-14)} - 9$	(subtraction)
$= \underbrace{5 - 9}$	(addition)
$= (-4)$	
Answer: (-4)	

Practice Exercise 1.3

1. Solve the following expressions.

a. $(-18) + (-15) - 24$ b. $(-21) + 14 + 21$

c. $(-16) + (-18) - (-20)$ d. $72 - (-20) + (-18)$

e. $(-19) + 42 - (-61)$

2. Solve the following expressions.

a. $(-24) + 15 \times (-2)$
b. $(-16) \times 2 + (-24)$
c. $(-8) \times 3 + 17 \times (-2) + (-68)$
d. $100 + 14 \times (-7) + 2 \times (-1)$
e. $16 \times (-4) + (-6) \times 6$

3. Solve the following.

a. $4 + (-8) \div (-2)$
b. $11 + 16 \div (-4)$
c. $18 + (-45) \div 5$
d. $21 \div (-3) + 3$
e. $(-100) \div (-5) + (-20)$

4. Solve the following.

a. $(-2) \times (-6) - 18$
b. $72 - (-10) \times 7$
c. $16 \times (-5) - (-81)$
d. $(-10) \times 0 - (-10)$
e. $100 - 7 \times (-5)$

5. Solve the following.

a. $17 - (-10) \div 2$
b. $98 \div (-7) - (-24) \div 3$
c. $(-100) \div (-5) - (-20) \div (-2)$
d. $121 \div (-11) - 50 \div (-5)$
e. $200 - 100 \div (-100)$

6. Solve the following.

a. $105 \div (-15) \times 6$
b. $14 \times 4 \div (-2)$
c. $81 \times (-9) \div (-9)$
d. $(-100) \div (-100) \times 10$
e. $(-63) \times 91 \div (-7)$

7. Simplify the following using the appropriate property in each case.

a. $420 \times (-10) + 420 \times (-15)$
b. $(-26) \times 72 + (-26) \times 28$
c. $(-101) \times 635 - (-1) \times 635$
d. $500 \times 15 - 500 \times 5$
e. $99 \times (-9) + 99 \times (-1)$

8. Calculate the answers to the following.

a. $19 - 18 \div 2 + 14 \times (-1)$
b. $(-16) + (-45) \div (-5) \times (-1)$
c. $65 \div (-13) + (-81) \div (-9)$
d. $77 + (-47) + (-95) \div 19$
e. $(-44) \times (-1) + 72 \div (-8)$

9. Put > or < in the boxes.

a. $15 - 16 \div 4 + 5$ ☐ $17 \div (-17) + 45 \div (-9)$
b. $16 - 18 \div (-9) + 6$ ☐ $23 \div (-1) + 16 \div (-4)$
c. $30 + (-16) \div (-4) - 8$ ☐ $65 \div (-13) - 8 \div (-2)$
d. $25 \div (-5) + 9 \div (-9)$ ☐ $32 \div (-8) - 17 \div (-17)$
e. $49 + (-55) \div 55$ ☐ $78 + 18 \div (-9)$

10. Classify the following statements as true or false.

a. If a and b are integers, then a ÷ b is an integer.
b. If a is an integer, then a ÷ 0 is an integer.
c. If a is an integer, then a ÷ a = 1 for all values of a.
d. If 0 is divided by any non-zero integer, the result is always 0.
e. The product of two negative integers is a negative integer.

Highlights

- Integers are a collection of numbers consisting of whole numbers and negative numbers.
- The additive inverse of an integer is a number of the same value as the integer but lying on the opposite side of 0 on the number line.
- To add integers with the *same* signs, we add their values and assign the same sign as the integers to the answer.
- To add integers with *different* signs, we subtract their values and assign the sign of the integer of the greater value to the answer.
- Integers follow the closure property for addition and subtraction, i.e., if a and b are integers, then $a + b$ and $a - b$ are also integers.
- The addition of integers obeys the commutative and associative properties, i.e., $a + b = b + a$ and $(a + b) + c = a + (b + c)$.
- For addition of integers, the integer 0 is the additive identity, i.e., $a + 0 = 0 + a = a$.
- The product of two integers with the same sign will be a positive integer.
- The product of two integers with different signs will be a negative integer.
- Integers follow the closure property for multiplication, i.e., if a and b are integers, then $a \times b$ is also an integer.
- The multiplication of integers obeys the commutative, associative and distributive properties, i.e,

  $a \times b = b \times a$ (commutative property)

  $(a \times b) \times c = a \times (b \times c)$ (associative property)

  $a \times (b + c) = a \times b + a \times c$ (distributive property)
- The integer 1 is the multiplicative identity for integers, i.e., $a \times 1 = 1 \times a = a$.
- For any integer a, where $(a \neq 0)$, $a \times 0 = 0 \times a = 0$.
- When an integer is divided by another integer of the same sign, the quotient is a *positive integer*.
- When an integxer is divided by another integer of a different sign, the quotient is a *negative integer*.

Highlights

- The closure, commutative and associative properties are not true for division of integers.
- For any integer a,

  $a \div a = 1, a \div 1 = a, 0 \div a = 0$

  $a \div 0$ is meaningless.
- When the four basic operations—addition, subtraction, multiplication and division—are to be performed on integers in a given expression, they follow a rule of precedence. It is given in short as DMAS where D $\rightarrow$ division, M $\rightarrow$ multiplication, A $\rightarrow$ addition, and S $\rightarrow$ subtraction.

  The operations are always performed in this order.

Higher Order Thinking Skills

HOTS

1. By how much does 2 exceed (-3)?
2. The product of three integers is (-85). If two of the integers are (-17) and (-5), find the third.
3. Find the quotient if the product of all integers from (-5) to $(+5)$ is divided by (-10).

Brainteaser

Use every number between 2 and 10 only once and fill in the squares in such a way that the total of each line-horizontally, vertically and diagonally is 18.

9		
2		10

(Answer for Brainteaser on page 19)

Magical Grid

Aim: To study the multiplication of integers.

Material required: a chart paper, colour pencils (any two colors of your choice), ruler and a pencil

Procedure:

Make a square of an appropriate size. Draw thirteen horizontal and vertical lines crossing each other at a distance of 2 cm. Write the integers (−5) to 5 horizontally and vertically. You will now have a grid. Multiply the integers and write the corresponding answers in the square. When the entire multiplication table is complete, colour the negative integers with one color and the positive with another colour.

×	−5	−4	−3	−2	0	1	2	3	4	5	5
−5											
−4											
−3											
−2											
−1											
1											
2											
3											
4											
5											

Your magical grid is ready!

Answer for Brainteaser on page 18

9	4	5
2	6	10
7	8	3

CHAPTER 2

Fractions and Decimals

All fractions have specific properties. A fraction is called a **proper fraction** when the numerator is less than the denominator.

In an **improper fraction**, the numerator is greater than the denominator.

If the numerator and the denominator of a fraction are equal, the fraction becomes a whole number.

Decimals are special types of fractions where the denominators are either 10, or powers of 10.

Any whole number can be written in the form of a fraction. For example, a can be written as $\frac{a}{1}$.

Two or more fractions with the same denominator are called **like fractions.**

Fractions with different denominators are called **unlike fractions.**

Unlike fractions can be converted into like fractions by converting them into ***equivalent fractions*** with the same denominator. To find equivalent fractions, we find the LCM of the denominators and then have a common or same denominator.

To add or subtract fractions, we add or subtract the numerators after making the denominators equal.

Practice Exercise 2.1

1. Write three equivalent fractions for each of the following.
   a. $\frac{1}{6}$ b. $\frac{2}{5}$ c. $\frac{9}{11}$ d. $\frac{15}{20}$ e. $\frac{25}{100}$
2. Add the following.
   a. $\frac{7}{12} + \frac{1}{12} + \frac{4}{12}$ b. $\frac{8}{13} + \frac{2}{13} + \frac{1}{13}$ c. $\frac{4}{5} + \frac{2}{3} + \frac{1}{15}$
   d. $\frac{7}{11} + \frac{3}{44}$ e. $\frac{1}{6} + \frac{5}{12} + \frac{7}{24}$
3. Add the following.
   a. $2\frac{1}{3} + 3\frac{1}{4}$ b. $8\frac{1}{5} + 3\frac{1}{2}$ c. $\frac{40}{21} + 2\frac{1}{7}$
   d. $1\frac{1}{5} + 2\frac{1}{3} + \frac{6}{15}$ e. $\frac{35}{25} + 2\frac{1}{5} + \frac{3}{125}$
4. Subtract the following.
   a. $\frac{16}{21} - \frac{7}{21}$ b. $\frac{20}{45} - \frac{15}{45}$ c. $\frac{2}{5} - \frac{1}{10}$ d. $\frac{5}{7} - \frac{8}{35}$ e. $\frac{11}{12} - \frac{6}{18}$
5. Subtract the following.
   a. $1\frac{2}{7}$ from $5\frac{1}{2}$ b. $2\frac{1}{2}$ from $3\frac{1}{6}$ c. $\frac{16}{25}$ from $2\frac{3}{10}$
   d. $6\frac{4}{9}$ from $10\frac{2}{3}$ e. $\frac{33}{20}$ from $5\frac{3}{4}$
6. Find the value of the following.
   a. $2\frac{1}{3} + 3\frac{1}{2} - 1\frac{1}{6}$ b. $4\frac{1}{5} - \frac{3}{10} - \frac{3}{5}$ c. $3\frac{1}{2} - 2\frac{2}{3} + 4\frac{2}{5}$

d. $2\frac{1}{7} + 1\frac{1}{14} - 2\frac{1}{21}$ e. $9\frac{2}{5} - 4\frac{1}{2} - 3\frac{1}{3}$

7. The sum of two numbers is $13\frac{1}{4}$. If one number is $5\frac{3}{4}$, find the other.
8. Which is greater — the sum of $2\frac{1}{4}$ and $5\frac{1}{2}$ or the sum of $3\frac{2}{3}$ and $2\frac{1}{3}$ and by how much?
9. Sunita bought a 10 kg box of grapes from the market. She gave $3\frac{1}{2}$ kg of the grapes to her friend Punita and $2\frac{1}{4}$ kg to Anita. How many kilograms of grapes were left with her?
10. A film show lasted $3\frac{3}{4}$ hours. Of this, $1\frac{2}{3}$ hours were spent on advertisements and trailers. What was the actual duration of the film?

Multiplication of Fractions

1. Multiplying a Fraction by a Whole Number

Multiplication is repeated addition.

Example 1: $3 \times \frac{1}{4}$

$= \frac{1}{4} + \frac{1}{4} + \frac{1}{4}$

$= \frac{1+1+1}{4} = \frac{3}{4}$

This can be represented as:

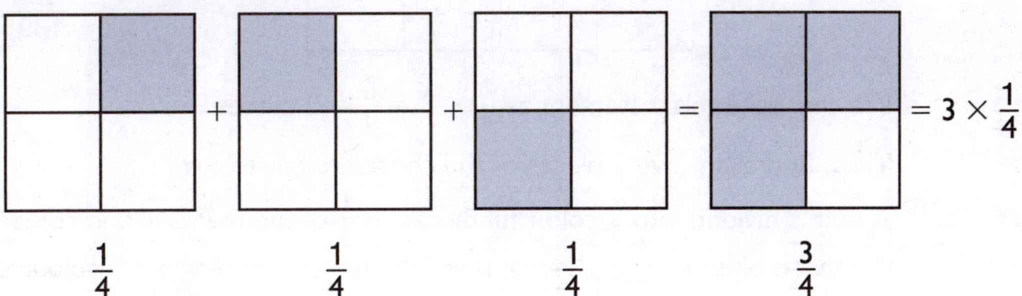

Example 2: $2 \times \frac{1}{3}$

$= \frac{1}{3} + \frac{1}{3}$

$= \frac{1+1}{3} = \frac{2}{3}$

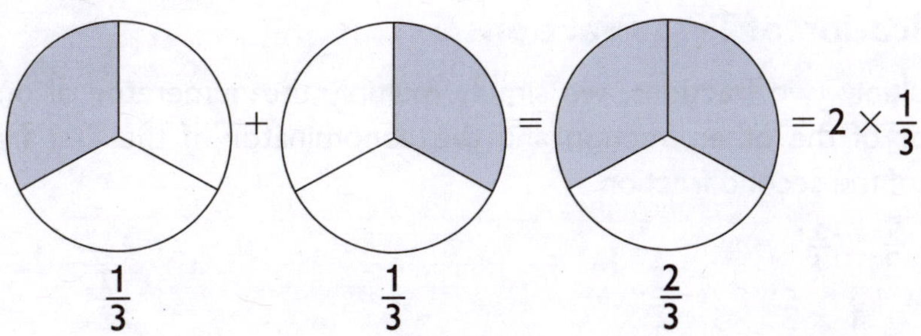

To multiply a fraction by a whole number, we multiply the numerator by the number while the denominator remains the same.

2. Multiplying a Mixed Number by a Whole Number

While multiplying a mixed number by a whole number, we first convert the mixed number into an improper fraction and then multiply it by the whole number.

Example 1: $3\frac{1}{2} \times 5$

$$= \frac{7}{2} \times 5 = \frac{7 \times 5}{2} = \frac{35}{2} = 17\frac{1}{2}$$

Example 2: $5\frac{3}{4} \times 7$

$$= \frac{23}{4} \times 7 = \frac{23 \times 7}{4} = \frac{161}{4} = 40\frac{1}{4}$$

3. Fraction as the Operation 'of':

Rudraksh had a bar of chocolate that had 8 pieces. He gave $\frac{1}{4}$ of the chocolate bar to his brother, Arnav. How many pieces of chocolate did Rudraksh give his brother?

Example 1: Consider a bar of chocolate that consists of 8 pieces. Rudraksh gave $\frac{1}{4}$ of the bar to his brother Arnav. $\frac{1}{4}$ out of 8 pieces is equal to 2 pieces.

We can write this statement as $\frac{1}{4} \times 8 = \frac{8}{4} = 2$ pieces.

Thus, Rudraksh gave 2 pieces of the chocolate bar to Arnav.

Example 2: A mat is divided into 9 colourful blocks. If $\frac{1}{3}$ of the mat is red in colour, $\frac{1}{3}$ of the mat is blue and $\frac{1}{3}$ of the mat is yellow, how many blocks are coloured with each colour?

Here $\frac{1}{3}$ of $9 = 3$

Hence 3 blocks are red, 3 are blue and 3 are yellow.

The word 'of' denotes multiplication.

4. Multiplication of Two Fractions

When we multiply two fractions, we simply multiply the numerator of one fraction with the numerator of the other fraction and the denominator of the first fraction with the denominator of the second fraction.

Example 1: $\frac{1}{2} \times \frac{3}{4}$

$$= \frac{1 \times 3}{2 \times 4} = \frac{3}{8}$$

Example 2: $\frac{3}{5} \times \frac{1}{2}$

$= \frac{3 \times 1}{5 \times 2} = \frac{3}{10}$

Alert!

1. In multiplication, we do not have to make the fractions into like fractions.
2. If there are more than two fractions, we follow the same method for multiplication. Numerators are multiplied together and denominators are multiplied together.

Example 1: Find the product of the following fractions and express it as a mixed fraction.

a. $\frac{3}{7} \times 8$

$= \frac{3 \times 8}{7} = \frac{24}{7} = 3\frac{3}{7}$

b. $\frac{5}{11} \times 6$

$= \frac{5 \times 6}{11} = \frac{30}{11} = 2\frac{8}{11}$

c. $\frac{6}{7} \times 7$

$= \frac{6 \times 7}{7} = \frac{42}{7} = 6$

Example 2: Find the product of the following fractions and express it as a mixed fraction.

a. $3\frac{1}{3} \times 6$

$= \frac{10}{3} \times 6 = \frac{10 \times 6}{3} = \frac{60}{3} = 20$

b. $6\frac{1}{2} \times 5$

$= \frac{13}{2} \times 5 = \frac{13 \times 5}{2} = \frac{65}{2} = 32\frac{1}{2}$

c. $5\frac{5}{9} \times 9$

$= \frac{50}{9} \times 9 = \frac{50 \times 9}{9} = \frac{450}{9} = 50$

Example 3: Find the values of the following.

a. $\frac{1}{3}$ of 60

$= \frac{1}{3} \times 60 = \frac{1 \times 60}{3} = \frac{60}{3} = 20$

b. $\frac{2}{7}$ of 35

$= \frac{2}{7} \times 35 = \frac{2 \times 35}{7} = \frac{70}{7} = 10$

c. $\frac{1}{9}$ of 72

$= \frac{1}{9} \times 72 = \frac{1 \times 72}{9} = \frac{72}{9} = 8$

Example 4: Multiply the following fractions and express the answer in the lowest term.

a. $3\frac{1}{2} \times \frac{1}{6}$

$= \frac{7}{2} \times \frac{1}{6} = \frac{7 \times 1}{2 \times 6} = \frac{7}{12}$

b. $4\frac{1}{5} \times 2\frac{3}{4}$

$= \frac{21}{5} \times \frac{11}{4} = \frac{21 \times 11}{5 \times 4} = \frac{231}{20} = 11\frac{11}{20}$

c. $\frac{3}{11} \times 3\frac{1}{2} \times 1\frac{1}{3}$

$= \frac{3}{11} \times \frac{7}{2} \times \frac{4}{3} = \frac{3 \times 7 \times 4}{11 \times 2 \times 3}$

$= \frac{84}{66} = \frac{42}{33} = \frac{14}{11} = 1\frac{3}{11}$

Example 5: In a box there are 50 balls. $\frac{3}{5}$ of these are red in colour and the rest are white balls. Find out how many balls of each colour are there in the box.

Number of red balls $= \frac{3}{5}$ of 50

$= \frac{3}{5} \times 50 = \frac{3 \times 50}{5} = \frac{150}{5} = 30$

Number of white balls = Total number of balls − number of red balls

= 50 − 30 = 20 balls

Example 6: Anita jogs $1\frac{1}{2}$ km in 1 hour. How many km can she cover in $2\frac{1}{2}$ hours?

In 1 hour Anita jogs $1\frac{1}{2}$ km $= \frac{3}{2}$ km

In $2\frac{1}{2}$ hours, Anita can jog $= \frac{3}{2} \times 2\frac{1}{2} = \frac{3}{2} \times \frac{5}{2}$ km

$= \frac{3 \times 5}{2 \times 2} = \frac{15}{4}$ km $= 3\frac{3}{4}$ km

Practice Exercise 2.2

1. Multiply the following and express their products in the lowest terms.

a. $\frac{4}{7} \times 5$ b. $\frac{6}{21} \times 8$ c. $11 \times \frac{3}{10}$ d. $\frac{2}{5} \times 13$ e. $\frac{3}{17} \times 4$

2. Multiply the following and express the products as mixed numbers.

a. $10 \times 4\frac{2}{5}$ b. $5 \times 3\frac{2}{7}$ c. $20 \times 3\frac{1}{2}$ d. $4\frac{3}{10} \times 18$ e. $1\frac{3}{11} \times 9$

3. Multiply the following and write their products in the lowest terms.

a. $\frac{1}{4} \times \frac{3}{4}$ b. $\frac{2}{5} \times \frac{7}{8}$ c. $\frac{5}{9} \times \frac{5}{8}$ d. $2\frac{1}{2} \times 3\frac{1}{4}$ e. $\frac{19}{8} \times 4\frac{1}{2}$

4. Find the values of the following.

a. $\frac{1}{6}$ of 72 b. $\frac{1}{5}$ of 85 c. $\frac{4}{5}$ of 90 d. $\frac{2}{3}$ of $\frac{3}{2}$ e. $\frac{4}{11}$ of $\frac{55}{72}$

5. Mrs Mehra gave $\frac{1}{3}$ of ₹90,00,000 to her daughter, $\frac{1}{5}$ to her grandson and the remaining to her sister. How much money did her daughter, grandson and sister receive?
6. From a ribbon 20 m long, Sneha cut off 3 pieces of $2\frac{1}{3}$ m each and Janani cut off 4 pieces of $2\frac{1}{4}$ m each. What length of the ribbon was left for Payal?
7. In a botanical garden, there are 1,080 flowers. Out of these, $\frac{3}{10}$ flowers are pink, $\frac{2}{5}$ are purple and the rest are yellow. How many pink, purple and yellow flowers are there in this garden?
8. Sapna earns ₹18,000 per month. She spends $\frac{7}{9}$ of her income and deposits the rest in the bank. How much money does she deposit in the bank each month? What will be her annual savings?
9. Find the area of a rectangular park which is $41\frac{2}{3}$ m long and $18\frac{3}{5}$ m broad.
10. In a multi-storey building, $\frac{1}{8}$ of the 728 residents watch the Discovery Channel, $\frac{3}{4}$ watch National Geographic and the rest watch Cartoon Network. What fraction of the total number of residents watch Cartoon Network?

Division of Fractions

Division of a fraction is the same as multiplication by its *reciprocal*.
Reciprocal of a fraction refers to the **inverse** of a fraction.

Example: Consider a fraction $\frac{3}{5}$.

Here the numerator is 3 and the denominator is 5.
Now, if we write it 'upside down' or in the inverse form, we get its reciprocal.
If 5 becomes the numerator and 3 becomes the denominator, the fraction becomes $\frac{5}{3}$.
Thus, the reciprocal of the fraction $\frac{3}{5}$ is $\frac{5}{3}$.
In general, if the fraction is $\frac{p}{q}$, where $q \neq 0$, then the *reciprocal* is $\frac{q}{p}$, where $p \neq 0$.
The product of a number and its reciprocal is equal to 1.

Alert!
The integer '0' has no reciprocal.

1. Division of a Fraction by a Proper Fraction

To perform division of a fraction by another fraction, we multiply it by its reciprocal. Thus,
dividend ÷ divisor = dividend × reciprocal of divisor

Example 1: $\frac{3}{4} \div \frac{1}{4}$

$= \frac{3}{4} \times \frac{4}{1} = \frac{3 \times 4}{4 \times 1} = \frac{12}{4} = 3$

Example 2: $\frac{2}{5} \div \frac{2}{11}$

$$= \frac{2}{5} \times \frac{11}{2} = \frac{2 \times 11}{5 \times 2} = \frac{22}{10} = \frac{11}{5} = 2\frac{1}{5}$$

2. Division of a Fraction by a Mixed Number

The division of a fraction by a mixed number or division between two mixed numbers involves the same method. First, we convert the mixed number into an improper fraction and then divide the two.

Example 1: $3\frac{1}{2} \div \frac{3}{4}$

$$= \frac{7}{2} \div \frac{3}{4}$$

$$= \frac{7}{2} \times \frac{4}{3} = \frac{7 \times 4}{2 \times 3} = \frac{28}{6} = \frac{14}{3} = 4\frac{2}{3}$$

Example 2: $4\frac{1}{3} \div 1\frac{1}{3}$

$$= \frac{13}{3} \div \frac{4}{3} = \frac{13}{3} \times \frac{3}{4}$$

$$= \frac{39}{12} = \frac{13}{4} = 3\frac{1}{4}$$

3. Division of a Fraction by a Whole Number

When we divide a fraction by a whole number, the same rule is applied. We multiply the dividend by the reciprocal of the divisor.

Example 1: $\frac{5}{7} \div 8$

$$= \frac{5}{7} \div \frac{8}{1} = \frac{5}{7} \times \frac{1}{8} = \frac{5 \times 1}{7 \times 8} = \frac{5}{56}$$

Example 2: $8\frac{1}{4} \div 6$

$$= \frac{33}{4} \div \frac{6}{1} = \frac{33}{4} \times \frac{1}{6} = \frac{33}{24} = \frac{11}{8} = 1\frac{3}{8}$$

Let us revise the division of fractions by observing more solved examples.

Example 1: Find the value of each of the following.

a. $\frac{2}{5} \div \frac{1}{3}$

$$= \frac{2}{5} \times \frac{3}{1} = \frac{6}{5} = 1\frac{1}{5}$$

b. $3\frac{1}{4} \div \frac{2}{3}$

$$= \frac{13}{4} \times \frac{3}{2} = \frac{13 \times 3}{4 \times 2} = \frac{39}{8} = 4\frac{7}{8}$$

c. $5\frac{1}{7} \div 2\frac{2}{3}$

$$= \frac{36}{7} \div \frac{8}{3} = \frac{36}{7} \times \frac{3}{8} = \frac{108}{56} = \frac{27}{14} = 1\frac{13}{14}$$

d. $\frac{7}{10} \div 10$

$= \frac{7}{10} \div \frac{10}{1} = \frac{7}{10} \times \frac{1}{10} = \frac{7 \times 1}{10 \times 10} = \frac{7}{100}$

e. $6\frac{1}{4} \div 25$

$= \frac{25}{4} \div \frac{25}{1} = \frac{25}{4} \times \frac{1}{25} = \frac{25 \times 1}{4 \times 25} = \frac{25}{100} = \frac{1}{4}$

Example 2: The product of two fractions is $13\frac{1}{4}$. If one of them is $5\frac{3}{4}$, find the other fraction.

The required fraction will be $13\frac{1}{4} \div 5\frac{3}{4}$

$13\frac{1}{4} \div 5\frac{3}{4} = \frac{53}{4} \div \frac{23}{4} = \frac{53}{4} \times \frac{4}{23} = \frac{53 \times 4}{4 \times 23} = \frac{212}{92} = \frac{53}{23} = 2\frac{7}{23}$

Answer: $2\frac{17}{23}$

Example 3: The cost of a book is ₹$25\frac{3}{4}$. How many books can be purchased for ₹2,472?

The number of books purchased will be $2,472 \div 25\frac{3}{4}$

$= 2472 \div 25\frac{3}{4} = 2472 \div \frac{103}{4}$

$= \frac{2472}{1} \times \frac{4}{103} = \frac{2472 \times 4}{1 \times 103} = \frac{9888}{103} = 96$

Answer: 96 books.

Example 4: The cost of $7\frac{1}{2}$ kg of rice is ₹$262\frac{1}{2}$. Find the cost of 1 kg of rice.

Cost of 1 kg rice $= \frac{\text{total cost}}{\text{amount of rice}}$

$= \frac{262\frac{1}{2}}{7\frac{1}{2}} = \frac{525}{2} \div \frac{15}{2}$

$= \frac{525}{2} \times \frac{2}{15} = \frac{525 \times 2}{2 \times 15} = \frac{1050}{30} = 35$

Answer: Cost of 1 kg of rice is ₹35.

Example 5: A tank is filled with $149\frac{1}{2}$ litres of water. How many buckets with a capacity of $6\frac{1}{2}$ litres can be filled from the tank?

Number of buckets $= \frac{\text{volume of water in the tank}}{\text{volume of the bucket}}$

$= 149\frac{1}{2} \div 6\frac{1}{2} = \frac{299}{2} \div \frac{13}{2} = \frac{299}{2} \times \frac{2}{13} = \frac{598}{26} = 23$

Answer: 23 buckets.

Practice Exercise 2.3

1. Find the reciprocals of the following.

   a. $\frac{7}{9}$ b. 18 c. $2\frac{3}{4}$ d. $\frac{15}{8}$ e. 101

2. Divide the following as indicated.

   a. $\frac{5}{8} \div \frac{2}{3}$ b. $\frac{11}{13} \div 22$ c. $6\frac{1}{4} \div 2\frac{3}{5}$ d. $\frac{14}{13} \div \frac{1}{3}$ e. $100 \div \frac{7}{10}$

3. If $5\frac{1}{3}$ litres of milk are to be divided between 8 children. How much milk will each child get?

4. If 7 identical books kept together weigh $6\frac{2}{9}$ kg, what is the weight of each book?

5. If the cost of $5\frac{2}{5}$ litres of milk is ₹$101\frac{1}{4}$, find its cost per litre.

6. The cost of $5\frac{3}{4}$ kg of mangoes is ₹184. Find the cost of 1 kg of mangoes.

7. A total of $4\frac{1}{8}$ kg of flour was used to bake 11 cakes. How much flour will be needed to bake 1 cake?

8. A roll of cloth measures 60 m. If $2\frac{1}{2}$ m of cloth are required to stitch a shirt, how many shirts can be stitched using this roll of cloth?

9. The area of a rectangular field is $286\frac{3}{4}$ sq. m. If the length of the field is $18\frac{1}{2}$ m, find the breadth of the field.

10. By selling tickets for a charity show, a group of students collected ₹$5272\frac{1}{2}$. If the cost of each ticket was ₹$55\frac{1}{2}$, find the number of tickets sold.

Decimals

Decimals are special fractions that have 10 or powers of 10 as their denominator. Fractions can be written in the decimal form and decimals can be converted into fractions.

Decimals can also be written in the expanded form.

Like decimals are two or more numbers with the same number of places of decimals. For example: 15.32 and 78.12 are like decimals. Unlike decimals have different number of places of decimals. For example: 32.17 and 13.328 are unlike decimals.

Unlike decimals can easily be converted into like decimals by adding zeroes after the decimal point on the right. This does not change the value of the number.

Addition and subtraction of decimals can be performed only after converting unlike decimals to like decimals.

Practice Exercise 2.4

1. Write the following decimal numbers in the expanded notation.

   a. 72.302 b. 293.007 c. 99.999 d. 500.005 e. 68.32

2. Add the following decimal numbers.

a. 432.24 + 23.268 b. 89.427 + 901.28 c. 68.68 + 7.818

d. 1009.99 + 910.9 e. 505.25 + 25.505

3. Subtract the following decimal numbers.

a. 3.25 from 15.8 b. 69.2 from 150.83 c. 41.287 from 100

d. 0.89 from 5.721 e. 88.88 from 90.01

4. Aparna rode 12.25 km on her new scooty on Monday, 13.1 km on Tuesday, 15.36 km on Wednesday and 11.9 km on Thursday. What was the total distance Aparna covered in the four days?

5. Lalita set out with a ₹500 note to the market. She bought the following items: tomato sauce for ₹48.15; mixed fruit jam for ₹39.25; corn flakes for ₹105.62; chocolates for ₹62.10; cereal for ₹89.36. How much money did she get back after paying the bill at the cash counter?

6. Tony and Mony got ₹250 each as pocket money to spend at the school canteen. Tony spent ₹158.85 and Mony saved ₹65.65 from his total allowance. Who spent more and how much?

7. An overhead water tank had 950.75 litres of water in the morning. During the day, 650.15 litres of water was consumed by the residents. In the evening, 750.35 litres of water was pumped up. How much water was in the tank the next morning?

8. A triangular park needs to be fenced. The dimensions of its lengths are 16.13 m, 12.48 m and 21.39 m. How much barbed wire will be required for the fence?

9. Solve the following.

a. By how much should 32.67 be increased to get 60.1?

b. By how much should 74.3 be decreased to get 26.87?

10. A particular airline allowed 46.5 kg of baggage to be checked-in. Arvind carried two suitcases weighing 24.3 kg and 28.25 kg. How much extra baggage did Arvind carry?

Multiplication of Decimals

1. Multiplication of a Decimal by Powers of 10 (10, 100, 1,000 ...)

This is simple multiplication and easy to perform.

The basic rule is that the decimal point is shifted to the *right* according to the number of zeroes in multiples of 10.

Example 1: $67.24 \times 1\underline{0} = 672.4$

Example 2: $6.724 \times 1\underline{00} = 672.4$

Example 3: $0.6724 \times 1\underline{000} = 672.4$

Example 4: $0.4\,9\,3 \times 1\underline{0} = 4.93$

Example 5: $68.2\,9\,7 \times 1\underline{00} = 6{,}829.7$

Example 6: $46.3\,8\,1 \times 1\underline{000} = 46{,}381.0 = 46{,}381$

Alert!

If we multiply a decimal number by $1\underline{0}$ (i.e. 1 zero), we have to shift the decimal point by one place to the right.

If we multiply a decimal number by $1\underline{00}$ (i.e. 2 zeroes), we have to shift the decimal point by two places to the right.

2. Multiplication of a Decimal by a Whole Number

This multiplication involves multiplying the decimal number without considering the decimal point by the given whole number. After this step, the decimal point is marked in the product according to the number of places in the given original decimal number.

Find the products of the following.

Example 1: 5.42×12	Example 2: 0.327×15	Example 3: 0.029×9
$= 542 \times 12$	$= 327 \times 15$	$= 29 \times 9$
$= 6504 = 65.04$	$= 4905$	$= 261$
	$= 4.905$	$= 0.261$

3. Multiplication of a Decimal Number by Another Decimal Number

Here, we first multiply the two decimal numbers without considering the decimal point as whole numbers. In the next step, we mark the decimal point in the product, which is the sum of decimal places in the given decimal numbers.

Example 1: Multiply 74.68 by 4.6.

$74.68 \times 4.6 = 7468 \times 46 =$

$$\begin{array}{r} 7468 \\ \times\ 46 \\ \hline 44808 \\ 298720 \\ \hline 343528 \\ \hline \end{array}$$

Since the sum of the decimal places in the two numbers is $2 + 1 = 3$, we place the decimal point after three places counting from the extreme right. So, the answer is 343.528.

Example 2: Multiply 0.098 by 0.78.

$0.098 \times 0.78 = 0098 \times 078 =$

$$\begin{array}{r} 98 \\ \times\ 78 \\ \hline 784 \\ 6860 \\ \hline 7644 \\ \hline \end{array}$$

Since the sum of the decimal places in the two given numbers is $3 + 2 = 5$, we place the decimal point after five places counting from the extreme right.

Since there are only four digits in the product, we write a zero to make five places and then place the decimal. So the answer is 0.07644.

Example 3: Multiply $5.8 \times 2.341 \times 7.69$.

First we multiply the number without taking into consideration the decimal points.

So, $58 \times 2341 \times 769 = 104413282$

Now, we count the number of decimal places in the original numbers. It is $= 6$. So counting from the extreme right, we place the decimal after the 6th digit and the answer is 104.413282.

Division of Decimals

1. Division of a Decimal by Powers of 10 (10, 100, 1,000 ...)

On dividing a decimal by the power of 10, we shift the decimal point to the left according to the number of zeroes.

Example 1: Divide 24.62 by 10.

$\frac{24.62}{10} = 2.462$ We shift the decimal point one place to the left

Example 2: Divide 463.5 by 100.

$\frac{463.5}{100} = 4.635$ We shift the decimal point two places to the left

Example 3: Divide 379.64 by 1000.

$\frac{379.64}{1000} = 0.37964$ We shift the decimal point three places to the left

Example 4: Divide 2.34 by 100.

$\frac{02.34}{100} = 0.0234$

We have to shift two places to the left but there is only one place before the decimal, so we add a zero and make two places and then place the decimal.

Example 5: Divide 6.27 by 1000.

$\frac{6.27}{1000} = 0.00627$

We have to shift three places to the left but there is only one place before the decimal, so we add two zeroes and make three places and then place the decimal.

Alert!

The quotient has the same number of digits as the dividend but the decimal point shifts to the left by as many places as there are zeroes in the divisor.

2. Division of a Decimal Number by a Whole Number

The division is performed in the normal manner by first ignoring the decimal point.

The decimal point is then placed in the quotient after counting the same number of digits as in the dividend.

Example 1: Divide 401.25 by 15.

The first step is to carry out the division.

```
15) 401.25(26.75
   −30
    101
   −90
     11.2
    −10 5
       75
      −75
        0
```

Then we place a decimal point in the quotient.

Example 2: Divide 883.26 by 42.

```
42) 883.26(21.03
   −84
     43
    −42
      126
     −126
        0
```

Example 3: Divide 2.32 by 16.

```
16) 2.32(0.145
   −0
    23
   −16
     72
    −64
      80
     −80
       0
```

We can insert a zero to continue with division and when we do this, we need to increase the number of decimal places to the right.

Alert!

Zeroes can be added at the end of the last decimal place, if required, to complete the division.

3. Division of a Decimal Number by a Decimal Number

The first step is to convert the divisor into a whole number by multiplying the dividend and divisor by suitable powers of 10 so that the decimal point in the divisor is removed and it becomes a whole number. In the next step, we proceed by long division method and divide the decimal number by the whole number.

Example 1: Divide 23.94 by 6.3.

$$\frac{23.94}{6.3} = \frac{23.94 \times 10}{6.3 \times 10} = \frac{239.4}{63}$$

```
63) 239.4 (3.8
   −189
    504
   −504
      0
```

The decimal point is placed after one digit from the right.

Example 2: Divide 110.52 by 3.07.

$$\frac{110.52}{3.07} = \frac{110.52 \times 100}{3.07 \times 100} = \frac{11052}{307}$$

```
307) 110.52 (36
     −921
      1842
     −1842
         0
```

The decimal point is placed after two digits from the right.

Example 3: Divide 365.04 by 15.6.

$$\frac{365.04}{15.6} = \frac{365.04 \times 10}{15.6 \times 10} = 3650.4 \times 156$$

```
156) 3650.4 (23.4
    −312
      530
     −468
      624
     −624
        0
```

The decimal point is placed after one digit from the right.

Commonly Used Decimal-based Units

1. 100 cm = 1 m
   To convert m to cm, we multiply the number by 100.
   To convert cm to m, we divide the number by 100.
2. 1000 m = 1 km
   To convert km to m, we multiply by 1000.
   To convert m to km, we divide by 1000.
3. 1000 g = 1 kg
   To convert kg to g, we multiply the number by 1000.
   To convert g to kg, we divide the number by 1000.
4. 1000 ml = 1litre
   To convert litre/s to ml, we multiply the number by 1000.
   To convert ml to litre/s, we divide the number by 1000.
5. 100 p = 1₹
   To convert ₹ to p, we multiply the number by 100.
   To convert p to ₹, we divide the number by 100.

Alert!

To convert a *larger* unit to a *smaller* unit we multiply by the powers of 10.
To convert a *smaller* unit to a *larger* unit we divide by the powers of 10.

Practice Exercise 2.5

1. Multiply the following.
   a. 6.89×10 b. 5.638×100 c. 0.053×1000 d. 10×741.8
   e. 100×98.6 f. 1000×3.29 g. 45.73×10 h. 3.685×100
   i. 9.005×1000 j. 100×96.8
2. Find the products of the following.
   a. 17.12×46 b. 5.4×16 c. 0.0146×67 d. 0.00125×326
   e. 104.06×75 f. 28.5×38 g. 756.3×91 h. 8.329×24
   i. 40.001×44 j. 86.66×66
3. Multiply the following.
   a. 2.4×1.6 b. 6.89×7.8 c. 9.234×82.5 d. 470.05×5.7
   e. 0.623×0.75 f. 0.007×70.1 g. $2.1 \times 0.21 \times 0.021$ h. $55.5 \times 5.55 \times 55$
   i. $0.9 \times 5.6 \times 3.3$ j. 54.5×1.76
4. One kg of apples cost ₹75.75. Find the cost of 6.50 kg of apples.
5. Find the cost of three dozen notebooks if the cost of each notebook is ₹27.45.
6. Divide the following.
   a. 42.8 by 10 b. 837.68 by 100 c. 354.26 by 1000 d. 7.8 by 100
   e. 0.04 by 10 f. 4.93 by 1000 g. 8.005 by 100 h. 9191.9 by 1000
   i. 3.923 by 10 j. 68.515 by 100
7. Divide the following.
   a. 117.6 by 21 b. 25.75 by 25 c. 883.26 by 42 d. 11.5968 by 96
   e. 4.032 by 96 f. 3293.6 by 23 g. 948.75 by 55 h. 217.44 by 18
   i. 604.8 by 12 j. 1.001 by 14
8. Divide the following.
   a. 3.28 by 0.8 b. 20.484 by 1.8 c. 219.76 by 1.64 d. 0.288 by 0.9
   e. 22.8 by 3.8 f. 25.395 by 1.5 g. 4.2336 by 0.56 h. 1845.12 by 4.8
   i. 806.08 by 9.16 j. 41.736 by 88.8
9. The cost of 15.5 litres of milk is ₹395.25. Find the cost of 1 litre of milk. Also find the cost of 30 litres of milk.
10. The weight of 37 bags of sugar is 3644.5 kg. What is the weight of each bag, if they weigh the same?

Highlights

- Fractions can be added or subtracted after being converted to *like* fractions.
- Only the numerators are added or subtracted. The denominator remains the same.
- 'Of' indicates multiplication, like $\frac{2}{3}$ of 15 is $\frac{2}{3} \times 15 = \frac{30}{3} = 10$.
- When we multiply two fractions, the numerator is the product of the numerators and the denominator is the product of the denominators.
- The reciprocal of a fraction is obtained by *inverting* it. The numerator becomes the denominator and the denominator becomes the numerator. Thus, the reciprocal of $\frac{7}{19}$ is $\frac{19}{7}$.
- To divide a fraction by another fraction, we *multiply* the dividend by the *reciprocal* of the divisor.
- Decimals are special fractions with denominators 10, 100, 1000 and so on.
- Numbers that have the same number of places of decimal are called *like decimals*. Numbers with different number of places of decimal are called unlike decimals.
- Addition or subtraction of decimals are performed after converting them into like decimals.
- To multiply two decimal numbers, we first multiply the number without taking into consideration the decimal points. Then, in the product we put the decimal point according to the sum of decimal places in the numbers given. The decimal point is placed after counting the places from the extreme right.

Higher Order Thinking Skills

HOTS

1. Find the reciprocal of the sum of $1\frac{7}{9}$ and $1\frac{9}{7}$.
2. Find the product of $0.2 \times 0.2 \times 0.2$.
3. By what number should $16\frac{2}{3}$ be divided to get 5?

Brainteaser

A vegetable vendor is 5 feet 8 inches tall. What does he weigh?

(Answer for Brainteaser on page 36)

Maths Lab Activity

Grids and Decimals

Objective: To represent the product of decimal numbers 0.4 and 0.6 on a grid paper.

Material required: Grid paper, yellow, light blue and purple-coloured sketch pens

Procedure:

Step 1 Take the grid paper and cut three 10×10 square pieces from it. Number each square.

Step 2 Now, colour four columns of the 10×10 grid paper on all grids from one to hundred. This would denote 0.4. Similarly colour six rows of another grid with light blue to represent 0.6

Step 3 Take the third grid paper and colour all the numbered squares that are common to the first two grids purple.

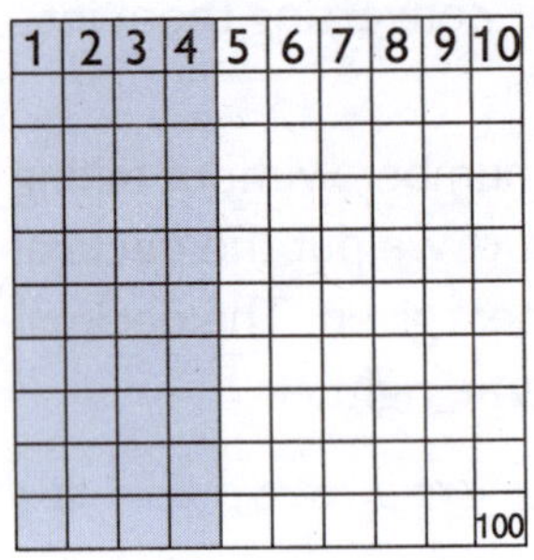

Decimal number 0.4

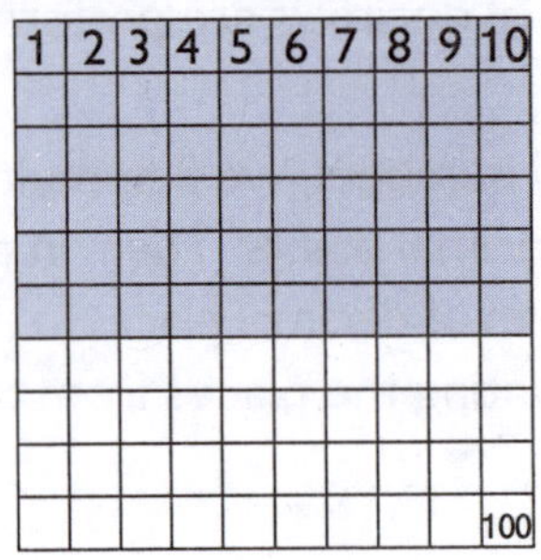

Decimal number 0.6

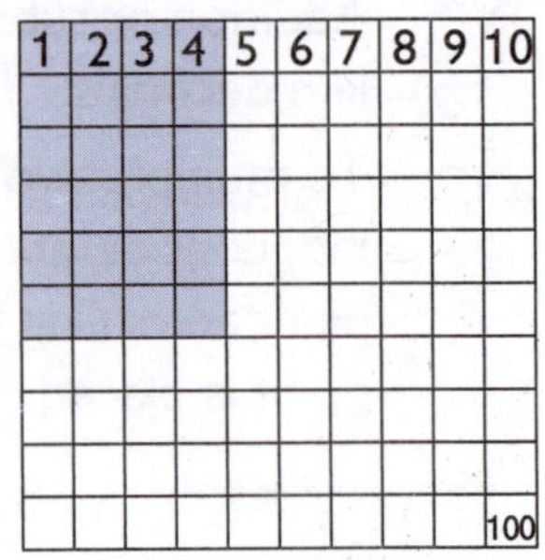

Intersection product

The common region represents 24 squares, which is the product of $0.4 \times 0.6 = 0.24$

This implies that 24 squares out of 100 are common.

Answer for Brainteaser from page 35

The vegetable vendor weighs vegetables.

Rewind

CHAPTERS 1–2

1. Classify the following statements as true or false.
   a. The sum of two integers can never be 0.
   b. The difference of two integers can never be 0.
   c. The product of two integers can never be 0.
   d. The product of two integers with opposite signs is always negative.
   e. The sum of two integers is always greater than their difference.

2. Using properties of integers simplify the following.
   a. $30 \times (-17) + 30 \times (-13)$
   b. $40 \times 18 + 12 \times 40$
   c. $250 \times 4 \times 317$
   d. $50 \times 39 + (-29) \times 50$
   e. $39(87 + 13)$

3. A boy is standing on the top of a building that is 45 m high. He throws a stone high in the air. If the stone reaches the highest point and falls 61 m to the ground below, how high did the boy throw the stone from the roof?

4. A monkey climbs 2 m per second up a slippery pole and slips down 1 m over the next second. If the pole is 11 m high, how much time will he take to reach the top?

5. State which of the two is greater.
   a. $(18 + 19) \times 20$ or $18 + 19 \times 20$
   b. $(6 - 9) \times 15$ or $6 - 9 \times 15$
   c. $[(-5) - 6] \times (-8)$ or $(-5) - 6 \times (-8)$
   d. $[(-14) + 14] \times (-14)$ or $(-14) + 14 \times (-14)$
   e. $5 \times (-6) \times 7$ or $(-5) \times (-6) \times 7$

6. Perform the following divisions.
   a. $48 \div (-3)$
   b. $(-125) \div (-25)$
   c. $120 \div 30$
   d. $0 \div (-36)$
   e. $(-42) \div (-42)$

7. Multiply the following.
   a. $6 \times \frac{3}{9}$
   b. $\frac{1}{8} \times \frac{1}{8}$
   c. $5\frac{3}{7} \times \frac{1}{19}$
   d. $\frac{3}{5}$ of 75
   e. $\frac{3}{7} \times \frac{14}{27}$

CHAPTERS 1–2 Rewind

8. Find the product of the following.

a. $6\frac{1}{3} \times 1\frac{1}{19} \times \frac{4}{5}$ b. $7\frac{3}{5} \times \frac{7}{25} \times 2\frac{2}{19}$ c. $9\frac{1}{3} \times 3\frac{1}{2} \times 4\frac{2}{7}$

d. $2\frac{3}{4} \times 3\frac{3}{4} \times \frac{4}{11}$ e. $\frac{7}{8} \times 4\frac{4}{5} \times 3\frac{3}{4}$

9. Simplify the following.

a. $\frac{2}{3} \div \frac{6}{7}$ b. $\frac{9}{11} \div \frac{3}{22}$ c. $\frac{31}{33} \div \frac{62}{121}$

d. $3\frac{1}{7} \div 4\frac{5}{7}$ e. $20\frac{2}{5} \div 10\frac{1}{5}$

10. A family spent $\frac{1}{5}$ of the monthly income of ₹26,500 on transport. Find out their monthly expenditure on transport.

11. At a party, $\frac{5}{9}$ of the persons were dressed in black and $\frac{4}{9}$ of them were in white. If there were a total of 1,800 people at the party, how many were dressed in black and how many were in white?

12. Monya wants to pour $5\frac{1}{3}$ litres of juice equally into 8 glasses. How much juice should she pour in each glass?

13. A total of 6 cartons weigh $42\frac{1}{2}$ kg. Find the weight of 1 carton.

14. If 30 packets of sweets weigh $7\frac{1}{2}$ kg, find the weight of 1 packet. Also find the weight of 100 packets.

15. If $2\frac{1}{2}$ m of cloth is required to make 1 shirt, how much cloth will be required to make 60 similar shirts?

Rational Numbers

CHAPTER 3

Let's briefly recap the different kinds of numbers we have shared so far:

The numbers 1, 2, 3, 4 ... are called **natural numbers** and denoted by the letter N. When 0 is introduced along with the natural numbers, they become **whole numbers** and are denoted by the letter W. In between two whole numbers, we get **fractions**, which comprise whole numbers in the numerator and the denominator. We cannot have 0 in the denominator of a fraction. Zero and the numbers that lie on either side of 0 on the number line, are termed integers and are denoted by Z or I.

At a glance let us see the numbers.

Natural numbers	$N = \{1, 2, 3, 4 \ldots\}$
Whole numbers	$W = \{0, 1, 2, 3, 4 \ldots\}$
Integers	$I = \{\ldots -3, -2, -1, 0, 1, 2, 3 \ldots\}$
Fractions	$F = \left(\frac{1}{4}, \frac{2}{4}, \frac{5}{9}, \frac{7}{12} \ldots\right)$

We will now learn about special types of fractions that are called **rational numbers** and are denoted by the letter Q.

Rational numbers are numbers that can be expressed in the form $\frac{p}{q}$, where p and q are integers and $q \neq 0$.

Rational numbers are similar to fractions. The difference between rational numbers and fractions is that fractions have whole numbers in the numerator and denominator while rational numbers have integers in the numerator and denominator. Hence a rational number can be positive or negative.

Example: $\frac{2}{3}, \frac{1}{5}, \frac{7}{8}$ are all fractions but $\left(-\frac{2}{3}\right), \left(-\frac{7}{8}\right), \frac{1}{(-5)}$ are not fractions. These are rational numbers since they are negative numbers.

Thus:

1. All fractions are rational numbers but all rational numbers are not fractions.
2. All decimal numbers are rational numbers.
3. All whole numbers are rational numbers.
4. All integers are rational numbers. Hence, all numbers we know till now can be expressed as rational numbers.

Example 1: A fraction $\left(-\frac{3}{4}\right)$ is a rational number.

Example 2: 0.21 is a decimal that can be written as $\frac{21}{100}$. A fraction is a rational number, therefore, a decimal is a rational number.

Example 3: 5 is a whole number. It can be written as $\frac{5}{1}$. $\left(\frac{p}{q} \text{ form, where } q \neq 0\right)$. Hence, a whole number is a rational number.

Example 4: The integer (-3) can be written as $\left(-\frac{3}{1}\right)$, which is a rational number.

Positive and Negative Rational Numbers

Rational numbers can be positive as well as negative. If the numerator and the denominator are both positive, then the rational number is positive, but if one of them is negative (either the numerator or the denominator), then the rational number is negative.

Example 1: Positive rational numbers: $\frac{3}{5}, \frac{9}{11}, \frac{5}{1}, \frac{15}{21}$

Example 2: Negative rational numbers: $\left(-\frac{4}{7}\right), \frac{16}{(-21)}, \left(-\frac{6}{13}\right), \left(-\frac{2}{5}\right)$

Alert!

If both the numerator and the denominator of a rational number are negative, then the rational number will be a positive number.

The number 0 is neither a positive number nor a negative one.

Equivalent Rational Numbers

We know how to express any fraction as an equivalent fraction by multiplying the numerator and the denominator by the same whole number.

Example: $\frac{2}{3} = \frac{2 \times 4}{3 \times 4} = \frac{8}{12}$ Here $\frac{8}{12}$ and $\frac{10}{15}$ are equivalent fractions.

$\frac{2}{3} = \frac{2 \times 5}{3 \times 5} = \frac{10}{15}$

Similarly, we can convert any rational number into an equivalent rational number by multiplying the numerator and the denominator by any integer (positive or negative).

$$\frac{2}{3} = \frac{2}{3} \times \frac{7}{7} = \frac{14}{21}$$

$$\frac{2}{3} = \frac{2 \times (-4)}{3 \times (-4)} = \frac{(-8)}{(-12)} = \frac{8}{12}$$

If both the numerator and the denominator are negative, the rational number will be positive.

Rational Number in a Standard Form

Fractions can be reduced to the lowest term by dividing the numerator and the denominator by their HCF. Similarly, rational numbers also can be reduced to their lowest term by dividing the numerator and the denominator by their HCF.

When rational numbers are in their lowest term, they are said to be in the standard form.

Example 1: Reduce $\left(-\frac{15}{45}\right)$ to it lowest term or write it in the standard form.

The HCF of 15 and 45 is 15. Hence $\frac{(-15) \div 15}{45 \div 15} = \left(-\frac{1}{3}\right)$

Example 2: Write $\frac{14}{(-21)}$ in the standard form.

The HCF of 14 and 21 is 7. Hence

$$\frac{14 \div 7}{(-21) \div 7} = \frac{2}{(-3)}$$

However the denominator has to be positive.

$$\text{so,} \quad \frac{2}{(-3)} \times \frac{(-1)}{(-1)} = \left(-\frac{2}{3}\right)$$

Alert!

The denominator of the rational number should always be positive.

Rational Numbers on the Number Line

Just as natural numbers, whole numbers, integers and fractions can be expressed on the number line, so also can the rational numbers.

All positive numbers lie on the right of zero and all the negative numbers on the left of zero. The same holds true for the rational numbers as well.

Example: Let us denote $\left(-\frac{2}{5}\right), \frac{3}{5}, \left(-\frac{6}{5}\right), \frac{4}{(-5)}, \frac{7}{5}$, on the number line.

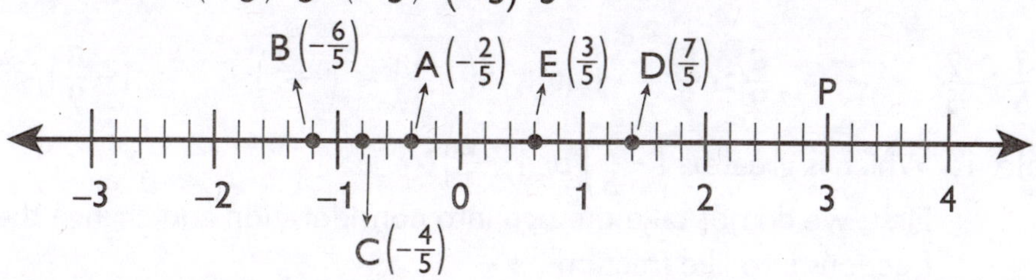

Since all the rational numbers have 5 in the denominator, we divide the distance between any two units into 5 equal parts.

$\left(-\frac{2}{5}\right)$ will lie between 0 and (-1). It is a negative rational number.

The point A represents $-\frac{2}{5}$.

$\frac{3}{1}$ is a whole number, written in the form of a rational number. It is represented by P.

$\left(-\frac{6}{5}\right)$ is smaller than -1 and lies between -1 and -2. It is represented by B.

$\frac{4}{(-5)}$ can be written as $\left(-\frac{4}{5}\right)$. It lies between 0 and -1. It is represented by C.

$\frac{7}{5}$ is greater than 1 and lies between 1 and 2. It is represented by D.

In integers, we have pairs equidistant from 0 but in opposite directions, for example, -5, 5 are a pair of integers where -5 is on the left of 0, whereas 5 is on the right of 0 on the number line.

Similarly, in rational numbers, we have pairs that are equidistant from 0 but in the opposite direction. For example, $\left(-\frac{3}{4}\right), \frac{3}{4}$ are a pair of rational numbers that are equidistant from 0 on either side of it on the number line.

Here are some examples to show pairs of rational numbers equidistant from 0 on the number line: $\left(-\frac{4}{5}\right)$ and $\frac{4}{5}$; $\left(-\frac{2}{7}\right)$ and $\frac{2}{7}$.

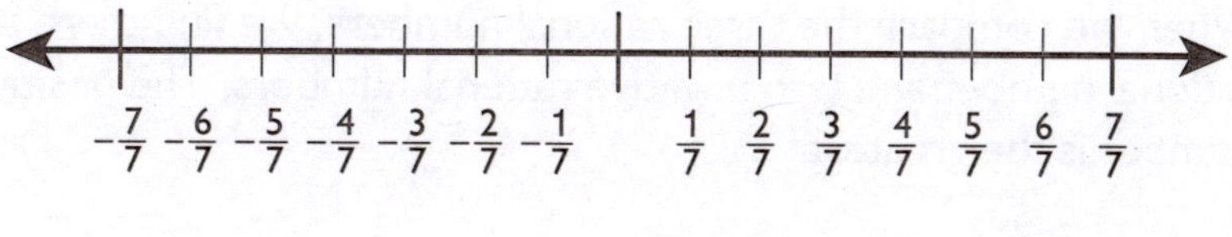

The number line on the previous page shows the pairs of rational numbers on the *right* of 0 (positive) and on the *left* of 0 (negative).

Comparing Rational Numbers

From the number line, we can see that numbers on the right of 0 are increasing, for example, $\frac{6}{7} > \frac{5}{7} > \frac{4}{7}$.

The numbers on the left of 0 are decreasing, for example, $\left(-\frac{6}{7}\right) < \left(-\frac{5}{7}\right) < \left(-\frac{4}{7}\right)$.

From the above examples we can conclude the following rules for rational numbers:

1. All positive rational numbers are greater than 0.
2. All positive rational numbers are greater than all negative numbers.
3. All negative rational numbers are smaller than 0.

Alert!

$\frac{3}{5} > \frac{2}{5}$; $\frac{8}{9} > \frac{5}{9}$ but $\left(-\frac{3}{5}\right) < \left(-\frac{2}{5}\right)$; $\left(-\frac{8}{9}\right) < \left(-\frac{5}{9}\right)$

Example 1: Which is greater, $\left(-\frac{2}{5}\right)$ or $\left(-\frac{2}{3}\right)$?

First, we do not take the sign into consideration and change these unlike fractions into like fractions.

So, $\frac{2}{5} \times \frac{3}{5} = \frac{6}{15}$ and $\frac{2}{3} \times \frac{5}{5} = \frac{10}{15}$.

By converting $\frac{2}{5}$ and $\frac{2}{3}$ into the fractions, we get $\frac{6}{15}$ and $\frac{10}{15}$ respectively.

At this stage we put the sign back is front of the fractions.

$\left(-\frac{6}{15}\right)$ and $\left(-\frac{10}{15}\right)$.

Clearly, $\left(-\frac{10}{15}\right)$ is smaller than $\left(-\frac{6}{15}\right)$ because it is to the left of $\left(-\frac{6}{15}\right)$ on the number line.

Hence: $\left(-\frac{6}{15}\right) > \left(-\frac{10}{15}\right)$ or $\left(-\frac{2}{5}\right) > \left(-\frac{2}{3}\right)$

Example 2: Which is greater, $\frac{6}{18}$ or $\left(-\frac{5}{15}\right)$?

Since one is a positive rational number and the other is a negative rational number, the positive rational will always be greater than the negative one.

Thus, $\frac{6}{18} > \left(-\frac{5}{15}\right)$

If two rational numbers are of the same sign, we need to compare them by making them into like fractions but if they are of opposite signs, the positive rational number will always be greater than the negative rational number.

Example 3: Arrange the following rational numbers in descending order.

$\frac{2}{7}, \left(-\frac{1}{4}\right), \frac{11}{(-55)}$

When we compare the three rational numbers, we find there is one positive rational number and two negative rational numbers. The positive rational number is the greatest.

Now, to compare $\left(-\frac{1}{4}\right)$ and $\frac{11}{(-55)}$, we need to first convert them into like fractions.

Thus, $\frac{11}{(-55)} = \left(-\frac{11}{55}\right) = \left(-\frac{1}{5}\right)$.

The LCM of 4 and 5 is 20.

Taking only the positive sign, we have $\frac{1}{4} \times \frac{5}{5} = \frac{5}{20}$

$\frac{1}{5} \times \frac{4}{4} = \frac{4}{20}$

Now $5 > 4$ so $\frac{5}{20} > \frac{4}{20}$ or by simplifying $\frac{1}{4} > \frac{1}{5}$.

However, in negative numbers we have the opposite, that is greater.

Therefore $\left(-\frac{1}{4}\right) < \left(-\frac{1}{5}\right)$ or $\left(-\frac{1}{5}\right) > \left(-\frac{1}{4}\right)$.

To conclude, the rational numbers in descending order are:

$$\frac{2}{7}, \left(-\frac{1}{5}\right), \left(-\frac{1}{4}\right) \quad \text{or} \quad \frac{2}{7}, \frac{11}{(-55)}, \left(-\frac{1}{4}\right)$$

Rational Numbers Between Two Rational Numbers

We can find finite numbers between any two natural numbers, any two whole numbers or any two integers. For example, between numbers 1 and 5 there are three natural numbers—2, 3 and 4.

Again between the numbers 0 and 7, there are six whole numbers 1, 2, 3, 4, 5 and 6.

Also between the numbers (−3) and 2, there are four integers (−2), (−1), 0 and 1.

Case 1 Now let us write the rational numbers between $\frac{2}{15}$ and $\frac{7}{15}$. We can easily write these as $\frac{3}{15}, \frac{4}{15}, \frac{5}{15}$ and $\frac{6}{15}$.

Case 2 But we can write $\frac{2}{15}$ as $\frac{2}{15} \times \frac{2}{2} = \frac{4}{30}$ and $\frac{7}{15}$ as $\frac{7}{15} \times \frac{2}{2} = \frac{14}{30}$.

So between $\frac{4}{30}$ and $\frac{14}{30}$, the rational numbers would be $\frac{5}{30}, \frac{6}{30}, \frac{7}{30}, \frac{8}{30}, \frac{9}{30}, \frac{10}{30}, \frac{11}{30}, \frac{12}{30}, \frac{13}{30}$. These numbers are also between $\frac{2}{15}$ and $\frac{7}{15}$ as $\frac{4}{30}$ and $\frac{14}{30}$ and are like rational numbers.

Case 3 If we write $\frac{2}{15}$ as $\frac{2 \times 10}{15 \times 10} = \frac{20}{150}$ and $\frac{4}{15}$ as $\frac{4 \times 10}{15 \times 10} = \frac{40}{150}$,

we can write a new set of rational numbers between $\frac{20}{150}$ and $\frac{40}{150}$.

Case 4 If $\frac{2}{15}$ is written as $\frac{2 \times 100}{15 \times 100} = \frac{200}{1500}$ and $\frac{4}{15}$ is written as $\frac{4 \times 100}{15 \times 100} = \frac{400}{1500}$,

we get another set of rational numbers.

Hence, between $\frac{2}{15}$ and $\frac{7}{15}$ we get an unlimited number of rational numbers.

Example 1: Find six rational numbers between 0 and 1.

Let us write 0 and 1 as rational numbers

$$0 = \frac{0}{1} \quad \text{and} \quad 1 = \frac{1}{1}$$

When we multiply the numerator and the denominator of both the rational numbers by 8, we get $\frac{0 \times 8}{1 \times 8} = \frac{0}{8}$ and $\frac{1 \times 8}{1 \times 8} = \frac{8}{8}$.

Case 1 Now between $\frac{0}{8}$ and $\frac{8}{8}$ we can write the following rational numbers $\frac{1}{8}, \frac{2}{8}, \frac{3}{8}, \frac{4}{8}, \frac{5}{8}, \frac{6}{8}, \frac{7}{8}$. We can select any six of them.

Case 2 We could have multiplied $\frac{0}{1}$ and $\frac{1}{1}$ by 10 also and got $\frac{0 \times 10}{1 \times 10} = \frac{0}{10}$ and $\frac{1}{1} \times \frac{10}{10} = \frac{10}{10}$.

Now between $\frac{0}{10}$ and $\frac{10}{10}$ we can write rational numbers as $\frac{1}{10}, \frac{2}{10}, \frac{3}{10}, \frac{4}{10}, \frac{5}{10}, \frac{6}{10}, \frac{7}{10}, \frac{8}{10}, \frac{9}{10}$. Out of these, any six rational numbers can be selected.

Example 2: Find eight rational numbers between $\left(-\frac{2}{3}\right)$ and $\frac{1}{(-5)}$.

The first step is to write the rational numbers in the standard form. The LCM of 3 and 5 is 15 so, $\left(-\frac{2}{3}\right) = \frac{(-2) \times 5}{3 \times 5} = \left(-\frac{10}{15}\right)$ and $\frac{1}{(-5)} = \left(-\frac{1}{5}\right) = \frac{(-1) \times 3}{5 \times 3} = \left(-\frac{3}{15}\right)$

Now between $\left(-\frac{10}{15}\right)$ and $\left(-\frac{3}{15}\right)$ we have the rational numbers $\left(-\frac{9}{15}\right)$, $\left(-\frac{8}{15}\right), \left(-\frac{7}{15}\right), \left(-\frac{6}{15}\right), \left(-\frac{5}{15}\right), \left(-\frac{4}{15}\right)$. These are only six, so we write, $\left(-\frac{10}{15}\right)$ as $\frac{(-10) \times 2}{15 \times 2} = \left(-\frac{20}{30}\right)$ and $\left(-\frac{36}{15}\right)$ as $\frac{(-3) \times 2}{15 \times 2} = \left(-\frac{6}{30}\right)$

Now the rational numbers between them are as follows:

$\left(-\frac{19}{30}\right), \left(-\frac{18}{30}\right), \left(-\frac{17}{30}\right), \left(-\frac{16}{30}\right), \left(-\frac{15}{30}\right), \left(-\frac{14}{30}\right), \left(-\frac{13}{30}\right), \left(-\frac{12}{30}\right), \left(-\frac{11}{30}\right), \left(-\frac{10}{30}\right), \left(-\frac{9}{30}\right), \left(-\frac{8}{30}\right), \left(-\frac{7}{30}\right)$

We can select any eight out of them.

Example 3: Find seven rational numbers between $\left(-\frac{1}{5}\right)$ and $\frac{1}{5}$.

$\left(-\frac{1}{5}\right)$ can be written as $\frac{(-1) \times 4}{5 \times 4} = \left(-\frac{4}{20}\right)$ and $\frac{1}{5}$ can be written as $\frac{1 \times 4}{5 \times 4} = \frac{4}{20}$.

Now, between $\left(-\frac{4}{20}\right)$ and $\frac{4}{20}$ we have the following rational numbers $\left(-\frac{3}{20}\right)$, $\left(-\frac{2}{20}\right), \left(-\frac{1}{20}\right), \frac{0}{20}, \frac{1}{20}, \frac{2}{20}, \frac{3}{20}$. These are the seven rational numbers between $\left(-\frac{1}{5}\right)$ and $\frac{1}{5}$.

Practice Exercise 3.1

1. Write the following as rational numbers in the form $\frac{p}{q}$, where $q \neq 0$.

   a. 15 b. 2.7 c. (−18) d. 0.67 e. 0

2. Identify the positive and negative rational numbers. Write them in two separate columns.

a. $\frac{7}{(-8)}$ b. $\frac{63}{67}$ c. $\frac{(-10)}{(-21)}$ d. $\left(-\frac{4}{17}\right)$ e. $\frac{17}{39}$

f. $\left(-\frac{100}{9}\right)$ g. $\frac{(-2)}{(-5)}$ h. $\frac{6}{15}$ i. $\left(-\frac{11}{19}\right)$ j. $\frac{7}{(-13)}$

3. Write the following rational numbers in the standard form.

a. $\frac{(-16)}{(-20)}$ b. $\frac{100}{(-300)}$ c. $\left(-\frac{14}{70}\right)$ d. $\frac{11}{121}$ e. $\frac{(-19)}{(-38)}$

4. Write three equivalent rational numbers for each of the following.

a. $\frac{3}{10}$ b. $\left(-\frac{4}{5}\right)$ c. $\frac{7}{(-8)}$ d. $\frac{(-10)}{(-20)}$ e. $\left(-\frac{9}{11}\right)$

5. Draw a number line and mark the following rational numbers on it: $\left(-\frac{6}{5}\right)$, $\left(-\frac{3}{5}\right)$, $\frac{0}{5}$, $\frac{2}{5}$, $\frac{4}{5}$.

6. Identify the greater rational number from each of the following pairs.

a. $\frac{7}{8}$ and $\left(-\frac{2}{15}\right)$ b. $\left(-\frac{1}{7}\right)$ and $\frac{2}{(-5)}$ c. $\frac{8}{(-17)}$ and $\frac{9}{17}$

d. $\left(-\frac{12}{25}\right)$ and $\left(-\frac{6}{5}\right)$ e. $\frac{12}{13}$ and $\frac{13}{39}$

7. Arrange the following rational numbers in ascending order.

a. $\frac{9}{18}$, $\frac{3}{(-4)}$ and $\left(-\frac{10}{50}\right)$ b. $\frac{2}{7}$, $\left(-\frac{1}{4}\right)$ and $\frac{11}{(-55)}$ c. $\frac{3}{(-21)}$, $\frac{0}{5}$, $\left(-\frac{2}{7}\right)$, $\frac{1}{3}$

d. $\frac{4}{9}$, $\left(-\frac{2}{6}\right)$, $\frac{4}{(-18)}$ e. $\left(-\frac{6}{7}\right)$, $\frac{3}{14}$, $\frac{7}{21}$

8. Arrange the following rational numbers in descending order.

a. $\left(-\frac{3}{8}\right)$, $\left(-\frac{7}{12}\right)$, $\left(-\frac{1}{4}\right)$ b. $\frac{11}{12}$, $\left(-\frac{3}{4}\right)$, $\frac{7}{(-6)}$ c. $\left(-\frac{3}{4}\right)$, $\frac{0}{8}$, $\frac{6}{(-16)}$

d. $\frac{2}{7}$, $\left(-\frac{3}{7}\right)$, $\frac{8}{(-21)}$ e. $\frac{11}{13}$, $\left(-\frac{1}{3}\right)$, $\left(-\frac{10}{13}\right)$

9. Find four rational numbers between the following numbers.

a. $\left(-\frac{2}{3}\right)$ and 0 b. $\frac{9}{10}$ and $\left(-\frac{1}{5}\right)$ c. $\left(-\frac{4}{7}\right)$ and $\frac{1}{7}$

d. $\frac{11}{12}$ and $\left(-\frac{1}{2}\right)$ e. $\left(-\frac{4}{13}\right)$ and $\frac{13}{39}$

10. Find ten rational numbers between the following numbers.

a. 0 and $\frac{5}{10}$ b. (-10) and $\frac{3}{10}$ c. $\frac{5}{16}$ and $\left(-\frac{5}{4}\right)$

d. $\left(-\frac{4}{9}\right)$ and $\frac{1}{(-3)}$ e. $\frac{2}{(-17)}$ and $\frac{1}{17}$

Addition of Rational Numbers

Like for the addition of fractions and integers, a similar set of rules apply for the addition of rational numbers. The rules here are a combination of the rules for fractions and integers.

Just like fractions, rational numbers with the same denominator are called **like rational numbers** and those with different denominators are called **unlike rational numbers.**

Rules for Addition of Rational Numbers

Step 1: Write the rational numbers in their standard form.

Step 2: If they are like rational numbers (if the denominators are the same), then add the numerators and leave the denominator as is.

Step 3: If they are unlike rational numbers (if the denominators are different), then convert them into like rational numbers and then add as in step 2.

Step 4: Write the answer in the standard form.

Example 1: Add $\frac{7}{9}$ and $\frac{(-4)}{9}$.

The two rational numbers are in the standard form.

The denominators are the same so we can add the numerators.

$$\frac{7}{9} + \frac{(-4)}{9}$$

$$= \frac{7 + (-4)}{9} = \frac{3}{9} = \frac{1}{3}$$

Example 2: Add $\left(-\frac{5}{11}\right)$ and $\frac{(-4)}{(-11)}$.

Writing $\frac{(-4)}{(-11)}$ in the standard form, we get $\frac{4}{11}$

$$\left(-\frac{5}{11}\right) + \frac{4}{11} = \frac{(-5) + 4}{11} = \left(-\frac{1}{11}\right)$$

Example 3: Add $\left(-\frac{5}{12}\right)$ and $\frac{2}{3}$.

These are unlike rational numbers, so first we convert them into like rational numbers. For this, we find the LCM of 12 and 3, which is 12.

Thus, $\left(-\frac{5}{12}\right) \times \frac{1}{1} = \left(-\frac{5}{12}\right)$ and $\frac{2}{3} \times \frac{4}{4} = \frac{8}{12}$

Now $\frac{(-5)}{12} + \frac{8}{12} = \frac{(-5) + 8}{12} = \frac{3}{12} = \frac{1}{4}$

Example 4: Add $\left(-\frac{4}{5}\right)$ and $\frac{3}{(-4)}$.

$\left(-\frac{4}{5}\right)$ is in the standard form.

$\frac{3}{(-4)}$ can be written as $\left(-\frac{3}{4}\right)$ to bring it to the standard form.

$$\left(-\frac{4}{5}\right) + \left(\frac{-3}{4}\right) = \left(-\frac{4}{5}\right) - \frac{3}{4}$$

The LCM of the denominator 5 and 4 is 20.

Thus, $\left(-\frac{4}{5}\right) \times \frac{4}{4} = \left(-\frac{16}{20}\right)$ and $\left(-\frac{3}{4}\right) \times \frac{5}{5} = \left(-\frac{15}{20}\right)$

Now $\frac{(-16)}{20} + \frac{(-15)}{20} = \frac{(-16) + (-15)}{20} = \left(-\frac{31}{20}\right)$

Subtraction of Rational Numbers

We can subtract two rational numbers by using a combination of the rules of the fractions and integers.

The additive inverse of a rational number is a number that has the same magnitude as the given number but on the opposite side of 0 lying at the same distance.

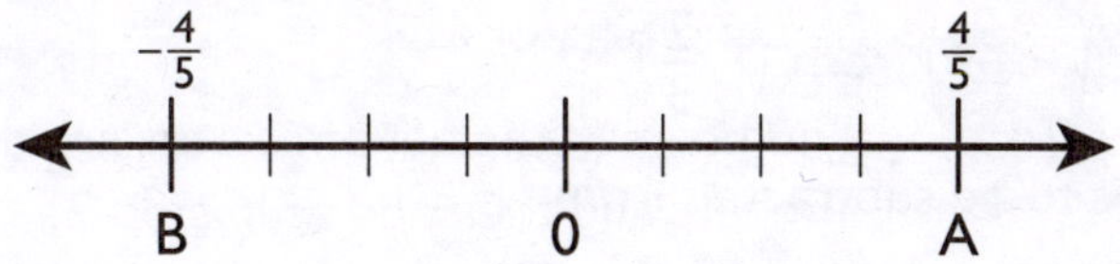

Thus the additive inverse of the rational number $\frac{4}{5}$ is $\left(-\frac{4}{5}\right)$ and the additive inverse of the rational number $\left(-\frac{4}{5}\right)$ is $\frac{4}{5}$.

Alert!

When we add the given number to its additive inverse, the sum is 0.

$$\frac{4}{5} + \frac{(-4)}{5} = \frac{4 + (-4)}{5} = 0$$

Rules for Subtraction of Rational Numbers

Step 1: Write the rational numbers in their standard form.

Step 2: Add the additive inverse of the rational number that is to be subtracted to the other rational number.

Step 3: Follow the rules of addition of rational numbers while adding the additive inverse.

Example 1: Subtract $\frac{2}{9}$ from $\left(-\frac{5}{9}\right)$.

The number to be subtracted is $\frac{2}{9}$. The additive inverse of $\frac{2}{9}$ is $\left(-\frac{2}{9}\right)$. So we write

$$\left(-\frac{5}{9}\right) - \frac{2}{9} = \frac{(-5) - 2}{9} = \left(-\frac{7}{9}\right)$$

Example 2: Subtract $\frac{2}{(-11)}$ from $\left(-\frac{5}{11}\right)$.

The number to be subtracted is $\frac{2}{(-11)}$ and its additive inverse is $\frac{2}{11}$.

We write $\left(-\frac{5}{11}\right) + \frac{2}{11} = \frac{(-5) + 2}{11} = \left(-\frac{3}{11}\right)$

Example 3: Subtract $\frac{11}{(-13)}$ from $\frac{1}{2}$.

$\frac{11}{(-13)}$ is to be subtracted from $\frac{1}{2}$. So we write the additive inverse of $\frac{11}{(-13)}$, which is $\frac{11}{13}$.

Now we add this to the number from which we have to subtract it. Thus, we get $\frac{1}{2} + \frac{11}{13}$

Now they are unlike rational numbers. The LCM of 2 and 13 is 26.

We change the unlike rational numbers to like rational numbers.

$$\frac{1 \times 26}{2 \times 26} = \frac{26}{52} = \frac{1 \times 13}{2 \times 13} = \frac{13}{26} \text{ and } \frac{11 \times 2}{13 \times 2} = \frac{22}{26}$$

Thus, $\frac{1}{2} + \frac{11}{13} = \frac{13}{26} + \frac{22}{26} = \frac{13 + 22}{26} = \frac{35}{26}$

Example 4: Subtract $\left(-\frac{9}{15}\right)$ from $\left(-\frac{2}{3}\right)$.

$\left(-\frac{9}{15}\right)$ is to be subtracted from $\left(-\frac{2}{3}\right)$

The additive inverse of $\left(-\frac{9}{15}\right)$ is $\frac{9}{15}$, which is to be added to $\left(-\frac{2}{3}\right)$

Thus, $\left(-\frac{2}{3}\right) + \frac{9}{15}$

Applying the rules of addition, we get

$$\frac{(-2) \times 5}{3 \times 5} + \frac{9 \times 1}{15 \times 1} = \left(-\frac{10}{15}\right) + \frac{9}{15} = \frac{(-10) + 9}{15} = \left(-\frac{1}{15}\right)$$

Example 5: Find the value of $\frac{4}{7} - \frac{(-1)}{3} + \frac{8}{21}$

In Step 1, we convert unlike rational numbers into like rational numbers. The LCM of 7, 3 and 21 is 21.

The additive inverse of $\left(-\frac{1}{3}\right)$ is $\frac{1}{3}$

Hence, $\frac{4}{7} + \frac{1}{3} + \frac{8}{21} = \frac{4 \times 3}{7 \times 3} + \frac{1 \times 7}{3 \times 7} + \frac{8 \times 1}{21 \times 1} = \frac{12}{21} + \frac{7}{21} + \frac{8}{21}$

$$= \frac{12 + 7 + 8}{21} = \frac{27}{21} = \frac{9}{7}$$

Alert!

Whenever you have to subtract a rational number, you add its additive inverse to the rational number from which it is to be subtracted.

Practice Exercise 3.2

1. Add the following rational numbers.

   a. $\frac{7}{8} + \frac{(-3)}{8} + \frac{1}{8}$ b. $\left(-\frac{6}{7}\right) + \frac{1}{(-7)} + \frac{3}{7}$ c. $\frac{4}{11} + \frac{6}{(-11)} + \frac{(-5)}{(-11)}$

   d. $\frac{1}{10} + \frac{4}{10} + \frac{(-3)}{10}$ e. $\frac{3}{5} + \left(-\frac{2}{5}\right) + \frac{7}{(-5)}$

2. Add the following rational numbers.

   a. $\frac{4}{7} + \left(-\frac{2}{3}\right) + \frac{4}{21}$ b. $\frac{2}{3} + \frac{13}{(-15)} + \frac{(-8)}{5}$ c. $\frac{2}{(-3)} + \left(-\frac{7}{12}\right) + \frac{5}{6}$

   d. $\frac{6}{7} + \frac{3}{14} + \left(-\frac{5}{21}\right)$ e. $\frac{7}{10} + \left(-\frac{11}{20}\right) + \frac{19}{30}$

3. Write the additive inverse of each of the following.

a. $\frac{7}{(-9)}$ b. $\frac{6}{11}$ c. $\frac{(-7)}{(-15)}$ d. $\left(-\frac{21}{100}\right)$ e. $\frac{17}{(-35)}$

4. Subtract the following.

a. $\frac{3}{16}$ from $\left(-\frac{8}{16}\right)$ b. $\frac{7}{14}$ from $\left(-\frac{6}{14}\right)$ c. $\left(-\frac{13}{19}\right)$ from $\frac{8}{19}$

d. $\left(-\frac{13}{16}\right)$ from $\left(-\frac{7}{16}\right)$ e. $\frac{18}{23}$ from $\left(-\frac{20}{23}\right)$

5. Subtract the following.

a. $\frac{11}{(-15)}$ from $\frac{1}{2}$ b. $\left(-\frac{9}{13}\right)$ from $\frac{2}{3}$ c. $\frac{5}{11}$ from $\left(-\frac{17}{22}\right)$

d. $\frac{13}{16}$ from $\frac{17}{24}$ e. $\frac{5}{8}$ from $\left(-\frac{11}{12}\right)$

6. Find the value of each of the following.

a. $\frac{4}{7}-\frac{(-1)}{3}+\frac{8}{21}$ b. $\frac{2}{5}+\frac{(-7)}{(-10)}-\frac{8}{15}$ c. $\frac{11}{12}+\frac{(-3)}{(-8)}+\frac{(-1)}{4}$

d. $\frac{(-1)}{(-4)}-\frac{11}{12}+\frac{(-7)}{8}$ e. $\frac{5}{6}-\frac{(-3)}{4}-\frac{(-9)}{12}$

7. What should be added to $\left(-\frac{11}{19}\right)$ to make the sum $\frac{3}{5}$?

8. The sum of two rational numbers is $\left(-\frac{7}{12}\right)$. If one of the numbers is $\left(-\frac{2}{3}\right)$, find the other.

9. The sum of three rational numbers is $\frac{15}{16}$. If two of the rational numbers are $\left(-\frac{7}{8}\right)$ and $\frac{3}{4}$, find the third rational number.

10. Which is greater—the sum of $\left(-\frac{3}{10}\right)$ and $\frac{7}{9}$ or the sum of $\frac{7}{8}$ and $\left(-\frac{15}{24}\right)$—and by how much?

Multiplication of Rational Numbers

The rules for the multiplication of rational numbers is a combination of the rules used for fractions and for integers.

Rules for Multiplication of Rational Numbers

Step 1: Write the rational number in the standard form.

Step 2: Multiply each numerator by using the rules for multiplication of integers.

Step 3: Multiply each denominator by using the rules for multiplication of integers.

Step 4: The product will be $\rightarrow \frac{\text{product of numerators}}{\text{product of denominators}}$

Step 5: Write the product in the standard form.

Example 1: Find the product of $\left(-\frac{7}{14}\right)\times\frac{4}{(-6)}$.

$$-\frac{\cancel{7}^{1}}{\cancel{14}_{2}}\times\frac{\cancel{4}^{2}}{\cancel{-6}_{3}}=\left(-\frac{7}{14}\right)\times\left(-\frac{4}{6}\right)$$

$$=\frac{(-1)\times(-2)}{2\times 3}=\frac{2}{6}=\frac{1}{3}$$

Example 2: Find the product of $\frac{15}{(-20)} \times \frac{3}{(-9)}$.

Writing in the standard form we get, $\left(-\frac{15}{20}\right) \times \left(-\frac{3}{9}\right)$

$$= \frac{(-15) \times (-3)}{20 \times 9} = \frac{45}{180} = \frac{1}{4}$$

Example 3: Find the product of $9 \times \left(-\frac{4}{27}\right)$.

$$\frac{9}{1} \times \frac{(-4)}{27} = \frac{9 \times (-4)}{1 \times 27} = \left(-\frac{4}{3}\right)$$

Example 4: Find the product of $(-8) \times \frac{10}{40}$.

$$\left(-\frac{8}{1}\right) \times \frac{10}{40} = \frac{(-8) \times 1}{1 \times 4} = \left(-\frac{8}{4}\right) = (-2)$$

Division of Rational Numbers

Similar to multiplication of rational numbers, we can also divide two rational numbers by using a combination of rules used in fractions and integers.

The reciprocal of a rational number is when we invert the rational number. The numerator becomes the denominator and the denominator becomes the numerator.

The reciprocal of $\left(-\frac{5}{16}\right)$ is $\frac{16}{(-5)}$ or $\left(-\frac{16}{5}\right)$.

The reciprocal of (-9) is $\left(-\frac{1}{9}\right)$ since (-9) is written as $\left(-\frac{9}{1}\right)$ as a rational number.

Alert!

1. The reciprocal of a negative number is negative. The sign does not change and only the digits are written in the inverted form. Thus, $\left(-\frac{x}{y}\right)$ becomes $\left(-\frac{y}{x}\right)$.
2. In the additive inverse, the sign of the rational number changes. Thus, $\left(-\frac{x}{y}\right)$ becomes $\frac{x}{y}$.

rational number	additive inverse of the rational number	reciprocal of the rational number
$\left(-\frac{3}{4}\right)$	$\frac{3}{4}$	$\left(-\frac{4}{3}\right)$

Rules for Division of Rational Numbers

Step 1: Write both the rational numbers in their standard form.

Step 2: Find the reciprocal of the divisor.

Step 3: Using the rules of multiplication of rational numbers, multiply the dividend by the reciprocal of the divisor.

Step 4: Write the quotient in the standard form.

Example 1: Solve $\left(-\frac{6}{11}\right) \div \frac{2}{(-5)}$

$$= \frac{(-6)}{11} \div \frac{(-2)}{5}$$

$$= \frac{(-6)}{11} \times \frac{5}{(-2)} = \frac{(-6)}{11} \times \frac{(-5)}{2} = \frac{(-6) \times (-5)}{11 \times 2} = \frac{30}{22} = \frac{15}{11}$$

Example 2: Solve $\frac{5}{7} \div \frac{(-13)}{22}$.

$$\frac{5}{7} \times \frac{(-22)}{13} = \frac{(-110)}{91}$$

Example 3: By which number should we multiply $\frac{6}{(-7)}$ to get $\frac{1}{3}$?

The required number will be $\frac{1}{3} \div \frac{6}{(-7)}$

$$\frac{1}{3} \div \frac{6}{(-7)} = \frac{1}{3} \times \frac{(-7)}{6} = \frac{1 \times (-7)}{3 \times 6} = \frac{(-7)}{18}$$

To check the answer, we multiply $\frac{6}{(-7)}$ by $\left(-\frac{7}{18}\right)$. We should get $\frac{1}{3}$.

$$\frac{6}{(-7)} \times \frac{(-7)}{18} = \frac{(-6)}{7} \times \frac{(-7)}{18} = \frac{(-6) \times (-7)}{7 \times 18}$$

$$= \frac{42}{126} = \frac{1}{3}$$

Hence, the required number is $\left(-\frac{7}{18}\right)$.

Example 4: The product of three rational numbers is $\left(-\frac{4}{5}\right)$. If two of the numbers are $\frac{1}{(-2)}$ and $\frac{3}{5}$, find the third.

The third number will be $\left(-\frac{4}{5}\right) \div \left[\frac{1}{(-2)} \times \frac{3}{5}\right]$

$$\left(-\frac{4}{5}\right) \div \left[\frac{1}{(-2)} \times \frac{3}{5}\right] = \frac{(-4)}{5} \div \left[\frac{(-1)}{2} \times \frac{3}{5}\right] = \frac{(-4)}{5} \div \left[\frac{(-1) \times 3}{2 \times 5}\right]$$

$$= \frac{-4}{5} \div \frac{-3}{10}$$

$$= \frac{(-4)}{5} \times \frac{10}{(-3)} = \frac{(-4)}{5} \times \frac{(-10)}{3} = \frac{(-4) \times (-10)}{5 \times 3} = \frac{40}{15} = \frac{8}{3}$$

To check the answer,

$$\frac{1}{(-2)} \times \frac{3}{5} \times \frac{8}{3} = \frac{(-1)}{2} \times \frac{3}{5} \times \frac{8}{3}$$

$$= \frac{(-1) \times 3 \times 8}{2 \times 5 \times 3} = \frac{(-24)}{30} = \frac{(-4)}{5}$$

Hence, the number is $\frac{8}{3}$.

Decimal Representation of Rational Numbers

A rational number is represented by $\frac{p}{q}$, where $q \neq 0$. Here $\frac{p}{q}$ means, p divided by q. Hence any rational number can be changed into the decimal form by dividing p by q. We perform the long division and write the required number of zeroes after the decimal point without changing the value.

When a rational number is converted into a decimal representation, there could be two possibilities.

Case 1 The division terminates after a few steps. This is called terminating decimal.

Case 2 The division continues indefinitely. This is called non-terminating decimal.

Example 1: Convert $\frac{1}{5}$ into the decimal form.

Write 1 as 1.0 and divide by 5.

```
5) 1.0 (0.2
    0
   10
  −10
    0
```

The decimal form of $\frac{1}{5}$ is 0.2.

Example 2: Convert $\left(-\frac{5}{8}\right)$ into the decimal form.
Write 5 as 5.0 and divide by 8.

```
8) 5.0 ( 0.625
    0
   50
  −48
    20
   −16
     40
    −40
      0
```

The decimal form of $\left(-\frac{5}{8}\right)$ is 0.625.

Example 3: Convert $\frac{1}{3}$ into the decimal form.
Write 1 as 0.1 and divide by 3.

```
3) 10 ( 0.333
    0
   10
   −9
    10
    −9
     10
     −9
      1
```

The decimal form of $\frac{1}{3}$ is 0.333.

Example 4: Convert $\frac{5}{6}$ into the decimal form.
Write 5 as 0.5 and divide by 6.

```
6 )0.5 ( 0.8333
    0
```

$$
\begin{array}{r}
6\,\overline{)\,0.5\,}\,(\,0.8333 \\
0 \\
\hline
50 \\
-48 \\
\hline
20 \\
-18 \\
\hline
20 \\
-18 \\
\hline
2
\end{array}
$$

The decimal form of $\frac{5}{3}$ is 0.8333.

Practice Exercise 3.3

1. Find the product of the following.

   a. $\frac{(-7)}{5} \times (-3)$ b. $\frac{11}{(-33)} \times \frac{3}{5}$ c. $\frac{(-9)}{11} \times \frac{2}{3} \times \frac{9}{16}$

   d. $\frac{5}{(-6)} \times \frac{(-5)}{6} \times \frac{12}{1}$ e. $\frac{3}{(-5)} \times \frac{(-10)}{3} \times \frac{5}{3}$

2. Write the reciprocal of the following.

   a. $\left(-\frac{3}{5}\right)$ b. $\frac{7}{(-9)}$ c. $\frac{(-10)}{(-35)}$ d. $\frac{15}{27}$ e. $\left(-\frac{17}{19}\right)$

3. Find the quotient of the following.

   a. $\frac{3}{5} \div \frac{(-1)}{6}$ b. $\frac{11}{15} \div \frac{3}{5}$ c. $\frac{6}{(-13)} \div (-5)$

   d. $\frac{100}{(-200)} \div \frac{1}{5}$ e. $(-13) \div \frac{2}{(-5)}$

4. Write the decimal representation of the following.

   a. $\frac{25}{8}$ b. $\frac{125}{(-16)}$ c. $\left(-\frac{324}{25}\right)$ d. $\frac{1041}{(-125)}$ e. $\frac{(-714)}{(-40)}$

5. The product of two rational numbers is $\left(-\frac{7}{9}\right)$. If one of the numbers is $\frac{1}{(-6)}$, find the other.

6. Divide the sum of $\left(-\frac{2}{5}\right)$ and $\frac{9}{(-10)}$ by the sum of $\frac{3}{7}$ and $\frac{4}{5}$.

7. Subtract the quotient of $\left(\frac{(-2)}{5} \div \frac{3}{5}\right)$ from the quotient of $\left(\frac{4}{3} \div \frac{(-8)}{9}\right)$.

8. To the product of $\left(-\frac{3}{15}\right)$ and $\frac{4}{(-17)}$, add the product of $\left(-\frac{2}{15}\right)$ and $\frac{3}{7}$.

9. The product of three rational numbers is $\left(-\frac{4}{11}\right)$. If two of the numbers are $\left(-\frac{2}{3}\right)$ and $\left(-\frac{1}{11}\right)$, find the third.

10. Evaluate the following.

    a. $\left[\frac{(-2)}{3} + \frac{1}{2}\right] \div \left[\frac{(-4)}{5} + 2\right]$ b. $\left(-7 \times \frac{1}{6}\right) - \left(\frac{3}{8} \times \frac{4}{9}\right)$

    c. $\left[\frac{4}{(-7)} + \frac{(-9)}{7}\right] \times \left[\frac{3}{5} + \frac{(-10)}{(-15)}\right]$ d. $\left[\frac{(-5)}{6} - \frac{1}{3}\right] \div \left[\frac{2}{3} - \frac{6}{(-5)}\right]$

    e. $\left[(-8) \times \frac{1}{5}\right] + \left[\frac{6}{11} \div \frac{1}{(-11)}\right] - \left[\frac{3}{(-5)} \times \frac{1}{7}\right]$

Highlights

- Rational numbers are those that can be expressed in the form $\frac{p}{q}$, where p and q are integers and $q \neq 0$.
- Rational numbers include fractions and integers.
- Rational numbers can be either positive or negative.
- Rational factors in the standard form have a positive denominator and no common factor between the numerator and denominator except 1.
- Rational numbers can be expressed on the number line.
- Between two rational numbers on the number line, we can find infinite rational numbers.
- For each positive rational number, these exists a negative rational number that lies at the same distance from 0 on the number lines, but in the opposite direction. This is known as its additive inverse.
- The additive inverse of a positive rational number is a negative rational number and vice-versa and the sum of the two is 0.
- Rational numbers with the same denominators are called like rational numbers.
- Rational numbers with different denominators are called unlike rational numbers.
- To add unlike rational numbers, we have to convert them into like rational numbers.
- To subtract a rational number, we add its additive inverse to the number from which we have to subtract it.
- To multiply rational numbers, we find the product of the numerators and the product of the denominators.

$$\frac{p}{q} \times \frac{r}{s} = \frac{p \times r}{q \times s}$$

- The reciprocal of a rational number is the inverse of the rational number. Thus, the reciprocal of $\frac{p}{q}$ is $\frac{q}{p}$.
- To divide by a rational number, we multiply the dividend by the reciprocal of the divisor.
- Rational numbers can be expressed as decimal numbers.

Question: What goes up and never comes down?

Answer for Brainteaser on page 55

Who Can Make the Longest Chain?

Objective: To find the longest chain of rational numbers between a given pair of rational numbers.

Material required: pencil, paper, stop watch and bell

Procedure: Here are a few pairs of rational numbers. The pairs constitute both positive and negative rational numbers.

a. $\left(-\frac{4}{15}\right)$ and $\frac{3}{6}$ b. $\frac{7}{18}$ and $\frac{2}{(-9)}$ c. $\frac{15}{(-5)}$ and $\left(-\frac{2}{25}\right)$

d. $\left(-\frac{3}{2}\right)$ and $\frac{8}{2}$ e. $\frac{11}{7}$ and $\frac{8}{(-7)}$

Work in pairs and each pair should select a pair of rational numbers. Set the timer for 5 minutes and start finding rational numbers between the pairs selected. At the end of 5 minutes, count how many rational numbers your team has found.

The pair of students who find the maximum number of rational numbers between two rational numbers is the winner.

Higher Order Thinking Skills

HOTS

1. Find the integer x such that $\frac{3}{8}$ and $\frac{x}{(-24)}$ are equivalent fractions.

2. Write the decimal representation of $\frac{42138}{625}$.

3. Which is greater—the sum of $\left(-\frac{7}{10}\right)$ and $\frac{3}{(-7)}$ or the sum of $\left(-\frac{1}{8}\right)$ and $\frac{15}{24}$ and by how much?

Answer for Brainteaser from page 54

Addition.

CHAPTER 4

Exponents and Powers

We know that multiplication is repeated addition of a number.

Example 1: $\underbrace{9 + 9 + 9 + 9 + 9 + 9}_{\text{6 times 9}} = 9 \times 6 = 54$

Example 2: $\underbrace{(-2) + (-2) + (-2) + (-2) + (-2)}_{\text{5 times } (-2)} = (-2) \times 5 = -10$

Example 3: $\underbrace{\frac{1}{3} + \frac{1}{3} + \frac{1}{3} + \frac{1}{3} + \frac{1}{3} + \frac{1}{3} + \frac{1}{3}}_{\text{7 times } \frac{1}{3}} = \frac{1}{3} \times 7 = \frac{7}{3}$

Now, we will study what is repeated multiplication.

For example: $2 + 2 + 2 = 6$, but $2 \times 2 \times 2 = 8$

$7 \times 7 \times 7 \times 7 \times 7$, that is, 5 times 7 is written as 7^5

Similarly $10 \times 10 \times 10 \times 10 \times 10 \times 10 \times 10$ or 7 times 10 is written as 10^7

Using exponents is a short way of saying "multiply the number by itself". The little number on top, the exponent, tells you how many times to multiply the number at the bottom, known as the base number.

Exponents

An exponent is a number to which a factor is raised.

Consider $7 \times 7 \times 7 \times 7 \times 7 = 7^5$

Here, 7 is called the base and 5 is called the power or exponent. We read it as "7 raised to the power of 5" or the fifth power of seven.

Let us look at a few more examples:

	Base	Exponent
Example 1: $2 \times 2 \times 2 \times 2 \times 2 = 2^5 = 32$	2	5
Example 2: $3 \times 3 \times 3 \times 3 = 3^4 = 81$	3	4
Example 3: $10 \times 10 \times 10 \times 10 \times 10 \times 10 = 10^6 = 10{,}00{,}000$	10	6

We can write repeated multiplication of negative integers in this form.

$$(-5) \times (-5) \times (-5) \times (-5) = (-5)^4 = +625$$
$$(-6) \times (-6) \times (-6) = (-6)^3 = (-216)$$

In negative integers, if the power or exponent is an **even** number, the answer will be **positive** and if the power or exponent is an **odd** number, the answer will be **negative**.

Alert!

$$(\text{negative integer})^{\text{even power}} = \text{positive answer}$$

$$(\text{negative integer})^{\text{odd power}} = \text{negative answer}$$

In an algebraic expression, when a variable is multiplied by itself many times, we can write it as an exponent.

Thus, $y \times y \times y \times y \times y = y^5$

Numbers raised to the power of 2 are called squared.

Numbers raised to the power of 3 are called cubed. For example,

$8 \times 8 = 8^2$ We read this as 8 **squared**.

$9 \times 9 \times 9 = 9^3$ We read this as 9 **cubed**.

A number raised to a certain power is said to be in its **exponential** form.

Example 1: Write down the base and exponent of each of the following.

$(3)^6$, $(7)^5$, $(-13)^4$, b^9, 10^7

Number	Base	Exponent
$(3)^6$	3	6
$(7)^5$	7	5
$(-13)^4$	(-13)	4
b^9	b	9
10^7	10	7

Example 2: Find the values of the following, after writing them in the exponential form.

a. $\underbrace{3 \times 3}_{9} \times \underbrace{3 \times 3}_{9} \times 3 = 3^5$

$9 \times 9 \times 3 = 243$

b. $\underbrace{7 \times 7}_{49} \times 7 = 7^3$

$49 \times 7 = 343$

c. $\underbrace{(-4) \times (-4)}_{16} \times \underbrace{(-4) \times (-4)}_{16} = (-4)^4$

$16 \times 16 = 256$

Example 3: Express the following as powers.

a. 512 as a power of 2.

b. 625 as a power of 5.

c. 729 as a power of 3.

We find the prime factors of the numbers above in terms of 2, 5 and 3 respectively.

a.

2	512
2	256
2	128
2	64
2	32
2	16
2	8
2	4
2	2
	1

b.

5	625
5	125
5	25
5	5
	1

c.

3	729
3	243
3	81
3	27
3	9
3	3
	1

Therefore, $512 = 2^9$ $\quad 625 = 5^4$ $\quad 729 = 3^6$

Example 4: Express the following numbers as a product of the powers of their prime factors.

a. 3969

3	3969
3	1323
3	441
3	147
7	49
7	7
	1

$3969 = 3 \times 3 \times 3 \times 3 \times 7 \times 7$

$= 3^4 \times 7^2$

b. 1600

2	1600
2	800
2	400
2	200
2	100
2	50
5	25
5	5
	1

$1600 = 2 \times 2 \times 2 \times 2 \times 2 \times 2 \times 5 \times 5$

$= 2^6 \times 5^2$

Powers of (+1) and (−1)

$1 \times 1 \times 1 \times 1 = 1^4 = 1$

Alert!

The number 1 raised to any power is always equal to 1.

$(-1)^2 = (-1) \times (-1) = 1$

$(-1)^3 = (-1) \times (-1) \times (-1) = (-1)$

$(-1)^4 = (-1) \times (-1) \times (-1) \times (-1) = 1$

$(-1)^5 = (-1) \times (-1) \times (-1) \times (-1) \times (-1) = (-1)$

(-1) raised to an even power is equal to 1 $\quad (-1)^{\text{even power}} = 1$

(-1) raised to an odd power is equal to (-1) $\quad (-1)^{\text{odd power}} = 1$

Practice Exercise 4.1

1. Write the base and exponent (power) of each of the following.

   a. 10^7 b. 9^4 c. $(-13)^5$ d. 8^3 e. 2^{10}

2. Write the following in the exponential form.

   a. $7 \times 7 \times 7 \times 7 \times 7$ b. $6 \times 6 \times 6 \times (-5) \times (-5)$
   c. $10 \times 10 \times 10 \times 10$ d. $4 \times 4 \times 4 \times 11 \times 11$
   e. $(-2) \times (-2) \times (-2) \times (-2) \times (-2) \times (-2)$

3. Find the values of the following.

   a. 2^7 b. $(-3)^5$ c. 5^4 d. $10^3 \times (-2)^4$ e. $4^3 \times (13)^2$

4. Which of the two is greater in each case?

   a. 2^9 or 9^2 b. 3^6 or 6^3 c. 10^2 or 2^{10} d. 6^5 or 5^6 e. 4^3 or 3^4

5. Express in the exponential form and also find the value of each of the following.

   a. $3 \times 3 \times 3 \times 5 \times 5$ b. $2 \times 2 \times 2 \times 2 \times 2 \times 7 \times 7$
   c. $10 \times 10 \times 10 \times 10 \times 9 \times 9$ d. $(-7) \times (-7) \times (-7) \times (-7) \times 6 \times 6$
   e. $(-4) \times (-4) \times (-4) \times (-3) \times (-3) \times (-3)$

6. Write the values of the following.

   a. $(-1)^{100}$ b. $(-1)^{101}$ c. $(-1)^{98}$ d. $(-1)^{37}$ e. $(-1)^{44}$

7. Express the following numbers as a product of the powers of their prime factors.

   a. 400 b. 2000 c. 5184 d. 6561 e. 50625

8. Write the base and power of each of the following.

   a. $(m)^3$ b. x^{10} c. p^q d. $(-r)^5$ e. y^z

9. Write the following variables in the power notation.

   a. $p \times p \times p \times p \times p$
   b. $t \times t \times t \times t \times t \times t \times t$
   c. $m \times m \times m \times n \times n$
   d. $(-a) \times (-a) \times (-a) \times (-a) \times (-a)$
   e. $y \times y \times y \times (-z) \times (-z) \times (-z) \times (-z)$

10. Find the values of the following if $a = 2$, $b = (-3)$ and $c = 5$.

a. $b \times b \times c \times c$

b. $a \times a \times a \times c \times c \times c$

c. $b \times b \times b \times a$

d. $a \times a \times a \times b \times b \times c$

e. $a^4b^2c^3$

Laws of Exponents

1. Power with the Same Bases

Let us consider the following examples of repeated multiplication.

Example 1: $2^3 \times 2^2 = 2 \times 2 \times 2 \times 2 \times 2 = 2^5$

Adding the powers $3 + 2 = 5$

Example 2: $3^4 \times 3^3 = 3 \times 3 \times 3 \times 3 \times 3 \times 3 \times 3 = 3^7$

Adding the powers $4 + 3 = 7$

Example 3: $(-5)^2 \times (-5)^4 = (-5) \times (-5) \times (-5) \times (-5) \times (-5) \times (-5) = (-5)^6$

Adding the powers $2 + 4 = 6$

In the above examples, the bases are 2, 3 and (-5).

When the bases are the same, we add their powers to get the result.

We can thus formulate the first law of exponents.

Law I:	$x^m \times x^n = x^{m+n}$, where $x \neq 0$

Now, let us consider examples of division with the same bases.

$$4^5 \div 4^3 = \frac{4^5}{4^3} = \frac{\cancel{4} \times \cancel{4} \times \cancel{4} \times 4 \times 4}{\cancel{4} \times \cancel{4} \times \cancel{4}} = 4^2$$

Subtracting the powers $5 - 3 = 2$

$$10^7 \div 10^3 = \frac{10^7}{10^3} = \frac{\cancel{10} \times \cancel{10} \times \cancel{10} \times 10 \times 10 \times 10 \times 10}{\cancel{10} \times \cancel{10} \times \cancel{10}} = 10^4$$

Subtracting the powers $7 - 3 = 4$

$$(-2)^8 \div (-2)^5 = \frac{(-2)^8}{(-2)^5} = \frac{\cancel{(-2)} \times \cancel{(-2)} \times \cancel{(-2)} \times \cancel{(-2)} \times \cancel{(-2)} \times (-2) \times (-2) \times (-2)}{\cancel{(-2)} \times \cancel{(-2)} \times \cancel{(-2)} \times \cancel{(-2)} \times \cancel{(-2)}}$$

$$= (-2)^3$$

Subtracting the powers $8 - 5 = 3$

In the above examples, the bases are 4, 10 and (-2). When the bases are the same, we subtract their powers to get the result.

We can thus formulate the second law of exponents.

Law II:	$x^m \div x^n = \frac{x^m}{x^n} = x^{m-n}$, where $x \neq 0$ and $m > n$

2. Numbers with Exponent 0

Let us look at the following division.

$$5^6 \div 5^6 = \frac{5^6}{5^6} = 5^{6-6} = 5^0$$

But $\frac{5^6}{5^6} = \frac{\cancel{5} \times \cancel{5} \times \cancel{5} \times \cancel{5} \times \cancel{5} \times \cancel{5}}{\cancel{5} \times \cancel{5} \times \cancel{5} \times \cancel{5} \times \cancel{5} \times \cancel{5}} = 1$

Therefore, $5^0 = 1$

Similarly, $7^3 \div 7^3 = \frac{7^3}{7^3} = 7^{3-3} = 7^0$

But $\frac{7^3}{7^3} = \frac{\cancel{7} \times \cancel{7} \times \cancel{7}}{\cancel{7} \times \cancel{7} \times \cancel{7}} = 1$

Therefore, $7^0 = 1$

Also $(-3)^4 \div (-3)^4 = \frac{(-3)^4}{(-3)^4} = (-3)^{4-4} = (-3)^0$

But $\frac{(-3)^4}{(-3)^4} = \frac{\cancel{(-3)} \times \cancel{(-3)} \times \cancel{(-3)} \times \cancel{(-3)}}{\cancel{(-3)} \times \cancel{(-3)} \times \cancel{(-3)} \times \cancel{(-3)}} = 1$

Therefore, $(-3)^0 = 1$

We can thus formulate the third law of exponents.

Law III:	$x^0 = 1$, where $x \neq 0$

Alert!

Any number raised to the power of 0 is equal to 1. Any number raised to the power of 1 is equal to the number itself.

3. Power of a Power

Let us consider the following expressions:

$(2^5)^3 = 2^5 \times 2^5 \times 2^5 = 2^{5+5+5} = 2^{15}$

Therefore, $(2^5)^3 = 2^{5 \times 3} = 2^{15}$

Similarly, $[(-6)^3]^4 = (-6)^3 \times (-6)^3 \times (-6)^3 \times (-6)^3$

$= (-6)^{3+3+3+3} = (-6)^{12}$

Therefore, $(-6^3)^4 = (-6)^{3 \times 4} = (-6)^{12}$

Similarly, $(10^2)^4 = 10^2 \times 10^2 \times 10^2 \times 10^2 = 10^{2+2+2+2} = 10^8$

Therefore, $(10^2)^4 = 10^8$

We can now write the fourth law of exponents.

Law IV:	$(x^m)^n = x^{m \times n}$, where $x \neq 0$

4. Power with the Same Exponents but Different Bases

Let us look at these examples.

$2^3 \times 5^3$ can be written as $2 \times 2 \times 2 \times 5 \times 5 \times 5$ or

$$(2 \times 5) \times (2 \times 5) \times (2 \times 5) \quad \text{or}$$

$$(2 \times 5)^3$$

Similarly $3^2 \times 4^2$ can be written as $3 \times 3 \times 4 \times 4$ or

$$(3 \times 4) \times (3 \times 4) \quad \text{or} \quad (3 \times 4)^2$$

Also $(-6)^2 \times (-7)^2$ can be written as $(-6) \times (-6) \times (-7) \times (-7)$

$$\text{or } \{(-6) \times (-7)\} \times \{(-6) \times (-7)\}$$

$$\text{or } \{(-6) \times (-7)\}^2$$

By observing the pattern in the above examples, we can write the fifth law of exponents.

Law V:	$x^m \times y^m = (xy)^m$, where $x \neq 0, y \neq 0$.

Now, let us look at some more expressions.

$$\frac{4^3}{5^3} = \frac{4 \times 4 \times 4}{5 \times 5 \times 5} = \frac{4}{5} \times \frac{4}{5} \times \frac{4}{5}, \text{ which is } \left(\frac{4}{5}\right)^3$$

Therefore, $\dfrac{4^3}{5^3} = \left(\dfrac{4}{5}\right)^3$

Similarly, $\dfrac{(-8)^2}{(-9)^2} = \dfrac{(-8) \times (-8)}{(-9) \times (-9)} = \left(\dfrac{-8}{-9}\right) \times \left(\dfrac{-8}{-9}\right) = \left(\dfrac{-8}{-9}\right)^2$

Therefore, $\dfrac{(-8)^2}{(-9)^2} = \left(\dfrac{-8}{-9}\right)^2$

Also, $\dfrac{(-6)^5}{(10)^5} = \dfrac{(-6) \times (-6) \times (-6) \times (-6) \times (-6)}{10 \times 10 \times 10 \times 10 \times 10}$

$$= \left(\frac{-6}{10}\right) \times \left(\frac{-6}{10}\right) \times \left(\frac{-6}{10}\right) \times \left(\frac{-6}{10}\right) \times \left(\frac{-6}{10}\right) = \left(\frac{-6}{10}\right)^5$$

Therefore, $\dfrac{(-6)^5}{(10)^5} = \left(\dfrac{-6}{10}\right)^5$

From the above examples, we can formulate the sixth law of exponents.

Law VI: $\frac{x^m}{y^m} = \left(\frac{x}{y}\right)^m$, where $x \neq 0, y \neq 0$.

Practice Exercise 4.2

1. Simplify and write the answers in the exponential form.

   a. $18^{15} \times 18^2$ b. $15^3 \times 15^4$ c. $19^5 \times 19$

   d. $(-7)^6 \times (-7)^5$ e. $4^2 \times 4^3 \times 4^4$

2. Simplify and write the answers in the exponential form.

   a. $17^5 \div 17^2$ b. $(-10)^8 \div (-10)^3$ c. $4^{11} \div 4^6$

   d. $(-13)^9 \div (-13)^5$ e. $8^m \div 8^n$

3. Simplify and write the answers in the exponential form.

   a. $\left(\frac{12^9}{12^4}\right) \div 12^3$ b. $(15^4 \times 15^7) \div 15^3$ c. $\left(\frac{9^{11}}{9^6}\right) \times 9^5$

   d. $\frac{(-3)^4 \times (-3)^7}{(-3)^2}$ e. $\frac{6^8 \times 6^4 \times 6}{6^{13}}$

4. Find the value of each of the following.

   a. $3^0 \times 7^0 \times (-4)^0$ b. $4^0 + 5^0 + (-7)^0$ c. $25 + 25^0$

   d. $\frac{15^2 \times 15^0}{15}$ e. $9^0 + 9^1 + 9^2$

5. Express the number 1 in the exponential form with five different bases.

6. Which term in each of the following pairs is greater and by how much?

   a. $2^3 \times 2^4$ or $3^2 \times 4^2$

   b. $5^2 \times 5^3$ or $2^5 \times 3^5$

   c. $10^2 \times 10^0$ or $2^{10} \times 2^0$

7. Simplify the following and write the answers in the exponential form.

   a. $(5^3)^8$ b. $[(-8)^3]^4$ c. $(11^7)^4$ d. $(9^2)^0$ e. $(7^0)^{10}$

8. Simplify the following and write the answers in the exponential form.

   a. $(2 \times 8)^5$ b. $(-9g)^7$ c. $(3 \times 9)^3$ d. $(11f)^4$ e. $(6 \times 8)^0$

9. Simplify the following and write the answers in the exponential form.

a. $\frac{(7)^0 \times 7^2}{7} + 7$ b. $(3^4 \div 3^2) \times 3^9$

c. $(4^3)^2 \times (4^2)^3$ d. $2^0 + 3^0 + 4^0 + 5^0 + 10^0$

e. $\frac{3^7}{8^7}$

10. Which of the two is larger—$(2^2)^4$ or $(4^2)^2$—and by how much?

Expanded Form of Numbers with Exponents

We have learnt how to write numbers in the expanded form. We can now simplify and write them using exponents.

Example 1: Express 86, 92, 345 in its exponential form.

86,92,345 = 80,00,000 + 6,00,000 + 90,000 + 2,000 + 300 + 40 + 5

= 8 × 10,00,000 + 6 × 100,000 + 9 × 10,000 + 2 × 1,000 + 3 × 100 + 4 × 10 + 5 × 1

$= 8 \times 10^6 + 6 \times 10^5 + 9 \times 10^4 + 2 \times 10^3 + 3 \times 10^2 + 4 \times 10^1 + 5 \times 10^0$

Example 2: Express 2, 46, 92, 82, 953 in its exponential form.

2,46,82,953 = 2,00,00,000 + 40,00,000 + 6,00,000 + 80,000 + 2,000 + 900 + 50 + 3

= 2 × 1,00,00,000 + 4 × 10,00,000 + 6 × 1,00,000 + 8 × 10,000 + 2 × 1,000 + 9 × 100 + 5 × 10 + 3 × 1

$= 2 \times 10^7 + 4 \times 10^6 + 6 \times 10^5 + 8 \times 10^4 + 2 \times 10^3 + 9 \times 10^2 + 5 \times 10^1 + 3 \times 10^0$

Alert!

It is simple to write the powers of 10. Count the number of zeros in the expanded form and 10 is raised to that power. If the first digit is 2 followed by 7 digits, then we will write it as: 2×10^7, 8 followed by 4 digits will be 8×10^4.

$5\underline{000} = 5 \times 1\underline{0}^3$ and not $(50)^3$

Standard Form or Scientific Notation

Expressing larger numbers with the help of exponents makes them easier to read, write and comprehend.

Let us take the example of the distance of the sun from the moon. It is 14,90,00,000 km. This large number can be written as:

$$14{,}90{,}00{,}000 = 149 \times 10{,}00{,}000 = 149 \times 10^6 \text{ km}$$
$$= 14.9 \times 1{,}00{,}00{,}000 = 14.9 \times 10^7 \text{ km}$$
$$= 1.49 \times 10{,}00{,}00{,}000 = 1.49 \times 10^8 \text{ km}$$

The distance of the moon from the earth is 38,44,00,000 m. This can be written as:

$$\begin{aligned} 38{,}44{,}00{,}000 &= 3844 \times 1{,}00{,}000 = 3844 \times 10^5 \text{ m} \\ &= 384.4 \times 10{,}00{,}000 = 384.4 \times 10^6 \text{ m} \\ &= 38.44 \times 1{,}00{,}00{,}000 = 38.44 \times 10^7 \text{ m} \\ &= 3.844 \times 10{,}00{,}00{,}000 = 3.844 \times 10^8 \text{ m} \end{aligned}$$

The answers that are expressed as a decimal number and multiplied by a power of 10 are said to be in the standard form or scientific notation.

Alert!

As we increase a position of the decimal point from the right to the left, the power of 10 increases.

Example: $152 \times 10^6 = 15.2 \times 10^7 = 1.52 \times 10^8$

Practice Exercise 4.3

1. Write the following numbers in the expanded forms with exponential notation.

   a. 3,70,295 b. 36,00,285 c. 23,89,060
   d. 70,78,282 e. 5,49,36,007

2. Write the following numbers in the compact forms.

   a. $7 \times 10^6 + 5 \times 10^5 + 3 \times 10^4 + 4 \times 10^3 + 8 \times 10^2 + 9 \times 10^1 + 2 \times 10^0$
   b. $9 \times 10^7 + 7 \times 10^6 + 5 \times 10^5 + 3 \times 10^4 + 1 \times 10^3 + 8 \times 10^2 + 6 \times 10^1 + 4 \times 10^0$
   c. $8 \times 10^7 + 6 \times 10^6 + 4 \times 10^5 + 2 \times 10^3 + 1 \times 10^2 + 3 \times 10^1 + 5 \times 10^0$

3. Express the following numbers in the standard form or in scientific notation.

   a. 7,82,00,00,00,00,000 b. 63,00,00,00,00,000 c. 48,75,00,00,00,000

4. Express the following numbers in the standard form or in scientific notation.

   a. 1496×10^5 b. 287.3×10^4 c. 98.37×10^6

5. Find the values of the following.

   a. $\dfrac{6^3 \times 4^3}{(24)^2}$ b. $\dfrac{9^2 \times 8^2}{72}$ c. $\left(\dfrac{5}{11}\right)^3 \div \left(\dfrac{5}{11}\right)^3$

Highlights

- Repeated multiplication is denoted by the exponential form.
- $(-1)^{\text{odd number}} = (-1)$ and $(-1)^{\text{even number}} = 1$
- The laws of exponents are:
  - $x^m \times x^n = x^{m+n}$
  - $x^m \times y^m = (xy)^m$
  - $x^m \div x^n = x^{m-n}$
  - $\frac{x^m}{y^m} = \left(\frac{x}{y}\right)^m$
  - $(x^m)^n = x^{mn}$
  - $x^0 = 1$
- Any number to the power of 0 is 1, i.e., $x^0 = 1$.

  Any number to the power of 1 is the number itself, i.e., $x^1 = x$.
- The scientific notation or standard form is when a number is written as the product of a decimal number between 1.0 and 10.0 (including 1.0) and a power of 10.

Higher Order Thinking Skills

HOTS

1. Find the value of $\left\{\left(\left(\frac{-1}{3}\right)^2\right)^{-2}\right\}^{-1}$.

2. Which of the following is in the scientific notation form?

   a. 0.9×10^3 b. 0.09×10^{-1} c. 9.9×10^4

   d. 0.9×10^{-3} e. 9.0×10^2

3. Find the value of 'a' for which the given expression is true.

$$\frac{9}{25}\left(\frac{3}{5}\right)^{4a} = \left[\left(\frac{3}{5}\right)^2\right]^3 \times \left[\left(\frac{3}{5}\right)^a\right]^3$$

Question: What did the plant grow with the maths influence?

Answer for Brainteaser on page 69

Scientific Notation!!

Aim: To gather information regarding the magnitude of the following quantities and express them in scientific notation.

Material required: information from internet or reference books

Method: Decode the following:

1. The speed of light in metres per second.
2. The distance between the sun and earth.
3. The numbers of seconds in 50 years.
4. The population of India.
5. The weight of the moon.
6. The surface area of the earth.
7. The diameter of the sun.
8. The distance between the moon and the earth.

Rewind

1. Write three rational numbers equivalent to each one of the following.

   a. $\frac{3}{8}$ b. $\frac{(-5)}{(-3)}$ c. $\left(-\frac{7}{5}\right)$ d. $\frac{2}{3}$ e) $\frac{5}{(-9)}$

2. Arrange the following rational numbers in ascending order.

   a. $\frac{4}{5}, \frac{3}{10}, \frac{7}{15}$ b. $\left(-\frac{5}{2}\right), \frac{7}{4}, \frac{9}{8}$ c. $\frac{7}{8}, \frac{2}{3}, \frac{11}{12}, \frac{5}{(-6)}$

   d. $\left(-\frac{2}{3}\right), \left(-\frac{3}{4}\right), \frac{5}{(-6)}$ e. $\left(-\frac{3}{10}\right), \frac{7}{(-15)}, \frac{8}{(-15)}, \frac{8}{(-3)}, \left(-\frac{3}{4}\right)$

3. Simplify the following.

   a. $\frac{(-3)}{10} + \frac{13}{(-10)} + \frac{25}{10}$ b. $\left(-\frac{1}{3}\right) + \frac{6}{3} + \frac{(-4)}{3}$ c. $\frac{(-1)}{2} + \frac{(-3)}{14} + \frac{1}{4}$

   d. $(-2) + \frac{2}{3} + \frac{(-3)}{4}$ e. $\left(-\frac{9}{11}\right) + \frac{2}{3} + \frac{(-5)}{4}$

4. Subtract the sum of $\frac{3}{7}$ and $\frac{5}{(-11)}$ from the sum of $\frac{8}{28}$ and $\left(-\frac{3}{14}\right)$.

5. What should be added to (-1) to get $\frac{7}{9}$?

6. Simplify the following.

   a. $\left(\frac{(-7)}{5} \times \frac{12}{6}\right) - \left(\frac{2}{8} \times \frac{6}{(-9)}\right)$

   b. $\left(\frac{5}{(-16)} \times \frac{7}{12}\right) + \left(\frac{(-4)}{9} \times \frac{8}{(-8)}\right)$

   c. $\left(\frac{3}{(-4)} \times \frac{5}{6}\right) - \left(\frac{3}{7} \times \frac{(-4)}{(-2)}\right) - \left(\frac{3}{2} \times \frac{(-6)}{5}\right)$

   d. $\left(\frac{15}{8} \times \frac{4}{3}\right) + \left(\frac{(-3)}{2} \times \frac{7}{4}\right)$

   e. $\left(\frac{9}{2} \times \frac{8}{3}\right) + \left(\frac{4}{3} \times \frac{5}{24}\right) - \left(\frac{3}{(-5)} \times \frac{(-7)}{6}\right)$

7. Divide the difference of $\frac{12}{7}$ and $\frac{13}{4}$ by the product of $\frac{4}{5}$ and $\frac{25}{2}$.

8. By what number should we multiply $\left(-\frac{15}{28}\right)$ so that the product is $\left(-\frac{5}{7}\right)$?

9. Find the product of each of the following.

   a. 63.2×0.11 b. 7.5×0.002 c. 11.6×0.2

   d. 10.71×0.05 e. 63.5×1.8

10. Five children weigh 45.2 kg, 63.75 kg, 36.125 kg, 35.896 kg and 55.138 kg each. Find their total weight.

11. Compute the following products.

a. 54×2^3 b. $4^3 \times 7^2$ c. $3^5 \times (-4)^2$

12. Find the square of the following.

a. (-17) b. (-1) c. $\left(-\frac{5}{14}\right)$ d. 25   e. $\left(-\frac{13}{17}\right)$

13. Express the following as a single exponent.

a. $\left[\left(\frac{3}{4}\right)^2\right]^4 \times \left[\left(\frac{3}{4}\right)^2\right]^4$ b. $\left[\left(\frac{2}{11}\right)^2\right]^5 \times \left[\left(\frac{2}{11}\right)^5\right]^3$ c. $\left[\left(\frac{-1}{3}\right)^3\right]^0 \times \left[\left(\frac{1}{3}\right)^2\right]^5$

d. $\left[\left(\frac{-3}{5}\right)^2\right]^7 \times \left[\left(\frac{-3}{5}\right)^7\right]^4$ e. $\left[\left(\frac{2}{3}\right)^4\right]^2 \times \left[\left(\frac{2}{3}\right)^3\right]^4$

14. Solve and find the value of x in each case.

a. $2^x = 64$ b. $x^2 = 36$ c. $3^x = 9^3$ d. $2^{2x} \div 2 = 8$ e. $5^x = 125$

15. Express the following in the power notation.

a. 512   b. $\frac{1000}{216}$ c. $\frac{1}{729}$ d. (-729) e. $\left(-\frac{243}{3125}\right)$

Answer for Brainteaser from page 66

Square roots

Test Yourself

Unit 1

1. Write the additive inverse of the following.

   a. (-10) b. 8 c. (-22) d. 40 e. (-51)

2. Find the values of the following products.

   a. $(-6) \times 15$ b. $18 \times (-5)$ c. $(-9) \times (-11)$
   d. $20 \times (-20)$ e. $(-45) \times (-5)$

3. Divide the following.

   a. (-625) by 5 b. 10,000 by (-100) c. (-4528) by 4528
   d. (-891) by (-891) e. (-23673) by (-3)

4. Find the values of the following.

   a. $(-6) \times 2 + 8$ b. $(-18) + (-20) + (-12)$
   c. $15 + 18 \div (-3)$ d. $(-20) \times (-1) + (-10) \div 10$
   e. $42 \times (-5) + (-10) \div (-1)$

5. Indicate whether the following statements are true (T) or false (F).

   a. The product of a positive and a negative integer is negative.
   b. The product of two negative integers is negative.
   c. The product of three negative integers is negative.
   d. The sum of two negative integers is positive.
   e. The quotient of two negative integers is positve.

6. Which is greater, the sum of $4\frac{1}{2}$ and $2\frac{1}{5}$ or the sum of $3\frac{2}{3}$ and $3\frac{1}{2}$, and by how much?

7. In a collection of 1,050 balloons at a party, $\frac{3}{10}$ of the balloons are blue, 2.5 of the balloons are red and the rest are green. How many blue, red and green balloons are there?

8. At a petrol station, there are $1351\frac{1}{2}$ litres of petrol in a tank. How many cars of capacity $25\frac{1}{2}$ litres can be completely filled by the petrol in the tank?

9. Lata bought 10.58 kg onions and 8.23 kg sugar, while Vibha bought 13.81 kg fruits and 5.32 kg tea. Who had more weight to carry and by how much?

10. Find the cost of 6.5 kg of watermelon at ₹24.75 a kg.

11. The weight of 53 cartons of books is 1947.75 kg. Find the weight of 1 carton of books. Also find the weight of 20 cartons.

12. Write the following as rational numbers.

a. 17 b. (−42) c. 0.05 d. 3.8 e. 0.63

13. The sum of three rational numbers is $\frac{11}{16}$. If two of the rational numbers are $\frac{3}{(-4)}$ and $\frac{7}{8}$, find the third rational number.

14. Find the following products.

a. $\frac{11}{(-22)} \times \frac{3}{4}$ b. $\frac{3}{(-5)} \times \frac{(-10)}{3}$ c. $\frac{(-7)}{9} \times \frac{2}{(-3)} \times \frac{9}{(-14)}$

d. $\frac{9}{(-11)} \times \frac{33}{41}$ e. $\frac{2}{(-3)} \times \frac{3}{(-5)} \times \frac{(-5)}{7} \times \frac{7}{(-9)}$

15. Find five rational numbers between (−2) and 3.

16. Express the following numbers as a product of the powers of their prime factors.

a. 1,600 b. 3,969 c. 6,561 d. 2,700 e. 10,648

17. Simplify the following and write the answer in the exponential form.

a. $19^4 \times 19^2 \times 19^1$ b. $(-18)^7 \div (-18)^3$ c. $(13^4 \times 13^5) \div 13^3$

d. $4^3 \times \left[\frac{4^{10}}{4^8}\right]$ e. $(9^{21} \div 9^{18}) \times 9$

18. Simplify the following and write the answer in the exponential form.

a. $(5^7)^3$ b. $[(-7)^2]^4$ c. $[(-10)6^5]^3$

d. $(n^8)^3$ e. $[-d^{65}]^7$

19. Write the following numbers in the expanded form with exponential notation.

a. 4,32,789 b. 18,69,593 c. 43,59,760

d. 70,06,08,940 e. 5,49,36,005

20. Simplify each of the following and express as rational numbers.

a. $\left(\frac{3}{2}\right)^4 \times \left(\frac{1}{5}\right)^2$ b. $\left(\frac{-2}{3}\right)^5 \times \left(\frac{-3}{7}\right)^3$

c. $\left(\frac{-1}{2}\right)^5 \times 2^3 \times \left(\frac{3}{4}\right)^2$ d. $\left(\frac{2}{3}\right)^3 \times \left(\frac{-3}{5}\right)^3 \times \left(\frac{7}{2}\right)^2$

e. $\left(\frac{23}{25}\right)^0 \times \left(\frac{25}{23}\right)^2 \times \left(\frac{23}{25}\right)^3$

CHAPTER 5

Algebraic Expressions

Algebra is a branch of mathematics that involves numbers and letters of the alphabets that are called literals. The numbers are fixed and are called constants. The letters are used for variables or literals, which are not constant. If we write $x + 5$, the value 5 is fixed but x can have any value and the value of the expression $x + 5$ depends on it. If $x = 3$, then $x + 5$ will be 8, if $x = (-3)$, then $x + 5$ will be 2 and so on.

The basic terminology in algebra includes:

Constant: A quantity having a fixed numerical value is called a constant. 1, 2, 3, etc. are constants.

Variable: A quantity that can have different numerical values is called a variable or literal. a, b, c, x, y, z, etc. are variables or literals.

Algebraic expressions: A combination of constants and variables connected by any or all the four fundamental operations $(+, -, \times, \div)$ is called an algebraic expression.

Example: $5abc$, $2x + 7y$, $p - q + r$, etc.

Terms: The different parts of the algebraic expression separated by the signs '+' or '−' are the terms of an expression.

Example: $5x + 2y - 3z$ consists of three terms $5x$, $2y$ and $-3z$, $5 + x$ consists of two terms 5 and x.

Alert!

$5x$ is one term.

$5 + x$ are two terms.

The terms are counted by the + or − sign between them, not the multiples.

Types of algebraic expressions:

1. **Monomials:** An algebraic expression that contains only one term is called a monomial.

   Example: $5x$, $7a^2b$, $-3ab$, -10, etc.

2. **Binomials:** An algebraic expression containing two terms is called a binomial.

   Example: $5x + 4$, $7a^2b - 3ab^2$, $p + 2q$, etc.

3. **Trinomials:** An algebraic expression containing three terms is called a trinomial.

   Example: $5x + 7y + 4$, $a - 2b + 3c$, $a^2b + ab + ab^2$, etc.

4. **Polynomials:** An algebraic expression containing two or more terms is called a polynomial. Example: $7x + 2y + 9z + 2a$, $x^3 + y^3 + 2a + 3y + 2m$, etc.

Factors of a term: Each term of an algebraic expression consists of a product of constants and variables. These constants and variables are called the factors of the term.

Example 1: $4x + 7y + 9z$

This is a trinomial because it consists of three terms: $4x$, $7y$ and $9z$.

The factors of $4x$ are 4 and x, the factors of $7y$ are 7 and y and the factors of $9z$ are 9 and z.

Example 2: $x^3 + y^3 + z^3 + 3xyz$.

This is a polynomial because it contains 4 terms, x^3, y^3, z^3 and $3xyz$.

The factors of x^3 are x, x and x; the factors of y^3 are y, y and y; the factors of z^3 are z, z and z and the factors of $3xyz$ are 3, x, y and z.

Coefficients: In a term of algebraic expression, any of the factors with the sign of the term is called the coefficient of the product of the other factors in that term.

Example 1: In $5x$, the coefficient of x is 5, which is a numerical factor.

Example 2: In $5x^2y$, the coefficient of y is $5x^2$, the coefficient of x^2 is $5y$.

Example 3: In $(-10x^2y^2)$, the coefficient of x^2 is $(-10y^2)$ and the coefficient of y^2 is $(-10x^2)$.

Example 4: In ab, the coefficient of a is b, the coefficient of b is a, the coefficient of ab is 1. When the coefficient is 1, it is generally not written.

Example 5: In $\frac{2}{3}x^2y$, the coefficient of y is $\frac{2}{3}x^2$, the coefficient of x^2 is $\frac{2}{3}y$.

Alert!

The coefficient is a numerical or constant quantity placed before and multiplying the variable in an algebraic equation.

Constant term: A term in the algebraic expression having no literal factor is called a constant term.

Example 1: $x^2 + 5x \times 10$ is a trinomial because it has three terms. Here the constant term is 10 because it has no literal factors.

Example 2: $x^3 - 27$ is a binomial because it has two terms. Here the constant term is (-27) as it has no literal factors.

Like terms: Algebraic terms that have the same literal factors are called like terms. The numerical factors can, however, be different.

Example 1: $8xy = 8 \times x \times y$

Example 2: $(-xy) = (-1) \times x \times y$

Example 3: $15xy = 15 \times x \times y$

These are all like terms because the literal factors are the same, i.e., 'xy'. The numerical factors are, however, different, i.e., 8, −1 and 15, respectively.

Unlike terms: Algebraic terms that have different literal factors are called unlike terms.

Example 1: $9xy = 9 \times x \times y$

Example 2: $-10x^2y = (-10) \times x \times x \times y$

Example 3: $15xy^2 = 15 \times x \times y \times y$

Example 4: $7x^2y^2 = 7 \times x \times x \times y \times y$

These are all unlike terms because the literal factors are different, i.e., xy, x^2y, xy^2 and x^2y^2, respectively.

Alert!

For like factors, xy and yx are the same. Also a^2b and ba^2 are the same. The order of letters may not be the same, but if the letters are the same they are like terms.

Power of a term: The power of a term is the exponent of the variable or variables in the term.

Example 1: In the term $6x^2$, the variable is x and its power is 2.

Example 2: In the term $10x^2y^3$, there are two variables — x and y. The power of x is 2 while the power of y is 3.

The power of the term is determined by adding the exponents of the variables, i.e., the power is $2 + 3 = 5$.

Example 3: In the term 6abc, there are three variables — a, b and c. The power of each variable is 1. The power of the term is $1 + 1 + 1 = 3$.

Hence, the exponent of a variable in a term is the degree of the variable. The degree of the whole term is the total of those exponents.

Degree of an expression: The highest power of the variable is the degree of an algebraic expression.

Example 1: In $x^2 + 2x + 3$, the degree of the expression is 2.

Example 2: In $xy + 2x + 3y + 4$, the degree of the expression is 2 because degree of the term xy is $(1 + 1) = 2$.

Hence, the degree of a polynomial is the degree of its highest degree term. The term with the highest degree decides the degree of the algebraic expression.

Finding the Value of an Algebraic Expression

If the values of the variables or literals are given for an algebraic expression, we can find their numerical value.

Replacing the values of the literals or variables in a given expression is called **substitution**. Evaluate the following if $x = 3$ and $y = (-2)$.

Example 1: Solve $2x + 3y$
$= 2(3) + 3(-2)$ (substituting the values of x and y)
$= 6 - 6 = 0.$

Example 2: Solve $x^2 + 2xy + y^2$
$= (3)^2 + 2(3)(-2) + (-2)^2$ (substituting the values of x and y)
$= 9 - 12 + 4 = 9 + 4 - 12 = 13 - 12 = 1$

We arrive at the answer by applying the DMAS rule for calculation.

Example 1: Write the factors of the following terms.

a. $9xy^2 = 9 \times x \times y \times y$

b. $(-12x^2y^3z) = (-12) \times x \times x \times y \times y \times y \times z$

c. $(-15a^2b^3c^2) = (-15) \times a \times a \times b \times b \times b \times c \times c$

Example 2: Classify the following expressions as monomials, binomials or trinomials and place them in the appropriate column in the table.

$5x$, $2a + 3b$, $a + 2b + 5c$, $x + y + z$, $-3a^2b$, -7, $8 - 3x$, $x^2 - 4xy^2$, $x^3 + y^3 + z^3$, $x + 2y - 3z$, $a^3 - b^3$, $9a^2b^2c^2$

Monomials	Binomials	Trinomials
$5x$	$2a + 3b$	$a + 2b + 5c$
$-3a^2b$	$8 - 3x$	$x + y + z$
-7	$x^2 - 4xy^2$	$x^3 + y^3 + z^3$
$9a^2b^2c^2$	$a^3 - b^3$	$x + 2y - 3z$

Example 3: Identify the coefficient of x in each of the following terms.

a. $3xy^2 \longrightarrow 3y^2$

b. $-7xy^2z \longrightarrow (-7y^2z)$

c. $4x + 3y \longrightarrow 4$

d. $x + y + z \longrightarrow 1$

Example 4: Identify the constant term in the following expressions.

a. $x^2 + y^2 - 16 \longrightarrow -16$

b. $2xy - 16x + 18 \longrightarrow 18$

c. $x^2 + 2x + 1 \longrightarrow 1$

d. $ab + bc + ca - 3abc$
no constant term

Example 5: Identify the coefficient of y^2 in the following terms.

a. $5xy^2 - y^3 + x^3 \longrightarrow 5x$ b. $x^2 - y^2 \longrightarrow (-1)$

c. $12y^2x^3 - 3xy \longrightarrow 12x^3$ d. $-10x^2y^2z^2 + 1 \longrightarrow (-10x^2z^2)$

Example 6: Identify the like and unlike terms and classify them.

a^2b, $-ba^2$, xy^2z, z^2x, $-7xy^2z$, m^3n^2, $-11z^2x$, $-10n^2m^3$, $4xy$, $3mn^2$, abc, $12pq$, $9x^2$, $-12xy$, $16p^2r^2$, $3xy$

Like terms	Unlike terms
$a^2b, -ba^2$	$3mn^2$
$xy^2z, -7xy^2z$	abc
$z^2x, -11z^2x$	$12pq$
$m^3n^2, -10n^2m^3$	$9x^2$
$4xy, -12xy, 3xy$	$16p^2r^2$

Example 7: Find the values of the following algebraic expressions when $x = (-1)$, $y = (-2)$ and $z = 3$.

a. $4x^2y + z$

Substituting the given values of x, y, z, we get

$4(-1)^2(-2) + 3 = 4(-1)(-1)(-2) + 3$

$= (-8) + 3 = (-5)$

b. $xyz - z^2$

Substituting the given values of x, y, z, we get

$= (-1)(-2)(3) - (3)^2 = 6 - 3 \times 3$

$= 6 - 9 = (-3)$

c. $x^2y^2z^2 - 3yz$

Substituting the given values of x, y, z, we get

$= (-1)^2(-2)^2(3)^2 - 3(-2)(3)$

$=(-1) \times (-1) \times (-2) \times (-2) \times 3 \times 3 - 3x(-2)3$

$= 36 + 18 = 54$

Practice Exercise 5.1

1. Write the factors of the following terms.

a. $11xyz$ b. $9x^2y$ c. $(-10xy^2)$ d. $-15yz^2$ e. $20abc$

f. $14a^3b^3$ g. $(-7pqr)$ h. $(-p^2q^2)$ i. $42axpm$ j. $(-lmn)$

2. Identify the following expressions as monomials, binomials or trinomials and classify them.

a. $4abc$ b. $a^3 + b^3 + c^3$ c. $x^2y^2 - xy$
d. $a^2 + b^2 + 2ab$ e. $7 + p$ f. $-18\,x^3y^2$
g. $xy + yz$ h. $xy + yz + zx$ i. $3p^2q^2$
j. $9a^2b^2c^2$

3. Identify the constant term from each of the given algebraic expressions.

a. $x^2 + 4x + 4$ b. $p^2q^2 - 10$ c. $20 + 9x + x^2$
d. $-100 + x^2$ e. $x^3 - 64$ f. $15a^2b^2 + 10ab - 9$
g. $-90x$ h. $x^2 + y^2 + z^2 - 1$ i. $x^3 + y^3 + z^3 - 3xyz$
j. -10

4. Write the coefficient of the variable indicated in the brackets.

a. $-2x^2y^2$ (y^2) b. $xyz - 10x^2$ (z)
c. $-21x^3y^2 - 11x^2y$ (y^2) d. $5x^3y^3 - 10y^3x^2$ (x^3)
e. $x^3 - y^3$ (y^3) f. $x^2 - 10x + 16$ (x)
g. $-25x^2y^2z^2 + 1$ (z^2) h. $7x + y + z$ (x)
i. $a^2b + ab^2 + c$ (b^2) j. $-p$ (p)

5. Identify the like terms in each set of algebraic expressions given below.

a. $3ab, 15ab^2, 9ab^2, 7ab$ b. $2ab^2, 3b^2a, a^2b, 7a^2b$
c. $pqr^2, qr^2p, r^2pq, pqr, 7pq$ d. $-xy, xy^2, -3xy^2, 10xy, 25xy$
e. $10xyz, 25x^2yz, 15xyz, -10zx^2y$ f. $pqr^2, -pqr, 10pqr^2, 7pqr$
g. $ab, bc, abc, ba, -3bc, -2abc$ h. $xyz, x^2y^2z, -3xyz, 12x^2y^2z$
i. $a^3, -7a^3, b^3a, 14ab^3, ab, 10ba$ j. $81c, 81d, -9c, -9d, c, d$

6. Write the algebraic expression whose terms are:

a. $3ab, -2c, +7b$ b. $x, -2y, z$
c. $x^2, -y^2, z^2, -3xyz$ d. $ab, bc, ca, -a^2, -b^2, -c^2$
e. $-x^2, y^2, -2xy$ f. $40, x^2, -y^2$
g. $100, -p^2$ h. $m^2, -m, (-10)$
i. $2x, -y^2, xy$ j. $a^3, -b^3, -3a^2b, 3ab^2$

7. Find the values of each of the following algebraic expressions if $x = 2$, $y = 3$ and $z = 1$.

a. $x - y + z$ b. $x^2 + y^2 + z^2$ c. $2x + y^2 - z^2 + 3$
d. $2x + 3y - 5z$ e. $xy - yz - zx$

8. Find the value of each of the following algebraic expressions if $a = 1, b = (-2)$ and $c = 3$.

a. $a^2 + b^2 + 2ab$ b. $a^3 - b^3 - 3a^2b + 3ab^2$ c. $a + b + c$

d. $a^3 + b^3 + c^3 - 3abc$ e. $a^2 + b^2 + c^2 - ab - bc - ca$

9. Find the value of each of the following algebraic expressions if $a = (-2), b = (-1)$ and $c = 0$.

a. $a + b + c$ b. $a^2 - b^2 - c^2$ c. $ab + bc + ac$

d. $3a^2b + 3ab^2 - 3abc$ e. $a^3 + b^3 + c^3$

10. Arrange the following polynomials in descending order.

a. $10 + xy^2 + xy - 15x^2y^2$ b. $15a^3 + 5a^3b^2 - 2b^2$

c. $21a - 10ab + 30a^2b^2$ d. $16x^3 - 64x^3y^3$

e. $15x^2y + 10x^2y$

Operations on Algebraic Expressions

We will now study the fundamental operations of addition and subtraction on algebraic expressions. We have learnt earlier that in fractions and decimals, we add like terms. In algebraic terms also we follow the same rule. Addition and subtraction is performed on like terms or those terms that have the same literal factors. We add or subtract the numerical coefficients of like terms, while the literal factors are written as such.

Addition of Algebraic Expressions

The sum of two or more like terms will be a like term with a numerical coefficient equal to the sum of the numerical coefficient of all the like terms.

The addition of binomials, trinomials and polynomials can be done by two methods:

1. The horizontal method (row method).
2. The vertical method (column method).

Example 1: Add the following monomials.

a. $7x, -2x, 4x$

$= (7 - 2 + 4)x = 9x$

b. $7ab^2, -9ab^2, 12ab^2$

$= (7 - 9 + 12)ab^2 = 10ab^2$

c. $5abc, -10bca, 5cab$

$= (5 - 10 + 5)abc = 0abc = 0$

Example 2: Add the following bionomials.

a. $4x - 2y, 7x + 3y$

Horizontal method	Vertical method
$(4x - 2y) + (7x + 3y)$	$\begin{array}{r} 4x - 2y \\ +\ 7x + 3y \\ \hline 11x + y \end{array}$
$= 4x - 2y + 7x + 3y$	
$= 4x + 7x - 2y + 3y$	
$= (4 + 7)x + (-2 + 3)y$	
$= 11x + y$	

b. $2x + 3, 3x + 2$

Horizontal method	Vertical method
$= 2x + 3 + 3x + 2$	$\begin{array}{r} 2x + 3 \\ +\ 3x + 2 \\ \hline 5x + 5 \end{array}$
$= 2x + 3x + 3 + 2$	
$= (2 + 3)x + (3 + 2)$	
$= 5x + 5$	

c. $-2x^2 + 5y^2, -x^2 + 3y^2$

Horizontal method	Vertical method
$(-2x^2 + 5y^2) + (-x^2 + 3y^2)$	$\begin{array}{r} -2x^2 + 5y^2 \\ +\ -x^2 + 3y^2 \\ \hline -3x^2 + 8y^2 \end{array}$
$= -2x^2 + (-x)^2 + 5y^2 + 3y^2$	
$= (-2 - 1)x^2 + (5 + 3)y^2$	
$= -3x^2 + 8y^2$	

Alert!

1. Only the numerical coefficients of like terms are added. The variables or literal factors remain the same in the answer.
2. If there is 'no' sign before a term, it means a positive sign. Hence, $5x$ means $+ 5x$.
3. The terms xy^2 and yx^2 have the same degree but they are unlike terms.

Example 1: Add $x - 3y + 4z$ and $y - 2x - 8z$ by both the horizontal and the vertical methods.

Horizontal method	Vertical method
$(x - 3y + 4z) + (y - 2x - 8z)$	(Writing the like terms in the same column.)
$= x - 3y + 4z + y - 2x - 8z$	$\begin{array}{r} x - 3y + 4z \\ +\ -2x + y - 8z \\ \hline -x - 2y - 4z \end{array}$
(Writing the like terms together)	
$= x - 2x - 3y + y + 4z - 8z$	
$= (1 - 2)x + (-3 + 1)y + (4 - 8)z$	
$= -x - 2y - 4z$	

Example 2: Add $2x^2 - 3y^2$, $5x^2 + 6y^2$, $-3x^2 - 4y^2$ by both the horizontal and the vertical methods.

Horizontal method

$(2x^2 - 3y^2) + (5x^2 + 6y^2) + (-3x^2 - 4y^2)$

$= 2x^2 + 5x^2 - 3x^2 - 3y^2 + 6y^2 - 4y^2$

(Writing the like terms together)

$= (2 + 5 - 3)x^2 + (-3 + 6 - 4)y^2$

$4x^2 - y^2$

Vertical method

(Writing the like terms in the same column)

$$\begin{array}{r} 2x^2 - 3y^2 \\ 5x^2 + 6y^2 \\ + \; -3x^2 - 4y^2 \\ \hline 4x^2 - y^2 \end{array}$$

Alert!

1. The vertical method of adding algebraic expressions is simpler to use. Chances of error are minimised in this method.
2. In the vertical method, we write the like terms in one column.

Subtraction of Algebraic Expressions

Similar to addition, the operation of subtraction is also carried out between like terms only. The difference of two like terms is a like terms whose coefficient is the difference of the numerical coefficients of the two like terms.

For subtraction, we change the sign of each term of the expression to be subtracted and then add. Changing the sign means adding the additive inverse. Thus, the additive inverse of $-(x - y)$ is $(x - y)$. Subtraction can also be done by the two methods used for addition — the horizontal method and the vertical method. The vertical method is simpler to use.

Examples 1: Subtract the following expressions.

a. $7x - 4x = (7 - 4)x = 3x$

b. $7x - (-3x) = 7x + 3x = (7 + 3)x = 10x$

c. $7x - (-5x) = 7x + 5x = (7 + 5)x = 12x$

Examples 2: Subtract the following expressions.

a. $3x + 5$ from $2x - 3$

Horizontal method

$(2x - 3) - (3x + 5)$

$= 2x - 3 - 3x - 5$ (signs changed)

$= 2x - 3x - 3 - 5$

$= (2 - 3)x\,(-3 - 5)$

$= -x - 8$

Vertical method

$$\begin{array}{r} 2x - 3 \\ \underset{-}{+}3x \underset{-}{+} 5 \\ \hline -x - 8 \end{array}$$ (signs changed)

b. $x + 3y$ from $2x - 3y$

Horizontal method

$(2x - 3y) - (x + 3y)$

$= 2x - 3y - x - 3y$

(signs changed)

$= 2x - x - 3y - 3y$

$= (2 - 1)x + (-3 - 3)y$

$= x - 6y$

Vertical method

$$\begin{array}{r} 2x - 3y \\ -\ \ x + 3y \\ \ominus\ \ \ominus\quad \\ \hline x - 6y \end{array}$$ (signs changed)

c. $x^2 - 3y^2$ from $5x^2 - 2y^2$

Horizontal method

$(5x^2 - 2y^2) - (x^2 - 3y^2)$

$= 5x^2 - 2y^2 - x^2 + 3y^2$ (signs changed)

$= 5x^2 - x^2 - 2y^2 + 3y^2$

$= (5 - 1)x^2 + (-2 + 3)y^2$

$= 4x^2 + y^2$

Vertical method

$$\begin{array}{r} 5x^2 - 2y^2 \\ -\ x^2 - 3y^2 \\ \ominus\ \ \oplus\quad \\ \hline 4x^2 + y^2 \end{array}$$ (signs changed)

Alert!

1. For subtraction, do not forget to change the sign of the term of the expression that is to be subtracted. First change the sign and then add.
2. In the vertical method, the algebraic expression that is to be subtracted is written below the other expression with a change of sign for each term.

Practice Exercise 5.2

1. Add the following monomials.

a. $4p, 3p, 6q, -3q, 2p$

b. $3ab, 4ab, 7ab, -ab$

c. $pq, -3pq, 4pq$

d. $x, 2x, -y, 3y, z$

e. $ab^2, 7ab^2, -10ab^2$

f. $2xy^2, -3x^2y, 4xy^2, 6x^2y$

g. $2a, 3b, 4c, -7a, -5c, -6b$

h. $2ab, 3bc, -5ca, 4ba, 5cb, 6ac$

i. $x, y, z, -xy, -yz, -zx$

j. $-6m^2, -2n^2, 10m^2, 8n^2$

2. Add the following algebraic expressions.

a. $a + 2b + 3c,\ a - 3b - 4c,\ -2a + b + 10c$

b. $6x^2 - 7x,\ 4x^2 + 10x,\ 3x - x^2$

c. $x^2 - y^2 + 10,\ 2x^2 - 7,\ 4y^2 + 5$

d. $p^2 + 3q^2 - 6r^2 + 2pqr,\ q^2 - 3p^2 + 2r^2 - 5pqr,\ r^2 - p^2 - 3q^2 + 2pqr$

e. $2x + 3y - 7z,\ -3x + y + 9z,\ 5x - 2y + 4z$

f. $x^3 + x^2 - 2x,\ 5x - 2x^2 + 7x^3,\ 8x^2 - 10x + 10x^3$

g. $4x^3 + 3x^2 - 7x + 4,\ 3x^3 - 4x^2 - 2x - 5,\ 2 + 3x - 4x^2 - 5x^3$

h. $2ab + 3bc - 5ca,\ 4bc - 3ab + 7ca,\ 2ca - ab - 5bc$

i. $10a^2b - 4ab,\ 6ab - a^2b,\ 9a^2b - ab$

j. $-3m + 5m^3,\ m^2 - 6m,\ m^3 - 7m^2$

3. Subtract the following algebraic expressions.

   a. $7x - 1$ from $14 + x$

   b. $16x^2 - 3x + 10$ from $10x - x^2 - 11$

   c. $x^3 - x^2$ from $3x^3 + 4x^2 + 7$

   d. $6xy + 4yz - 2xz$ from $-9xz + 2xy - 7yz$

   e. $3xyz - x^3 - y^2$ from $z^3 + 3x^3 - y^2 + xyz$

   f. $8a - 2b - 2c + 6$ from $6a + 2b + 2c + 5$

   g. $4pq + 3r$ from $10r - 7pq$

   h. $-m^3 + 4mn$ from $4m^3 - 3mn + 15$

   i. $a^2 + b^2 - 2ab$ from $a^2 + b^2 + 2ab$

   j. $x^2 - y^2$ from $2x^2 - 3y^2 + 6xy$

4. From the sum of $-3x + 4y - 7z$ and $x + y - 3z$, subtract $3x - y + 2z$.

5. From the sum of $3x^2 + 4xy$ and $-x^2 + xy$, subtract $10x^2 - 3xy$.

6. Subtract the sum of $2x + 3y + 5z$ and $-3x - y - 2z$ from the sum of $3x - 2y + z$ and $2x + 2y + 3z$.

7. From the sum of $11p^3 - 3q^2$ and $4p^3 + 6q^2$, subtract the sum of $9p^3 + q^2$ and $3p^3 - 4q^2$.

8. What should be added to $7x^2 + 8x + 10$ to get $15x^2 - x + 7$?

9. What should be subtracted from $9m^3 - 2m^2 + 4m$ to get $3m^3 + m^2 + 2m$?

10. The sum of three algebraic expressions is $5x^3 - 2x^2 + 10x + 1$. If two of the expressions are $x^3 - x^2 + 5x + 7$ and $2x^3 - 3x^2 + 7x - 9$, find the third.

Higher Order Thinking Skills

HOTS

1. What should be subtracted from $(2 - x + x^2)$ to obtain $x - 1$?

2. The perimeter of a triangle is $8 + 13a + 7a^2$ and two of its sides are $2a^2 + 3a + 2$ and $3a^2 - 4a - 1$. Find the third side of the triangle.

3. If $a = x + 2y$ and $b = x - 2y$, find $(2a + b) - (a - 2b)$ in terms of x and y.

Highlights

- A quantity having a fixed numerical value is called a constant.
- A quantity that can have different numerical values is called a variable or literal.
- A combination of constants and variables (literals) connected by the signs of addition, subtraction, multiplication and division is called an algebraic expression.
- The different parts of an algebraic expression that are separated by the signs '+' and '−' are called the terms of an expression.
- A term is a product of factors.
- An expression with only one term is called a monomial. An expression with two terms is called a binomial. An expression with three terms is called a trinomial. In general, an algebraic expression with more than two terms is called a polynomial.
- The product of all the factors except for a specified factor in an expression is the coefficient of that specified factor.
- The term with the highest power in a polynomial decides the degree of the polynomial.
- To find the value of an expression, we need to know the value of the variables in that expression.
- Terms that have the same literal factors are called like terms and terms with different literal factors are called unlike terms.
- When we add or subtract algebraic expressions, like terms are added or subtracted, while unlike terms are left as they are.
- The sum (or difference) of two like terms is another like term in which the coefficient is the sum (or difference) of those like terms.

Question: How do you expand $(a + b)^2$?

Answer for Brainteaser on page 85

Magical Formula

Aim: To form an algebraic formula using toothpicks or coloured straw.

Material required: A pack of toothpicks or coloured straw and a pair of scissors

Procedure: Cut each straw into four equal pieces.

Step 1 Arrange the straw pieces/toothpicks to form triangles as shown in the figure below.

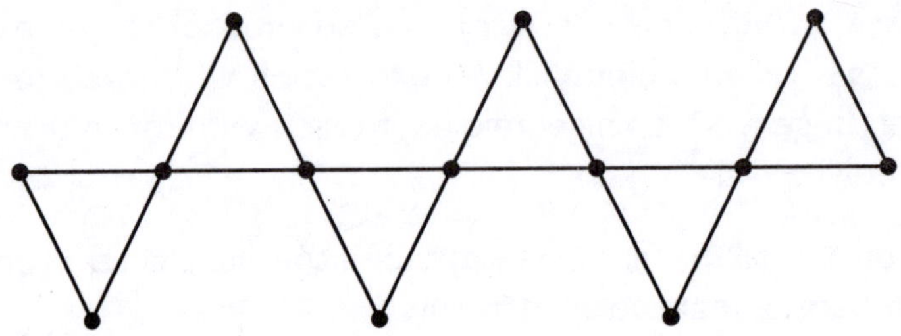

The formula for a triangle is as follows:

Number of triangles (x)	1	2	3	4	5	6
Number of straws/toothpicks required (y)	3	6	9			

Step 2 Arrange the straw pieces/toothpicks to form squares as shown below.

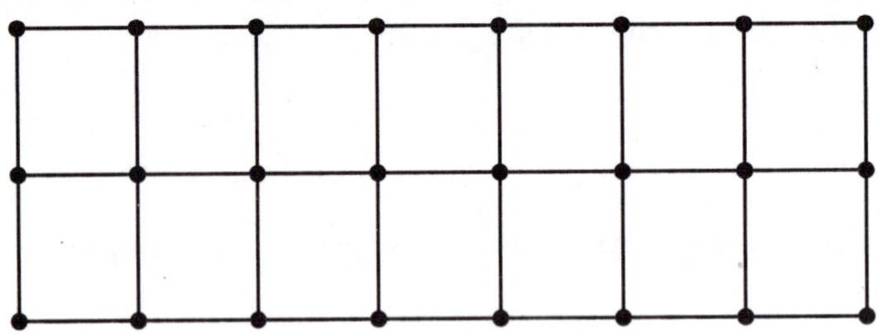

The formula for double squares is as follows:

Number of double squares (x)	1	2	3	4	5	6
Number of straws/toothpicks required (y)	7	12	17			

Step 3 Arrange the straw pieces/toothpicks to form a pattern comprising the letter H as shown below.

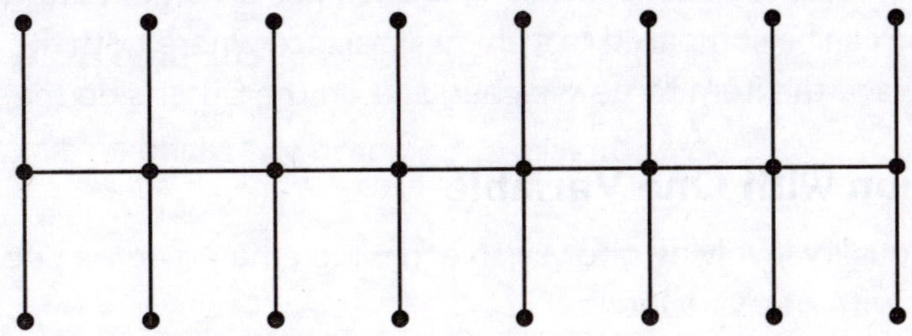

The formula for the letter H is as follows:

Number of letter H (x)	1	2	3	4	5	6	7	8
Number of straws/toothpicks required (y)	5	8	11					

Try this out with other shapes and patterns and deduce the formulae for the same.

Answer for Brainteaser from page 83

$(a \quad + \quad b)^2$

CHAPTER 6

Linear Equations with One Variable or Simple Equations

An algebraic expression with one variable, whose power or degree is one is called a simple or linear algebraic expression. For example, $x + 4$ or $2x + 3$ is a linear expression. Now if this expression 'is equal to' a constant or 0, it becomes an **algebraic equation**. Hence, an algebraic equation can be compared to a physical balance where both the pans are balanced—on one side we place the item to be weighed and on the other side the weights.

Linear Equation with One Variable

A statement of equality involving one variable in which the power is one is called a linear (or simple) equation with one variable.

The equations $x + 3 = 7$; $2p + 3 = 9$ and $\frac{x}{5} = 4$ are examples of linear equations.

In the example of a linear equation with one variable — $ax + b = 0$, $a \neq 0$ and a is any constant. The letter a is the numerical coefficient of x.

Alert!

The difference between an algebraic expression and algebraic equation is the 'equal to sign'.

$8x + 9$	algebraic expression
$8x + 9 = 17$	algebraic equation

Properties of Equations

1. If the left hand side (LHS) of an equation is interchanged with the right hand side (RHS), **the equation remains unchanged**.

   For example: $\underset{\text{(LHS)}}{4x + 2} = \underset{\text{(RHS)}}{2x - 6}$

   Now, if we write the equation as, $\underset{\text{(LHS)}}{2x - 6} = \underset{\text{(RHS)}}{4x + 2}$

   there will be no change in the solution of the equation.

   The entire expression on the LHS has been shifted to the RHS and vice versa.

2. If we add both sides of an equation with the same number, the equation remains the same. For example: $x - 3 = 5$

   $$x - 3 + 3 = 5 + 3$$

3. If we subtract both sides of an equation with the same number, the equation remains unaltered (the same). For example: $x + 5 = 7$

   $x + 5 - 5 = 7 - 5$

4. If we multiply both sides of an equation with the same number, the equation remains unaltered (the same). For example: $\frac{x}{4} = 5$

   $\frac{x}{4} \times 4 = 5 \times 4$

5. If we divide both sides of an equation by the same number, the equation remains unaltered (the same). For example: $5x = 20$

   $5x \div 5 = 20 \div 5$

Solution of an Equation

The value of the variable that makes the equation a true statement is called the solution or root of the equation. For a simple or linear equation with one variable, the variable can have only one value that makes the equation true.

Consider the equation $2x + 7 = 11$.

LHS $= 2x + 7$ RHS $= 11$

For the equation to be a true statement, we have to find a value of the variable x such that LHS = RHS. The value of 'x' must satisfy the equation or the equation should be balanced.

	LHS $2x + 7$	RHS 11
If $x = 1$,	$2 \times 1 + 7 = 2 + 7 = 9$	
If $x = 0$,	$2 \times 0 + 7 = 0 + 7 = 7$	
If $x = 2$,	$2 \times 2 + 7 = 4 + 7 = 11$	

Thus $x = 2$. This is the value of x that makes the LHS = RHS. Hence, it is the solution of the equation.

Example 1: Solve the equation $x - 5 = 20$.

$x - 5 = 20$ (add 5 to both sides of the equation)

$x - 5 + 5 = 20 + 5$ (using the addition property)

$x = 25$

To check the solution, if we put the value of x(25) in the given equation, it must satisfy it or make it a true statement.

$x - 5 = 20$

$25 - 5 = 20$

$20 = 20$

We can see that LHS = RHS

Therefore, $x = 25$ is the solution of the equation $x - 5 = 20$.

Example 2: Solve the equation $x + 8 = 20$.

$x + 8 = 20$ (subtract 8 from both sides of the equation)

$x + 8 - 8 = 20 - 8$ (using the subtraction property)

$x = 12$

To check the solution, if we put the value of x(12) in the given equation, it must satisfy it or make it a true statement.

$x + 8 = 20$

$12 + 8 = 20$

$20 = 20$

We can see that LHS = RHS

Therefore, $x = 12$ is the solution of the equation $x + 8 = 20$.

Example 3: Solve the equation $\frac{x}{5} = (-3)$.

$\frac{x}{5} = (-3)$ (multiply both sides of the equation by 5)

$\frac{x}{5} \times 5 = (-3) \times 5$ (using the multiplication property)

$x = (-15)$

To check the solution, if we put the value of x(−15) in the given equation, it must satisfy it or make it a true statement.

$\frac{x}{5} = (-3)$

$\frac{(-15)}{5} = (-3)$ or $(-3) = (-3)$

We can see that LHS = RHS, hence, $x = (-15)$ is the solution of the equation.

Example 4: Solve the equation $5x = 20$.

$5x = 20$ (divide both sides by 5)

$\frac{5x}{5} = \frac{20}{5}$ (using the division property)

$x = 4$

To check the solution, if we put the value of x(4) in the given equation, it must satisfy it or make it a true statement.

$5x = 20$

$5 \times 4 = 20$

$20 = 20$

We can see that LHS = RHS. Therefore, $x = 4$ is the solution of the equation.

Transposition

Transpose means to move to a different place. Instead of adding, subtracting, multiplying or dividing both sides of the equation by the same quantity, we move a term from the LHS to the RHS or from the RHS to the LHS. Any term of an equation may be taken from one side to the other with a **change in its sign**. This does not affect the equality of the statement. This process is called transposition.

When a term or a number crosses the equality sign and moves to the other side,

1. addition changes to subtraction (+ to −);
2. subtraction changes to addition (− to +);
3. multiplication changes to division (× to ÷); and
4. division changes to multiplication (÷ to ×).

Example 1: Solve $3p - 10 = 5$.

If we transpose −10 to the RHS, it will became +10.

Therefore, $3p = 5 + 10 = 15$

Now p is multiplied by 3. If we move it to the RHS, it will be divided.

$$3p = 15$$

$$\therefore \quad p = \frac{15}{3} = 5$$

Example 2: Solve $5(x + 3) = 25$.

We have to take 5 to the RHS. On the LHS, 5 is multiplied by (x + 3). When we shift it to the RHS, multiplication changes to division.

$$\therefore \quad x + 3 = \frac{25}{5} = 5$$

Now, $x + 3 = 5$

When we transpose +3 to the RHS, it changes to −3.

$$\therefore \quad x = 5 - 3 = 2$$

Thus, we see that transposition is an easier way to solve equations.

Example 1: Solve the equation $7x - 3 = 2x + 17$.

First, we shift −3 to the RHS, so we get

$$7x = 2x + 17 + 3$$

$$7x = 2x + 20$$

Next, we shift 2x to the LHS, we get

$$7x - 2x = 20$$

$$5x = 20$$

Now, we divide the RHS by 5 (as in LHS, 5 is multiplied by x).

$$\therefore \quad x = \frac{20}{5} = 4$$

$$x = 4$$

Now we need to substitute the value of x in the equation to check if it is correct.

LHS: $7x - 3 = 7 \times 4 - 3 = 28 - 3 = 25$

RHS: $2x + 17 = 2 \times 4 + 17 = 8 + 17 = 25$

Thus, LHS = RHS

Example 2: Solve $3x + \frac{1}{5} = 2 - x$.

We transpose $-x$ from the RHS to the LHS All variables need to be on one side

$$3x + x + \frac{1}{5} = 2 = 4x + \frac{1}{5} = 2$$

Again we transpose $\frac{1}{5}$ from the LHS to the RHS

$$\therefore \quad 4x = \frac{2}{1} - \frac{1}{5} = \frac{2 \times 5}{5} - \frac{1}{5}$$

$$4x = \frac{10}{5} - \frac{1}{5} = \frac{10 - 1}{5} = \frac{9}{5}$$

$$4x = \frac{9}{5}$$

When we transpose 4 to the RHS, multiplication changes to division.

$$x = \frac{9}{5} \times \frac{1}{4} = \frac{9}{20}$$

$$x = \frac{9}{20}$$

To check the answer, substitute the value of x in the equation.

$3x + \frac{1}{5} = 2 - x$

$$\text{LHS} = 3x + \frac{1}{5} = 3 \times \frac{9}{20} + \frac{1}{5}$$

$$= \frac{27}{20} + \frac{1}{5} = \frac{27}{20} + \frac{4}{20} = \frac{31}{20}$$

$$\text{RHS} = 2 - x = \frac{2}{1} - \frac{9}{20} = \frac{40 - 9}{20} = \frac{31}{20}$$

Thus, LHS = RHS, making the statement true when $x = \frac{9}{20}$.

Example 3: Solve $\frac{1}{4}x + \frac{1}{6}x = \frac{1}{2}x + \frac{3}{4}$.

The LCM of the denominators 4, 6, 2 and 4 is 12.

We multiply each term on both the sides by 12.

$$12 \times \frac{1}{4} \times x + 12 \times \frac{1}{6} \times x = 12 \times \frac{1}{2} \times x + 12 \times \frac{3}{4}$$

$$3x + 2x = 6x + 9$$

$$5x = 6x + 9$$

We transpose +6x from RHS to LHS to get $5x - 6x = 9$.

$$(-x) = 9$$

multiplying both sides by (-1), we get $x = (-9)$

To check the answer, substitute the value of x in the equation.

$$\frac{1}{4}x + \frac{1}{6}x = \frac{1}{2}x + \frac{3}{4}$$

LHS $\frac{1}{4}x + \frac{1}{6}x = \frac{1}{4}(-9) + \frac{1}{6}(-9)$

$$= \frac{(-9)}{4} - \frac{9}{6}$$

$$= \frac{(-9)}{4} \times \frac{6}{6} - \frac{9}{6} \times \frac{4}{4}$$

$$= \frac{(-54)}{24} - \frac{36}{24}$$

$$= \frac{(-90)}{24} = \frac{(-15)}{4}$$

RHS $\frac{1}{2}x + \frac{3}{4} = \frac{1}{2}(-9) + \frac{3}{4}$

$$= \frac{(-9)}{2} + \frac{3}{4}$$

$$= \frac{(-9)}{2} \times \frac{4}{4} + \frac{3}{4} \times \frac{2}{2}$$

$$= \frac{(-36)}{8} + \frac{6}{8}$$

$$= \frac{(-30)}{8} = \frac{(-15)}{4}$$

Thus, LHS = RHS, hence, $x = (-9)$ is the solution of the equation.

Practice Exercise 6.1

1. Form equations from the given statements.
   a. The sum of a number and 15 = 35.
   b. The product of a number and 9 = 54.
   c. Half of a number is 19.
   d. Three times a number plus 17 is 62.
   e. Twenty-five less than a number is 50.
   f. Ten times a number plus 11 is 121.
   g. One-fifth of a number plus 29 is 39.
   h. 15 less than 7 times a number is 48.
   i. Half the difference of a number and 20 is 40.
   j. 10 less than twice a number is 88.

2. Check whether the values of the variables given make the equation true.

a.	$3a + 7 = 22$	where	$a = 6$
b.	$14y = 7$	where	$y = 1$
c.	$2(x + 9) = 20$	where	$x = 2$
d.	$11b - 6 = 60$	where	$b = 7$
e.	$\frac{3m + 2}{11} = \frac{m + 5}{8}$	where	$m = 3$
f.	$7p + 10 = 45$	where	$p = 5$
g.	$5r + 12 = 67$	where	$r = 10$
h.	$\frac{t}{2} + \frac{t}{4} = \frac{1}{8}$	where	$t = 8$
i.	$8n - 1 = 9 - 2n$	where	$n = 1$
j.	$5(2d - 3) - 3(3d - 7) = 5$	where	$d = 4$

3. Solve the following equations and verify your answer.

a. $x - 5 = 3$ b. $p - 6 = -2$ c. $4y - 7 = 7$

d. $2a - 10 = 8 - a$ e. $5m - 7 = 9 - 3m$

4. Solve the following equations and verify your answer.

a. $x + 5 = 9$ b. $x + 7 = (-11)$ c. $5x + 5 = 20$

d. $7p + 5 = 19$ e. $3y + 7 = 22$

5. Solve the following equations and verify your answer.

a. $\frac{x}{5} = 3$ b. $\frac{x}{2} = 9$ c. $\frac{7p}{9} = 21$

d. $\frac{2}{3}x = \frac{3}{8}x + \frac{7}{12}$ e. $\frac{2m + 5}{3} = 3m - 10$

6. Solve the following equations and verify your answer.

a. $4x = 24$ b. $\frac{3}{4}x = 15$ c. $\frac{2y + 6}{9} + 10 = 14$

d. $\frac{8x}{3} + 4 = 12$ e. $\frac{3(m - 2)}{9} + 12 = 17$

7. Solve the following equations.

a. $5(2x - 3) - 3(3x - 7) = 5$

b. $13(y - 4) - 3(y - 9) = 5(y + 4)$

c. $p - (2p + 5) - 5(1 - 2p) = 2(3 + 4p) - 3(p - 4)$

d. $6(3a + 2) - 5(6a - 1) = 3(a - 8) - 5(7a - 6) + 9a$

e. $2(m - 2) - 3(m - 3) = 5(m - 5) - 4(m - 8)$

8. Solve the following equations.

a. $2x - \frac{1}{3} = \frac{1}{5} - x$ b. $\frac{1}{2}p - 3 = 5 + \frac{1}{3}p$

c. $\frac{x}{6} - \frac{x}{5} = \frac{x}{15} - \frac{x}{3} + 7$ d. $\frac{4x - 5}{7} - \frac{2x + 1}{2} = \frac{1}{2} - x$

e. $\frac{y - 1}{3} - \frac{y - 2}{4} = 1$

9. Solve the following equations and let the answers remain in fractions.

a. $2.45x + 1.5 = 3.7x - 2.25$
b. $2.4(2 - x) - 0.6(4x - 3) = 0$
c. $2.5x - 7 = 0.5x + 13$
d. $1.5x + 2.5 = 1.5x + 0.3x + 1$
e. $0.18(5x - 4) = 0.5x + 0.8$

10. Solve the following equations and verify your answer.

a. $\frac{2x + 3}{3} = \frac{3x - 8}{2}$
b. $\frac{2y - 1}{4y + 1} = \frac{1}{5}$
c. $\frac{9x + 7}{2} - \left(x - \frac{x - 2}{7}\right) = 36$
d. $2m - 3 = \frac{3}{10}(5m - 12)$
e. $\frac{2y + 4}{7} + \frac{y - 3}{2} = 3$

Word Problems Based on Linear Equations

Simple practical problems in everyday situations can be solved by applying simple equations. You can choose any letter of the English alphabet to denote a variable. The commonly used variables are x, y, z, m, n and p. The word problem should be read carefully and then the linear equation can be formulated with the unknown variable and the known quantities.

Example 1: Find a number, which when added to its half, gives the number 45.

Let the number be x, so half of the number x will be $\frac{x}{2}$.

According to the problem,

$$\frac{x}{1} + \frac{x}{2} = 45$$

$$\frac{2x + x}{2} = \frac{45}{1}$$

$$\frac{3x}{2} = 45$$

$$3x \times \frac{2}{2} = 45 \times 2 \quad \text{(multiplying both sides by 2)}$$

$$3x = 90$$

$$x = \frac{90}{3} = 30$$

The required number is 30.

Example 2: The sum of two natural numbers is 121. If one number is ten times the other, find the two numbers.

Let one number be x.

The other number is 10 times x = 10x.

According to the problem,

$$x + 10x = 121$$

$$11x = 121$$

$$x = \frac{121}{11} = 11$$

The number $x = 11$.

The other number is $10x = 10 \times 11 = 110$.

Their sum is $11 + 110 = 121$.

Therefore, the required numbers are 11 and 110.

Example 3: The length of a rectangle is 19 cm more than its breadth. If the perimeter of the rectangle is 138 cm, find its length and breadth.

Let the breadth of the rectangle be x cm. The length of the rectangle is $x + 19$ cm. We know that the perimeter of rectangle is 2(length + breadth).

$$\text{Perimeter} = 2[l + b] = 138$$

Substituting the values $l = x + 19$, $b = x$,

$$2[x + 19 + x] = 138$$
$$2[2x + 19] = 138$$
$$4x + 38 = 138$$
$$4x = 138 - 38$$
$$4x = 100$$
$$x = \frac{100}{4} = 25 \text{ cm}$$
$$x + 19 = 25 + 19 = 44 \text{ cm}$$

Thus, the length of the rectangle = 44 cm and the breadth of the rectangle = 25 cm.

Example 4: A number consists of two digits and the sum of the digits is 12. The digits are reversed (interchanged) if 18 is subtracted from the number. Find the number.

Let the digit in the unit's place be x. Then the digit in the ten's place is $12 - x$.

The two-digit number will be

$$10(12 - x) + x = 120 - 10x + x$$
$$= 120 - 9x \text{ (original number)}$$

On subtracting 18 from the given two-digit number, the digits are interchanged. So the digit in the unit's place is $12 - x$ and the digit in the ten's place is x. The number will be:

$$10x + (12 - x) = 10x + 12 - x$$
$$= 9x + 12 \text{ (new number)}$$

According to the problem,

$$\text{Original number} - 18 = \text{New number}$$
$$120 - 9x - 18 = 9x + 12$$

$$120 - 18 - 12 = 9x + 9x$$
$$90 = 18x$$
$$\frac{90}{18} = x \text{ or } 5 = x$$

Original number is $120 - 9x = 120 - 45 = 75$

Example 5: Amar's mother is nine times as old as Amar. Four years from now she will be five times as old as her son. Find their present ages.

Let Amar's present age be x years. His mother's age is 9x years.

Four years from now Amar will be $(x + 4)$ years old.

His mother will be $(9x + 4)$ years old.

According to the question, $9x + 4 = 5(x + 4)$

$$9x + 4 = 5x + 20$$
$$9x - 5x = 20 - 4$$
$$4x = 16$$
$$x = 4$$

$\therefore$ Amar is 4 years old, his mother is $9 \times 4 = 36$ years old.

Example 6: The price of a pair of jeans and two shirts is ₹2,440. A pair of jeans is ₹400 more than a shirt. Find the cost of one shirt and a pair of jeans.

Let the cost of one shirt be ₹x, then the cost of one pair of jeans is ₹$(x + 400)$.

The cost of a pair of jeans and two shirts is ₹2,440.

According to the problem, $2x + x + 400 = 2440$

$$3x + 400 = 2440$$
$$3x = 2040$$
$$x = \frac{2040}{3} = ₹680$$

The cost of a shirt is ₹680 and a pair of jeans is ₹1,080.

Example 7: The sum of three consecutive odd natural numbers is 153. Find the numbers.

Let the three consecutive odd numbers be x, $x + 2$, $x + 4$.

According to the problem, $x + x + 2 + x + 4 = 153$

$$3x + 6 = 153$$
$$3x = 153 - 6$$
$$3x = 147$$
$$x = \frac{147}{3} = 49$$

The three numbers are 49, 49 + 2, 49 + 4, that is, 49, 51 and 53.

Alert!

The units on the LHS and RHS of an equation should be the same.

Practice Exercise 6.2

1. Solve the following problems.

   a. A number when added to its half is equal to 84. Find the number.

   b. Four-fifth of a number is more than three-fourth of the number by 8. Find the number.

   c. Find three consecutive even natural numbers whose sum is 138.

   d. The sum of four consecutive numbers is 230. Find them.

   e. The length of a rectangular field exceeds its breadth by 5 m. If the perimeter of the field is 142 m, find the dimensions of the field.

   f. Two equal sides of an isosceles triangle are each 9 m less than twice the third side. If the perimeter of the triangle is 72 m, find the lengths of its sides.

   g. Rudy's grandmother's age is 15 times more than Rudy's age. After 10 years, Rudy's grandmother will be 5 times as old as Rudy. Find their present ages.

   h. A man is 30 years older than his son. In 12 years, the man will be 3 times as old as his son. Find their present ages.

   i. Bhairav collected ₹600 in his piggy bank by putting in ₹2 and ₹5 coins. The number of ₹5 coins are twice as many as ₹2 coins. Find the number of ₹2 and ₹5 coins.

   j. Lata bought a washing machine and two air conditioners for ₹56,000. The cost of a washing machine is one-third the cost of an air conditioner. Find the cost of each appliances.

   k. The numerator of a fraction is 4 less than its denominator. If 1 is added to both the numerator and the denominator, the fraction becomes $\frac{1}{2}$. Find the fraction.

   l. The denominator of a fraction is 5 more than its numerator. If 2 is subtracted from both the numerator and the denominator, the fraction becomes $\frac{4}{5}$. Find the fraction.

   m. The sum of the digits of a two digit numbers is 7. If we add 45 to the number, the digits are interchanged. Find the number.

   n. A two-digit number is such that its ten's digit is 6 more than the unit's digit. Also the ten's digit is three times the unit's digit. Find the number.

o. Mr. Singh left one fourth of his property to his son, one fifth of his property to his daughter and the remaining to his wife. If the wife's share is ₹2,20,000, what was the worth of his total property?

p. A man travelled $\frac{3}{5}$ of his journey by metro rail, $\frac{1}{4}$ by taxi, $\frac{1}{8}$ by bus and the remaining 10 km on foot. What is the length of his total journey? How much distance did he cover by rail?

q. A number is $\frac{3}{5}$ times another number. If their sum is 88, find the numbers.

r. The fifth part of a number when increased by 5 equals its fourth part decreased by 5. Find the number.

s. The cost of 2 tables and 8 chairs is ₹2,200. If a table costs ₹150 more than a chair, find the cost of each.

t. A mason was employed at a construction site for a period of 60 days. He was given ₹250 per day but if he was absent from work, a sum of ₹75 was deducted per day. At the end of 60 days he received ₹14,400. Find the number of days he was absent.

Higher Order Thinking Skills

HOTS

1. A number is as much greater than 17 as it is less than 31. Find the number.

2. A number consists of two digits. The digits in the ten's place exceeds the digit in the unit's place by 4. The sum of the digits is $\frac{1}{7}$ of the number. Find the number.

3. Ankur is now one-third the age of his father. Twelve years hence he will be half the age of his father. Determine the present age of Ankur and that of his father.

Highlights

- A linear equation is a statement of equality involving one variable and whose power is also one. The general linear equation is $ax + b = 0$, where $a \neq 0$.
- The value of the variable that makes the equation true is called the solution or root of the equation.
- If the LHS and RHS of an equation are interchanged, the equation remains unchanged.
- The equation remains unchanged or the same if:
  a. We add the same number to both sides of the equation.
  b. We subtract the same number from both sides of the equation.
  c. We multiply both sides of the equation by the same non-zero number.
  d. We divide both sides of the equation by the same non-zero number.
- Transposing a term means to take it from one side of the equation to the other.
- During transposition, the operation of the term reverses, thus

  (+) addition becomes (−) subtraction

  (−) subtraction becomes (+) addition

  (×) multiplication becomes (÷) division

  (÷) division becomes (×) multiplication
- The following steps are to be kept in mind while solving word problems:
  a. Read the question carefully understanding the language.
  b. Denote the unknown quantity or variable by a letter of the English alphabet (example x, y, z).
  c. Write the statement given in the form of a simple equation with the chosen variable.
  d. Solve the linear equation.

Replace the question marks with any of the following digits: 1, 2, 3, 4, 5 and 6. But remember that each digit can be used only once.

```
 ? ?
 x ?
 ----
 ? ? ?
```

Answer for Brainteaser on page 99

Balance the Equation

Objective: To change simple statements into algebraic equations and then solve them.

Material required: a box containing slips of paper with statements written on them. The students can write themselves or take the help of a group of students

Procedure: Form a pair and do this activity.

Each pair picks a slip from the box. One partner reads the statement and then writes it on the board as an algebraic equation. The other partner then finds the value of the variable using the trial and error method in solving the equation. Each pair is given 15 minutes to solve the equation. The pair that completes the equation is the winner.

Answer for Brainteaser from page 98

```
   54
  x 3
------
  162
-----
```

Rewind

1. If $x = 2$, $y = 3$ and $z = 1$, find the value of each of the following algebraic expressions.

   a. $x - y + z$ b. $2x + 3y - 5z$ c. $x^2 + y^2 - z^2$

   d. $xy - yz - zx$ e. $3xyz - x^2 + 7$

2. Add the following algebraic expressions.

   a. $3x - 5y + 1, 6x - 5y + 3$

   b. $4x^2 - 5x + 2, -5x^2 + 6x + 7$

   c. $12a + 9b - 10c - 16, 17 - 9c - 5b - a$

   d. $4x^3 + 3x^2 - 7x + 4, 3x^3 - 4x^2 - 2x - 5, 2 + 3x - 4x^2 - 5x^3$.

   e. $p^2 + 3q^2 - 6r^2 + 2pqr, q^2 - 3p^2 + 2r^2 - 5pqr, r^2 - p^2 - 3q^2 + 2pqr$

3. Subtract the following algebraic expressions.

   a. $x + y$ from $3x - y$

   b. $6xy + 4yz - 2xz$ from $-9xz + 2xy - 7yz$

   c. $3x^3 - 9xy - 3y^2$ from $-4x^3 + 8xy - 10y^2$

   d. $8a - 2b - 2c + 6$ from $6a + 2b + 2c + 5$

   e. $-m^3 + 4mn$ from $4m^3 - 3nm + 7$

4. Subtract the sum of $2x + 3y - 5z$ and $-3x + y - 2z$ from the sum of $3x - 2y - z$ and $2x + 2y - 3z$.
5. What must be subtracted from $7xyz^2 + 6cd + 3c$ to make it $2xyz^2 + 3cd + c$?
6. Solve the equation $4(x - 2) = 2(5 - x)$.
7. Solve the equation $4(5 - x) - 2(x - 3) = (x - 4) - 3(x + 2)$.
8. Solve the equation $\frac{x+1}{2} - \frac{5x+9}{28} = \frac{x+6}{21} + 5 - \frac{x-12}{3}$.
9. Solve the equation $\frac{3}{4}(7x - 1) - \left(2x - \frac{1-x}{2}\right) = \frac{x+3}{2}$.
10. Solve the equation $\frac{y+5}{6} - \left(\frac{14-y}{2} - \frac{1}{4}\right) = \frac{2y-7}{12}$.
11. Divide 64 into two parts such that one part is three times the other.
12. Ten years ago the father was six times as old as his daughter. After ten years, he will be twice as old as his daughter. Determine their present ages.
13. The width of a rectangle is two-thirds its length. If the perimeter of the rectangle is 135 cm, find the dimensions of the rectangle.
14. A number consists of two digits whose sum is equal to 8. If 18 is added to the number, the digits interchange their places. Find the number.
15. The measure of the angles of a triangle are $(x + 20)°$, $(2x - 30)°$ and $(3x - 50)°$. Find each of its angles.

Comparing Quantities

CHAPTER 7

Ratio

We know that *ratio is a fraction* that shows how many times a quantity is of another quantity of the same kind.

The ratio of two numbers, a and b, where ($b \neq 0$), is $a \div b$ or $\frac{a}{b}$ and is denoted by a : b. In the ratio a : b, a is called the first term or **antecedent** and b is called the second term or **consequent**.

A ratio remains unchanged if both its terms are multiplied or divided by the same non-zero quantity

Example 1: $\frac{a}{b} = \frac{ma}{mb}$, thus $a:b = ma:mb$

Example 2: $\frac{a}{b} = \frac{\frac{a}{m}}{\frac{b}{m}}$, thus $a:b = \frac{a}{m}:\frac{b}{m}$

The ratio a : b is said to be in its simplest form if the HCF of a and b is 1.

Alert!

Quantities written in a ratio must have the same *units*. A ratio has no units. It is a pure number.

Example 1: The cost of an eraser is ₹1.50 and the cost of a pencil is ₹5. What is the ratio of their costs in the simplest form?

Cost of an eraser = ₹1.50 = 150 p

Cost of an pencil = ₹5.00 = 500 p

Cost of an eraser:cost of a pencil or 150:500

$= \frac{150}{50} : \frac{500}{50}$ (HCF of 150 and 500 is 50)

$= 3:10$

The required ratio is 3:10.

Example 2: Divide 840 sweets among three sections A, B, C of Class VII in the ratio 5:7:8.

Sum of the ratios = $5 + 7 + 8 = 20$

Section A will receive $\frac{5}{20} \times 840 = 210$ sweets

Section B will receive $\frac{7}{20} \times 840 = 294$ sweets

Section C will receive $\frac{8}{20} \times 840 = 336$ sweets

Example 3: If $2A = 3B = 4C$, find A : B : C.

Let $2A = 3B = 4C = k$

$A = \frac{k}{2}, B = \frac{k}{3}, C = \frac{k}{4}$

$$A:B:C = \frac{k}{2}:\frac{k}{3}:\frac{k}{4}$$

LCM of (2, 3, 4 = 12)

$$\therefore \quad \frac{k}{2} \times 12 : \frac{k}{3} \times 12 : \frac{k}{4} \times 12$$

A:B:C = 6k : 4k : 3k

Dividing throughout by 'k', we get

A:B:C = 6:4:3

Proportion

When two ratios are equal, they are said to be in proportion. Four quantities or numbers a, b, c, d are said to be in proportion if a:b = c:d and we write a:b :: c:d.

If a:b :: c:d then,

1. a, b, c, d are known as first, second, third and fourth terms, respectively.
2. a and d are called extremes while b and c are called means.
3. $a \times d = b \times c$, that is the product of extremes = the product of means.
4. d is called the fourth proportional to a, b, c.

If a:b :: b:c then

1. a, b, c are said to be in continued proportion.
2. c is called the third proportional to a, b, and fourth proportional to a, b, c.
3. $\frac{a}{b} = \frac{b}{c} \Leftrightarrow b^2 = ac \Leftrightarrow b = \sqrt{ac}$
   and "b" is called the mean proportional or geometric mean between a and c.

Example 1: The first three terms of a proportion are 3, 5 and 21, respectively. Find its fourth term.

Let the fourth term be x, then

3:5 :: 21:x

$3x = 5 \times 21$ (since the product of extremes = product of means)

$$x = \frac{5 \times 21}{3} = 35$$

Hence, the fourth term is 35.

Example 2: If 25, 35 and x are in continued proportion, find the value of x.

Since 25, 35 and x are in continued proportion, we have

25:35 :: 35:x

$25x = 35 \times 35$ (since the product of extremes = product of means)

$$x = \frac{35 \times 35}{25}$$

Hence, x = 49.

Example 3: Find the third proportional to 16 and 12.

Let the third proportional to 16 and 12 be x, then

16 : 12 :: 12 : x

$16x = 12 \times 12$ (since the product of extremes = product of means)

$$x = \frac{12 \times 12}{16}$$

Hence, $x = 9$.

Example 4: Find the mean proportional between 3 and 27.

Let the mean proportional between 3 and 27 be x, then

3 : x :: x : 27

$x^2 = 3 \times 27$ (since the product of extremes = products of means)

$x^2 = 81$

Hence, the mean proportional between 3 and 27 is 9.

Alert!

1. If 3 terms (or numbers) are in continued proportion, then the central number is repeated. If a, b, c are in continued proportion, then b is repeated, i.e., a : b :: b : c.
2. If we have to find the *third proportional* to a and b, then we assume the third proportional to be 'x' and write a : b :: b : x.
3. If we have to find the mean proportional between two numbers a and b, we assume the mean proportional to be x. The third proportional between a and b is a : x :: x : b.
4. All values can be found by using the fact that product of the extremes = product of the means.

Direct Proportion

If two quantities are so related that the *increase* in one causes the corresponding *increase* in the other, they are said to be in *direct proportion.* Similarly, if a *decrease* in one quantity corresponds to a *decrease* in the other, they are said to be in direct proportion.

Some examples of *direct proportion* are:

1. The quantity purchased is *proportional* to the amount spent.
2. The quantity of food required is *proportional* to the number of people served.
3. The consumption of fuel is *proportional* to the distance travelled.
4. Profit is *proportional* to the investment.

Example 1: The cost of a dozen bananas is ₹40. Find the cost of 30 bananas.

One dozen bananas is 12, hence 12 bananas cost ₹40 and 30 bananas cost ₹x.

12 : 30 :: 40 : x

$12x = 30 \times 40$

$$x = \frac{30 \times 40}{12} = \frac{1200}{12} = 100$$

Thus, 30 bananas cost ₹100.

Example 2: In a hostel, 150 students consume 60 kg of rice per month. If 50 students of Class XII left after their board examination, what will be the consumption of rice in the next month?

If 150 students consume 60 kg of rice, 100 students will consume x kg of rice

$150:100::60:x$

$150x = 100 \times 60$

$x = \frac{100 \times 60}{150} = 40$

Thus, the remaining 100 students will consume 40 kg of rice.

Inverse Proportion

If two quantities are so related that the increase in one causes the corresponding decrease in the other, they are said to be in inverse proportion. Similarly, if a decrease in one causes an increase in the other, they are said to be in **inverse proportion.**

In an inverse proportion, the ratio of one kind of like terms is equal to the inverse ratio of the second kind of like terms.

Some examples of inverse proportion are:

1. the number of people and the time taken to complete the same work.
2. the number of people and the number of days to consume a fixed amount of food.
3. the number of articles purchased from a fixed amount if price increases.
4. the relation between pressure and volume of a fixed amount of gas when temperature is constant.

Example 1: Bhairvi can finish reading a book in 25 days, if she reads 18 pages of it every day. How many days will she take to finish reading it if she reads 15 pages everyday?

When Bhairvi reads 18 pages per day, she finishes reading the book in 25 days.

When Bhairvi reads 15 pages per day, she will finish the book in x days.

18 pages   25 days

15 pages   x days

$18:15::x:25$

$15x = 18 \times 25$

$x = \frac{18 \times 25}{15} = 30$ days

Bhairvi will finish reading the book in 30 days.

Example 2: A battalion of 600 soldiers had food provisions for 24 days. A fresh batch of 300 soldiers joined them. How many days will the food last now?

For 600 soldiers, the food provision will last for 24 days.
So, for 900 soldiers the food provisions will last for x days

600 soldiers　　24 days
900 soldiers　　x days

$600:900 :: x:24$

$900 \times x = 600 \times 24$

$$x = \frac{600 \times 24}{900} = 16 \text{ days}$$

Thus, the food will last for 16 days.

Practice Exercise 7.1

1. Express each of the following ratios in the simplest form.

   a. 75 paise : ₹5　　b. 9 months : 2 years　　c. 1 hour 15 minutes : 45 minutes
   d. 1 m 10 cm : 55 cm　　e. 2 kg 250 g : 3 kg

2. Divide 450 in the ratio 7:8.

3. Divide 560 in the ratio $\frac{1}{3}:\frac{1}{4}$.

4. a. If 2:9 :: x:27, find the value of x.

   b. If 8:x :: 16:35, find the value of x.

   c. If x:35 :: 48:60, find the value of x.

5. Find the third proportional to the following numbers.

   a. 36 and 54　　b. 27 and 36　　c. 7 and 14.

6. Find the mean proportional between the following numbers.

   a. 9 and 16　　b. 0.4 and 0.9　　c. 21 and 84

7. If the cost of 15 books is ₹240, find the cost of 39 books.

8. If the weight of 6 sheets of paper is 62 grams, find how many sheets of paper there are if a bundle of paper weighs 15.5 kg?

9. A bus covers a certain distance in 3 hours 20 minutes at an average speed of 45 km/hr. How long will it take to cover the same distance at a speed of 36 km/hr?

10. A gas cylinder lasts for 30 days in a family of 4 members. Six guests join the family. How long will the cylinder last?

Unitary Method

The unitary method is a method in which the value of unit (one) quantity is obtained first and that is used to find the value of any required quantity.

In direct proportion and inverse proportion, we apply the proportion formula directly. In the unitary method, we use either direct or inverse variation but after finding the value for one unit.

Let us compare the methods of proportion and unitary method to solve problems. The answer will, in any case, be the same irrespective of the method used.

Example 1: The cost of 30 shirts is ₹3,500. Find the cost of 18 shirts.

Method 1: Proportion method

30 shirts cost ₹3,500

18 shirts will cost ₹x

$30 : 18 :: 3,500 : x$

$30 \times x = 3,500 \times 18$

$x = \dfrac{3,500 \times 18}{30} = ₹2,100$

The cost of 18 shirts is ₹2,100.

Method 2: Unitary method

30 shirt cost ₹3,500

∴ 1 shirt will cost ₹$\dfrac{3,500}{30}$

Thus 18 shirts will cost ₹$\dfrac{3,500}{30} \times 18$ (we multiply by the number of units)

= ₹2,100

The cost of 18 shirts will be ₹2,100.

Example 2: Suhas has to send his paintings abroad for an exhibition. It is possible to pack 120 paintings in 15 cartons. How many cartons of the same size will be needed to pack 280 paintings that are all of the same size?

Method 1: Proportion method

120 paintings fit in 15 cartons

280 paintings fit in x cartons

$120 : 280 :: 15 : x$

$120 \times x = 280 \times 15$

$x = \dfrac{280 \times 15}{120} = 35$

Method 2: Unitary method

15 cartons can hold 120 paintings

1 carton can hold $\frac{120}{15} = 8$ paintings

8 paintings fit in 1 carton

280 paintings fit in x cartons

$\frac{280}{8} = 35$ cartons

35 cartons will be required for packing 280 paintings.

Example 3: If 36 men can finish constructing a boundary wall in 25 days, how many days will 15 men take to complete the construction?

Method 1: Proportion method

36 men finish in 25 days

15 men will finish in x days

$$\frac{36}{15} = \frac{x}{25} \quad \text{or } 36:15::x:25$$

$$15x = 36 \times 25$$

$$x = \frac{36 \times 25}{15} = 60 \text{ days}$$

Method 2: Unitary method

36 men complete the work in 25 days

1 man will complete the work in 36×25 days

If there are less men, they will require more days

15 men will complete the work $\frac{36 \times 25}{15}$

$\frac{36 \times 25}{15} = 60$ days.

Thus, 15 men will complete the work in 60 days.

Practice Exercise 7.2

1. Use the proportion method and unitary method to solve each of the following problems.

    a. The cost of 18 geometry boxes is ₹450. What would be the cost of 425 geometry boxes?

    b. If 1,152 bars of chocolate can be packed in 8 cartons of the same size, how many such cartons will be required to pack 3,888 bars of chocolate?

    c. If 56 men can complete paving a stretch of road in 18 days, how long will 24 men take to complete the same work?

    d. A military camp has provisions for 630 men to last for 25 days. How many men must be transferred to another camp so that the food lasts for 30 days?

e. The cost of 9 kg of dal is ₹414. How much dal can be bought for ₹552?

f. If the thickness of a pile of 15 tin sheets is 54 mm, how many tin sheets will be there in a pile that is 72 mm thick?

g. The yield of wheat from 11 hectares of land is 539 quintals. Find the number of hectares of land required for a yield of 490 quintals.

h. A taxi covers a certain distance in 4 hours at a speed of 60 km/hr. How much time will the taxi take to cover the same distance at a speed of 80 km/hr?

Percentage

Per cent comes from the Latin words *per centum* meaning out of hundred.

The symbol for per cent is %.

Thus 20% or 20 per cent implies twenty out of every hundred.

This is a very simple and widely used method to compare quantities.

If two quantities are given in different units, they can be compared by converting the quantities as percentage.

Anil secured 150 marks out of 200 and Sunil secured 180 marks out of 250. Which of the two secured higher marks?

We can compare Anil and Sunil's scores by converting into percentage.

Anil's marks expressed as a percentage: $\frac{150}{200} \times 100 = 75\%$

Sunil's marks expressed as a percentage: $\frac{180}{250} \times 100 = 72\%$

So, Anil secured a higher score than Sunil.

In daily life we come across statements such as

1. Dhruv scored 98% in mathematics.
2. The bank pays 5% interest on savings bank accounts.
3. A 40% discount during Diwali sale.
4. About 70% of the population of India lives in villages.
5. The pass percentage in the board examination is 33%.

Converting Fractions to Percentage

Per cent means out of hundred, so we multiply the fraction by 100 and add the % sign.

Example 1: $\frac{1}{4}$ as a percentage: $\frac{1}{4} \times 100 = 25\%$ or 25 per cent

Example 2: $\frac{17}{40}$ as a percentage: $\frac{17}{40} \times 100 = \frac{1700}{40} = 42\frac{1}{2}\%$

Example 3: $\frac{13}{100}$ as a percentage: $\frac{13}{100} \times 100 = 13\%$

Converting Percentage to Fractions

To convert a percentage to a fraction, we divide the percentage by 100 and remove the % sign.

Example 1: 30% as a fraction: $= \frac{30}{100} = \frac{3}{10}$

Example 2: 57% as a fraction: $= \frac{57}{100}$

Example 3: 48.5% as a fraction: $= \frac{48.5}{100} = \frac{485}{1000} = \frac{97}{200}$

Expressing a Percentage as a Ratio

To convert a percentage to a ratio, we divide the given value by 100.

Example 1: 27% as a ratio: $= \frac{27}{100} = 27:100$

Example 2: 45% as a ratio: $= \frac{45}{100} = \frac{9}{20} = 9:20$

Example 3: 22.5% as a ratio: $= \frac{22.5}{100} = \frac{225}{1000} = \frac{45}{200} = \frac{9}{40} = 9:40$

Converting a Ratio to a Percentage

To convert a ratio to a percentage, we first write the ratio as a fraction. The fraction is then multiplied by 100 to get the percentage.

Example 1: 16:25 as a percentage: $= \frac{16}{25} = \frac{16}{25} \times 100 = 64\%$

Example 2: 7:8 as a percentage: $= \frac{7}{8} = \frac{7}{8} \times 100 = \frac{700}{8}\% \quad = 87\frac{4}{8}\% = 87\frac{1}{2}\%$

Example 3: 100:150 as a percentage: $= \frac{100}{150} = \frac{100}{150} \times 100 \quad = \frac{200}{3} = 66\frac{2}{3}\%$

Converting Percentage to the Decimal Form

To convert a percentage to the decimal form, we write the percentage as a fraction and then convert it to the decimal form.

Example 1: $35\% = \frac{35}{100} = 0.35$

Example 2: $40\% = \frac{40}{100} = 0.40$

Example 3: $75\% = \frac{75}{100} = 0.75$

Converting Decimal to the Percentage Form

To convert a decimal to the percentage form, we simply multiply it by 100.

Example 1: $0.465 = 0.465 \times 100 = 46.5\%$

Example 2: $7.85 = 7.85 \times 100 = 785\%$

Example 3: $0.36 = 0.36 \times 100 = 36\%$

Converting Percentage into Actual Numbers

We know that 'of' means multiplication and % means per cent.

Example 1: $60\% \text{ of } 50 = \frac{60}{100} \times 50 = 30$

Example 2: $8\% \text{ of } 125 = \frac{8}{100} \times 125 = 10$

Example 3: $9\% \text{ of } ₹700 = \frac{9}{100} \times 700 = ₹63$

To Find the Entire Amount From the Percentage Amount Known

Example 1: If 20% of x is 400, find x.

$20\% \text{ of } x = 400$

$\frac{20}{100} \times x = 400$

$x = 400 \times \frac{100}{20}$

$x = 2000$

Example 2: If 40% of Ravi's salary is ₹8,000, find his entire salary.

40% of total salary = ₹8,000

$\frac{40}{100} \times \text{total salary} = 8,000$

Let the total salary be ₹x.

$\frac{40}{100} \times x = 8,000$

$x = 8,000 \times \frac{100}{40}$

$x = ₹20,000$

Example 3: If 12% of the total eggs in a basket is 42, find the total number of eggs.

12% of total eggs = 42

$\frac{12}{100} \times \text{total eggs} = 42$

Let the total number of eggs be x

$\frac{12}{100} \times x = 42$

$x = 42 \times \frac{100}{12}$

x = 350 eggs

Cancellation of Terms in Calculations

When fractions are multiplied, we can simplify the calculations by cancelling terms in the numerator and denominator. A term in the numerator is cancelled with a term in the denominator by a common factor. A 0 at the end of a number in the numerator is cancelled with a 0 at the end of a number in the denominator.

Example 1: $\frac{70}{100} = \frac{7}{10}$

Here we have cancelled 0 from the numerator as well as the denominator and simplified it. Cancelling 0 means we are dividing the numerator and the denominator by the common factor, 10.

Example 2: $\frac{13}{65} = \frac{1}{5}$

Here we are dividing the numerator and the denominator by the common factor, 13.

Example 3: $\frac{125}{625} = \frac{25}{125} = \frac{5}{25} = \frac{1}{5}$

Here we first divide the numerator and the denominator by a common factor, 5 and get $\frac{25}{125}$.

Here, we again divide the numerator and the denominator by a 5 and get $\frac{5}{25}$.

We again divide the numerator and the denominator by 5 and get $\frac{5}{25}$. We divide the numerator or the denominator one more time by 5 and bring the fraction to its lowest term, $\frac{1}{5}$.

Example 4: $\frac{7}{42} \times \frac{14}{70} = \frac{1}{30}$

Here, we cancel 7 and 70 by the common factor, 7. Also 14 and 42 can be cancelled by 7 twice or directly by 14 to get the simplified result.

$$= \frac{\overset{1}{\cancel{7}}}{\underset{3}{\cancel{42}}} \times \frac{\overset{1}{\cancel{14}}}{\underset{10}{\cancel{70}}} = \frac{1}{30}$$

Example 5: $\frac{17}{250} \times \frac{1000}{170} = \frac{100}{250} = \frac{10}{25} = \frac{2}{5}$

Here, we cancel one 0 in 1000 with a 0 in 170. Next, we cancel 17 and 17. Now, we can cancel another 0 in the numerator with a 0 in the denominator. Finally, we can cancel the numerator and the denominator by the common factor 5 to obtain the result.

Alert!

1. Cancellation can be done **only** when the fractions are being multiplied.
2. Only the 0 at the end of a number in the numerator can be cancelled with a 0 at the end of a number in the denominator.
3. When the numerator and the denominator are the same, they can be cancelled and the answer is 1 since that is the common factor. For example $\frac{18}{18} = \frac{1}{1} = 1$.

Practice Exercise 7.3

1. Convert the following fractions into percentage form.

   a. $\frac{1}{5}$ b. $\frac{6}{25}$ c. $\frac{13}{20}$ d. $7\frac{3}{4}$ e. $\frac{216}{500}$

2. Convert the following percentages into fractions in their lowest terms.

   a. 27% b. 35% c. 43% d. 52% e. 61%

3. Write the following percentages in the decimal forms.

   a. 28% b. 35% c. 12% d. 7.5% e. 0.5%

4. Convert the following decimal forms into percentages.

   a. 0.625 b. 0.025 c. 3.75 d. 0.008 e. 1.5

5. Find answers for the following.

   a. 30% of ₹240 b. 60% of 600 hours c. 10% of 400 km

   d. 15% of 650 kg e. 75% of 800 marbles

6. Find the value of x in each of the following.

   a. 30% of x is ₹600.

   b. 25% of x is ₹1500 sweets.

   c. 48% of x is 240 computer sets.

   d. 90% of x is 2,700 shirts in a shop.

   e. $33\frac{1}{3}$% of x is 900 marks.

7. Convert the following ratios into percentages.

   a. The ratio of yellow flowers to white flowers in a garden is 17:9.

   b. The ratio of chocolate ice cream to vanilla ice cream at an ice cream parlour is 45:55.

   c. The ratio of boys to girls in a class room is 13:12.

   d. The ratio of cricket to hockey as a popular sport is 35:15.

   e. The ratio of blue ball pens to black ball pens in a stationery shop is 7:5.

8. Anuj spends 10% of his salary on rent, 15% on transport, 50% on grocery, 5% on newspaper and magazines, 8% on bills and 12% on entertainment. If his monthly salary is ₹50,000, find out how many rupees he spends on each of them during the month.

9. The ratio of fiction books, non-fiction books and magazines in a school library is 3:5:2. Express this as a percentage. If the total number of books in the library is 10,000, find the numbers of books in each category.

10. Chalk contains 3% carbon, 10% calcium and 12% oxygen. Find the amount in grams of each of these substances in 1 kg chalk.

Higher Order Thinking Skills

HOTS

1. If 2A = 3B = 5C, then find A:B:C.

2. The present ages of A and B are in the ratio 7:5. Ten years hence, the ratio of their ages will be 9:7. Find the present ages of A and B.

3. What must be added to each of the numbers 5, 9, 7 and 12 to get the numbers that are in proportion?

Highlights

- The ratio of two numbers, a and b, is $a \div b$, and is denoted by $a:b$.
- The ratio of two quantities is always expressed in the simplest form and has no units.
- An equality of two ratios is called a proportion if $\frac{a}{b} = \frac{c}{d}$.
- The first and fourth terms of a proportion are called extremes while the second and third terms are called means.
- The numbers a, b, c and d are in proportion if $ad = bc$, that is, the product of the extremes = the product of the means.
- If a, b and c are in continued proportion, then $b^2 = ac$ and the middle term is called the mean proportional.
- In the unitary method, we find the value of one unit and then of many.
- More articles cost more. To get more we multiply (×). Cost of required number of articles = Cost of one article × Number of articles.
- Less articles cost less. To get less we divide (÷). Cost of one article $= \frac{\text{Cost of given number of articles}}{\text{Number of articles}}$.
- Percentage is another way of comparing quantities. A percentage is a fraction with the denominator as 100. Hence, 25% means 25 per cent $= \frac{25}{100}$.
- To convert a fraction or a ratio to a percentage, we multiply it by 100.
- To convert a decimal to a percentage, we shift the decimal point two places to the right.
- To convert a percentage to a fraction, we divide it by 100 and drop the % sign.
- To convert a percentage to a decimal, we shift the decimal point two places to the left and drop the % sign.
- We can find the exact number when a certain per cent of total quantity is given.
- When we know the value of a certain per cent of the whole, we can find the value of the whole.

Comparing Quantities

Objective: To learn the concept of ratio and percentage.

Material required: chart paper, sketch pens or colour pencils, ruler, pencil and eraser

Procedure: Students should collectively form a pool of a few ratio and percentage examples.

Example 1:

Shaded 20%
Dotted 50%
Unshaded 30%

Use your imagination and creativity to draw different figures and shapes or colour them according to the ratio.

Example 2: 2:8 can be represented as

Ratio of shaded parts:
Ratio of unshaded parts:

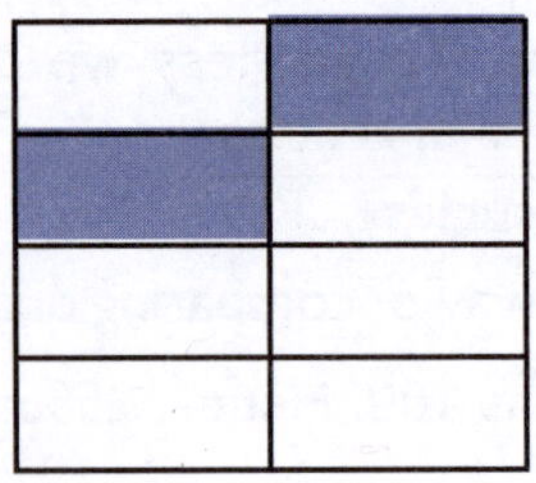

Example 3: 1:3:5 can be represented as

Ratio of shaded parts:
Ratio of dotted parts:
Ratio of unshaded parts:

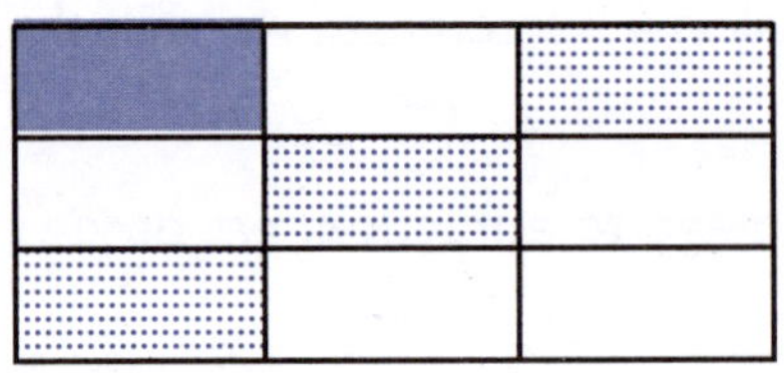

You can also use different shapes and figures to represent different percentages and ratios.

In which case can you add (2) to (11) and get (1) as the correct answer?

Answer for Brainteaser on page 115

Maths Lab Activity

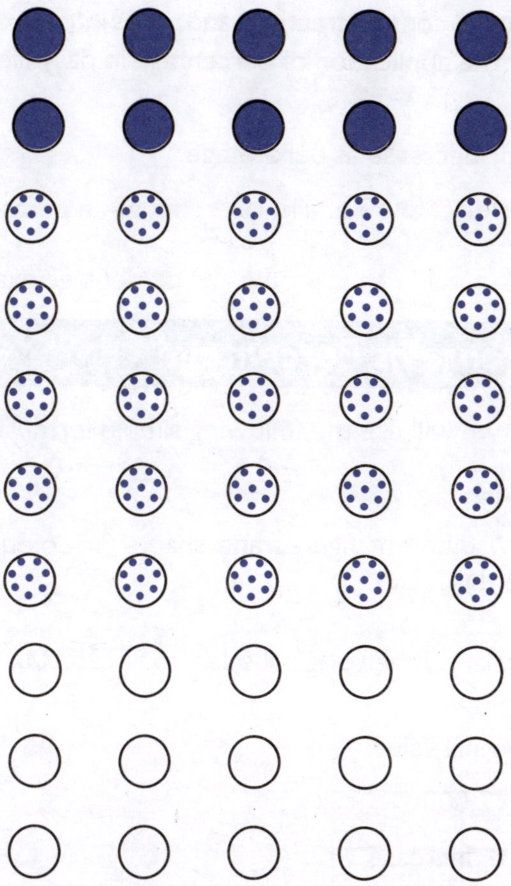

$$20\% = \frac{20}{100} \times 50 = 10$$

$$50\% = \frac{50}{100} \times 50 = 25$$

$$30\% = \frac{30}{100} \times 30 = 15$$

Answer for Brainteaser from page 114

When you add two hours to eleven o'clock the answer is one o'clock.

CHAPTER 8

Application of Percentage

We have studied percentage and we know how to convert fractions and ratios into percentage and vice versa. In this chapter, we will study the application of percentage in daily life under three broad categories:

1. Word problems related to increase or decrease as percentage.
2. Profit and loss.
3. Simple interest.

Increase or Decrease as Percentage

To find the increase or decrease in per cent we will use the following simple formulae:

$$\text{Increase \%} = \left[\frac{\text{Increase}}{\text{Original value}} \times 100\right]\%$$

$$\text{Decrease \%} = \left[\frac{\text{Decrease}}{\text{Original value}} \times 100\right]\%$$

Example 1: Avni got an 8% raise in her salary. If her original salary was ₹25,000, what is her new salary?

Increase in salary = 8% of original value

$$\text{Increase} = \frac{8}{100} \times 25{,}000 = ₹2{,}000$$

New salary = Original salary + Increase

= ₹25,000 + ₹2,000

= ₹27,000

Avni's new salary will be ₹27,000.

Example 2: The cost of an air conditioner before the budget was ₹18,000. The new price is ₹23,000. What is the per cent increase in the price of the air conditioner?

Original price = ₹18,000

New price = ₹23,000

Increase in price = ₹23,000 − ₹18,000 = ₹5,000

$$\text{Increase\%} = \left[\frac{\text{Increase}}{\text{Original price}} \times 100\right]\%$$

$$= \left[\frac{5{,}\cancel{000}}{18{,}\cancel{000}} \times 100\right]\%$$

$$= \frac{500}{18}$$

$$= 27\frac{7}{9}\%$$

Example 3: The cost of a mobile phone is ₹6,000. After discount, it costs ₹4,800. What is the per cent decrease in the price of the phone?

Original price = ₹6,000

New price = ₹4,800

Decrease in price = ₹6,000 − ₹4,800

= ₹1,200

$$\text{Decrease\%} = \left[\frac{\text{Decrease}}{\text{Original price}} \times 100\right]\%$$

$$= \frac{\overset{2}{\cancel{1200}}}{\cancel{6000}} \times 1\cancel{0}0$$

= 20%

Example 4: Namita purchased a basket of apples containing 180 apples. Due to heat, 15% of the apples got spoiled. Find the number of good apples in the basket.

Total number of apples in the basket = 180.

If 15% of the apples got spoiled, the number of rotten apples = 15% of 180

$$= \frac{\overset{3}{\cancel{15}}}{\underset{\underset{1}{\cancel{2}}}{\cancel{100}}} \times \overset{9}{\cancel{180}} = 27$$

Good apples = Total apples − Spoiled apples

= 180 − 27

Good apples in the basket = 153

Example 5: If the price of sugar rises by 25%, by how much per cent should a family reduce their consumption of sugar so that the expenditure on sugar may remain the same?

Suppose 100 units of sugar costs ₹100.

Increase in price = 25% [₹25 on every ₹100]

Cost of 100 units = ₹100 + 25 = ₹125

Now for ₹125 the quantity of sugar purchased will be 100 units. But the amount to be spent on sugar is ₹100 only.

Quantity of sugar for ₹100 = $\frac{100}{125} \times 100 = 80$ units

Hence, consumption of sugar is to be reduced by (100 − 80)% = 20%

Practice Exercise 8.1

1. Find the increase per cent if:

   a. the sale of cars in a showroom increases from 9,700 to 10,185 before the budget.

   b. Radha's salary is increased from ₹36,000 to ₹39,600.

c. the consumption of electricity increases from 9,000 units to 9,900 units in a family.

d. the population of a town increases from 75,000 to 85,000.

e. Rohit's marks in mathematics increase from 40 to 85.

2. Find the per cent decrease if:

a. the price of a pair of shoes decreases from ₹300 to ₹270.

b. the temperature drops from 40°C to 25°C at night.

c. in a village school the number of students in the primary section was 600 and at the secondary level 480.

d. The consumption of petrol by Mr Kumar's car dropped from 100 litres a month to 85 litres a month with the 20% hike in petrol prices.

e. the sale of ice cream in winter at a shop dropped from 500 to 375 ice creams per day.

3. Mr A's salary is ₹6,800 and he gets a raise of 15%. Mr B has a salary of ₹7,200 and he gets a raise of 12%. Who gets a higher raise and by how much?

4. Anuradha got a discount of 5% on a dress and she paid ₹760 for it. What was the original price of the dress?

5. Lata receives ₹25,000 as her monthly salary. She pays 15% of her salary as rent. What is the house rent? If she spends ₹8,500 on grocery, what per cent of her salary does she spend on grocery?

6. A total of 36,000 candidates appeared for the mathematics olympiad examination. Of them, 40% were girls and the remaining boys. If 15% boys and 10% girls got prizes, find the percentage of students who got prizes.

7. In an election, there were two candidates, A and B. The total number of voters in the constituency were 60,000 of out which 75% of the total votes were polled. If 80% of the polled votes were cast in favour of A, how many votes did B receive?

8. A fruit vendor stored 420 watermelons. Out of these, 10% turned rotten due to heat. How many watermelons could the fruit vendor sell?

9. If the price of petrol increases by 20%, by what per cent should Mr Brown reduce his consumption of petrol so that his expenditure on petrol remains the same?

10. Harsh attended school for 165 days during a year. His attendance is 75% of the total number of working days. How many working days were there in the academic year? If his attendance is 5% short of the required school attendance, how many days is he short of attendance?

Profit and Loss

Suppose you go to the market to buy a loaf of bread for ₹15. The shopkeeper would have either made the bread himself or bought it from a baker for a lower price (say ₹13).

The money that the shopkeeper spends to make an article or buy it from the manufacturer is called the cost price (CP). Here the CP is ₹13.

The price at which the shopkeeper sells the article is called selling price (SP). In this case it is ₹15.

The difference in price ₹15 − ₹13 = ₹2 is the profit or gain to the shopkeeper.

So, if SP is greater than CP, there is a profit of

$$\text{Profit} = \text{SP} - \text{CP} \text{ (when SP} > \text{CP)}$$

Sometimes a shopkeeper sells articles at a price less than his CP. He then suffers a loss.

$$\text{Loss} = \text{CP} - \text{SP} \text{ (when SP} < \text{CP)}$$

Profit or loss is always calculated on the CP.

Find the profit or loss in each of the following cases.

Example 1: SP = ₹250   CP = ₹200

SP > CP

∴ Profit = SP − CP

= 250 − 200

= ₹50

Example 2: SP = ₹1,987   CP = ₹1,988

SP > CP

Loss = CP − SP

= ₹1,988 − ₹1,987

= ₹1

Example 3: CP = ₹4,625   SP = ₹6,425

SP > CP

∴ Profit = SP − CP

= ₹6,425 − ₹4,625

= ₹1,800

Example 4: CP = ₹2,880   SP = ₹2,865

SP < CP

∴ Loss = CP − SP

= ₹2,880 − ₹2,865

= ₹15

Example 5: SP = ₹5,000 CP = ₹4,500

SP > CP

$\therefore$ Profit = SP − CP

= ₹5,000 − ₹4,500

= ₹500

Alert!

1. Profit or loss is always calculated on the basis of the CP.
2. If SP > CP, there is a profit.
3. If SP < CP, there is a loss.

Profit or Loss as a Percentage

Profit or loss is found with respect to the CP. We can also find the profit or loss per hundred units or the per cent.

Thus,

$$\text{Profit\%} = \frac{\text{Profit}}{\text{CP}} \times 100 \qquad \text{Loss\%} = \frac{\text{Loss}}{\text{CP}} \times 100$$

where Profit = SP − CP   where Loss = CP − SP

If the profit% or loss% are given and we have to find the actual profit or actual loss, we can determine it by using the formulae:

$$\text{Profit} = \frac{\text{Profit\%} \times \text{CP}}{100} \qquad \text{Loss} = \frac{\text{Loss\%} \times \text{CP}}{100}$$

Example 1: Amar bought a tricycle for ₹550 and sold it for ₹600. Find his profit and profit per cent.

SP = ₹600 CP = ₹550

SP > CP

Profit = SP − CP

= ₹600 − ₹550

Profit = ₹50

$$\text{Profit\%} = \frac{\text{Profit}}{\text{CP}} \times 100$$

$$= \frac{\overset{1}{\cancel{50}}}{\underset{11}{\cancel{550}}} \times 100 = \frac{100}{11} = 9\frac{1}{11}\%$$

Example 2: Raman bought a set of books for ₹400 and sold them for ₹380. Find his loss and the loss per cent.

SP = ₹380 CP = ₹400

SP < CP

Loss = CP − SP

= ₹400 − ₹380

Loss = ₹20

$$\text{Loss\%} = \frac{\text{Loss}}{\text{CP}} \times 100$$

$$= \frac{\cancel{20}^{5}}{\cancel{400}} \times \cancel{100} = 5\%$$

Example 3: A house was purchased for ₹5,00,000 and sold at a profit of 25%. Find the selling price of the house.

Here the profit% is given as 25%

$$\text{Actual profit} = \frac{\text{Profit\%} \times \text{CP}}{100}$$

$$= \frac{25 \times 5,000,\cancel{00}}{\cancel{100}}$$

Profit = ₹1,25,000

SP − CP = Profit

∴ SP = CP + Profit

= 5,00,000 + 1,25,000

= 6,25,000

Example 4: A man sells his television set for ₹15,500 at a loss of 20%. Find his CP

Here the loss% is given as 20%

SP = ₹15,500 loss% = 20%

If CP was 100, the SP would be ₹80

When SP is ₹80, CP is ₹100

When SP is ₹15,500 CP is $\frac{100}{80} \times 15,500$

CP = ₹19,375

Example 5: By selling a refrigerator for ₹18,000, Sonu lost 20%. At what price should he have sold it to make a profit of 10%?

SP = ₹18,000 loss = 20% CP = ?

If CP was 100, the SP would be ₹80 (loss 20%)

When SP is ₹80, CP is ₹100

When SP is ₹18,000 CP is $\frac{100}{80} \times 18,000$

CP = ₹22,500

If Sonu wanted to make a profit of 10%,

$$\text{The actual profit} = \frac{10}{\cancel{100}} \times 22,5\cancel{00}$$

= ₹2250

SP = CP + Profit

= ₹22,500 + ₹2250

SP = ₹24,750

Thus, Sonu should have sold the refrigerator for ₹24,750 to get a profit of 10%.

Practice Exercise 8.2

1. Find the profit% or loss% in each of the following cases.

   a. CP = ₹600 SP = ₹720 b. CP = ₹5,000 SP = ₹4,970

   c. SP = ₹1,250 CP = ₹1,000 d. SP = ₹1,900 CP = ₹2,000

   e. CP = ₹800 SP = ₹800

2. Find the SP in each of the following cases.

   a. CP = ₹950 profit = 6% b. CP = ₹9,600 profit = $16\frac{2}{3}\%$

   c. CP = ₹760 loss = 5% d. CP = ₹3,800 profit = 8%

   e. CP = ₹600 profit = 15%

3. Find the CP if:

   a. SP = ₹924 gain = 10% b. SP = ₹1,755 gain = $12\frac{1}{2}\%$

   c. SP = ₹851 loss = 8% d. SP = ₹1,904 gain = 12%

   e. SP = ₹10,240 loss = 20%

4. Arun bought a dining table set for ₹12,500 and sold it for ₹14,000. Find his profit or loss per cent.

5. Ritu bought a pair of gold bangles for ₹25,000 and sold them at a profit of 8%. Find the selling price of the gold bangles.

6. Rahim sold a water cooler for ₹8,010 at a loss of 11%. Find his CP.

7. Anubhav and Sambhav bought a carpet each for ₹25,000. Anubhav sold the carpet at a loss of 10% and Sambhav sold the carpet at a profit of 10%. Find the price at which each sold his carpet.

8. By selling a television set for ₹4,500, Ganga incurred a loss of 10%. Had she sold it for ₹4,900, would she have made a profit or loss? What would be her loss or profit per cent?

9. A shopkeeper bought 6 dozen eggs at the rate of ₹50 per dozen. On the way to the shop, 6 eggs broke. At what rate per egg does he need to sell the remaining to make a profit of 10%?

10. A dealer bought 18 chairs for ₹300 each. He sold 12 of them at ₹400 each and 6 of them at ₹250 each. Find his gain or loss per cent.

Simple Interest

When we need money to buy an essential commodity or pay a medical bill in case of an emergency and we do not have extra money for an eventuality, we borrow money. The money can be borrowed from a bank, a finance company or a money lender. We borrow the money for a specified time and then pay back the borrowed money plus some additional money. There are specific terms used for borrowing, lending and the additional money.

The borrowed money is called the **principal** (P).

The additional money paid by the borrower is called the **interest**.

The borrowed money plus the additional money is called the **amount** (A).

The interest on ₹100 for one year is known as the **rate per cent per annum** (R).

The term for which the money is borrowed is called the **time** (T).

If the interest is calculated uniformly on the original principal throughout the loan period, it is called **simple interest** (SI).

If P is the principal, R is the rate of interest per annum and T is the time (number of years), the simple interest is calculated as below.

Interest on ₹100 for one year = ₹R

∴ Interest on ₹1 for one year = ₹$\frac{R}{100}$

Interest on ₹P for one year = ₹$\frac{P \times R}{100}$

Interest on ₹P for T years = ₹$\frac{P \times R \times T}{100}$

Thus, the formula for calculating simple interest is given by

Simple interest (SI) = $\frac{P \times R \times T}{100}$

There are four variables (or unknowns) in the formula, SI, P, R and T. If any three of them are known, we can calculate the fourth.

To summarise:

1. $SI = \frac{P \times R \times T}{100}$
2. Amount = Principal + SI
3. Principal = $\frac{SI \times 100}{R \times T}$
4. Rate = $\frac{SI \times 100}{P \times T}$
5. Time = $\frac{SI \times 100}{P \times R}$

Alert!

If time is given in months or days, we should convert it to years.

To convert months to years, divide by 12 (÷ 12).

To convert days to years, divide by 365 (÷ 365).

Example 1: Find the simple interest on ₹5,000 for 2 years at the rate of 6% per annum.

Here P = ₹5,000 R = 6% pa T = 2 yrs

$$SI = \frac{P \times R \times T}{100}$$

Substituting the values of P, R and T, we get,

$$SI = \frac{5,000 \times 6 \times 2}{100} = ₹600$$

Thus, SI is ₹600.

Example 2: Anupam borrowed ₹7,500 from a money lender for 3 years at the rate of 8% per annum. How much money will Anupam have to return to the money lender at the end of three years?

Here, P = ₹7,500 R = 8% T = 3yrs

Substituting the values in the formula for SI,

$SI = \frac{P \times R \times T}{100}$. We get,

$$SI = \frac{7,500 \times 8 \times 3}{100} = 75 \times 24 = ₹1,800$$

Now, amount = principal + simple interest

Amount = ₹7,500 + ₹1,800 = ₹9,300

Hence, Anupam has to return ₹9,300 at the end of 3 years.

Example 3: Rati borrowed ₹5,000 from Ravi at the rate of 12% per annum. After a certain time period she paid Ravi ₹6,450. For how much time did Rati borrow the money?

Here, P = ₹5,000 A = ₹6,450, R = 12%

SI = A − P

= 6,450 − 5,000 = ₹1,450

$$T = \frac{SI \times 100}{P \times R}$$

Substituting the known values in the formula we get:

$$T = \frac{\overset{29}{\cancel{1450}} \times \cancel{100}}{\underset{1}{\cancel{5000}} \times 12} = \frac{29}{12} \text{ years}, = 2\frac{5}{12} \text{ years}$$

Rati borrowed the money for 2 years and 5 months.

Example 4: Shamli borrowed ₹6,000 from the State Bank of India for 3 years 8 months. She paid an amount of ₹8,640 at the end of the time period. How much rate of interest did the bank charge her?

Here, P = ₹6,000 A = ₹8,640 Time = 3 years 8 months = $3\frac{8}{12}$ years

= $3\frac{2}{3}$ years

SI = A − P

= 8,640 − 6,000 = ₹2,640

Now, $R = \frac{SI \times 100}{P \times T}$.

Substituting the known values in the formula we get:

$$R = \frac{2,640 \times 100}{6,000 \times 3\frac{2}{3}}$$

$$R = \frac{2,640 \times 100}{6,000 \times \frac{11}{3}}$$

$$R = \frac{\overset{\overset{12}{1,32}}{\cancel{2,640}} \times \cancel{100} \times \overset{1}{\cancel{3}}}{\underset{\underset{1}{2}}{\cancel{6,000}} \times \underset{1}{\cancel{11}}} = 12\%$$

Rate of interest is 12% per annum.

Example 5: Mini lent a certain sum of money to her friend Bindu for which she got an interest of ₹3,600 in 6 years at the rate of 8% per annum. What sum of money did Bindu borrow from Mini?

Here, SI = ₹3,600, T = 6 years, R = 8%

$$P = \frac{SI \times 100}{R \times T}$$

Substituting the known values in the formula we get:

$$P = \frac{\overset{\overset{75}{600}}{\cancel{3,600}} \times 100}{\underset{1}{\cancel{8}} \times \underset{1}{\cancel{6}}} = ₹7,500$$

Bindu borrowed ₹7,500 from Mini.

Practice Exercise 8.3

1. Calculate the simple interest for the following cases:

a. P = ₹6,500	R = 5% pa	and	T = 3 years
b. P = ₹9,000	R = 10% pa	and	T = 2 years 6 months
c. P = ₹1,500	R = 12% pa	and	T = 146 days
d. P = ₹7,200	R = $7\frac{1}{2}$% pa	and	T = 7 months
e. P = ₹1,00,000	R = 8% pa	and	T = 5 years

2. Find the rate of interest per annum for the following cases.

a. P = ₹6,400	SI = ₹1,152	and	T = 2 years
b. P = ₹5,000	SI = ₹1,650	and	T = 3 years
c. P = ₹5,200	SI = ₹975	and	T = $2\frac{1}{2}$ years
d. A = ₹768	P = ₹640	and	T = 2 yrs 6 month
e. A = ₹4,734	P = ₹3,600	and	T = $3\frac{1}{2}$ years

3. Find the time period for the following cases.

P = ₹8,250	SI = ₹1,100	and	R = 10%
A = ₹6,720	P = ₹5,600	and	R = 8%
P = ₹3,650	SI = ₹876	and	R = 6%
A = ₹11,036	P = ₹8,900	and	R = 12%
P = ₹5,000	SI = ₹650	and	R = $6\frac{1}{2}$%

4. Find the principal and the amount for the following cases.

a. SI = ₹720	R = 6% pa	and	T = 4 years
b. SI = ₹3,600	R = 8% pa	and	T = 6 years
c. SI = ₹829.50	R = 10% pa	and	T = 3 years
d. SI = ₹375	R = 6% pa	and	T = 2 years 6 months
e. SI = ₹90	R = 10% pa	and	T = 73 days

5. Rita lent ₹6,800 for 5 years at 5% pa interest, whereas Mita lent ₹8,600 for 4 years at 4% pa. Who earned more interest? How much more interest did this person earn?

6. Raghavi borrowed ₹5,600 and had to return ₹7,865 after 5 years. Shivika borrowed ₹6,500 and had to return ₹8,775 after 7 years. Who paid a higher rate of interest per annum?

7. Mrs Malhotra deposited her provident fund of ₹5,00,000 in a bank for 5 years at the rate of 8% pa. How much money will she receive at the end of 5 years?

8. Yoginder lent ₹7,500 to Rakshit on interest at the rate of 15% per annum. After 3 years and 3 months, Rakshit returned the money to Yoginder. How much interest did Rakshit pay? What was the amount that Yoginder received?

9. Nidhi borrowed ₹1,00,000 for 3 years at the rate of 5 % pa as an education loan. After 3 years, she paid the interest money and kept the same amount again for 3 years for higher education at the same rate. Find the amount she has to return after 3 years.

10. Vijaya borrowed a certain sum of money from her friend. At the end of 4 years, at a rate of interest of 3% pa, she returned ₹9,520 to her friend. Find the sum of money Vijaya borrowed from her friend.

Highlights

- If two quantities are given, we can find what percentage one quantity is of the other.
- If the increase or decrease in a quantity is given as a percentage, we can find the actual increase or decrease.
- During a transaction, there is either a profit or a loss.
- The amount we pay to buy goods is called its cost price (CP).
- The price at which a good is sold is called its selling price (SP).
- If SP > CP, there is a profit or gain. Profit or gain = SP − CP.
  If CP > SP, there is a loss. Loss = CP − SP.
- Profit or loss can also be calculated as a percentage.
  $\text{Profit \%} = \frac{\text{Profit}}{\text{CP}} \times 100$, $\text{Loss \%} = \frac{\text{Loss}}{\text{CP}} \times 100$
- Profit or loss is always calculated on the cost price (CP)
- To find the CP when the profit or loss per cent is given
  $\text{CP} = \frac{\text{SP} \times 100}{(100 + \text{profit \%})}$ (when there is a profit)
  $\text{CP} = \frac{\text{SP} \times 100}{(100 - \text{loss \%})}$ (when there is a loss)
- To find the SP when the profit or loss per cent is given
  $\text{SP} = \frac{\text{CP} \times (100 + \text{gain \%})}{100}$ (when there is a profit)
  $\text{SP} = \frac{\text{CP} \times (100 - \text{loss \%})}{100}$ (when there is a loss)
- When a sum of money is borrowed, an additional amount of money is charged for using that money. The borrowed money is called the principal, the money charged for using the principal is called the interest.
- $\text{Simple interest} = \frac{\text{Principal} \times \text{Rate of interest} \times \text{Time (in years)}}{100}$
  or simply, $\text{SI} = \frac{\text{P} \times \text{R} \times \text{T}}{100}$
- The rate of interest is usually given as a percentage per annum (per annum means per year).
- The sum of money returned after a given time period is called the amount.
  Amount = Principal + Interest
- If any three quantities are given out of the four–P, R, T, or SI, we can calculate the fourth. Thus,
  $\text{P} = \frac{\text{SI} \times 100}{\text{R} \times \text{T}}, \text{R} = \frac{\text{SI} \times 100}{\text{P} \times \text{T}}, \text{T} = \frac{\text{SI} \times 100}{\text{P} \times \text{R}}$

Higher Order Thinking Skills

HOTS

1. Find the difference between 1% of 100 and 100% of 1.
2. What per cent of one day is 36 minutes?
3. If 11% of a number exceeds 7% of the number by 18, find the number.
4. A mobile phone dealer marks a mobile phone with a price that is 20% more than its cost price. He allows a discount of 10% on this price. Find his gain %.
5. At what rate per cent per annum simple interest will a sum become three times itself in 12 years?

Divide 110 into two numbers in such a way that one of them will be 150 per cent of the other. What are the two numbers?

Answer for Brainteaser on page 132

Application of Percentage
PROFIT OR LOSS

Aim: To understand the concept of profit and loss.

Material required: a collection of items including school bag, textbooks, notebooks, tiffin box, water bottle, geometry box, pencils, pen, eraser, coloured pencils, sketch pens, etc., colourful stickers for price marking the price, coupons of different denominations—₹1, ₹5, ₹10, ₹20, ₹50 and ₹100 made of different coloured chart paper to make each denomination distinct

Method: Students need to work in pairs for this activity. Student A pretends to be the shopkeeper while student B pretends to be the customer. First student A needs to decide the cost price of the various items on sale. Student A then needs to put stickers on the articles marking the selling price of those articles. Items that are in a good state can have a selling price greater than the cost price, while items that are damaged should have a selling price less than the cost price. Student B now needs to 'buy' these articles using the coupons he/she has. Once the transaction is complete, each pair calculates the loss/profit percentage for the shopkeeper (Student A).

CHAPTERS 7–8

Rewind

1. Write the ratio of each of the following in the simplest form.

   a. 160 kg to 4.5 kg b. ₹5.50 to ₹2.50 c. 5 kg to 450 g

   d. 2 m to 50 cm e. 2 hours to 36 minutes.

2. Divide ₹108 in the ratio 2:3:4.

3. In a school, 500 students appeared in an examination in which 450 passed and the rest failed. Find the following ratios.

   a. Those who passed to those who appeared for the examination.

   b. Those who failed to those who appeared for the examination.

   c. Those who passed to those who failed.

4. The ratio of the length of a park to its width is 7:3. If the width of the park is 240 m, find its length.

5. Find x in the following proportions.

   a. $20 : x = 160 : 32$ b. $8 : 20 = x : 70$ c. $120 : 18 = 20 : x$

6. Write each of the following percentages as fractions.

   a. 36% b. 81% c. 95% d. 28% e. 44%

7. The population of a town was 25,00,000 in a certain year. Three years later, it increased to 38,00,000. By what percentage did the population increase?

8. The price of sugar was reduced from ₹45 per kg to ₹42 per kg. Find the percentage decrease in the price of sugar.

9. Arpit bought a mobile phone for ₹10,000 and sold it for ₹8,100. Find his percentage loss.

10. Kamlesh bought a saree for ₹2,500 and sold it for ₹2,800. Find her profit percentage.

11. Find the sum for which the simple interest for 3 years at 9% per annum is ₹4,320.

12. Urmi bought a table for ₹1,880. She spent ₹50 on polishing it and sold it at a profit of 3%. Find the selling price.

13. Ashok invested ₹3,000 for 2 years and ₹2,500 for 3 years at the same rate of interest. He received a total interest of ₹810. Find the rate of interest.

14. A shopkeeper bought 300 eggs at the rate of ₹120 per 100. Out of these, 40 eggs broke in transit and he sold the remaining at the rate of ₹1.30 per egg. Find his loss or profit per cent.

15. Find the simple interest on ₹30,000 for 219 days at 8% per annum (1 year = 365 days).

Test Yourself

Unit II

1. Identify the following expressions as monomials, binomials or trinomials.

   a. $(-7a^2b^2c^2)$ b. $18abc - b^2c^2$ c. $11a^3 - b^3 + 7c^3$
   d. $x^2 - y^2$ e. $42x^2$

2. Write the following polynomials in descending order.

   a. $10 + p^2q + pq - 15p^2q^2$ b. $16a^3 + 4a^3b^2 - 3b^2$
   c. $18x + 10xy + 9x^2y^2$ d. $15x^3 - 13x^2y^3$
   e. $18a^2b + 27a^2b$

3. Add the following algebraic expressions.

   a. $6x^2 - 7x,\ 4x^2 + 10x,\ 3x - x^2$
   b. $x^3 - y^3 + 1,\ 2x^3 - 7,\ 4y^3 - 6$
   c. $12p^2q - 6pq + 10,\ 3pq - 15,\ p^2q - 3$
   d. $8a^2 - b^2 - 4,\ a^2 + b^2,\ 3b^2 - 16$
   e. $11p + 5p^2,\ 9p^2 - 10,\ 4 + 9p$

4. What should be subtracted from $9p^3 - 2p^2 + 4p$ to get $3p^3 + p^2 + 2p$?

5. From the sum of $11x^3 - 3y^2$ and $4x^3 + 6y^2$ subtract the sum of $9x^3 + y^2$ and $3x^3 - 4y^2$.

6. Solve the equations.

   a. $3\left(y - \frac{1}{3}\right) = 2(2y - 6)$ b. $\frac{2a - 1}{4a + 1} = \frac{1}{5}$
   c. $\frac{x - 1}{3} - \frac{x - 2}{4} = 1$

7. The sum of three consecutive odd numbers is 147. Find the numbers.

8. There are some ₹1 and ₹2 coins in a piggy bank. The number of ₹1 coins is half the number of ₹2 coins. If the total amount of money in the piggy bank is ₹315, how many ₹1 and ₹2 coins are there in the piggy bank?

9. The sum of five consecutive natural numbers is 325. Find the numbers.

10. The numerator of a fraction is 4 less than its denominator. If 2 is added to both the numerator and the denominator, the fraction becomes $\frac{7}{11}$. Find the original fraction.

11. Check whether the following quantities are in proportion or not.

a. 8, 10, 16 and 20 b. 15, 19, 75 and 95 c. 11, 22, 6 and 18

d. 20, 25, 80 and 100 e. 16, 24, 8 and 14

12. Convert the following as indicated.

a. $\frac{9}{10}$ as a percentage b. 1.4 as a percentage c. 78% as a fraction

d. 45% as a decimal e. 0.00% as a percentage

13. Calculate the following:

a. 10% of ₹3,000 b. 15% of 300 bulbs c. 25% of 400 pens

d. 45% of 600 trees e. 68% of 500 marks

14. Sagnik, Magi and Raunaq are members of a reading club. Sagnik read 20% of a 150 page book in a day; Magi read 16% of a 200 page book in a day and Raunaq read 18% of a 300 page book in a day. Who reads the maximum number of pages in a day?

15. The ratio of yellow, red and white flowers in a garland is 3:4:5. Find the percentage of each type of coloured flowers in the garland.

16. Decrease the following quantities by 10%.

a. 3,600 scooters b. 45,100 cars c. 9,750 books

d. 8 kg e. 5 hours

17. Ivan bought a scooter for ₹38,000 and sold it at a profit of 5%. At what price did he sell the scooter?

18. By selling a television set for ₹13,500, Anubhav incurs a loss of 10%. At what price did he buy the television set? If he works a profit of 10%, at what price should he sell it?

19. In how many years will ₹7,320 amount to ₹13,176 at the rate of 8% per annum?

20. What sum of money will yield an interest of ₹3,600 in 8 years at the rate of 9% pa?

Answer for Brainteaser from page 128

The two numbers are: 66 and 44

Lines and Angles

CHAPTER 9

A line can be extended indefinitely on either sides and is denoted as $\overleftrightarrow{AB}$. A line is represented by any capital letters of the English alphabet.

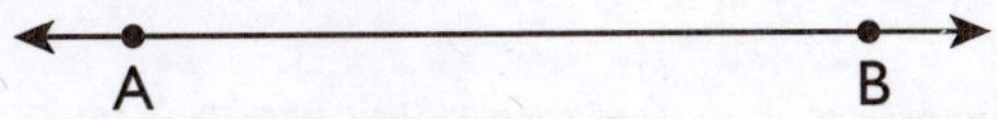

A line is sometimes denoted by a single letter.

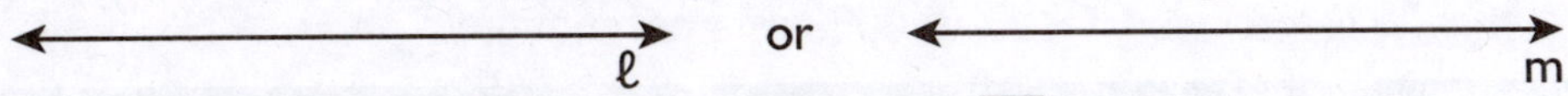

A line segment is a part of a line and is represented as $\overline{AB}$.

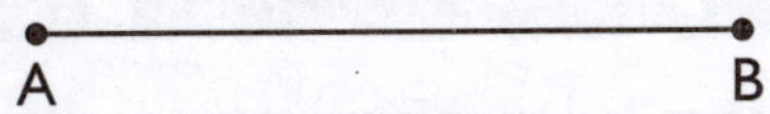

A ray starts from a point and extends indefinitely on one side as $\overrightarrow{AB}$.

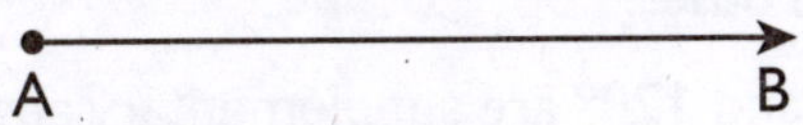

Two rays make the two arms of an angle. The point from which the two rays start is called the vertex of the angle.

An angle is represented as ∠AOB. Angles are named by any three letters of the English alphabet. The letter in the centre represents the vertex.

The measure of an angle does not depend on the length of its arms but the distance between the arms.

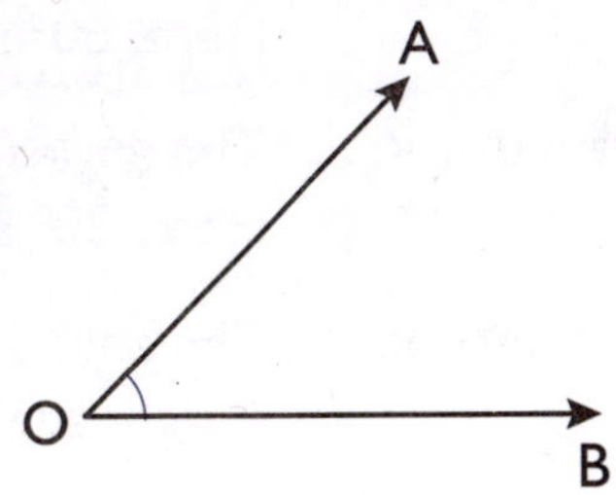

Examples:

The different angles that have been classified according to their measures are listed below.

Acute angle	between 0° to 90°	Right angle	90°
Obtuse angle	between 90° to 180°	Straight angle	180°
Reflex angle	between 180° to 360°	Complete angle	360°
Zero angle	0°		

Various angles can be constructed with the help of a protractor and a compass.

We shall now study the following pairs of angles.

1. Complementary angles
2. Supplementary angles
3. Adjacent angles
4. Linear angles
5. Vertically opposite angles

Complementary Angles

Two angles or a pair of angles are called complementary angles if the sum of the angles is 90°. Each angle is called the complement of the other.

Example 1: The angles 60° and 30° are complementary angles as their sum is 90°. Here 60° is the complement of 30° and 30° is the complement of 60°.

Example 2: The angles 50° and 40° are complementary angles as their sum is 90°. Here 50° is the complement of 40° and 40° is the complement of 50°.

Example 3: The angles 25° and 65° are complementary angles as their sum is 90°. Here 25° is the complement of 65° and 65° is the complement of 25°.

Alert!

For angles to be complementary, the pair of angles have to be acute angles, since their sum has to be 90°.

Supplementary Angles

Two angles or a pair of angles are called supplementary angles if their sum is 180°. Each angle is called the supplement of the other.

Example 1: The angles 60° and 120° are supplementary angles as their sum is 180°. Here, 60° is the supplement of 120° and 120° is the supplement of 60°.

Example 2: The angles 30° and 150° are supplementary angles as their sum is 180°. Here, 30° is the supplement of 150° and 150° is the supplement of 30°.

Example 3: The angles 90° and 90° are supplementary angles.
A right angle is the supplement of another right angle since their sum is 180°.

Alert!

For a pair of angles to be supplementary, one angle will have to be an acute angle, while the other angle will have to be an obtuse angle.

The exception to the case is 90°. Here both angles are right angles.

Adjacent Angles

A pair of angles that have a common vertex, a common arm and lie on the opposite sides of the common arm are called adjacent angles.

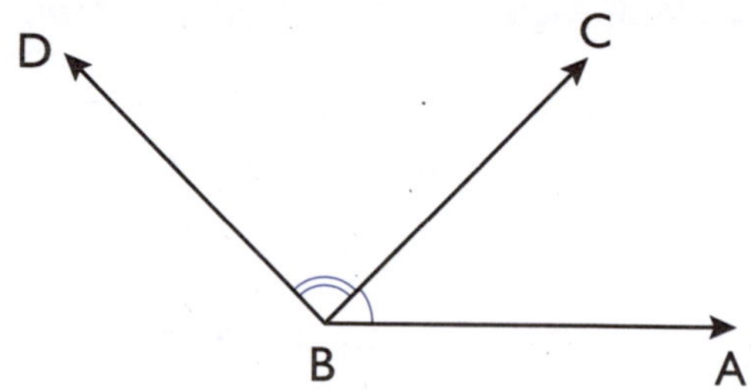

Example 1: Here ∠ABC and ∠CBD are a pair of adjacent angles. The common vertex is B and the common arm is $\overrightarrow{BC}$

The angles ∠ABC and ∠CBD lie on opposite sides of the common arm BC.

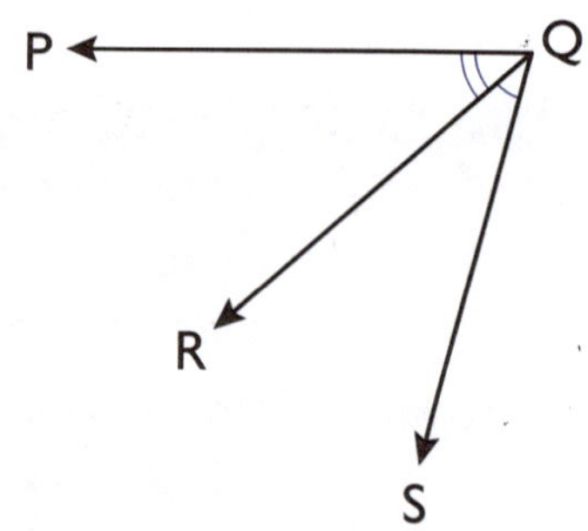

Example 2: Here ∠PQR and ∠RQS are adjacent angles. The common vertex is Q and the common arm is QR.

Angels ∠PQR and ∠RQS lie on opposite sides of the common arm QR.

Example 1: Angles ∠AOC and ∠AOB have a common arm AO and a common vertex O, but ∠AOC and ∠AOB are not adjacent angles as they are not on opposite sides of the arm AO.

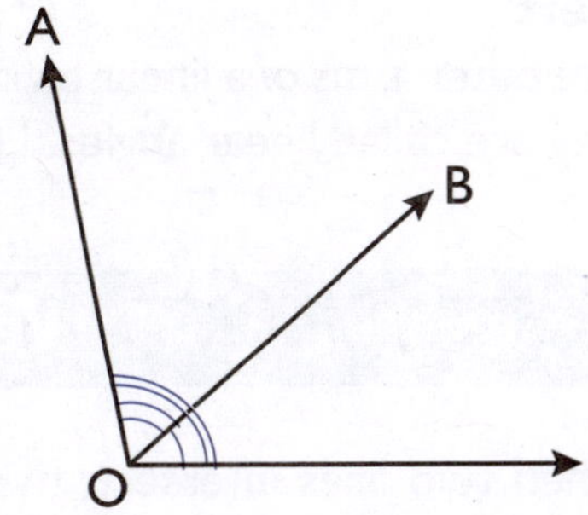

Example 2: Angles ∠AOB and ∠COD are not adjacent angles since they have a common vertex O but do not have a common arm.

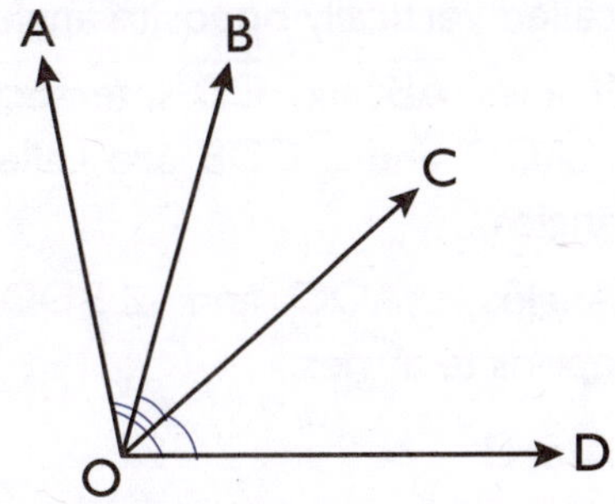

Here the adjacent angles are ∠AOB and ∠BOC as well as ∠BOC and ∠COD.

Alert!

A pair of angles may have an arm and vertex in common but if the angles do not lie on opposite sides of the common arm, the pair of angles are not adjacent angles

Linear Pair

A pair of angles that is supplementary and adjacent formed a linear pair.

Example 1: In the diagram, ∠AOB = 30° and ∠BOC = 150°. This makes them supplementary angles as ∠AOB + ∠BOC = 180°. Also, ∠AOB and ∠BOC share a common vertex (O) and common arm (OB). Hence they are adjacent angles. Since they are supplementary angles and adjacent angles, they are a linear pair.

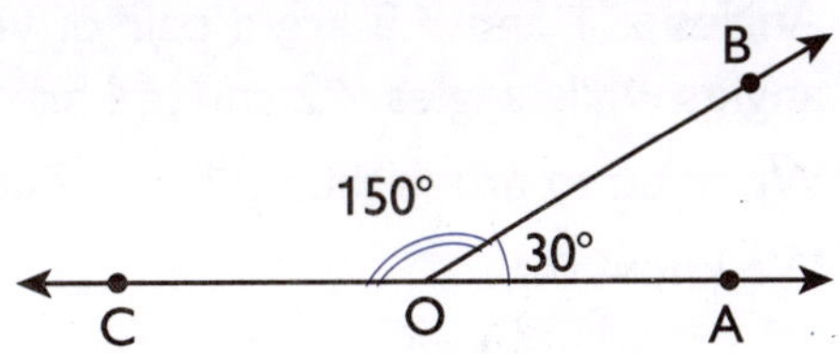

Example 2: In the diagram, ∠POQ = 60° and ∠QOR = 120°. This makes them supplementary angles as ∠POQ + ∠QOR = 180°. Also, ∠POQ and ∠QOR share a common vertex (O) and common arm (OQ). Hence they are adjacent angles. Since they are supplementary angles and adjacent angles, they are a linear pair.

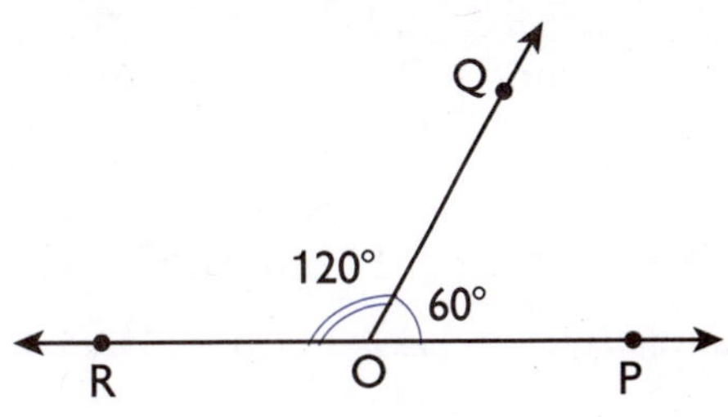

Example 3: In the diagram, ∠XOY = 90° and ∠YOZ = 90°. This makes them supplementary angles as ∠XOY + ∠YOZ = 180°. Also, ∠XOY and ∠YOZ share a common vertex (O) and common arm (OY). Hence they are adjacent angles. Since they are supplementary angles and adjacent angles, they are a linear pair.

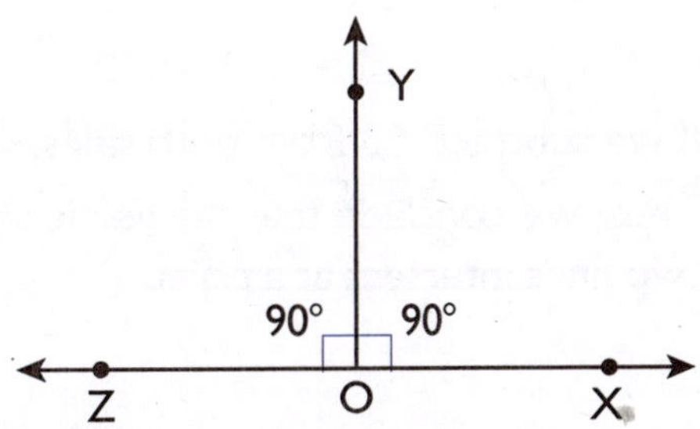

Alert!

The outer arms of a linear pair of angles form a straight line or a straight angle of 180°, hence they are called linear angles. Linear means in one line.

Vertically Opposite Angles

When two lines intersect, the two pairs of angles so formed without a common arm are called vertically opposite angles.

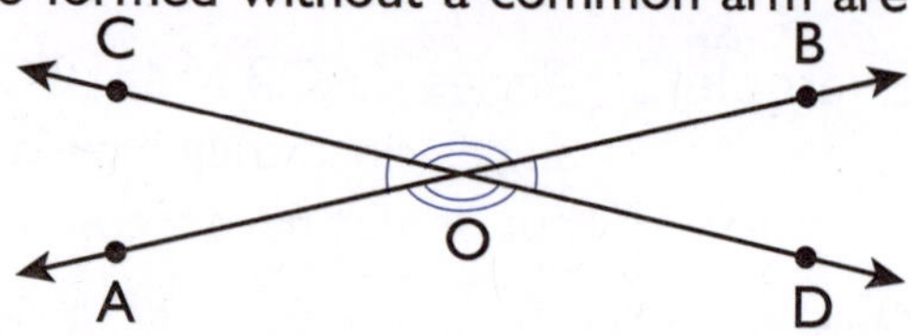

If lines $\overleftrightarrow{AB}$ and $\overleftrightarrow{CD}$ intersect at a point O then $\angle AOD$ and $\angle COB$ are called vertically opposite angles.

Angles $\angle AOC$ and $\angle BOD$ are also vertically opposite angles.

Alert!

Vertically opposite angles have a common vertex but no common arm.

Vertically opposite angles are equal to each other.

Example 1:

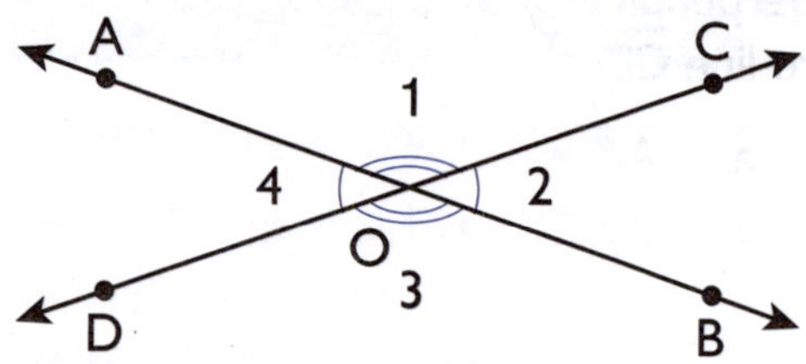

Lines $\overleftrightarrow{AB}$ and $\overleftrightarrow{CD}$ intersect at the point O. The four angles formed are $\angle AOC$, $\angle COB$, $\angle BOD$ and $\angle DOA$, which have been numbered 1, 2, 3 and 4, respectively.

Angles $\angle 1$ and $\angle 3$ are a pair of vertically opposite angles while angles $\angle 2$ and $\angle 4$ are another pair of vertically opposite angles.

We need to prove that $\angle 1 = \angle 3$ and $\angle 2 = \angle 4$.

We know that

$\angle 1 + \angle 2 = 180°$ (linear pair)

and $\angle 2 + \angle 3 = 180°$ (linear pair)

So, $\angle 1 + \angle 2 = \angle 2 + \angle 3 = 180°$

If we subtract $\angle 2$ from both sides, we get $\angle 1 = \angle 3$. (i)

Similarly $\angle 2 + \angle 3 = 180°$ (linear pair)

$\angle 3 + \angle 4 = 180°$ (linear pair)

So, $\angle 2 + \angle 3 = \angle 3 + \angle 4 = 180°$

If we subtract $\angle 3$ from both sides, we get $\angle 2 = \angle 4$. (ii)

Thus, we conclude that the vertically opposite angles are always equal to each other, when two lines intersect at a point.

Example 2:

The lines $\overleftrightarrow{PQ}$ and $\overleftrightarrow{RS}$ intersect at O. If ∠POR is 20°, find the other angles.

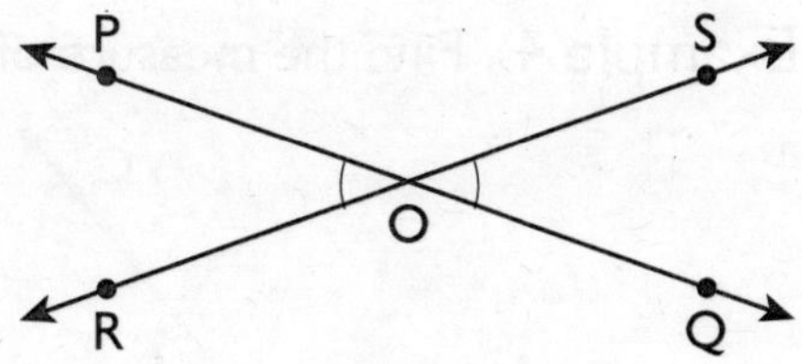

∠POR = ∠SOQ (since they are vertically opposite angles)

∠POR = 20° (given)

∴ ∠SOQ = 20°

Angles ∠POR and ∠POS form a linear pair, hence ∠POR + ∠POS = 180°

∠POR = 20° (given)

∴ ∠POR + ∠POS = 180°

20° + ∠POS = 180°

∠POS = 180° − 20° = 160°

∠POS and ∠ROQ are vertically opposite angles.

If ∠POS = 160°, ∠ROQ is also equal to 160° (since vertically opposite angles are equal)

Example 3: In the figure given below, name each of the angles mentioned.

The lines $\overleftrightarrow{AB}$ and $\overleftrightarrow{CD}$ intersect at O. The ray $\overrightarrow{OE}$ is perpendicular to line ray $\overleftrightarrow{AB}$ and $\overrightarrow{OF}$ is perpendicular to line $\overleftrightarrow{CD}$.

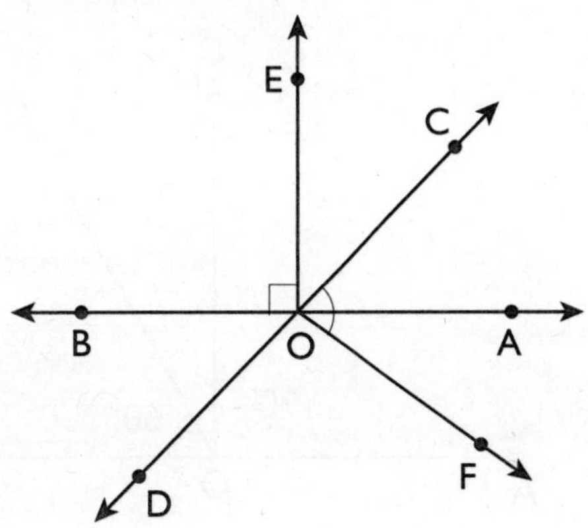

a. Adjacent angles:

∠AOC and ∠COE (with common vertex O and common arm OC)

∠DOB and ∠BOE (with common vertex O and common arm OB)

b. Linear pair:

∠AOC and ∠COB (adjacent and supplementary angles)

∠AOC and ∠AOD (adjacent and supplementary angles)

c. Complementary angles:

∠AOC and ∠COE (sum of the angles is 90°)

∠AOC and ∠AOF (sum of the angles is 90°)

d. Supplementary angles:

∠AOC and ∠COB (sum of the angles is 180°)

∠COB and ∠BOD (sum of the angles is 180°)

e. Vertically opposite angles:

∠AOC and ∠BOD (lines $\overleftrightarrow{AB}$ and $\overleftrightarrow{DC}$ intersect at O)

∠BOC and ∠AOD (lines $\overleftrightarrow{AB}$ and $\overleftrightarrow{BC}$ intersect at O)

Example 4: Find the measure of the unknown angles in the following figures.

a.

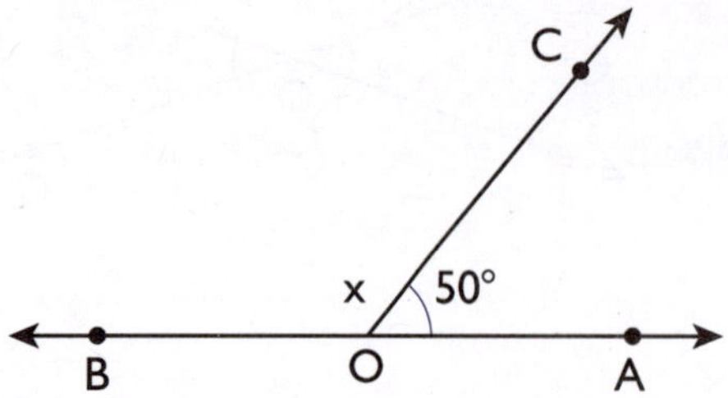

$\angle AOC + \angle BOC = 180°$ (linear pair)

$50° + \angle BOC = 180°$

$\therefore \angle BOC = 180° - 50° = 130°$

$\angle BOC = 130°$

b.

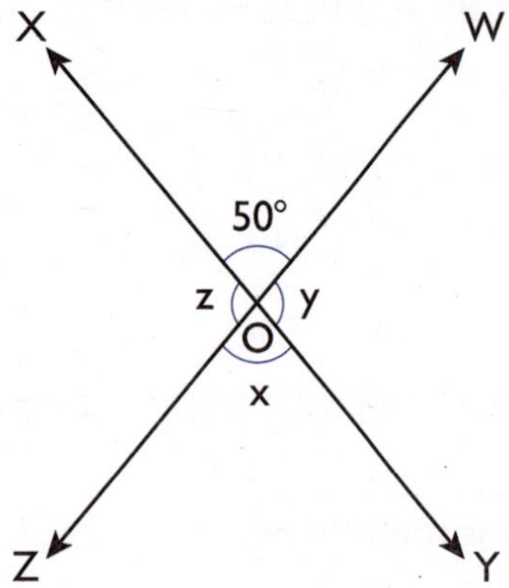

$\angle YOZ = \angle XOW$ (vertically opposite angles)

$\angle YOZ = 50°$

$\angle XOW + \angle WOY = 180°$ (linear pair)

$50° + \angle WOY = 180°$

$\angle WOY = 180° - 50° = 130°$

$\angle WOY = 130°$

$\angle XOZ = \angle WOY$ (vertically opposite angles)

$\angle XOZ = 130°$

c.

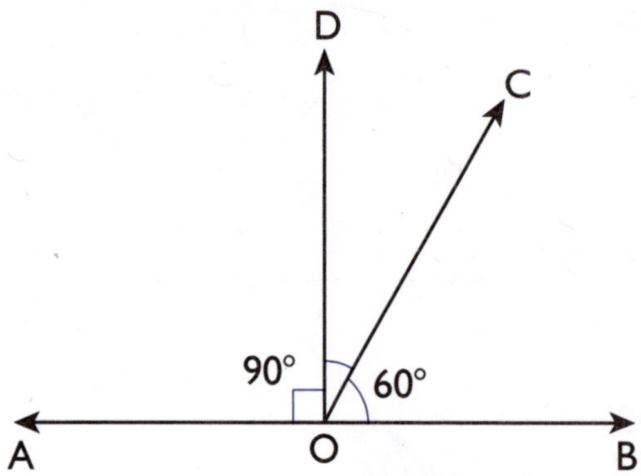

$\angle BOC + \angle COD = 90°$ (complementary angles)

$60° + \angle COD = 90°$

$\therefore \angle COD = 30°$

Practice Exercise 9.1

1. Write the complements of each of the following angles.

   a. 62° b. 72° c. 48° d. 44° e. 58°
   f. 53° g. 75° h. 12° i. 21° j. 6°

2. Write the supplements of each of the following angles.

   a. 91° b. 20° c. 46° d. 115° e. 62°
   f. 100° g. 132° h. 18° i. 77° j. 135°

3. Classify the following statements as true (T) or false (F).

   a. If two angles are adjacent, they are equal.
   b. Two complementary angles always form a linear pair.
   c. Two obtuse angles can be supplementary.
   d. Two acute angles can be complementary.
   e. Adjacent angles can be complementary.
   f. Two adjacent angles are always supplementary.

g. The supplement of an obtuse angle is always an acute angle.

h. The complement of an acute angle is always an acute angle.

i. If two lines intersect each other, the vertically opposite angles are equal.

j. If two lines intersect, one pair of vertically opposite angles must always be an acute angle.

4. a. An angle is $\frac{2}{3}$ of its complement. What is its magnitude?

b. An angle is $\frac{4}{5}$ of its supplement. What is its magnitude?

c. Two angles are equal and they form a pair of supplementary angles. Find their magnitude.

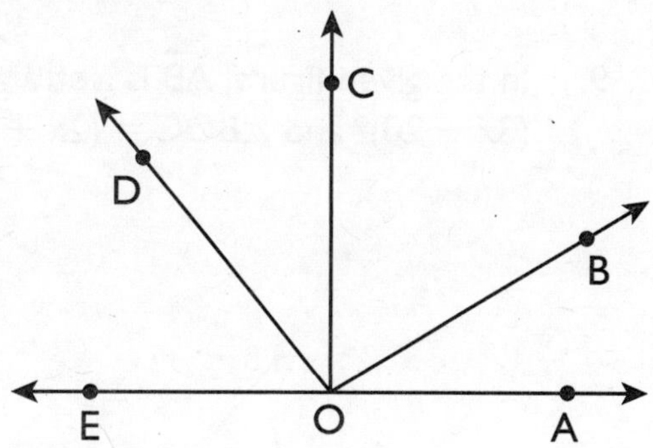

5. a. Study the figure given here and list three pairs of adjacent angles.

b. Study the figure given here and list the following: (i) adjacent angles, (ii) vertically opposite angles and (iii) a linear pair.

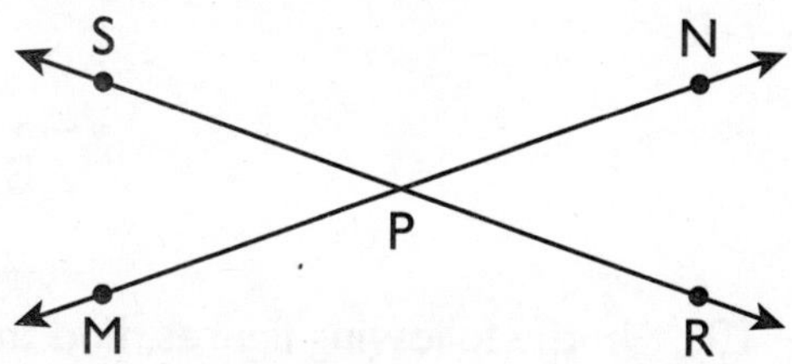

6. In the given figure, if $\angle XOY = 40°$, find all the other angles.

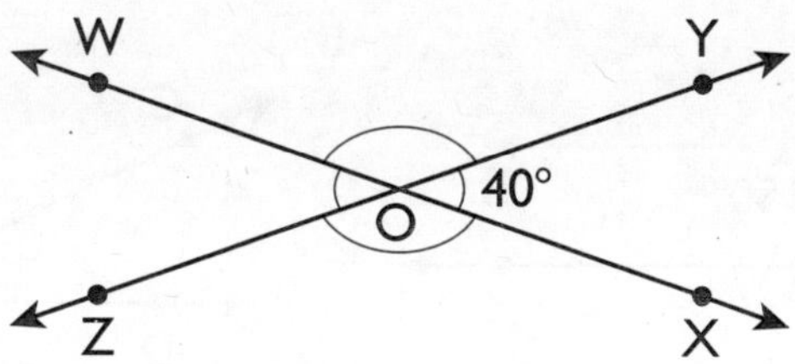

7. In the given figures, find the value of x.

a.

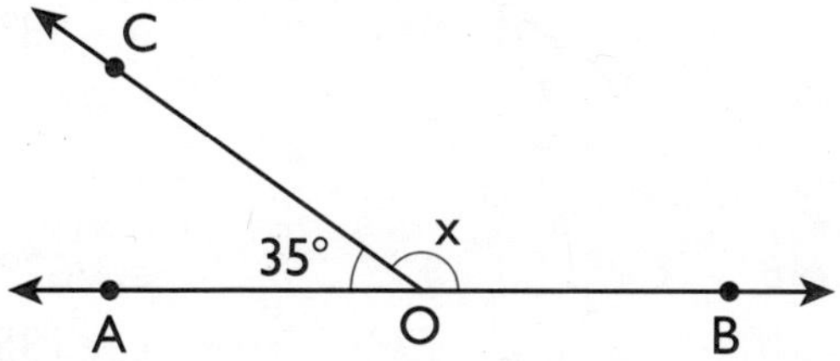

b.

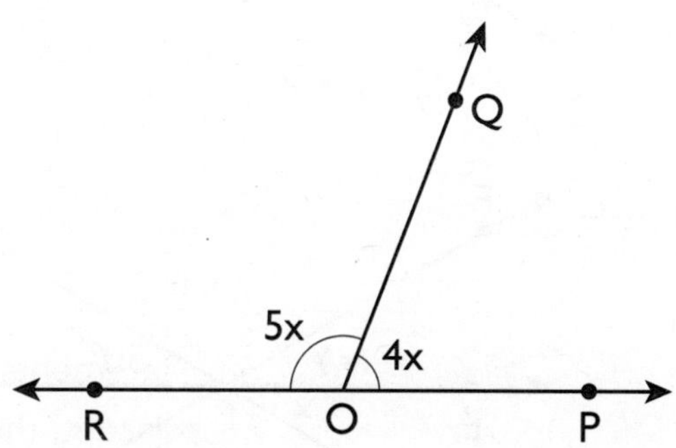

c.

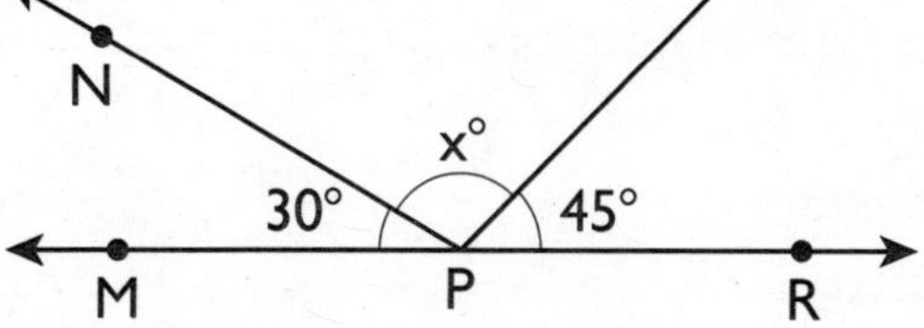

8. In the following figures, find the value of x given that $\angle ABC$ is a right angle.

a.

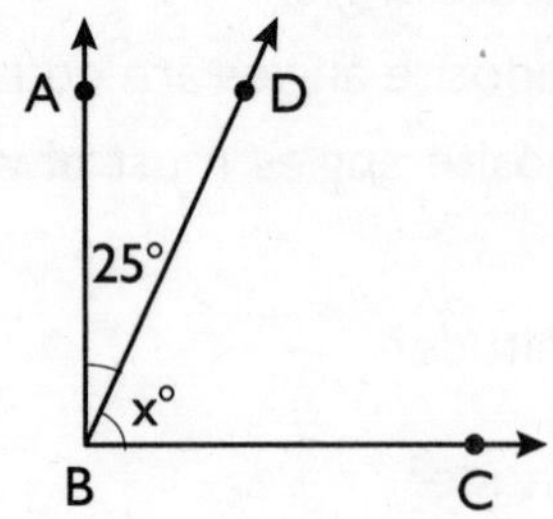

b.

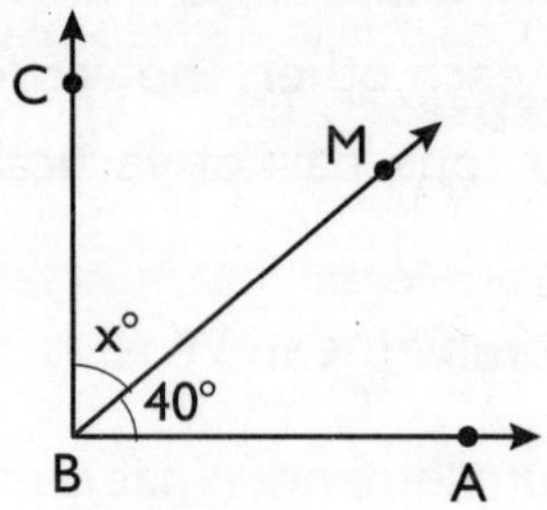

c.

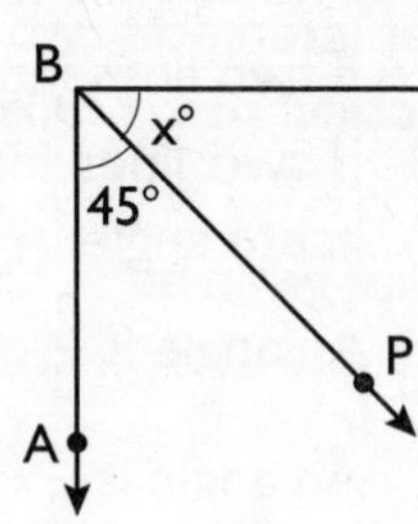

9. In the given figure, $\overleftrightarrow{AB}$ is a straight line and the ray $\overrightarrow{OC}$ stands on it. If $\angle AOC = (3x - 20)°$ and $\angle BOC = (2x + 30)°$, find the value of x, $\angle AOC$ and $\angle BOC$.

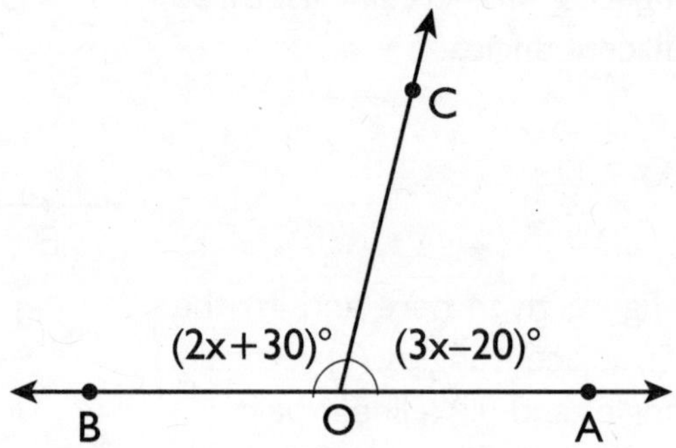

10. In the following figures, find the values of x and y.

a.

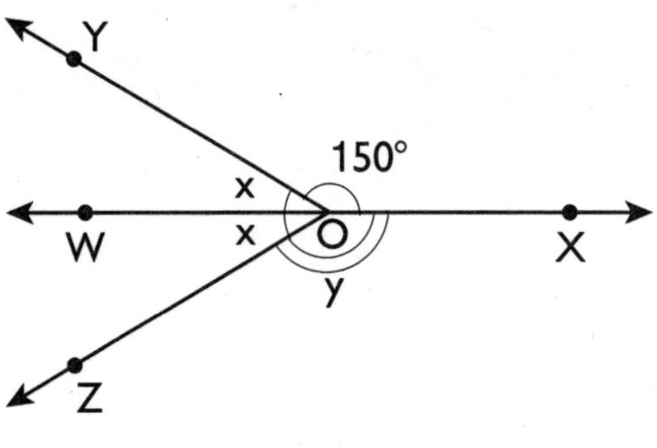

b.

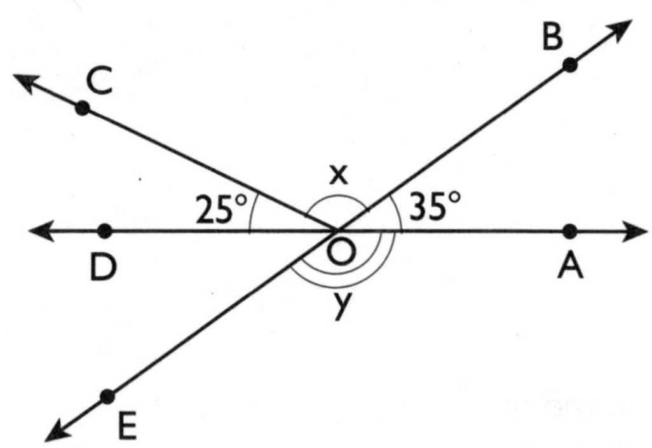

c.

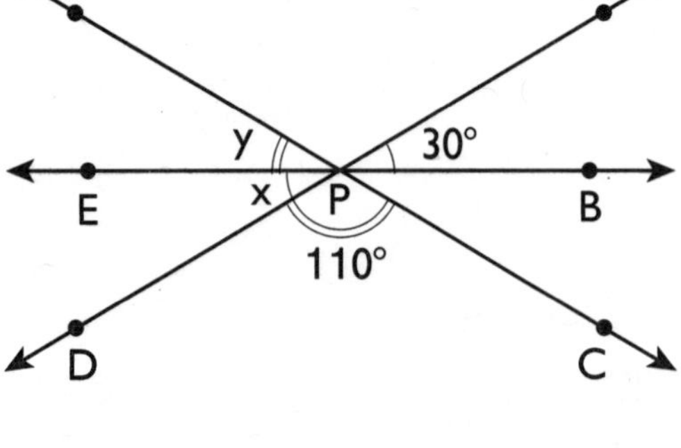

The Transversal

A line that intersects two or more lines in a given plane at **distinct points** is called a **transversal**.

In the figure given here, t is the transversal that intersects the lines ℓ and m at two distinct points A and B.

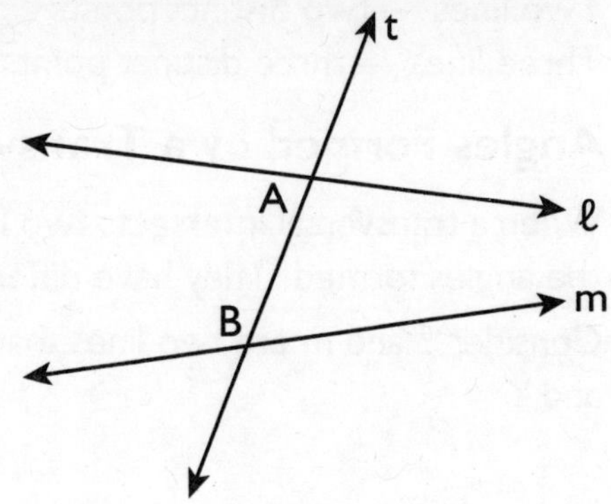

In figure given here, p and q are two parallel lines that are intersected by the transversal 'r' at two distinct points, X and Y.

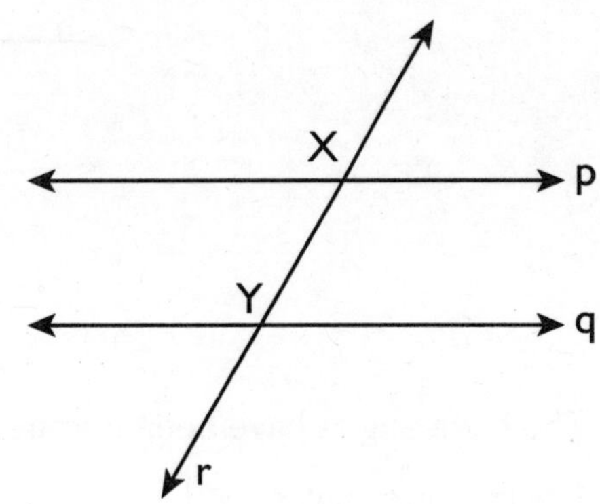

In this figure, the transversal 'S' intersects the lines ℓ and m at distinct points A and B, respectively.

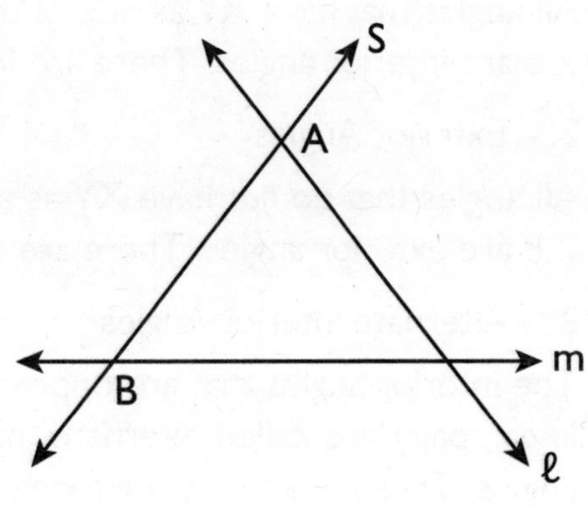

In the figure given here, there is no transversal as the three lines intersect or meet at one point—O. The lines are said to be concurrent and O is the point of concurrency.

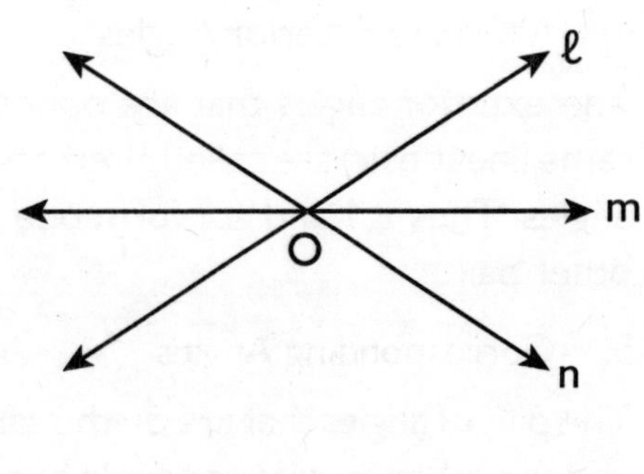

Alert!

A transversal will intersect two or more lines at *distinct* points.
Two lines — two distinct points
Three lines — three distinct points

Angles Formed by a Transversal with Two Lines

When a transversal intersects two lines, **eight** angles are formed. Special names are given to the angles formed. They have different relationships with each other.

Consider ℓ and m are two lines that are intersected by a transversal t at *two* distinct points, X and Y.

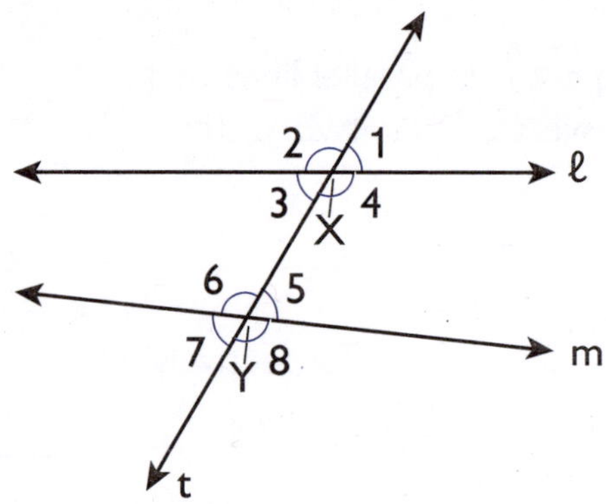

The eight angles have been numbered from 1 to 8.

1. Interior Angles

All angles that have XY as one of the arms are called interior angles. Thus ∠3, ∠4, ∠5 and ∠6 are interior angles. There are four interior angles.

2. Exterior Angles

All angles that do *not* have XY as an arm are called exterior angles. Thus ∠1, ∠2, ∠7 and ∠8 are exterior angles. There are four exterior angles.

3. Alternate Interior Angles

The interior angles that are opposite to each other in separate linear pairs (not in the same linear pair) are called alternate interior angles. There are two pairs of alternate interior angles. Thus ∠3 and ∠5 form one pair of alternate interior angles and ∠4 and ∠6 form the other pair.

4. Alternate Exterior Angles

The exterior angles that are opposite to each other in the separate linear pairs (not in the same linear pair) are called alternate exterior angles. There are two pairs of alternate exterior angles. Thus ∠1 and ∠7 form one pair of alternate exterior angles and ∠2 and ∠8 form the other pair.

5. Corresponding Angles

The pair of angles that are on the same side of the transversal, one of which is an interior angle and the other an exterior angle but they do not form a linear pair, are a pair of corresponding angles. There are four pairs of corresponding angles. Thus ∠1 and ∠5, ∠2 and ∠6, ∠4 and ∠8 and ∠3 and ∠7 are four pairs of corresponding angles.

6. Consecutive Interior Angles or Co-Interior Angles

The pair of interior angles on the same side of the transversal are called consecutive interior angles. There are two such pairs.

Angles ∠4 and ∠5 form one pair of co-interior angles on the same side of the transversal and ∠3 and ∠6 form the other pair

Example:

In the given figure, a pair of lines, $\overleftrightarrow{PQ}$ and $\overleftrightarrow{RS}$, are intersected by a transversal $\overleftrightarrow{MN}$. Name the:

a. Interior angles
b. Exterior angles
c. Alternate interior angles
d. Alternate exterior angles
e. Corresponding angles
f. Co-interior angles

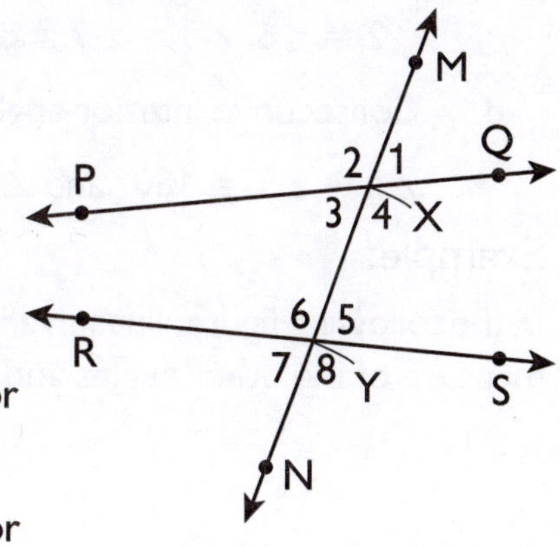

a. The four interior angles are ∠3, ∠4, ∠5 and ∠6, or ∠PXY, ∠QXY, ∠RYX and ∠SYX, respectively

b. The four exterior angles are ∠1, ∠2, ∠7 and ∠8 or ∠QXM, ∠PXM, ∠RYN and ∠SYN, respectively.

c. The two pairs of alternate interior angles are ∠3 and ∠5 and ∠4 and ∠6 or ∠PXY and ∠SYX and ∠QXY and ∠RYX.

d. The two pairs of alternate exterior angles are ∠1 and ∠7 and ∠2 and ∠8 or ∠QXM and ∠RYN and ∠PXM and ∠SYN.

e. The four pairs of corresponding angles are ∠1 and ∠5, ∠2 and ∠6, ∠3 and ∠7 and ∠4 and ∠8 or ∠QXM and ∠SYX, ∠PXM and ∠RYX, ∠PXY and ∠RYN and ∠QXY and ∠SYN, respectively.

f. The two pairs of co-interior angles are ∠4 and ∠5 and ∠3 and ∠6 or ∠QXY and ∠SYX and ∠PXY and ∠RYX, respectively.

Parallel Lines

Two lines ℓ and m in the *same plane* are said to be parallel if they do not meet or intersect however far they are produced in either direction.

Alert!

For two lines to be parallel it is important for them to be in the same plane since there can be two lines in different planes that are neither parallel nor do they meet each other at a point. Such lines are called skew lines.

Parallel Lines and a Transversal

If two lines ℓ and m are parallel and a transversal t cuts the line at two distinct points A and B, eight angles are formed. These angles have special properties in relation to each other.

The special properties of *parallel lines* cut by a transversal are:

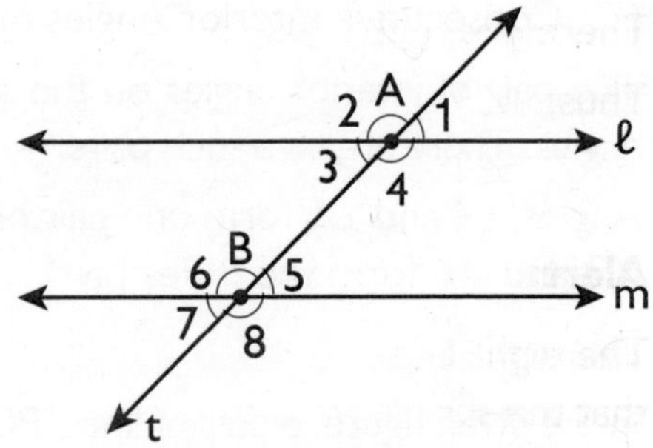

a. Alternate interior angles are equal, i.e., $\angle 3 = \angle 5$ and $\angle 4 = \angle 6$.

b. Alternate exterior angles are equal, i.e., $\angle 1 = \angle 7$ and $\angle 2 = \angle 8$

c. Corresponding angles are equal, i.e., $\angle 1 = \angle 5$, $\angle 2 = \angle 6$, $\angle 3 = \angle 7$ and $\angle 4 = \angle 8$.

d. Consecutive interior angles or co-interior angles are supplementary, i.e., $\angle 4 + \angle 5 = 180°$ and $\angle 3 + \angle 6 = 180°$.

Example:

In the following figure, lines m and n are parallel and t is the transversal. If $\angle 1 = 50°$, find the measure of the other angles and give reasons.

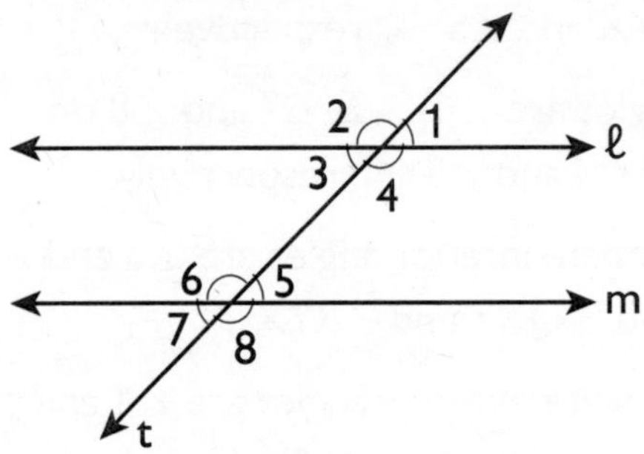

Lines ℓ and m are parallel and t is the transversal.

$\angle 5 = \angle 1$	(corresponding angles)
$\angle 5 = 50°$	
since $\angle 1 = 50°$	(given)
$\angle 7 = \angle 5$	(vertically opposite angles)
Therefore, $\angle 7 = 50°$	(since $\angle 5 = 50°$ as proved above)
$\angle 3 = \angle 5$	(alternate interior angles)
Therefore, $\angle 3 = 50°$	(since $\angle 5 = 50°$ as proved above)
$\angle 3 + \angle 6 = 180°$	(co-interior angles)
$50° + \angle 6 = 180°$	
Therefore, $\angle 6 = 180° - 50° = 130°$	
$\angle 8 = \angle 6$	(vertically opposite angles)
Therefore, $\angle 8 = 130°$	
$\angle 4 + \angle 5 = 180°$	(co-interior angles)
$\angle 4 + 50° = 180°$	
Therefore, $\angle 4 = 180° - 50° = 130°$	
$\angle 2 = \angle 4$	(vertically opposite angles)

Therefore, $\angle 2 = 130°$

Thus, $\angle 1 = \angle 3 = \angle 5 = \angle 7 = 50°$ and

$\angle 2 = \angle 4 = \angle 6 = \angle 8 = 130°$.

Alert!

The eight angles formed by a transversal intersecting two parallel lines will always be such that the sum of each pair formed at the intersection will be 180°. If four angles measure 40° each, the remaining four angles will measure 140° each. If four angles measure 135° each, the other four angles will measure 45° each.

If we have to check whether two lines are parallel or not when a transversal intersects them, any one of the following conditions must be true.

1. The interior alternate angles should be equal.
2. The corresponding angles should be equal.
3. The sum of the co-interior angles should be 180°.

Practice Exercise 9.2

1. In the following figures, identify and write the transversal.

a.

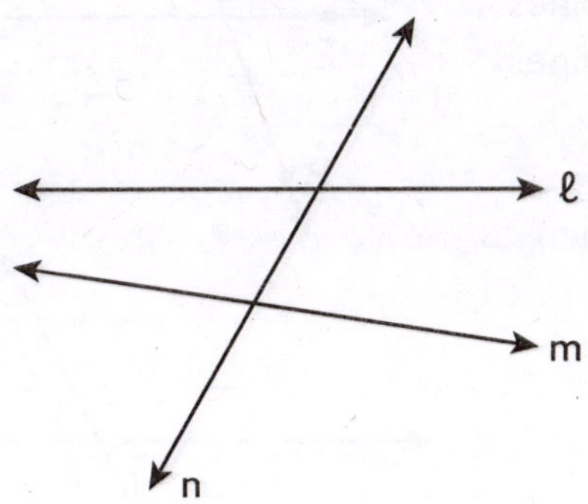

b.

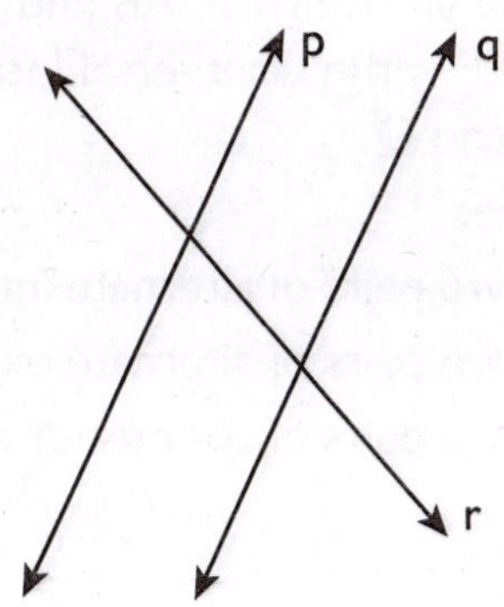

c.

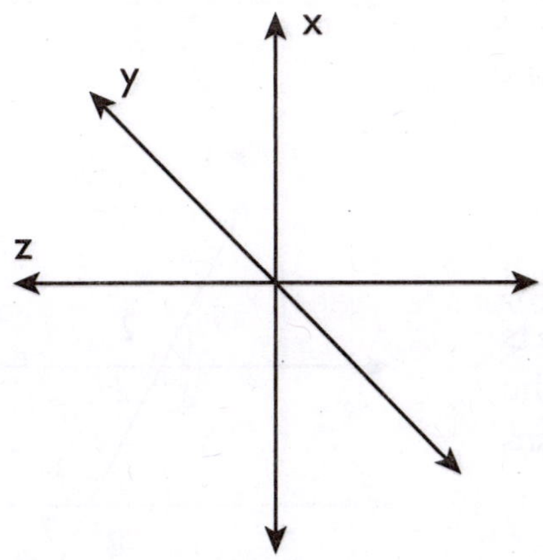

d.

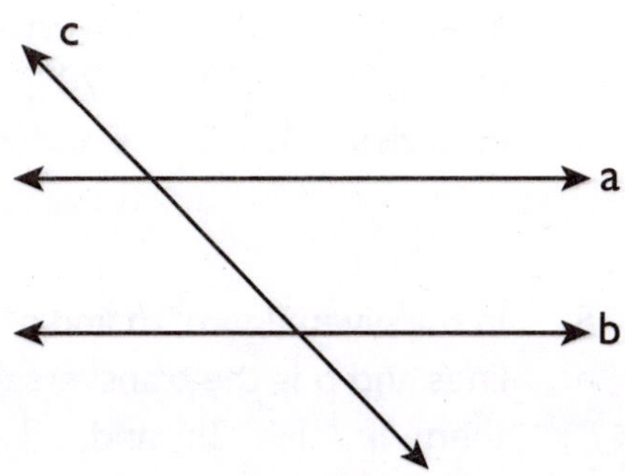

e.

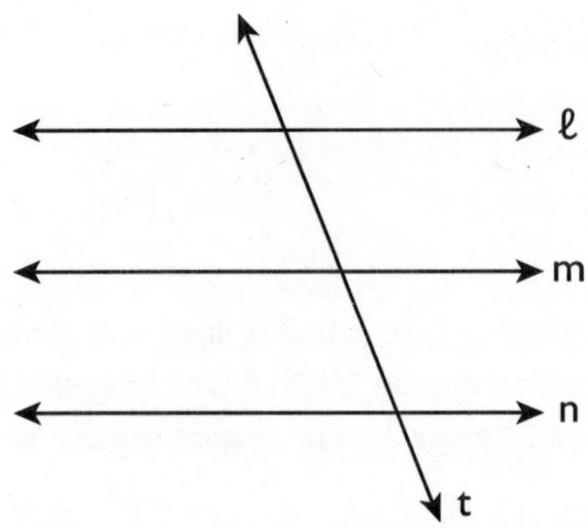

2. In the given figure, ℓ and m are two lines and t is the transversal.

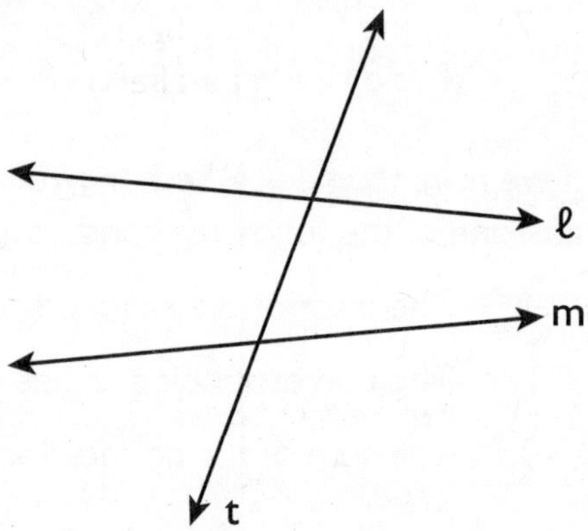

   Number the angles formed. Write all the:
   a. interior angles
   b. exterior angles
   c. pairs of alternate interior angles
   d. pairs of alternate exterior angles
   e. pairs of corresponding angles
   f. pairs of co-interior angles

3. In the given figure, AB and CD are two lines and EF is the transversal intersecting the lines at P and Q.

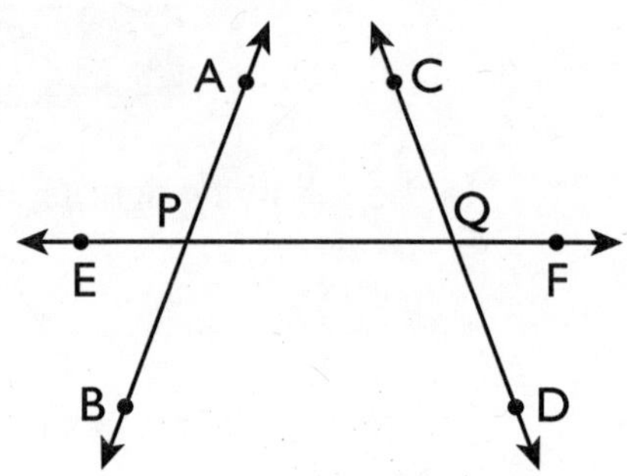

   Name:
   a. two pairs of alternate interior angles
   b. two pairs of alternate exterior angles
   c. two pairs of co-interior angles

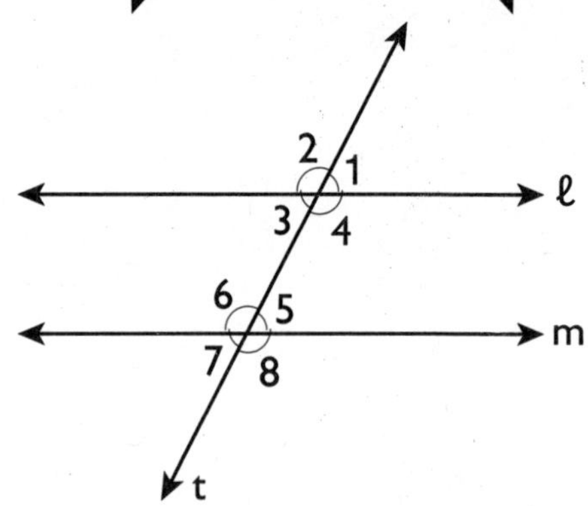

4. In the given figure, ℓ and m are two parallel lines and t is the transversal that intersects the two lines. If $\angle 5 = 70°$, find the measure of angles $\angle 1$, $\angle 3$, $\angle 4$ and $\angle 8$.

5. In the given figure, m and n are two parallel lines and p is the transversal that intersects them. If $\angle 1 = 2x°$ and $\angle 2 = 3x°$. Find the value of x and the measures of all the angles.

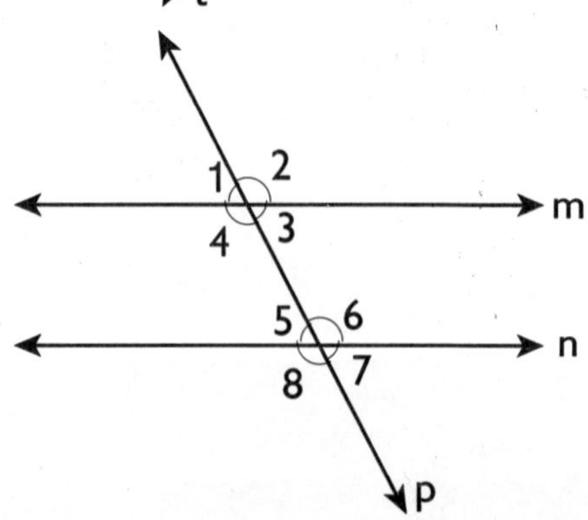

6. In the given figure, ℓ and m are two parallel lines, s and t are two transversals that are not parallel. Find the values of x and y.

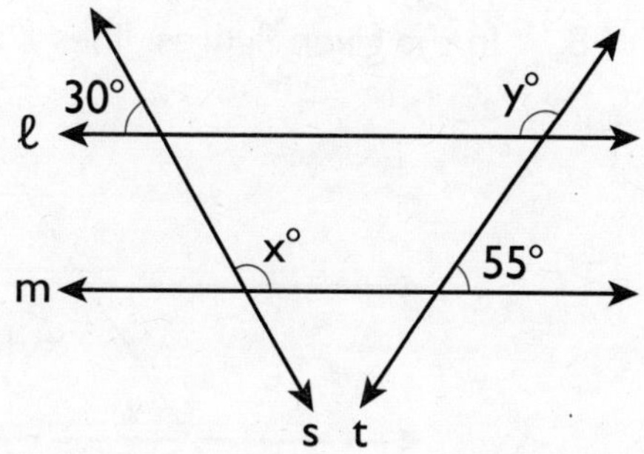

7. In the following figures, indicate whether lines ℓ and m are parallel or not. Give reasons for your answer.

a.

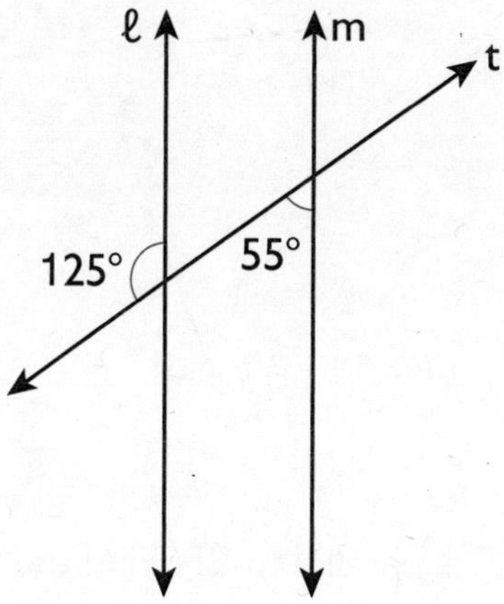

b.

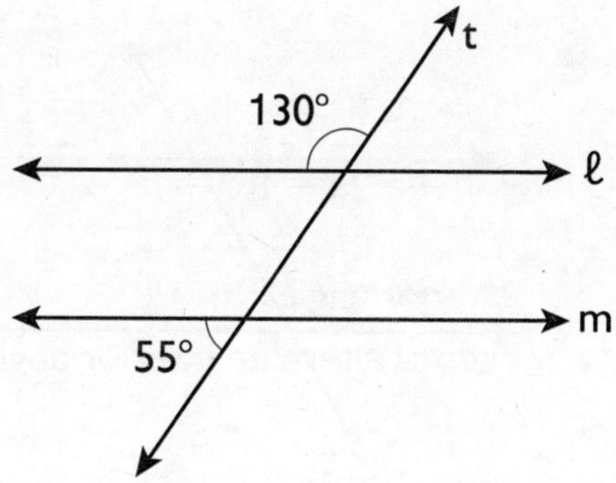

c.

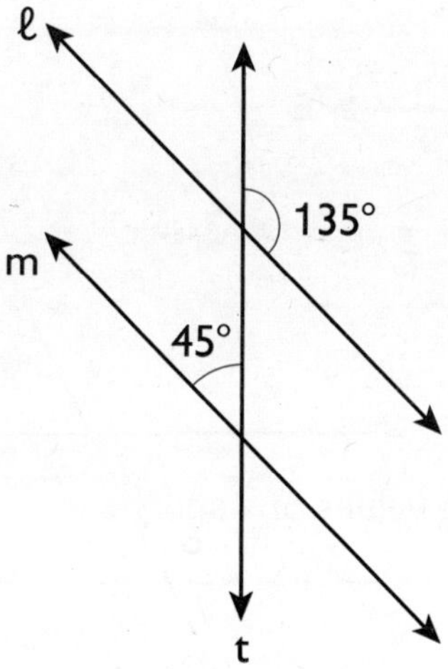

d.

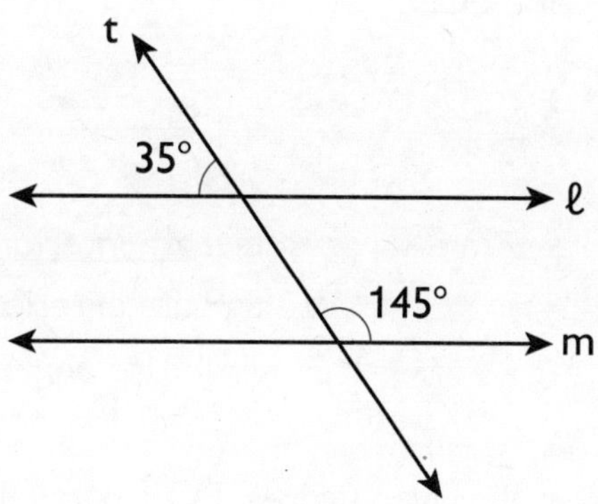

e.

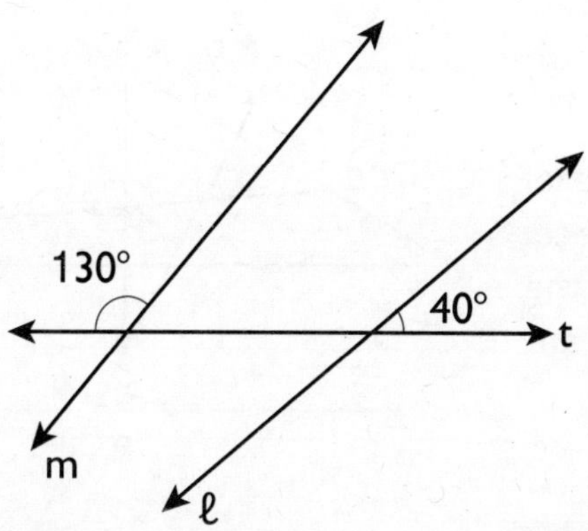

8. In the given figures, lines ℓ and m are parallel to each other. Find the value of x.

a.

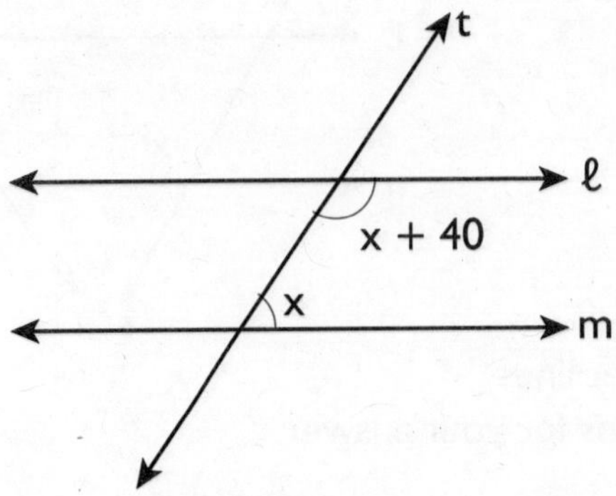

b.

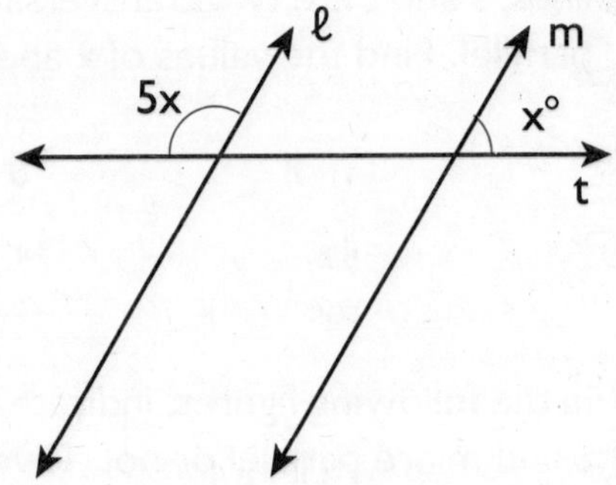

c.

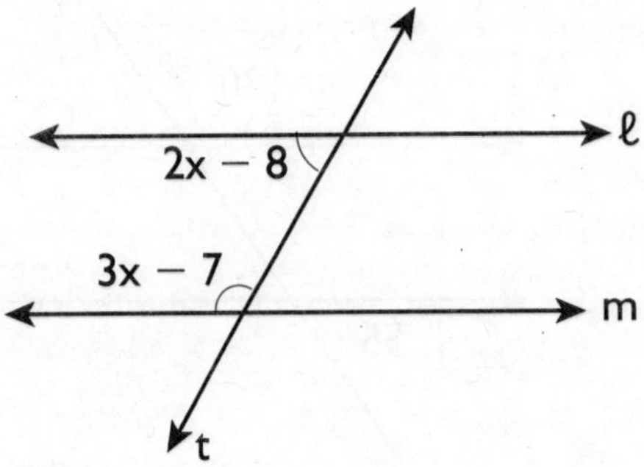

9. In the given figure, AB is parallel to CD and CE is parallel to BF. Find the measure of $\angle ECD$.

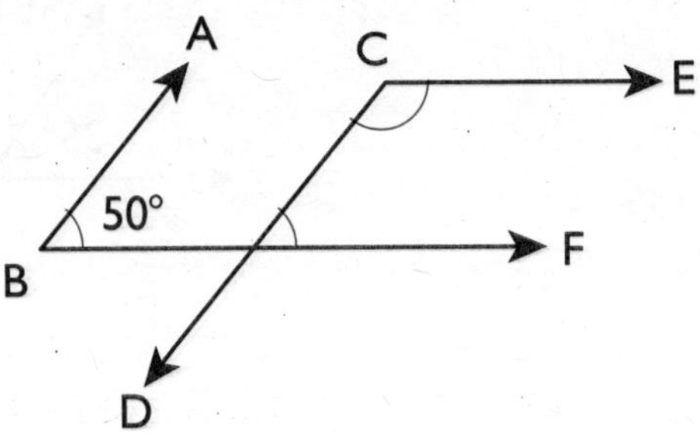

10. In the given figures, PQ is parallel to RS. Find the values of x and y.

a.

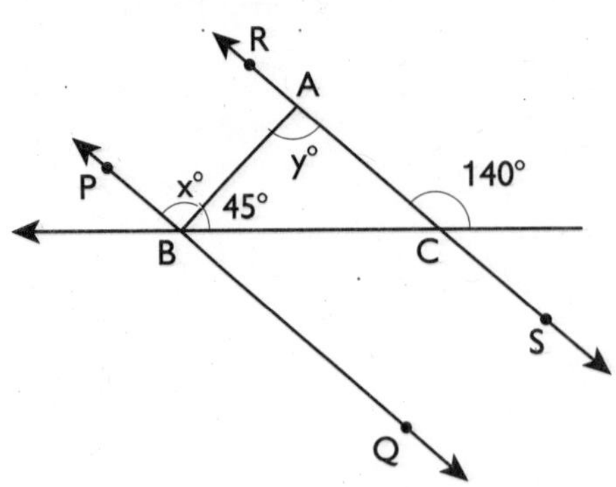

b.

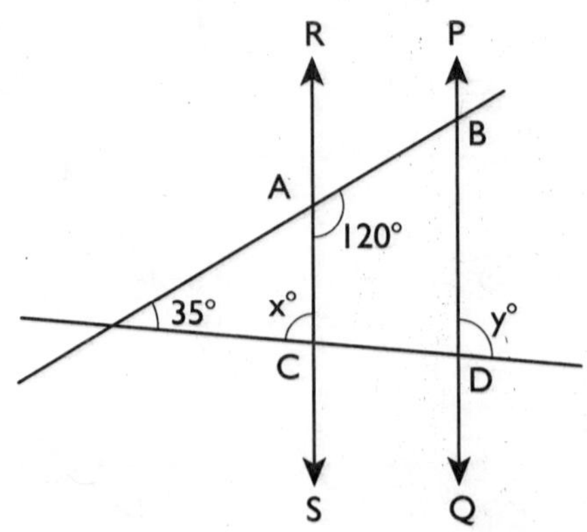

Highlights

- If the sum of two angles is 90°, they are said to be complementary angles.
- If the sum of two angles 180°, they are said to be supplementary angles.
- Two angles that have a common vertex, a common arm and lie on opposite sides of the common arm are said to be adjacent angles.
- Two supplementary adjacent angles form a linear pair.
- When two lines intersect, the two pairs of angles formed without any common arm are called vertically opposite angles. Vertically opposite angles are equal.
- A transversal is a line that intersects two or more lines in a plane at distinct points.
- When a transversal intersects two lines, eight angles are formed, of which four are exterior angles and four are interior angles.
- When a transversal intersects two lines, we get, two pairs of interior alternate angles, two pairs of exterior alternate angles, four pairs of corresponding angles and two pairs of interior angles on the same side of the transversal, called co-interior angles.
- The interior angles that are opposite to each other in separate linear pairs form a pair of alternate interior angles.
- The exterior angles that are opposite to each other in separate linear pairs form a pair of alternate exterior angles.
- The pairs of angles on the same side of the transversal, one of which is exterior and the other interior but do not form a linear pair, form a pair of corresponding angles.
- When a transversal intersects a pair of parallel lines, the alternate angles are equal to each other, the corresponding angles are equal to each other and the interior angles on the same side of the transversal or co-interior angles are supplementary.
- If the two lines are intersected by a transversal and the alternate angles are equal, or the corresponding angles are equal, or the co-interior angles are supplementary, then the two lines are parallel.
- When a transversal intersects a pair of parallel lines, the eight angles thus formed either have two sets of values that are supplementary or *all* are right angles.

Question: What do you call a crushed angle?

Answer for Brainteaser on page 150

Maths Lab Activity

Parallel Lines

Objective: To identify the different angles formed when parallel lines are intersected by a transversal as well as their relationship.

Material required: chart paper, pencil, coloured wool, glue and a pair of scissors

Method: Draw three parallel lines on the chart paper so that they are easily visible from a distance. Draw a transversal.

Now, stick different coloured pieces of wool on the three lines to show lines ℓ, m and n.

Use another piece of wool of a different colour to mark transversal 't'.

Measure any one angle made by the transversal on line ℓ. Mark this on the chart.

Ask your partner to give the measure of all 12 angles formed and indicate the relationship between them.

This activity can be done in pairs. The pair of students who completes the activity first is the winner. Their chart can be displayed on the class bulletin board.

Higher Order Thinking Skills

HOTS

1. If two parallel lines are intersected by a transversal, which pair of angles are equal and which pairs are supplementary?

2. In the given figure, rays OA, OB, OC and OD are such that $\angle AOB = 50°$, $\angle BOC = 90°$, $\angle COD = 70°$ and $\angle AOD = x°$. Find the value of x.

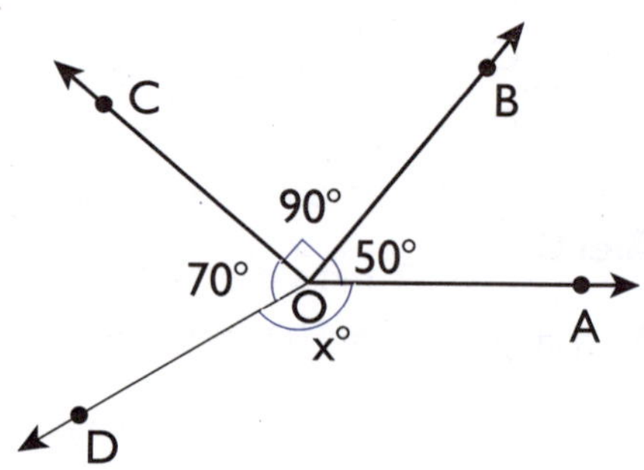

3. An angle is 58° more than its supplement. What is the measure of the angle?

Answer for Brainteaser from page 149

A Rectangle

CHAPTER 10

Properties of Triangles

We know that a triangle is a three-sided closed figure. It is the simplest polygon. As the name suggests, tri means three, hence a triangle has three sides and three angles. The sides and angles of a triangle are called its elements.

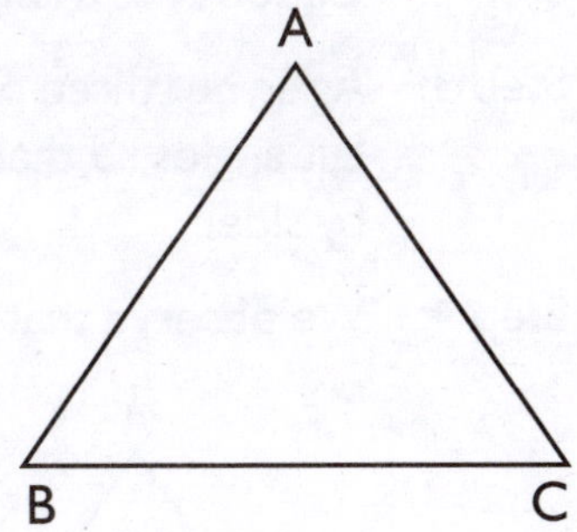

Thus, if ABC is a triangle, it is denoted as $\triangle ABC$ where the $\triangle$ is the symbol used to denote a triangle..

The sides of $\triangle ABC$ are AB, BC and CA and the angles of $\triangle ABC$ are $\angle ABC$, $\angle BCA$ and $\angle CAB$. The sides of a triangle are also denoted by the small letters of the English alphabet.

Thus,

AB is denoted by 'c' (C is the vertex with opposite side AB) BC is denoted by 'a' (A is the vertex with opposite side BC) and CA is denoted by 'b' (B is the vertex with opposite side CA).

Types of Triangles

Triangles can be classified on the basis of two criteria:

1. the measure of their sides.
2. the measure of their angles.

On the basis of the measure of its sides, there can be three kinds of triangles:

a. Equilateral triangle in which all sides are equal.
b. Isosceles triangle in which two sides are equal.
c. Scalene triangle in which no two sides are equal.

On the basis of the measure of its angles there can be three kinds of triangles:

a. Acute-angled triangle in which all angles are acute.
b. Right-angled triangle in which one angle is a right angle and the other two are acute angles.
c Obtuse-angled triangle in which one angle is an obtuse angle and the other two are acute angles.

Alert!

All triangles have two acute angles; the third angle can be an acute, right or obtuse angle.

Angle Sum Property of a Triangle

We have learnt in earlier classes that the sum of the three angles of a triangle is 180°. Now we shall learn how to prove this statement with the help of practical examples as well as theoretically.

Experiment 1

Step 1: Draw a triangle ABC on a cardboard.

Step 2: Cut out the triangular region ABC along its sides with a pair of scissors.

Step 3: Again cut three parts from this triangle as shown in the figure b. Arrange the three cut angles so that the vertex of each is at O as in figure c. and each angle lies side by side.

Step 4: We observe that the three angles A, B and C form a straight angle or 180°.

a.

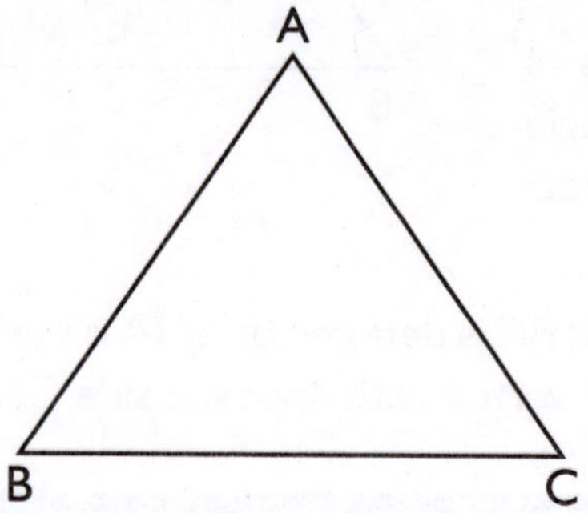

b.

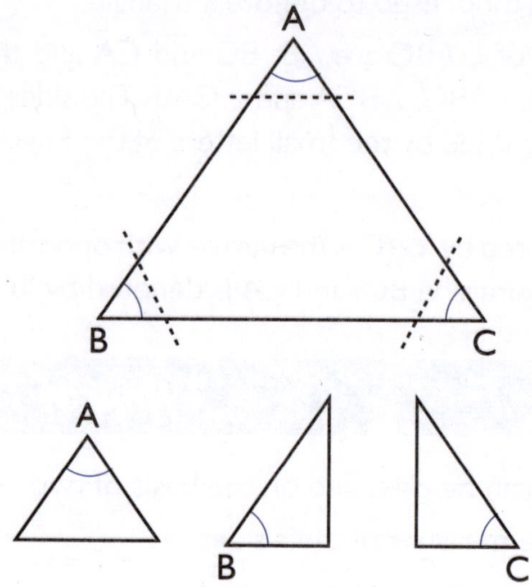

c.

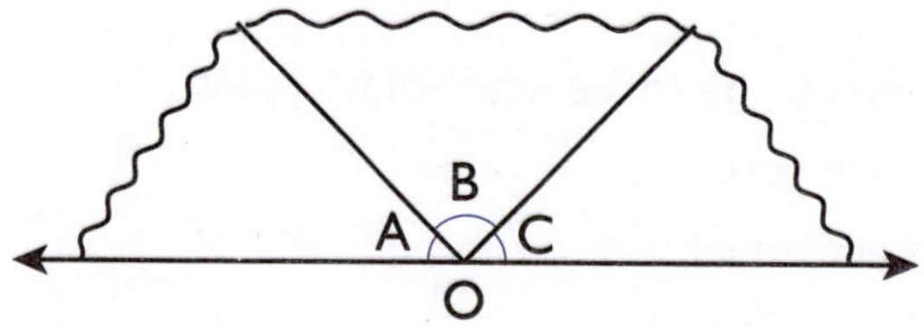

Therefore, $\angle A$, $\angle B$ and $\angle C$ combine to give 180°.

Experiment 2

Step 1: Draw three types of triangles:

a. An acute-angled triangle where all angles are acute.

b. A right-angled triangle where one angle is 90° .

c. An obtuse-angled triangle where one angle is obtuse.

a.

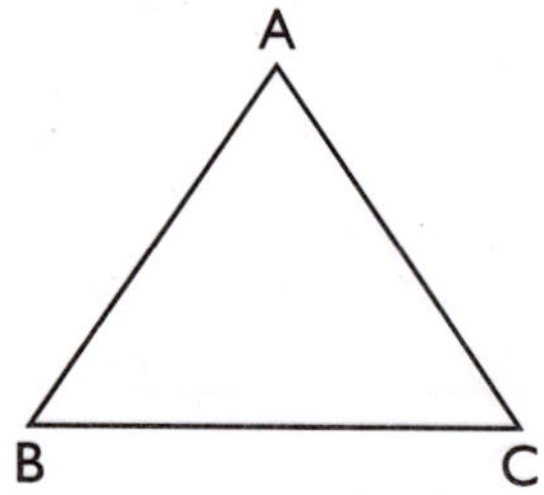

b.

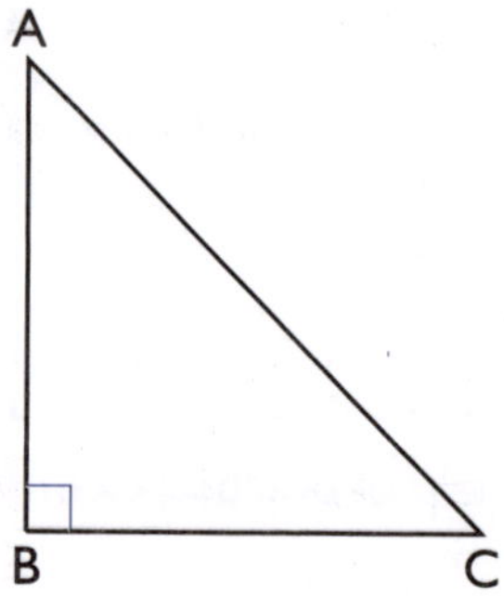

c.

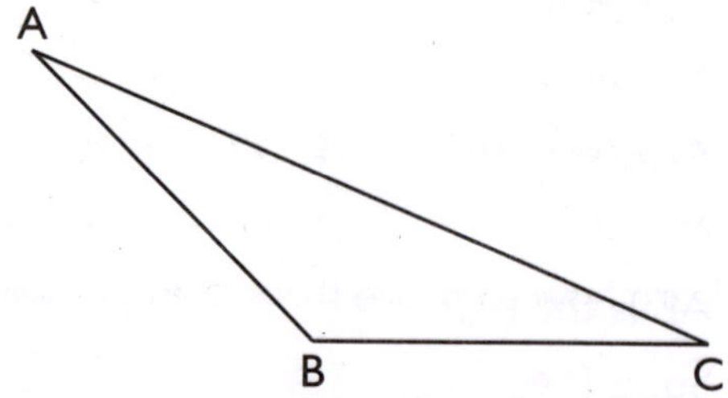

Step 2: We measure the angles with the help of a protractor. Record the measures of the angles in the table.

Figure	∠A	∠B	∠C	∠A+∠B +∠C
a				
b				
c				

Step 3: We observe that the last column, ∠A + ∠B + ∠C, is the same, that is, 180°. Thus the sum of the three angles of a triangle is 180°.

Experiment 3

Step 1: Draw a triangle ABC on a sheet of chart paper (say yellow chart paper). Cut out the triangle with the help of a pair of scissors. Now keep this cut out on the chart paper again and cut out another triangle. In a similar manner cut-out a third triangle. Now we have three triangles of the same size as in figures a, b and c. Place the three cut-outs of equal size as shown in figure d.

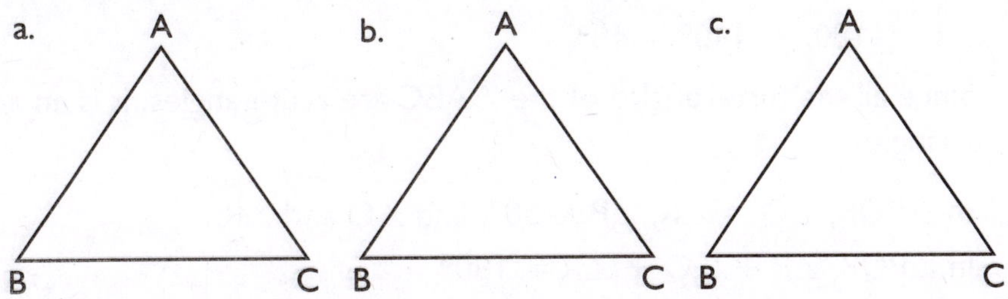

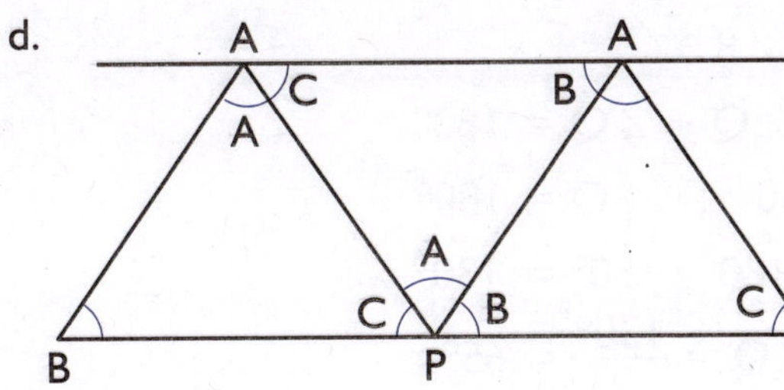

It is observed that both the arms at point P are linear, that is, ∠C + ∠A + ∠B is a straight angle of 180°.

Hence the sum of the angles of a triangle is 180°, which is proved by the experiments. Now let us prove it theoretically.

Proof of the Angle Sum Property

Given: △ABC

To prove: ∠ABC + ∠BAC + ∠ACB = 180°.

Construction: Through the point A, draw a line DE that is parallel to BC.

Proof: DE is parallel to BC (by construction).

AB is the transversal, which intersects the parallel lines at two distinct points, A and B.

So, ∠DAB = ∠ABC (since they are alternate interior angles)

Also, AC is the transversal that intersects the parallel lines at two distinct points A and C.

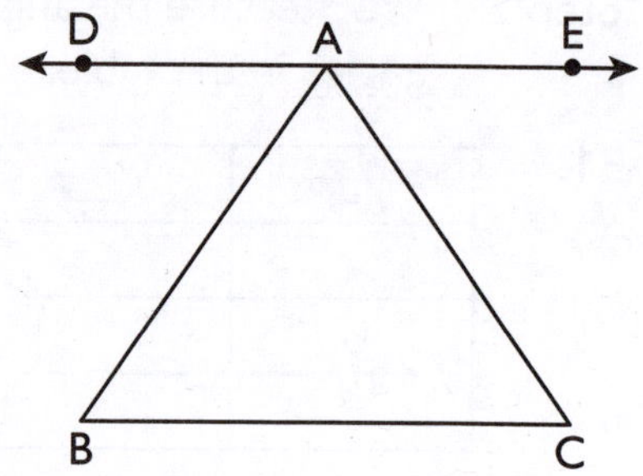

So ∠EAC = ∠ACB (since they are alternate interior angles)

As DE is a straight line, we know that ∠DAB + ∠BAC + ∠EAC = 180°

So ∠ABC + ∠BAC + ∠ACB = 180° (since ∠DAB = ∠ABC and ∠EAC = ∠ABC)

Hence, the sum of the three angles of a triangle is 180°.

In any triangle, the sum of the three angles of a triangle is always 180°.

Example 1: A triangle ABC is such that ∠A = 60° and ∠B = 80°. Find ∠C. What type of triangle is this?

In △ABC, we have

∠A + ∠B + ∠C = 180°

60° + 80° + ∠C = 180°

140° + ∠C = 180°

∠C = 180° − 140° = 40°

Since all the three angles of the △ABC are acute angles, it is an acute-angled triangle.

Example 2: In △PQR, ∠Q = ∠R, ∠P = 50°, find ∠Q and ∠R.

In △PQR, ∠P + ∠Q + ∠R = 180°

50° + ∠Q + ∠R = 180°

But ∠Q = ∠R

∴ 50° + ∠Q + ∠Q = 180°

50° + 2∠Q = 180°

2∠Q = 180° − 50° = 130°

$\angle Q = \frac{130°}{2} = 65°.$

∴ ∠R = ∠Q ∴ ∠R = ∠65°

Example 3: In △ABC, DE is parallel to BC. If ∠ADE = 50° and ∠ACB = 40°, find ∠ABC and ∠BAC.

In △ABC, DE is parallel to BC, thus ∠ADE = ∠ABC (since they are corresponding angles)

∠50° = ∠ABC

In △ABC, ∠A + ∠B + ∠C = 180°

∠A + 50° + 40° = 180°

∠A + 90° = 180°

∠A = 180° − 90° = 90°

∴ ∠A = 90°

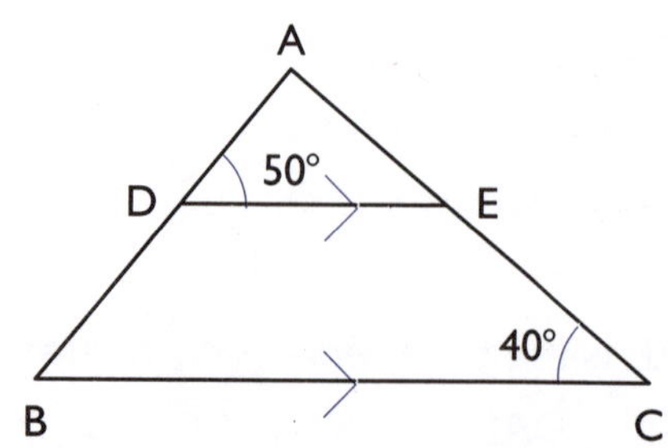

Practice Exercise 10.1

1. The measures of two angles of a triangle are given. Find the measure of the third angle.

a. 65°, 45° b. 90°, 40° c. 130°, 30°
d. 53°, 42° e. 100°, 27° f. 25°, 45°
g. 110°, 30° h. 38°, 65° i. 22°, 38°
j. 75°, 35°

2. The measures of three angles are given. State which of them will form a triangle.

a.	$\angle A = 30°$	$\angle B = 60°$	$\angle C = 90°$
b.	$\angle D = 45°$	$\angle E = 65°$	$\angle F = 70°$
c.	$\angle G = 100°$	$\angle H = 50°$	$\angle I = 30°$
d.	$\angle J = 120°$	$\angle K = 40°$	$\angle L = 50°$
e.	$\angle M = 75°$	$\angle N = 65°$	$\angle O = 75°$
f.	$\angle P = 28°$	$\angle Q = 42°$	$\angle R = 110°$
g.	$\angle S = 48°$	$\angle T = 58°$	$\angle U = 68°$
h.	$\angle V = 48°$	$\angle W = 38°$	$\angle X = 94°$
i.	$\angle X = 100°$	$\angle Y = 80°$	$\angle Z = 0°$
j.	$\angle A = 90°$	$\angle B = 90°$	$\angle C = 90°$

3. The two angles of a triangle are equal and the third angle measures 70°. Find the measure of the equal angles.

4. In the given figure, find the values of x, y and z if AB is parallel to CD.

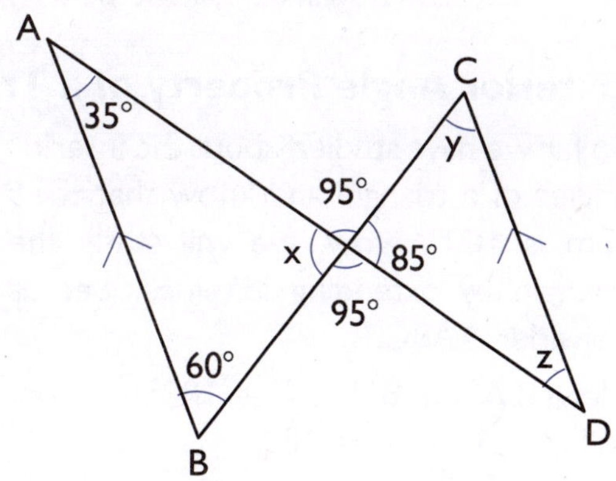

5. In the given figure, find the values of x, y and z.

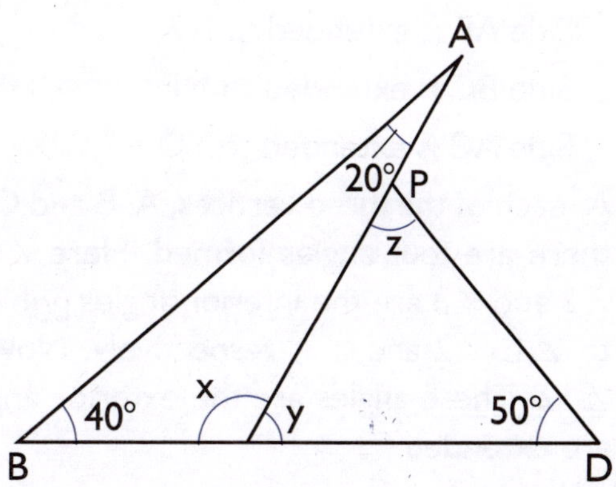

6. In the given figure, find the values of x, y and z.

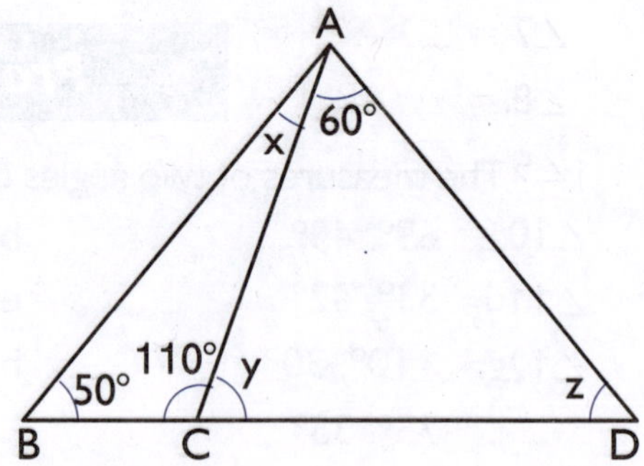

7. In the given figure, there are three triangles, $\triangle ABC$, $\triangle CDE$ and $\triangle EFG$.
$\angle A = 45°$ $\angle D = 95°$
$\angle B = 100°$ $\angle F = 55°$.
Find the measure of $\angle G$.

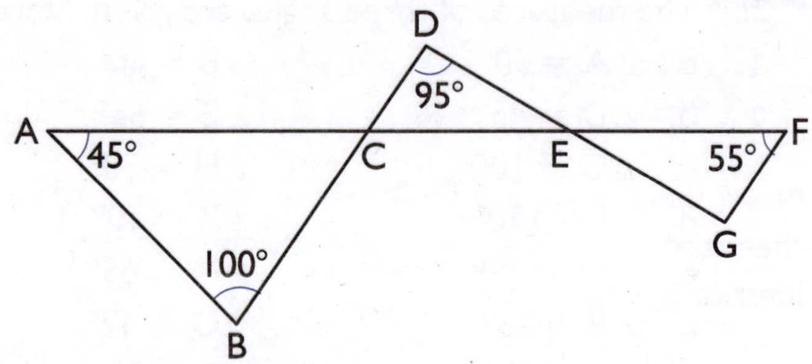

8. Answer each of the following questions with a yes or no.
   a. Can an isosceles triangle be a right-angled triangle?
   b. Can a right-angled triangle be a scalene triangle?
   c. Can a right-angled triangle be an equilateral triangle?
   d. Can an obtuse triangle be an isosceles triangle?
   e. Can a scalene triangle be a right-angled triangle?

Exterior Angle Property of a Triangle

So far we have studied about the interior angles of a triangle and know that their sum is 180°. Now, we will study the triangle by extending its sides. Let us consider $\triangle ABC$,

Here $\angle A + \angle B + \angle C = 180°$ or
$\angle 1 + \angle 2 + \angle 3 = 180°$

Let us extend sides AB, BC and CA.

Side AB is extended to NX

Side BC is extended to MP

Side AC is extended to YQ

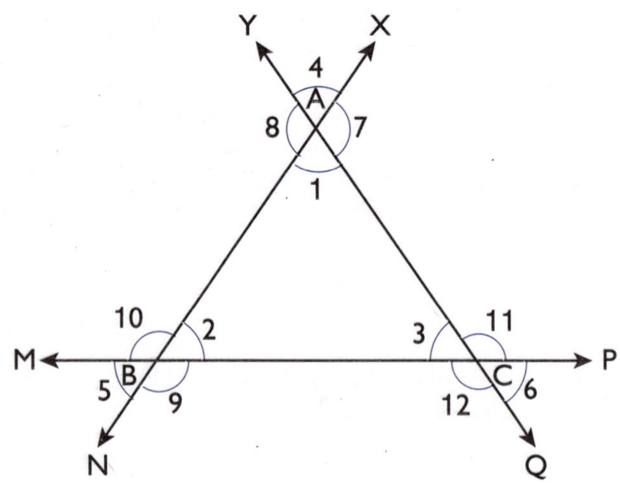

At each of the three vertices, A, B and C, there are four angles formed. Here $\angle 1$, $\angle 2$ and $\angle 3$ are the interior angles, while $\angle 4$, $\angle 5$ and $\angle 6$ are the vertically opposite angles to $\angle 1$, $\angle 2$ and $\angle 3$, respectively. Now observe the angles $\angle 7$, $\angle 8$, $\angle 9$, $\angle 10$, $\angle 11$ and $\angle 12$. These angles are the exterior angles, which are formed when the sides of a triangle are extended.

$\left.\begin{array}{r}\angle 7 = \angle XAC \\ \angle 8 = \angle YAB\end{array}\right\}$ at vertex A

$\left.\begin{array}{r}\angle 9 = \angle NBC \\ \angle 10 = \angle MBA\end{array}\right\}$ at vertex B

$\left.\begin{array}{r}\angle 11 = \angle PCA \\ \angle 12 = \angle QCB\end{array}\right\}$ at vertex C

Alert!

1. The angles — $\angle 4$, $\angle 5$ and $\angle 6$ are not exterior angles but vertically opposite angles.
2. The exterior angles at a vertex are equal to each other.

Now, we shall prove the exterior angle property with the help of experiments as well as theoretically. Let us determine the relation between the exterior angle of a triangle and its interior angles.

Experiment 1

Step 1: Draw a triangle ABC and extend BC to D.

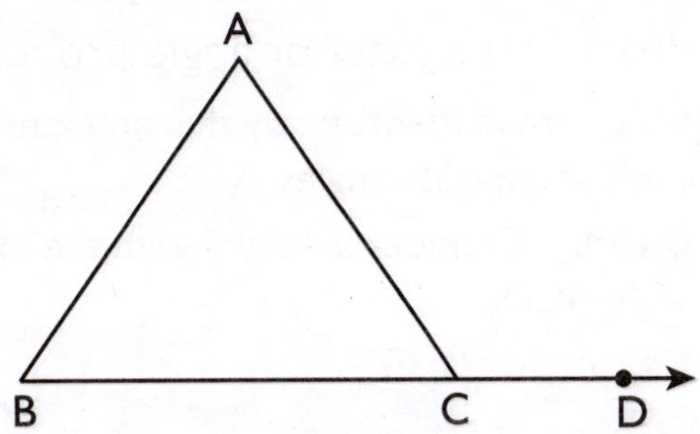

Step 2: Trace out this triangle on another paper and cut off $\angle b$ and $\angle a$ as shown in the figures given here.

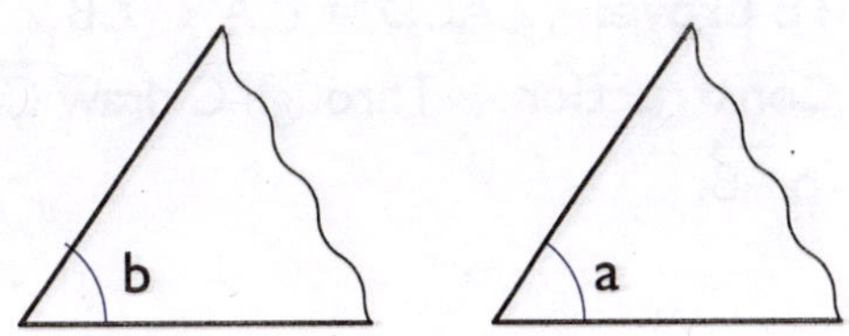

Step 3: Arrange these angles alongside by keeping the vertex of each on C and placing an arm of $\angle B$ along CA. Let the other arm be along CE. Similarly, place one arm of $\angle A$ along CE and let the other arm be along CD, as shown in the figure.

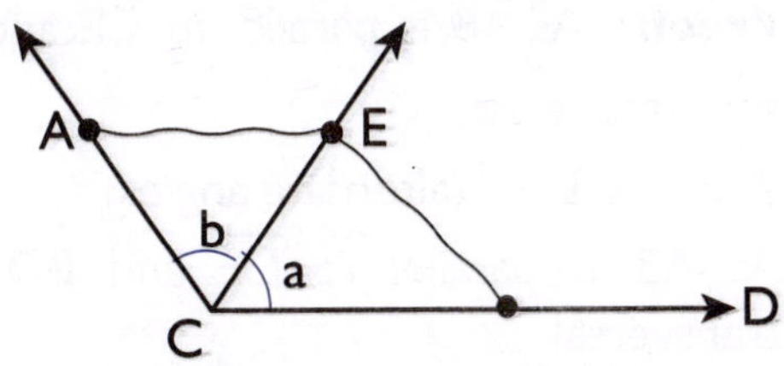

It is observed that $\angle A + \angle B = \angle ACD$.

Thus, we observe that the exterior angle of a triangle is equal to the sum of the interior opposite angles.

Experiment 2

Step 1: Draw a $\triangle ABC$ and extended its side BC to D.

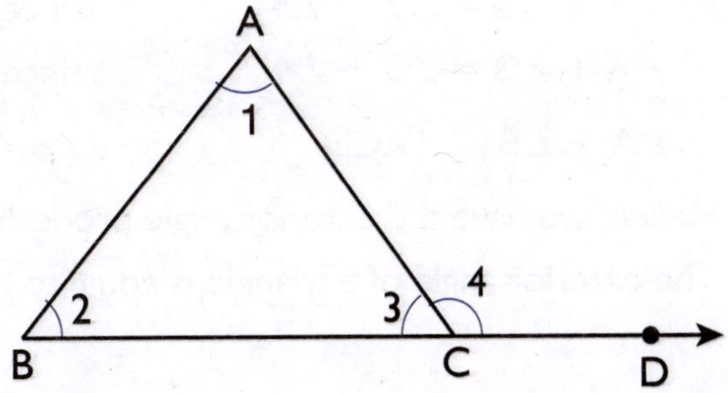

Step 2: Using a protractor, measure ∠ACD, ∠ABC, and ∠BAC.

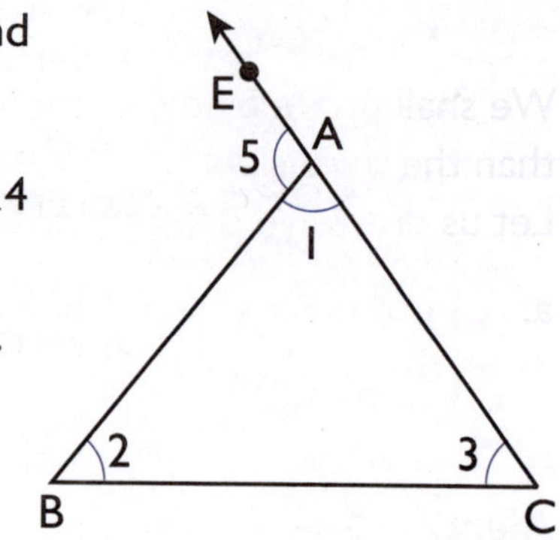

Step 3: It is observed that ∠ACD = ∠ABC + ∠BAC or ∠4 = ∠2 + ∠1.

Step 4: Repeat the experiment by extending the side CA to E.
It is observed that ∠BAE = ∠ABC + ∠ACB or ∠5 = ∠2 + ∠3.

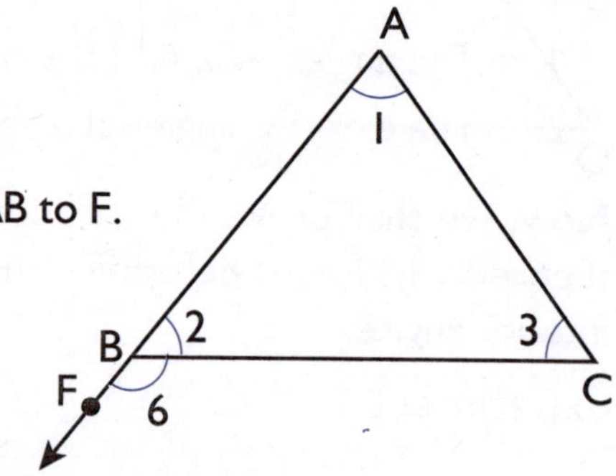

Step 5. Repeat the experiment by extending the side AB to F.
It is observed that ∠CBF = ∠BAC + ∠ACB or ∠6 = ∠1 + ∠3.

Proof of the exterior angle property

Let us prove theoretically that an exterior angle of a triangle is equal to the sum of the interior opposite angles.

Given: Consider a △ABC with the exterior angle ACD.

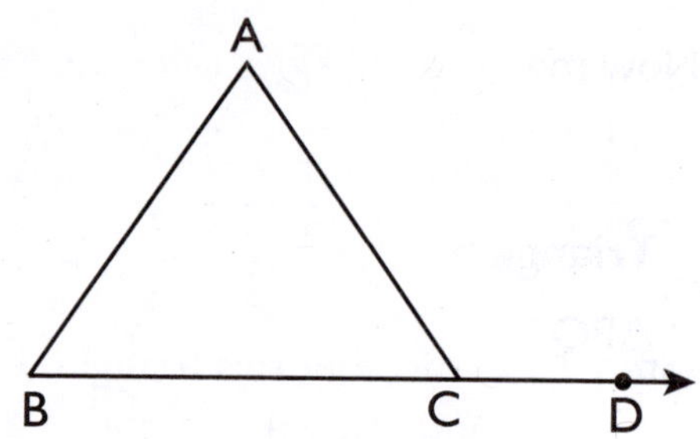

To prove: ∠ACD = ∠A + ∠B

Construction: Through C draw $\overrightarrow{CE}$ parallel to $\overrightarrow{AB}$.

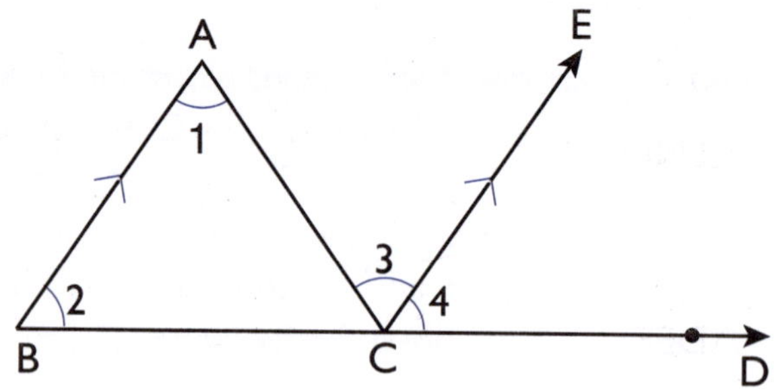

Proof: As $\overrightarrow{AB}$ is parallel to $\overrightarrow{CE}$ and $\overrightarrow{AC}$ is the transversal.

∠1 = ∠3 (alternate angles)

As $\overrightarrow{AB}$ is parallel to $\overrightarrow{CE}$ and BD is the transversal

∠2 = ∠4 (corresponding angles)

so, ∠1 + ∠2 = ∠3 + ∠4 (since ∠1 = ∠A)

∠A + ∠B = ∠3 + ∠4 (since ∠2 = ∠B)

∴ ∠A + ∠B = ∠ACD (∠3 + ∠4 = ∠ACD)

Hence, we have the exterior angle properly of a triangle.

The exterior angle of a triangle is equal to the sum of the interior opposite angles.

The Relation Between the Three Sides of a Triangle

We shall prove by experiments that the sum of any two sides of a triangle is always greater than the third side.

Let us draw five different triangles of various shapes and sizes.

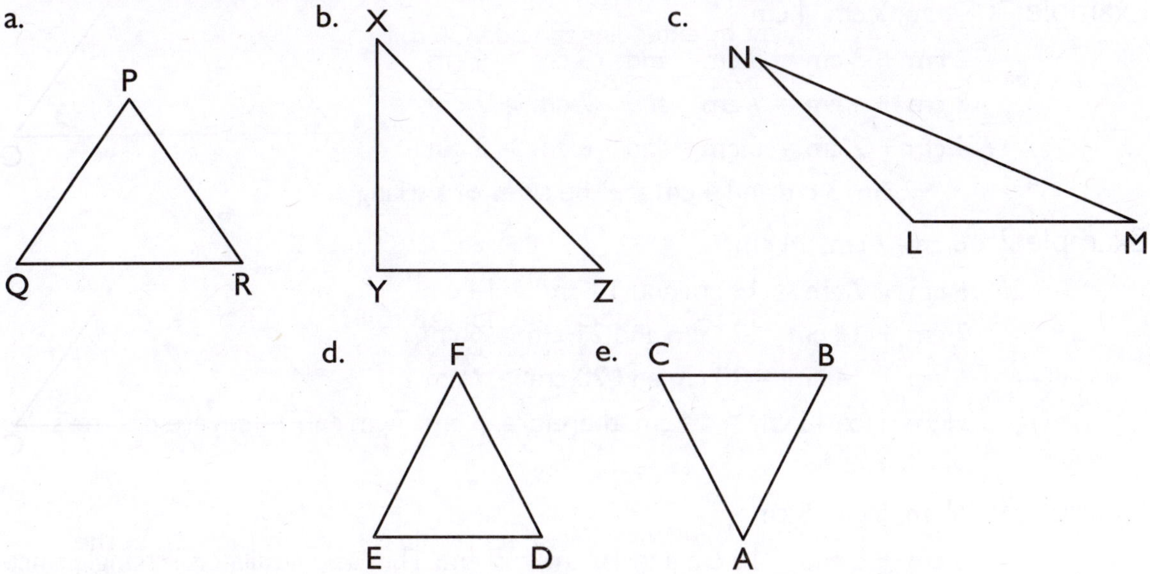

Now measure the sides of each of the triangles and fill in the following table.

TABLE 10.1

Triangle	Length of sides	Sum of lengths of other two sides
△PQR	PQ =	QR + RP =
	QR =	RP + PQ =
	RP =	PQ + QR =
△XYZ	XY =	YZ + ZX =
	YZ =	ZX + XY =
	ZX =	XY + YZ =
△LMN	LM =	MN + NL =
	MN =	NL + LM =
	NL =	LM + MN =
△DEF	DE =	EF + FD =
	EF =	FD + DE =
	FD =	DE + EF =
△ABC	AB =	BC + CA =
	BC =	CA + AB =
	CA =	AB + BC =

In each triangle, we observe that *the* sum of the lengths *of two sides of a triangle is always greater than the third side.*

Alert!

If in a figure the sum of any two sides is *not* greater than the third side, then it is not a triangle.

State whether the following are the sides of a triangle or not.

Example 1: 2 cm, 3 cm, 4 cm

2 cm + 3 cm = 5 cm and 5 cm > 4 cm.

3 cm + 4 cm = 7 cm and 7 cm > 2 cm.

4 cm + 2 cm = 6 cm and 6 cm > 3 cm.

$\therefore$ 2 cm, 3 cm and 4 cm are the sides of a triangle.

Example 2: 6 cm, 7 cm, 14 cm

6 cm + 7 cm = 13 cm and 13 cm $\ngtr$ 14 cm.

7 cm + 14 cm = 21 cm and 21 cm > 6 cm.

6 cm + 14 cm = 20 cm and 20 cm > 7 cm.

Here since 13 cm $\ngtr$ 14 cm, therefore, 6 cm, 7 cm and 14 cm are not the sides of a triangle.

Example 3: 5 cm, 5 cm, 5 cm

5 cm + 5 cm = 10 cm and 10 cm > 5 cm. This is an equilateral triangle since all the sides are equal.

Two Special Triangles

We have studied about triangles. Two special triangles are discussed below.

Equilateral triangles have all sides equal as well as all angles equal. Since the sum of all the angles of a triangle is equal to 180°, each angle of an equilateral triangle is 60°.

Consider ABC an equilateral triangle. Thus, AB = BC = CA.

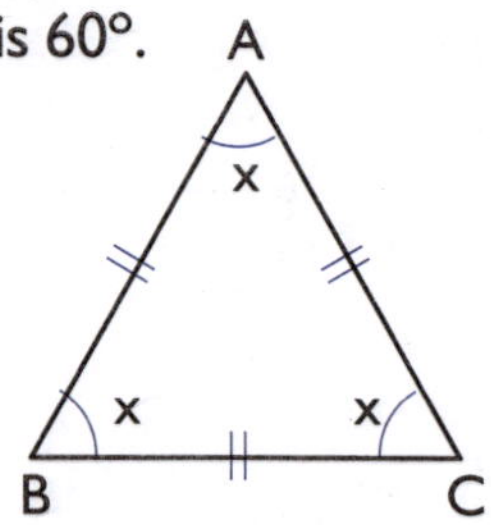

$$\text{Also, } \angle A = \angle B = \angle C = x^\circ$$
$$\text{so } \angle A + \angle B + \angle C = 180^\circ$$
$$x^\circ + x^\circ + x^\circ = 180^\circ$$
$$3x^\circ = 180^\circ \Rightarrow x^\circ = 60^\circ.$$

Isosceles triangles have two sides equal. The third side, which is not equal, is called the base of the triangle. The angles that are opposite to the equal sides are equal. If ABC is an isosceles triangle, the sides AB and AC are equal. The angles opposite to these sides are equal.

$$\angle ABC = \angle ACB = x^\circ$$
$$\therefore \quad \angle A + \angle B + \angle C = 180^\circ$$
$$30^\circ + x^\circ + x^\circ = 180^\circ$$
$$2x^\circ = 180^\circ - 30^\circ$$
$$2x^\circ = 150^\circ$$
$$x^\circ = 75^\circ$$

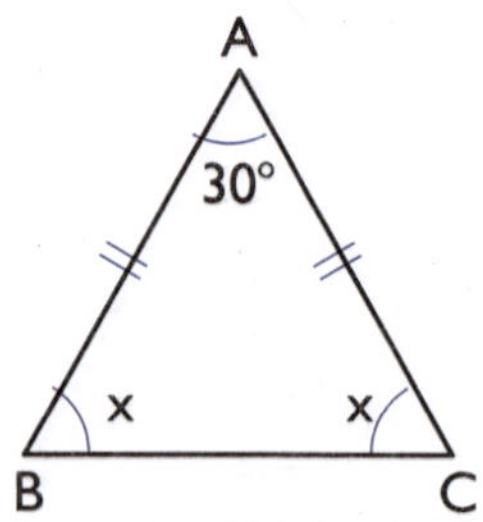

The $\angle$B and $\angle$C are called base angles and BC is the base.

A right-angled triangle can be an isosceles triangle. One angle will be the right angle (90°) and the equal angles will be 45° each.

Practice Exercise 10.2

1. In the following figures, name the exterior angles of the triangles.

a.

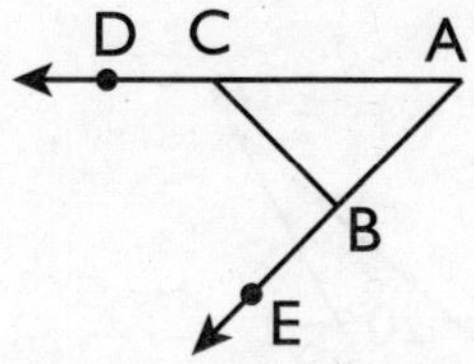

b.

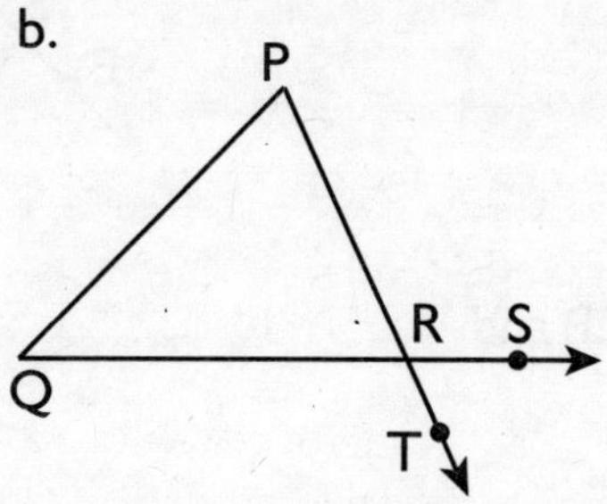

c.

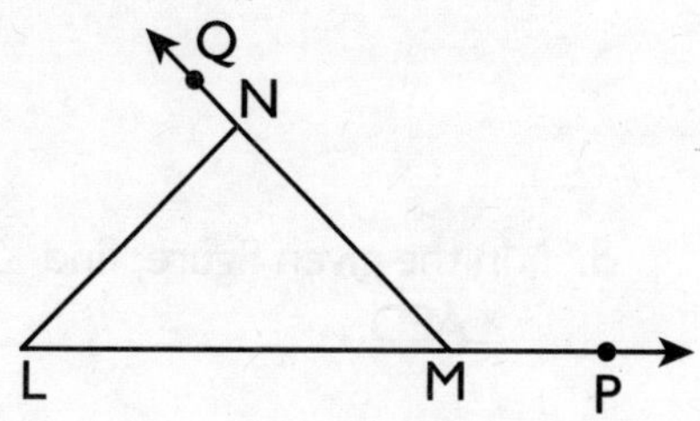

d.

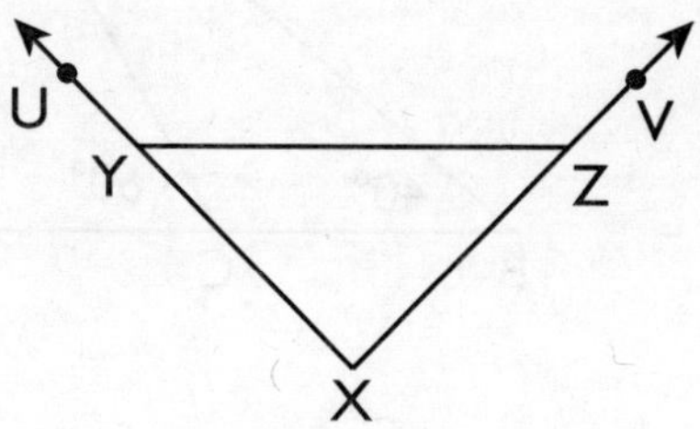

e.

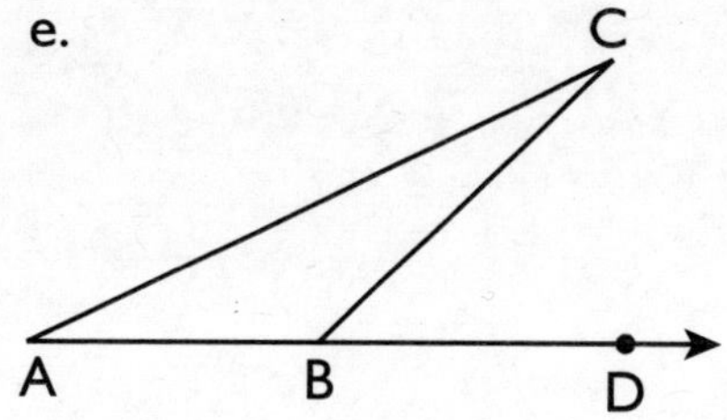

2. In the following figures, find the value of x.

a.

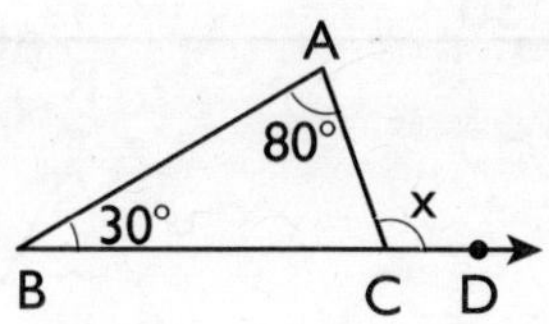

b.

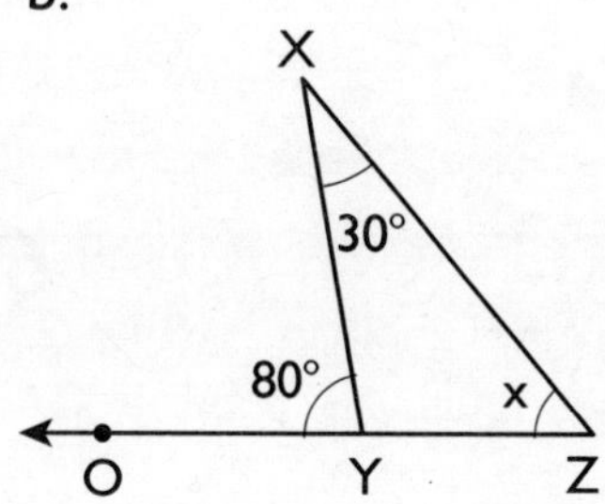

c.

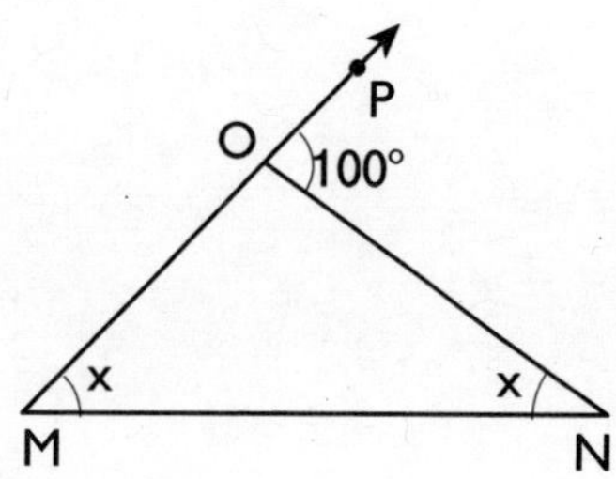

d.

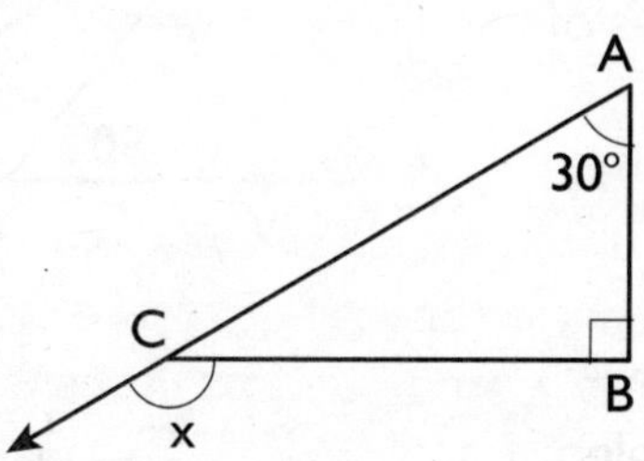

e.

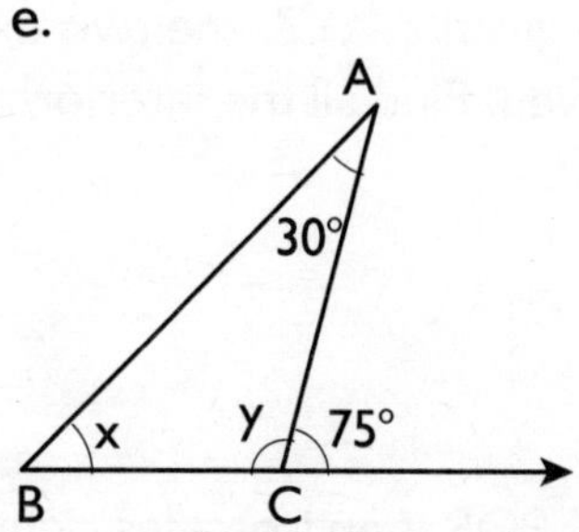

3. In the given figure, PQ is parallel to MS and PS is the transversal. Here ∠QPS = 90° and ∠PQR = 60°. Find the measures of angles 1, 2, 3 and 4.

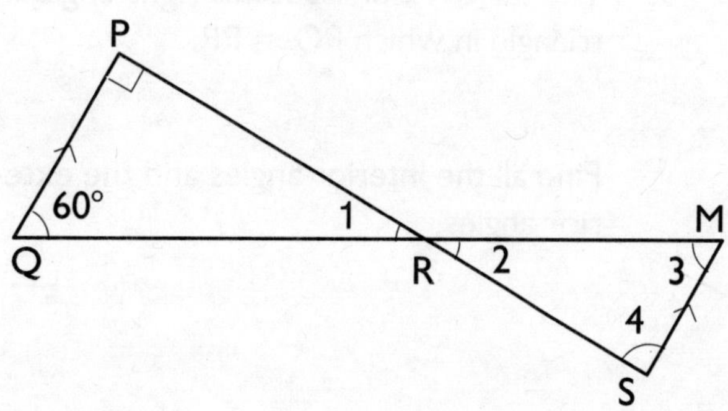

4. In the given isosceles triangle ABC, AB is equal to BC. If the measure of the exterior angle ∠EBC is 100°, find the measures of ∠BCD and ∠A. Also find the base angles.

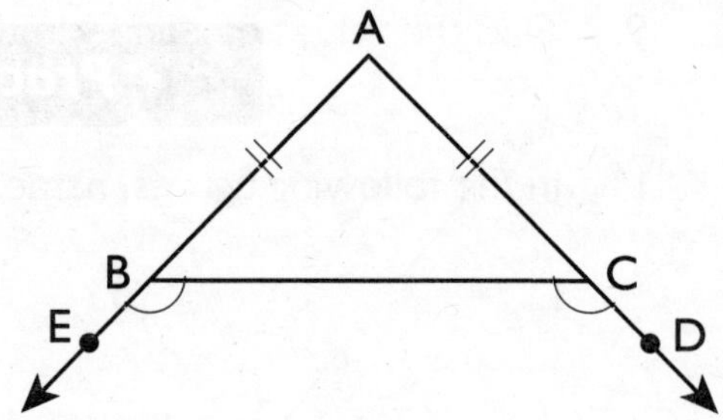

5. In the given figure, find ∠ACB and ∠AED.

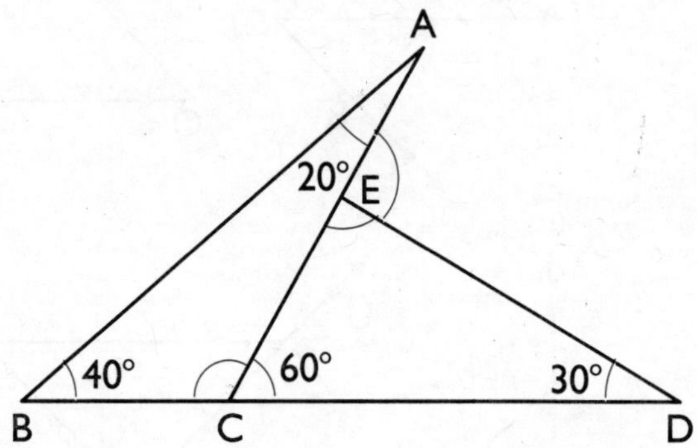

6. In the given figure, find ∠PRS, ∠PSR and ∠SPM.

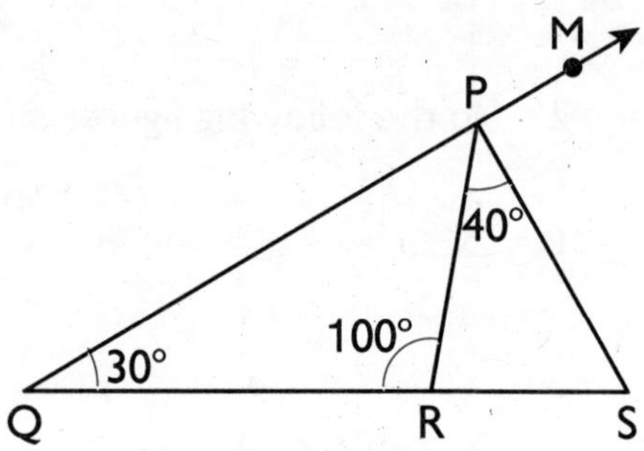

7. In the given △XYZ, the two exterior angles are given. Find all the interior angles of △XYZ.

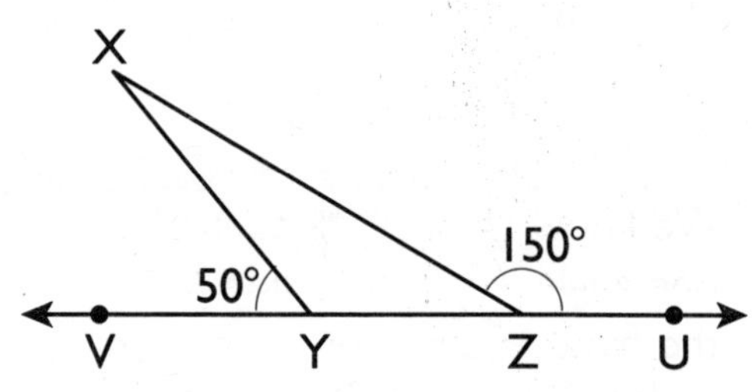

8. The △PQR is an isosceles right-angled triangle in which PQ = PR.

Find all the interior angles and the exterior angles.

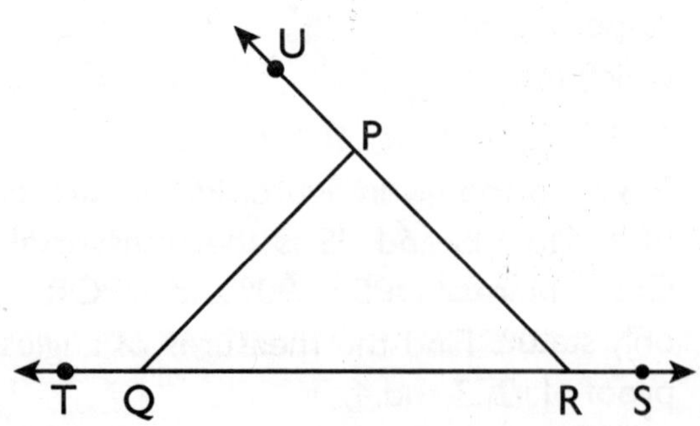

9. Find the values of x and y in the following figures.

a.

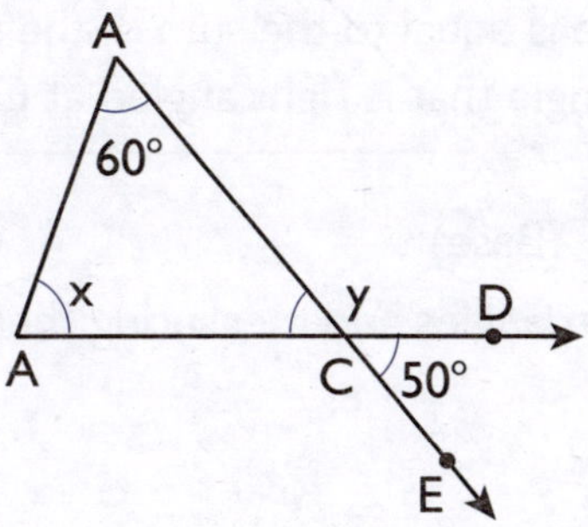

b.

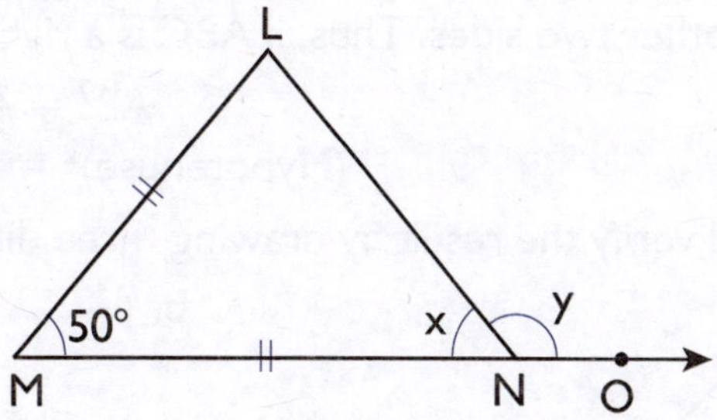

c.

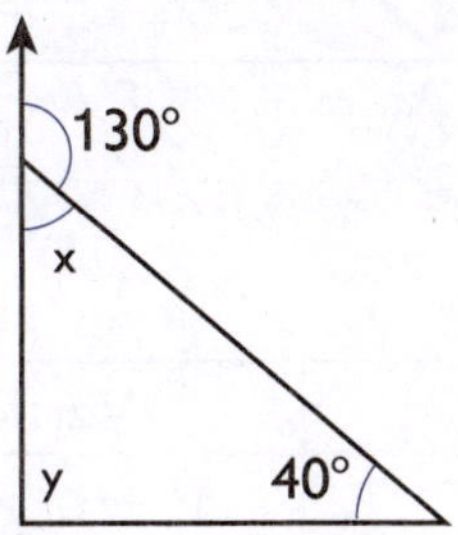

d.

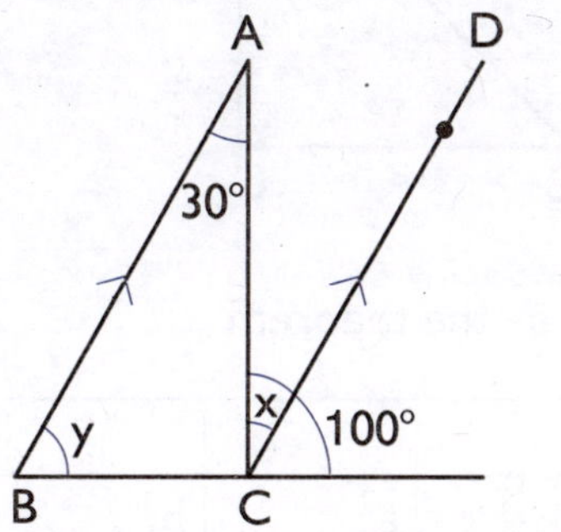

e.

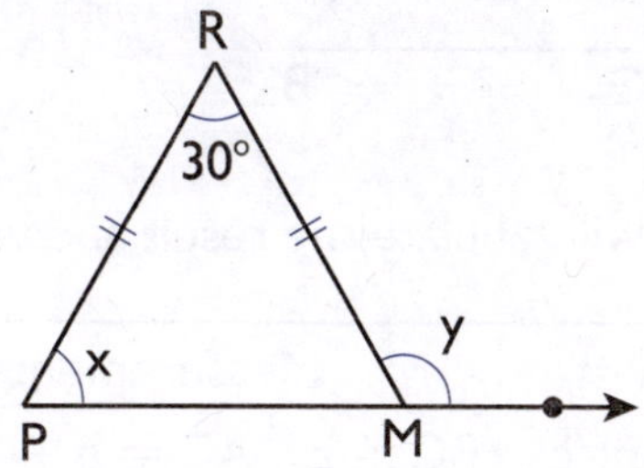

10. State whether the following lengths are sides of a triangle or not.

a. 6 cm, 7 cm, 9 cm
b. 10.2 cm, 6.8 cm, 8.4 cm
c. 15 cm, 6.2 cm, 7.8 cm
d. 9.5 cm, 15.3 cm, 6.1 cm
e. 3.8 cm, 4.7 cm, 9.2 cm
f. 5 cm, 3 cm, 2 cm
g. 7.1 cm, 11.4 cm, 8.2 cm
h. 7.8 cm, 16.7 cm, 8.5 cm
i. 5 cm, 3 cm, 4 cm
j. 8 cm, 10 cm, 12 cm

The Right Triangle

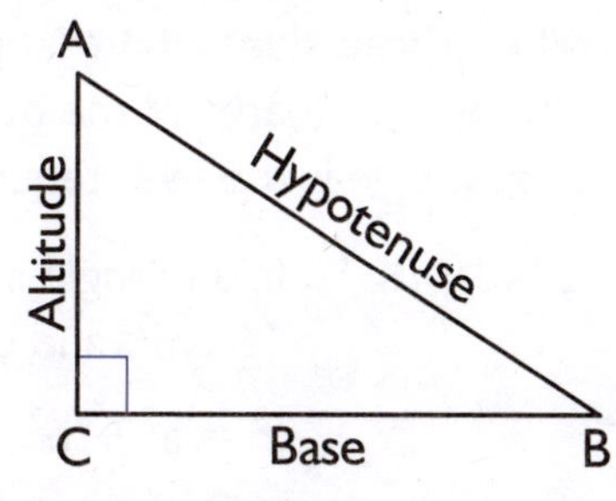

We know that a right triangle is a special triangle in which one angle is 90°. The side opposite the right angle is called the hypotenuse. The other two sides are named the base and perpendicular (or altitude) and are called the legs of the triangle.

A special right triangle is an isosceles right-angled triangle in which the base and altitude are of the same length and the angles other than 90° are equal, each measuring 45°.

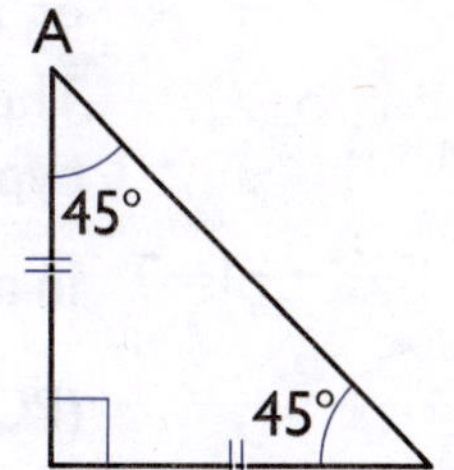

A very special relation between the length of the sides of a right-angled triangle was discovered by the famous Greek philosopher Pythagoras (580 BC – 500 BC). He not only stated the important result but also gave the analytical proof of it.

Pythagoras Theorem

In any right-angled triangle, the square on the hypotenuse is equal to the sum of the squares of the other two sides. Thus, if ABC is a right-angled triangle that is right angled at C then,

$$AB^2 = AC^2 + BC^2$$
$$(\text{Hypotenuse})^2 = (\text{Altitude})^2 + (\text{Base})^2$$

We will verify the result by drawing three different right triangles and measuring their sides.

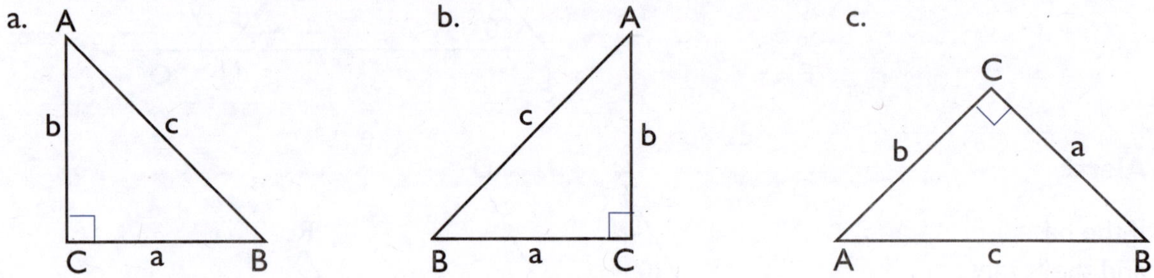

We will tabulate the result and verify the theorem.

	Measurements						Verify	
Triangles	BC = a	AC = b	AB = c	a^2	b^2	c^2	$a^2 + b^2 = c^2$	
a.								
b.								
c.								

We find in each case, $c^2 = a^2 + b^2$.

The Pythagoras theorem is a very important theorem and is widely used in all branches of mathematics as well as for higher mathematical calculations.

Converse of the Pythagoras Theorem

When three sides of a triangle are such that the square on the longest side is equal to the sum of the squares of the other two sides, then the triangle is a right-angled triangle and the longest side is the hypotenuse.

Example 1: In a triangle if a = 3 cm, b = 4 cm and c = 5 cm, then $a^2 = 9$ cm^2, $b^2 = 16$ cm^2, and $c^2 = 25$ cm^2.

$c^2 = a^2 + b^2$

or $25 = 9 + 16$.

Thus, the given triangle is a right-angled triangle with side C = 5 cm as the hypotenuse.

Example 2: In any $\triangle PQR$, if PQ = 8 cm, QR = 10 cm, and RQ = 12 cm, we have

$(PQ)^2 = 64$ cm^2 $\quad$ $(QR)^2 = 100$ cm^2 and $\quad$ $(RQ)^2 = 144$ cm^2

$PQ^2 + QR^2 \neq RQ^2$

since $64 + 100 \neq 144$

Therefore, the given $\triangle PQR$ is not a right-angled triangle.

Example 3: In any $\triangle XYZ$, if XY = 6 cm, YZ = 8 cm and ZX = 10 cm, we have

$(XY)^2 = 36 \text{ cm}^2$ $(YZ)^2 = 64 \text{ cm}^2$ and $(ZX)^2 = 100 \text{ cm}^2$

$XY^2 + YZ^2 = ZX^2$

or $36 + 64 = 100$

Thus, $\triangle XYZ$ is a right-angled triangle, right angled at Y.

Alert!

If the base and altitude are XY and YZ, then the right angle will be at the common vertex Y, and the hypotenuse will be ZX.

If in $\triangle ABC$, AB is the base and BC is perpendicular, then the right angle is at B and hypotenuse is AC. Right angle is at vertex B.

Pythagorean Triplets

When three natural numbers are such that the square of the largest number is equal to the sum of the squares of the other two numbers, they form a Pythagorean triplet.

Some examples of Pythagorean triplets are

3, 4, 5 as $3^2 + 4^2 = 5^2 \Rightarrow 9 + 16 = 25$

6, 8, 10 as $6^2 + 8^2 = 10^2 \Rightarrow 36 + 64 = 100$

5, 12, 13 as $5^2 + 12^2 = 13^2 \Rightarrow 25 + 144 = 169$

8, 15, 17 as $8^2 + 15^2 = 17^2 \Rightarrow 64 + 225 = 289$

7, 24, 25 as $7^2 + 24^2 = 25^2 \Rightarrow 49 + 576 = 625$

Here the longest side in each case will be the hypotenuse; the other two sides will be the base and the perpendicular.

The Pythagoras theorem is used to solve many problems. To use this theorem we should learn the square of numbers so that the application of the theorem is simple.

A number multiplied by itself is called its square. Thus, $2 \times 2 = 4$ and $5 \times 5 = 25$.

The square of 2 is 4 or $2^2 = 4$.

The square of 5 is 25 or $5^2 = 25$.

Now from a square if we have to find the number, we find its square root. Thus, the square root of $\sqrt{4} = 2$ and $\sqrt{25} = 5$.

The symbol for square root is $\sqrt{\ }$.

The symbol for square is the exponent 2. For ready reference, see the given table:

Table 10.2

Square of numbers		Square roots of a number	
$1^2 = 1$	$11^2 = 121$	$\sqrt{1} = 1$	$\sqrt{121} = 11$
$2^2 = 4$	$12^2 = 144$	$\sqrt{4} = 2$	$\sqrt{144} = 12$
$3^2 = 9$	$13^2 = 169$	$\sqrt{9} = 3$	$\sqrt{169} = 13$
$4^2 = 16$	$14^2 = 196$	$\sqrt{16} = 4$	$\sqrt{196} = 14$
$5^2 = 25$	$15^2 = 225$	$\sqrt{25} = 5$	$\sqrt{225} = 15$
$6^2 = 36$	$16^2 = 256$	$\sqrt{36} = 6$	$\sqrt{256} = 16$
$7^2 = 49$	$17^2 = 289$	$\sqrt{49} = 7$	$\sqrt{289} = 17$
$8^2 = 64$	$18^2 = 324$	$\sqrt{64} = 8$	$\sqrt{324} = 18$
$9^2 = 81$	$19^2 = 361$	$\sqrt{81} = 9$	$\sqrt{361} = 19$
$10^2 = 100$	$20^2 = 400$	$\sqrt{100} = 10$	$\sqrt{400} = 20$

Example 1: The legs of a right triangle are 5 cm and 12 cm. Find the length of the hypotenuse.

Let the hypotenuse be c, then

$$c^2 = a^2 + b^2$$
$$c^2 = 5^2 + 12^2$$
$$c^2 = 25 + 144$$
$$c^2 = 169$$
$$c = \sqrt{169} = 13 \text{ cm.}$$

∴ The hypotenuse of the right triangle is 13 cm.

Example 2: Find the altitude of a right-angled triangle whose hypotenuse is 15 cm and base is 9 cm.

The base b = 9 cm, hypotenuse c = 15 cm, thus altitude a = ?

$$c^2 = a^2 + b^2$$
$$15^2 = a^2 + 9^2$$
$$225 = a^2 + 81$$
$$225 - 81 = a^2$$
$$144 = a^2$$
$$\sqrt{144} = a$$
$$12 \text{ cm} = a$$

∴ The altitude of the triangle is 12 cm.

Example 3: A ladder 10 m long is placed along a wall in such a way that it reaches a height of 8 m on the wall. How far is the foot of the ladder from the wall?

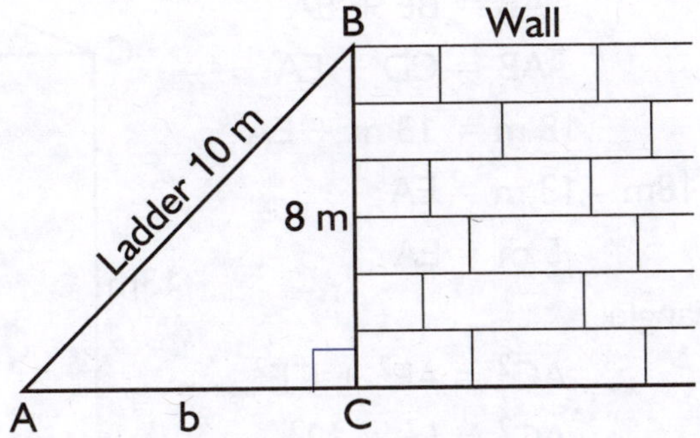

Here, $\triangle ABC$ is a right triangle, the wall being the perpendicular.
The ladder AB is the hypotenuse and the height of the wall is BC,

$$\therefore \quad AB^2 = BC^2 + AC^2$$
$$10^2 = 8^2 + AC^2$$
$$100 = 64 + AC^2$$
$$100 - 64 = AC^2$$
$$36 = AC^2$$
$$\sqrt{36} = AC$$
$$6 \text{ cm} = AC$$

Thus, the foot of the ladder is 6 m away from the wall.

Example 4: The sides of a rectangle are 12 cm and 16 cm. Find the length of its diagonal.

Let ABCD be a rectangle with length AB = CD = 16 cm and breadth AD = BC = 12 cm.

We know that all angles of a rectangle are 90°. We have to find the length of the diagonal AC. Let us consider the right triangle ABC,

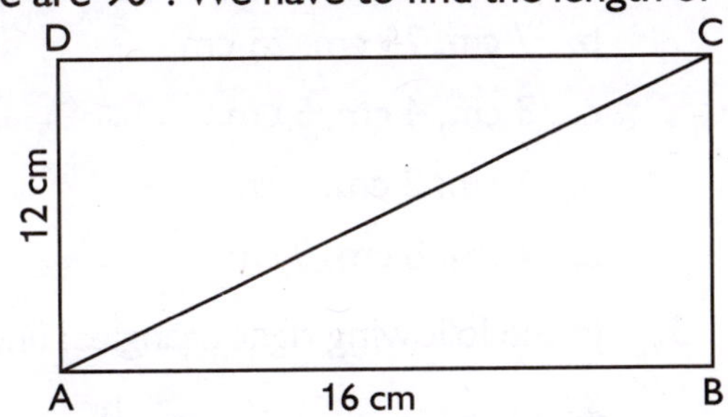

$$AC^2 = AB^2 + BC^2$$
$$AC^2 = 16^2 + 12^2$$
$$AC^2 = 256 + 144$$
$$AC^2 = 400$$
$$\therefore \quad AC = \sqrt{400} = 20 \text{ cm.}$$

The length of the diagonal is 20 cm.

Example 5: Two poles—18 m and 13 m high—stand upright in a playground. If their feet are 12 m apart, find the distance between their tops.

The height of the two poles are 18 m and 13 m. Let AB = 18 m and CD = 13 m. The distance between their feet is 12 m. Thus, DB = 12 m. We have to find the distance between their tops that is AC.

The two poles are parallel to each other, therefore, the distance between them is constant, which is 12 m.

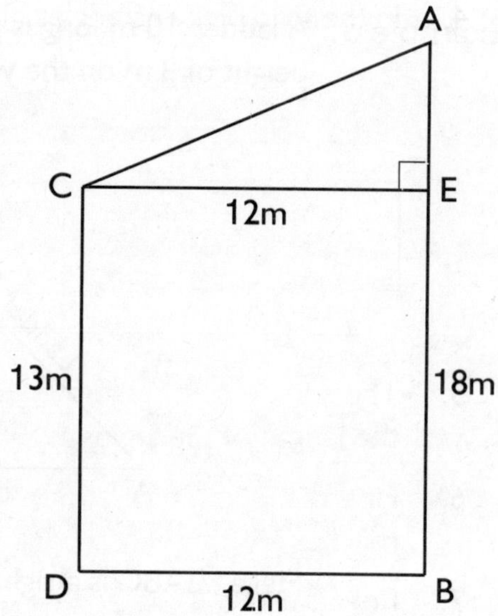

$$AB = BE + EA$$
$$AB = CD + EA$$
$$18\text{ m} = 13\text{ m} + EA$$
$$18\text{m} - 13\text{ m} = EA$$
$$5\text{ m} = EA$$

$\triangle ACE$ is a right triangle.

$$\therefore\ AC^2 = AE^2 + CE^2$$
$$AC^2 = 5^2 + 12^2$$
$$AC^2 = 25 + 144$$
$$AC^2 = 169$$
$$\therefore AC = \sqrt{169} = 13\text{ m}$$

The distance between the tops is 13 m.

Practice Exercise 10.3

1. Find the length of the hypotenuse in the following right triangles.
   a. $\triangle ABC$, where $\angle C = 90°$, $BC = 8$ cm and $CA = 6$ cm.
   b. $\triangle PQR$, where $\angle P = 90°$, $PQ = 3$ cm and $PR = 4$ cm.
   c. $\triangle XYZ$, where $\angle Y = 90°$, $XY = 5$ cm and $YZ = 12$ cm.
2. Use the Pythagoras theorem to check which of the triplets given below will form a right triangle.
   a. 6 cm, 8 cm, 10 cm
   b. 7 cm, 24 cm, 25 cm
   c. 3 cm, 4 cm, 5 cm
   d. 1 cm, 2 cm, 3 cm
   e. 7 cm, 8 cm, 9 cm
   f. 20 cm, 25 cm, 15 cm
   g. 12 cm, 16 cm, 20 cm
   h. 17 cm, 23 cm, 19 cm
   i. 8 cm, 9 cm, 13 cm
   j. 40 cm, 30 cm, 50 cm
3. In the following right triangles, find the length of x.

a.

b.

c.

4. In the following rectangles, find the measure of the diagonal in each case.

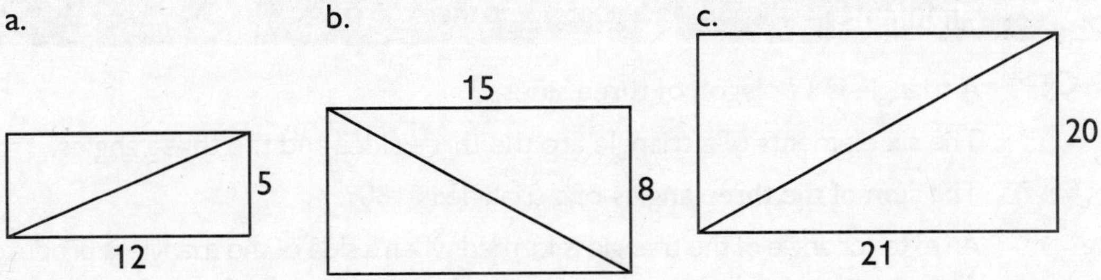

5. The square of the hypotenuse of a right-angled isosceles triangle is 288 cm. Find the length of the legs.

6. Find the length of a ladder kept at a distance of 16 m from the foot of a wall that reaches a window at a height of 30 m.

7. Rohan drove 7 km to the east and then 24 km to the north. Find the distance between his starting point and the final destination.

8. Two poles of height 10 m and 25 m stand on the plane ground. If the distance between their feet is 36 m, find the distance between their tops.

9. A fire engine ladder 17 m long reaches a window that is 8 m above the ground on one side of the street. Keeping the foot of the ladder at the same point, the ladder is turned to the other side of the street to reach a window at a height of 15 m. Find the width of the street.

10. In the given figure, ABCD is a square with side 24 cm. If the length of MD is 31 cm, find the length of MB.

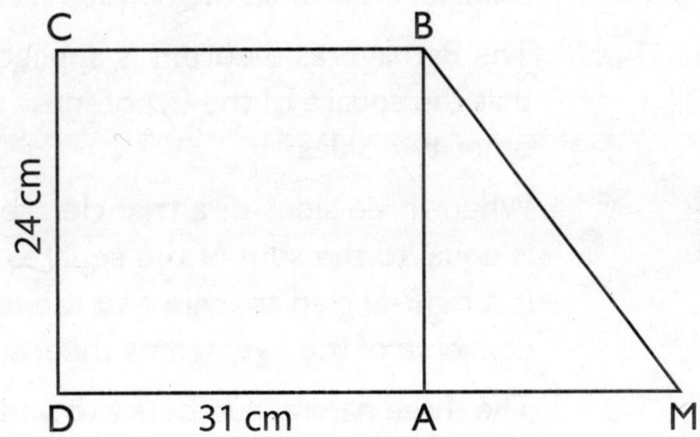

The numbers 1, 2, 3, 4, 5, 6, 7, 8, and 9 must be put in the triangle shown alongside, in such a way that the sums of the numbers on each side are equal.

Answer for Brainteaser on page 171

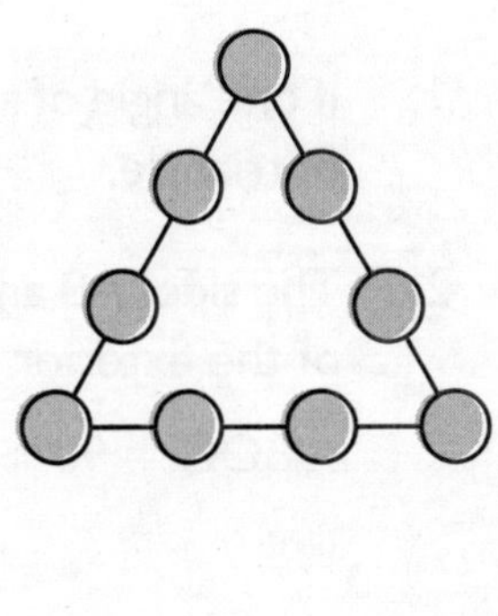

Highlights

- A triangle is a polygon of three sides.
- The six elements of a triangle are the three sides and the three angles.
- The sum of the three angles of a triangle is 180°.
- An exterior angle of the triangle is formed when a side of the triangle is produced. At each vertex of the triangle, two exterior angles can be formed.
- The measure of an exterior angle of the triangle is equal to the sum of the two opposite interior angles.
- An equilateral triangle has three equal sides and three equal angles, so each angle is 60°. Each exterior angle is 120°.
- An isosceles triangle has two equal sides. The angles opposite to the equal sides are also equal.
- The sum of the lengths of two sides of a triangle is always greater than the length of the third side.
- In a right triangle, the side opposite the right angle is called the hypotenuse. The hypotenuse is the longest side in a right triangle.
- An isosceles right triangle is a special right triangle in which two sides of a triangle, other than the hypotenuse, are equal.
- The Pythagoras theorem is applied to any right-angled triangle and it states that the square of the hypotenuse is equal to the sum of the squares on the other two sides.
- When three sides of a triangle are such that the square of the longest side is equal to the sum of the squares of the other two sides, then the triangle is a right-angled triangle and the longest side is the hypotenuse. This is the converse of the Pythagoras theorem.
- The three natural numbers a, b and c are said to form a Pythagorean triplet if $c^2 = a^2 + b^2$.

Higher Order Thinking Skills

HOTS

1. If one angle of a triangle is equal to the sum of the other two angles, name the type of triangle.

2. The sides AB and AC of $\triangle ABC$ are extended to D and E, respectively. The bisector of the exterior angles at B and C of $\triangle ABC$ intersect each other at O. Prove that $\angle BOC = 90° - \frac{1}{2}\angle A$.

Verification of the Pythogoras Theorem

Objective: To verify that the square of the hypotenuse is equal the sum of the square of the other two sides.

Material required: chart paper, coloured sketch pens, pencil, ruler and eraser

Procedure:

Step 1 Draw a line segment BC that is 3 cm long.

Step 2 At point B, draw a right angle with the help of a protractor.

Step 3 Match AB such that AB = 4 cm.

Step 4 Join AC, which will be 5 cm long.

Step 5 Now construct squares on the three sides of the triangle, i.e., BC, AB and CA of 3 cm, 4 cm and 5 cm, respectively. Make lines at a distance of 1 cm, each horizontal and vertical. There will nine squares on the 3 cm side BC, sixteen squares on the 4 cm side BC and twenty five squares on the side AC 5 cm.

The sum of the squares will be:
9 + 16 = 25

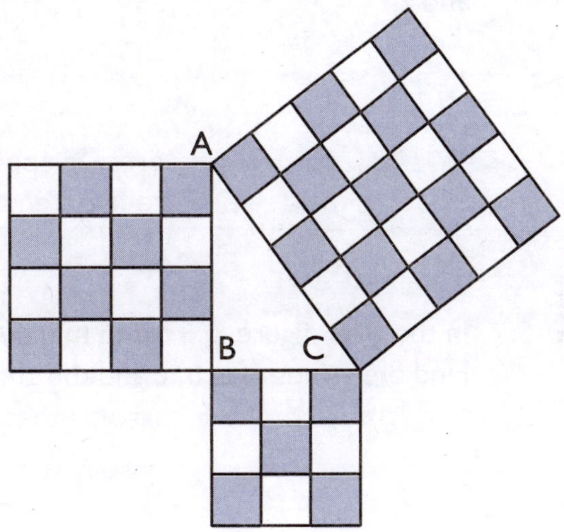

Answer for Brainteaser from page 169

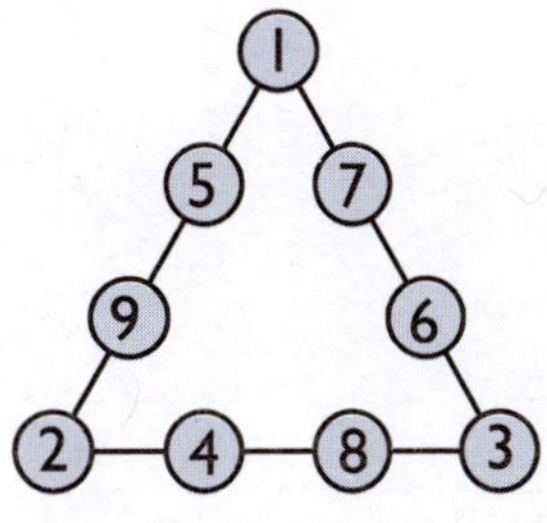

Rewind

1. Indicate whether the following statements as true (T) or false (F).
   a. If two angles are adjacent, they are equal.
   b. Two complementary angles always form a linear pair.
   c. Two complementary angles can be supplementary.
   d. The complement of an acute angle is always an acute angle.
   e. The supplement of an acute angle is always an acute angle.
2. a. The measures of the angles in a linear pair are $x°$ and $(x + 10)°$. Find the measure of each angle.
   b. The measure of two complement any angle are $x°$ and $(x + 50)°$. Find the measure of each angle.
3. a. An angle is $\frac{2}{3}$ of its complement. What is its magnitude?
   b. An angle is $\frac{4}{5}$ of its supplement. What is its magnitude?
4. In the given figure, DE || BC. Find the value of x, y and z.

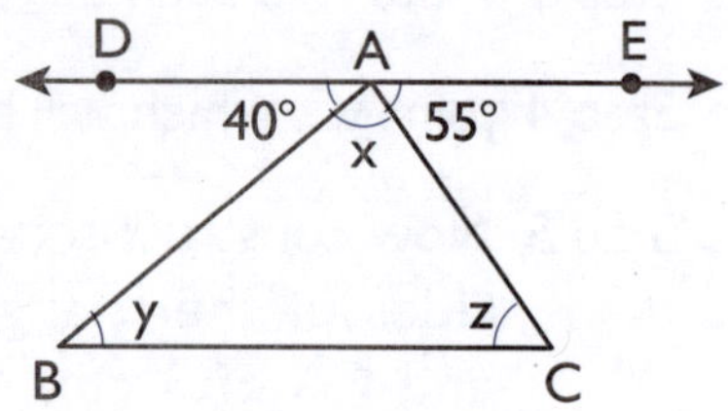

5. In the given figure, p || q and m || n. Find the values of a, b, c and d.

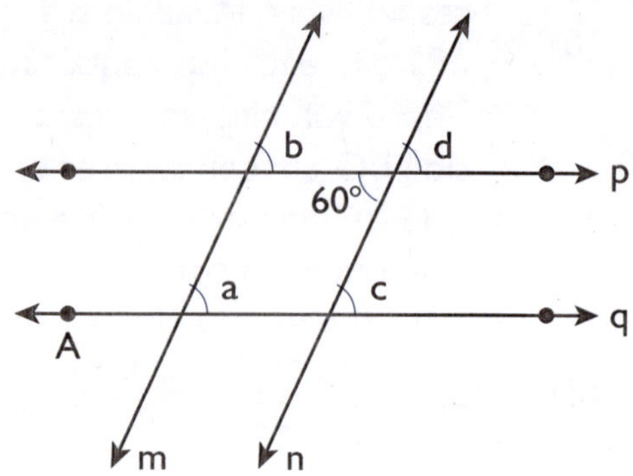

6. In the given figure, PQ || RS. Find the values of x and y.

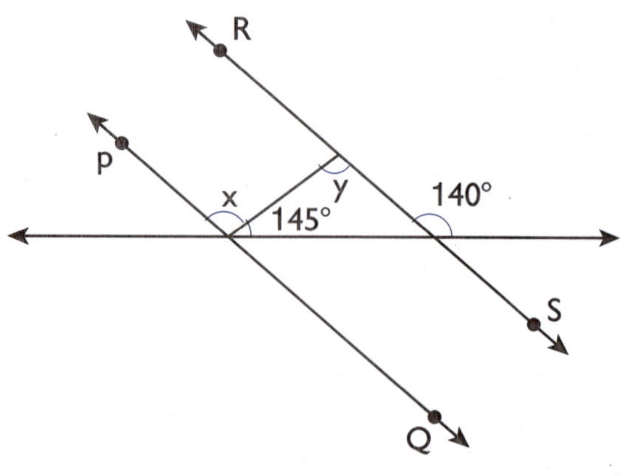

7. In the given figure, find the value of x and y.

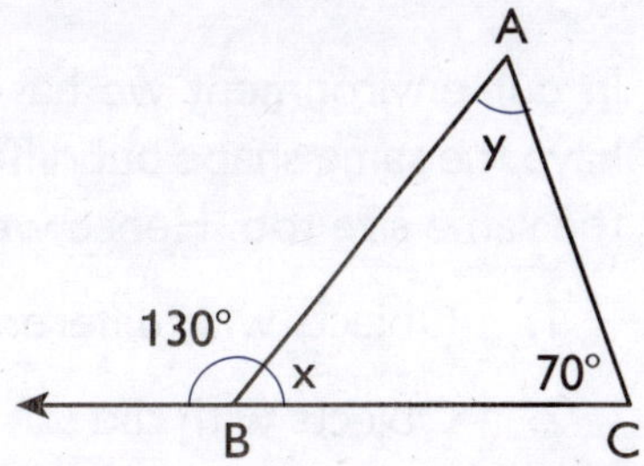

8. In the given figure, find the value of angles x, y and z.

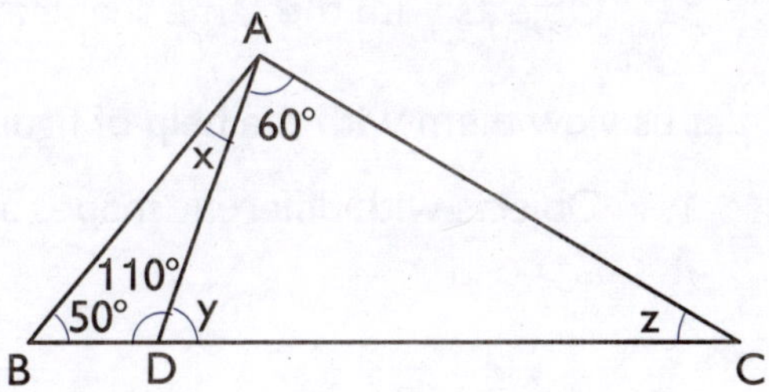

9. Find x, y and z in the given figure, where ABC is a triangle and DE || BC.

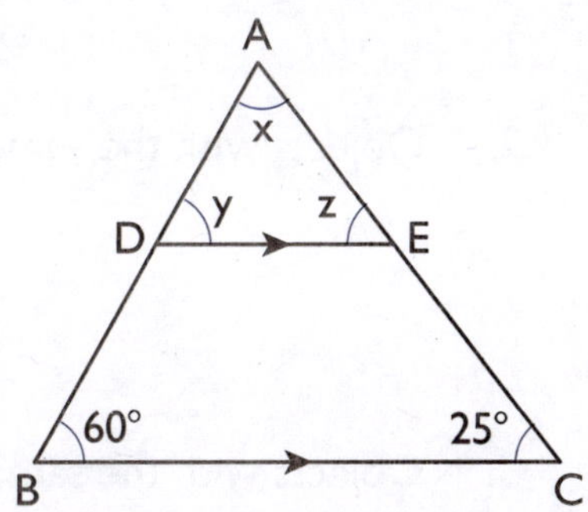

10. Fill in the blanks.
    a. In a right-angled triangle, the ________ is the longest side.
    b. The numbers 10, 24, 26 form a Pythagorean triplet because ________.
    c. In a right angled triangle, if c denotes the length of the hypotenuse and a and b are the lengths of the other sides then c^2 is _______.
11. How much shorter it is to walk diagonally across a rectangular field that is 80 m long and 60 m wide than along two of its adjacent sides?
12. The square of the hypotenuse of a square is 128 cm^2. Find the length of the side of the square.
13. Find the length of a ladder kept at a distance of 16 m from the foot of a wall that just reaches a window at a height of 30 m.
14. Show that the sum of the exterior angles of a triangle ABC is 360°.
15. The angles of a triangle are $(x - 5)°$, $(x + 15)°$ and $(2x - 30)°$. Find the measure of the angles.

CHAPTER 11

Congruence

In our environment we have different objects that have different shapes and sizes. Some have the same shape but different size. There are some others that have the same shape and the same size too. Hence we can classify them in three categories.

1. Objects with different shapes and different sizes.
2. Objects with the same shape but different sizes.
3. Objects with the same shape and the same size.

Let us view them with the help of figures.

1. Objects with different shapes and different sizes.

2. Objects with the same shape but different sizes.

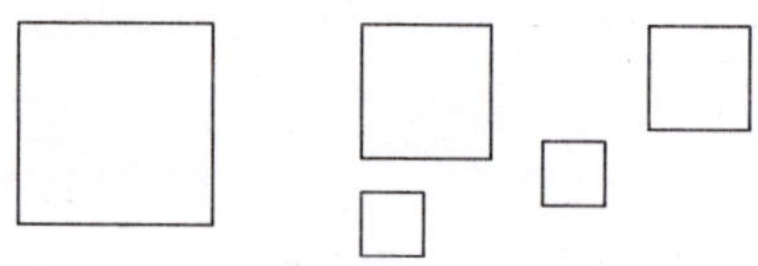

3. Objects with the same shape and the same size.

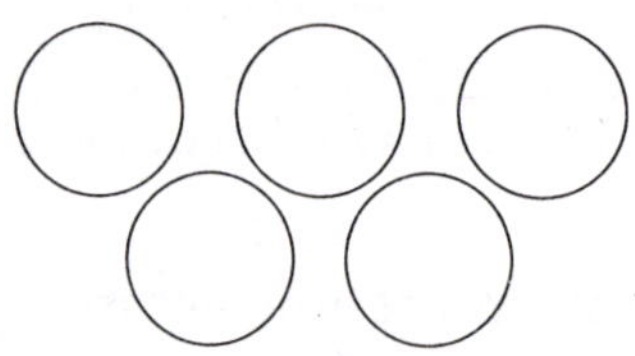

Articles manufactured in a factory are of the same size and same shape. A jam bottle, notebooks, cars of the same model, school uniform are a few examples.

In this chapter, we shall study objects with the same shape and the same size. Such figures are identical figures.

Figures that have the same shape and same size are said to be congruent figures or are said to be congruent to each other. The symbol for congruency is $\cong$. If ABCD is a square and it has the same size as square PQRS, then we say that ABCD is congruent to PQRS. It is expressed symbolically as PQRS $\cong$ ABCD.

Alert!

To show two equal numbers or values, we use the 'equal to' symbol, for example, $10 = 10$. To show two plane figures of the same size and shape, we use the 'congruence' symbol ($\cong$) for example, $\triangle ABC \cong \triangle PQR$.

Congruence of Plane Figures

Just by observing two figures, it may not be possible to decide whether the size of the two plane figures is the same or not. The easiest way to decide if figures of the same shape have the same size is to cut them and place them one over the other. If one can completely cover the other then it can be said they have the same size and so are congruent figures.

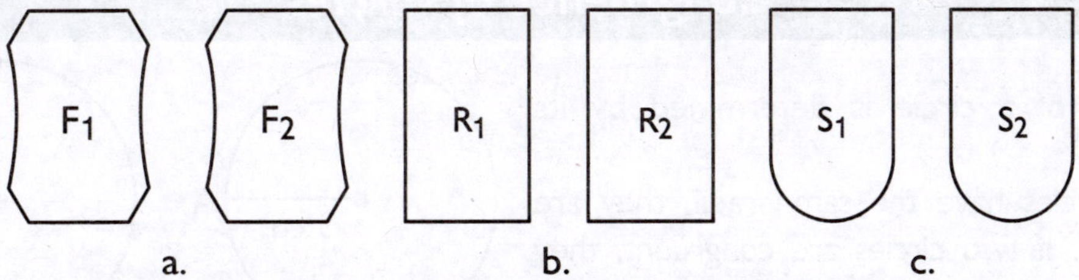

The figures in a, b and c seem to be of the same size. If we cut them out and place them one over the other, that is, use the method of superposition, they should cover each other completely. If that happens, we conclude that the two figures are congruent. We can write it as:

$$F_1 \cong F_2, \quad R_1 \cong R_2 \quad \text{and} \quad S_1 \cong S_2$$

Congruence of Line Segments

Line segments have only length. So if two line segments have the same length, they should be congruent.

Let us consider $\overline{AB}$ and $\overline{CD}$.

If we use a tracing paper and make a copy of $\overline{AB}$ and place it on $\overline{CD}$, we find that both segments superpose each other. So, $\overline{AB} \cong \overline{CD}$.

For congruence, both the figures must cover each other completely.

If two line segments have equal length, they are congruent. If two line segments are congruent, they have equal length.

Congruence of Angles

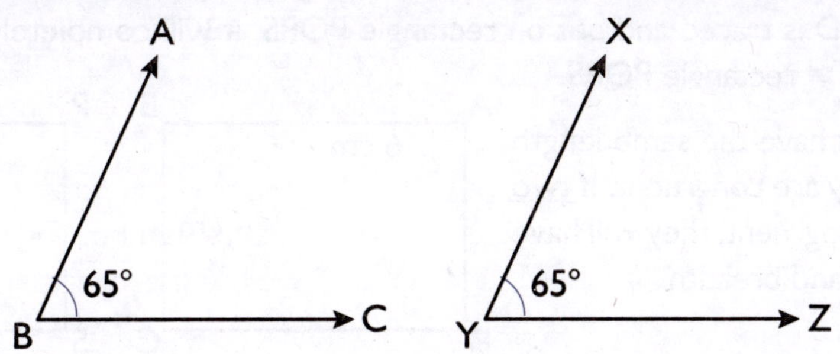

In the given figures, we have two angles, $\angle ABC$ and $\angle XYZ$. If we trace $\angle ABC$ and place it over $\angle XYZ$ so that the vertex B coincides with vertex Y, the angles will cover each other completely and so are congruent. Hence, $\angle ABC \cong \angle XYZ$.

If two angles have the same measure, they are congruent. If two angles are congruent, they have the same measure.

Congruence of Circles

The size of a circle is determined by its radius.

If two circles have the same radii, they are congruent. If two circles are congruent, they have the same radii.

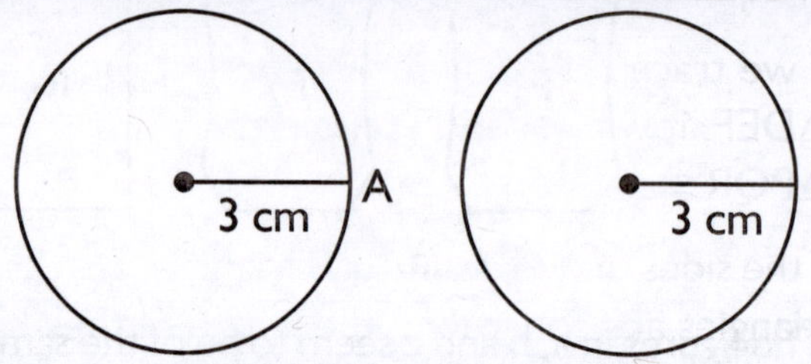

Congruence of Squares

We know that a square has four equal sides and that all its four angles measure 90°. Hence, the size of a square depends on the length of its side. If the length of the sides of two squares is the same then they will be congruent.

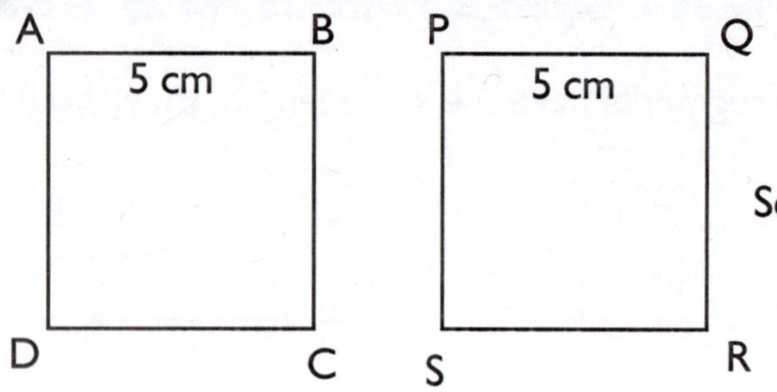

Square ABCD $\cong$ Square PQRS

If two squares have the same length, they are congruent. If two squares are congruent, the length of their sides will be equal.

Congruence of Rectangles

We know that a rectangle has four sides and the opposite sides are equal. The four angles of a rectangle are equal and each is 90°. The shape and size of a rectangle depends on its length and breadth.

If rectangle ABCD is traced and put on rectangle PQRS, it will completely cover it. Hence, rectangle ABCD $\cong$ rectangle PQRS.

If two rectangles have the same length and breadth, they are congruent. If two rectangles are congruent, they will have the same length and breadth.

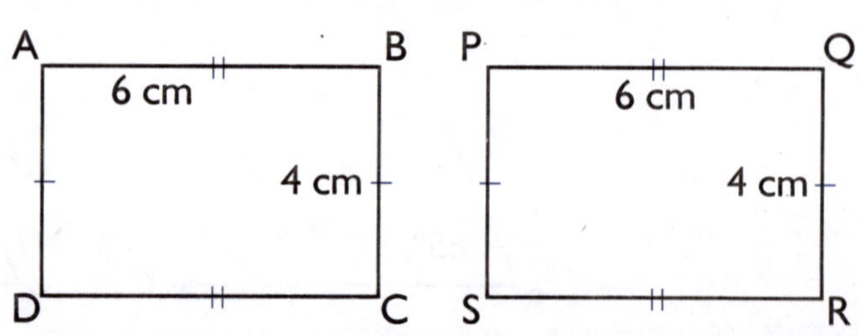

Congruence of Equilateral Triangles

An equilateral triangle has three equal sides and all its angles measure 60° each. However, all equilateral triangles are not congruent. For equilateral triangles to be equal, their sides should be of equal measure.

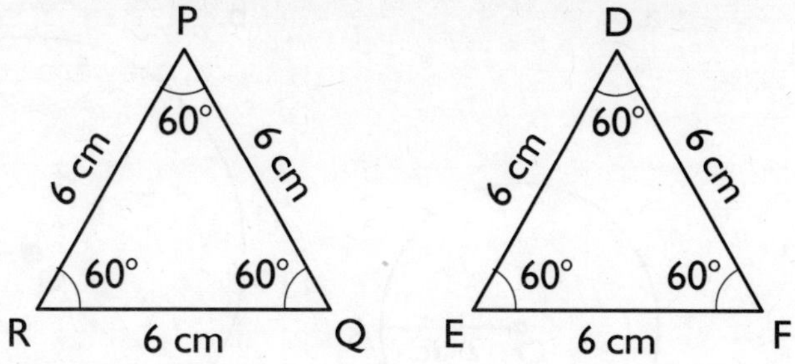

If we trace $\triangle PQR$ and superpose it on $\triangle DEF$, it will cover it completely. Thus $\triangle PQR \cong \triangle DEF$.

If the sides of two equilateral triangles are the same then they are congruent. If two equilateral triangles are congruent, the length of their sides are equal.

Conditions of Congruence

Figure	Congruence depends upon
Line segments	Length of the line segments
Angles	Measure of the angle
Circles	Measure of radius
Squares	Length of a side
Rectangles	Length and breadth
Equilateral triangles	Length of a side

Practice Exercise 11.1

1. Draw line segments congruent to the following using a ruler.

a.

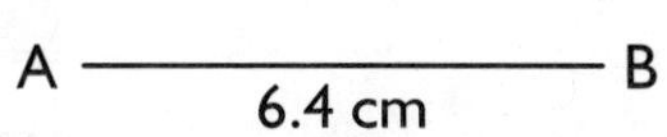

b.

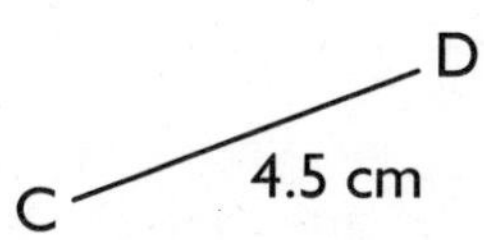

c.

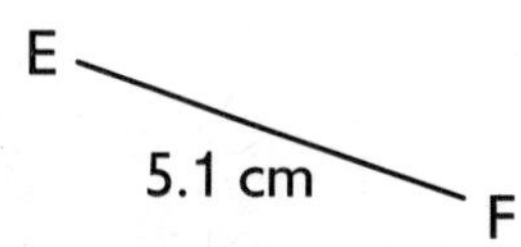

2. Draw angles congruent to the following angles using a protractor.

a.

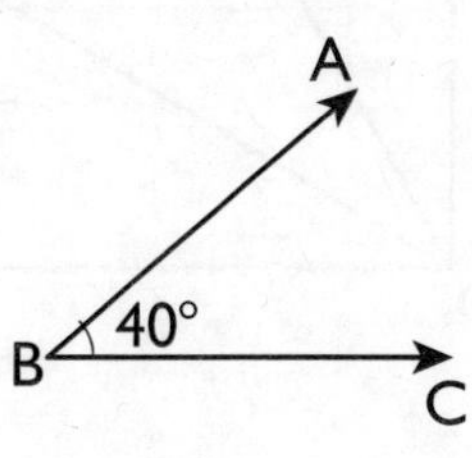

b.

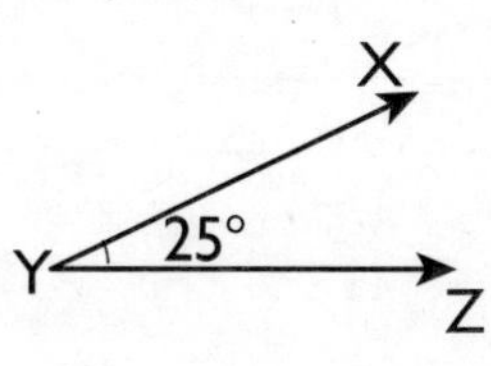

c.

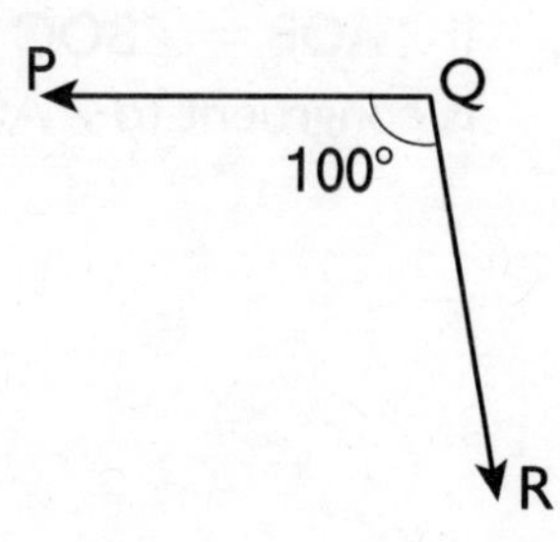

3. In the following circles, identify the congruent pair and give reasons for their congruency.

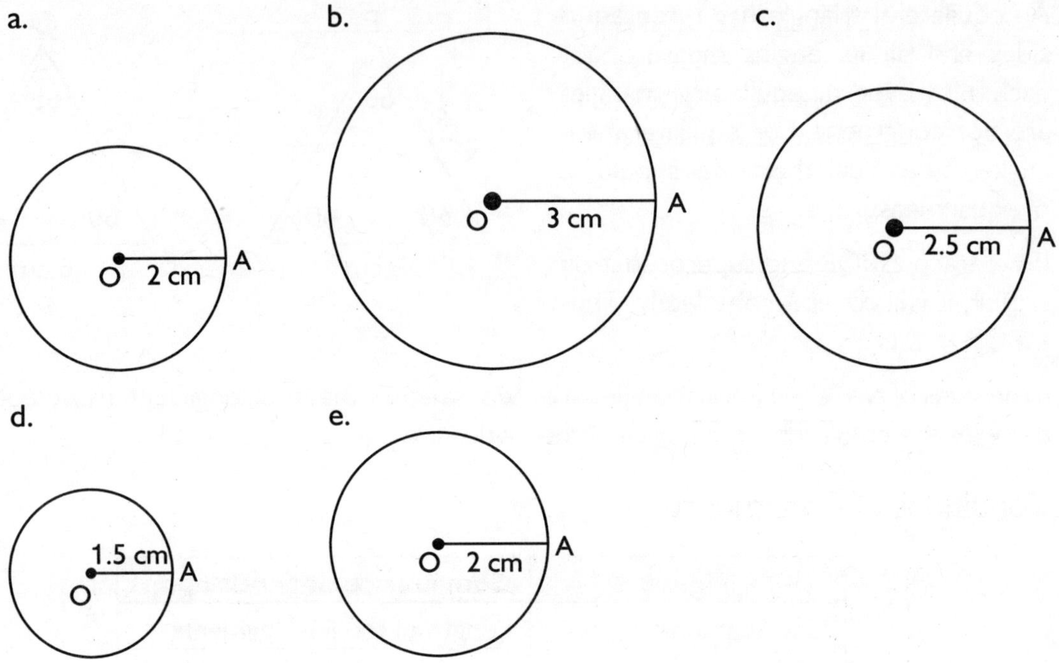

4. If $\angle AOB = \angle COD$, show that $\angle AOC \cong \angle BOD$.

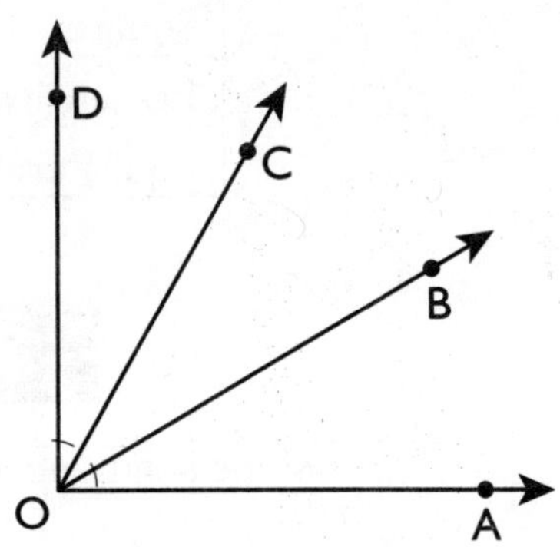

5. If $\angle AOB = \angle BOC = \angle COD$, name the angle which is congruent to $\angle AOC$.

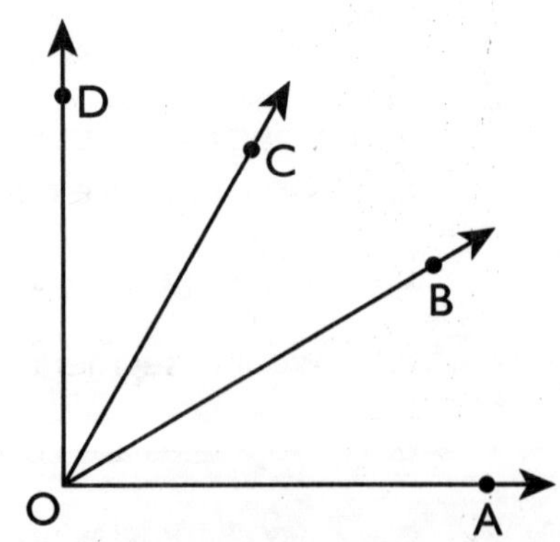

6. Identify the pairs of congruent rectangles from the figures given below.

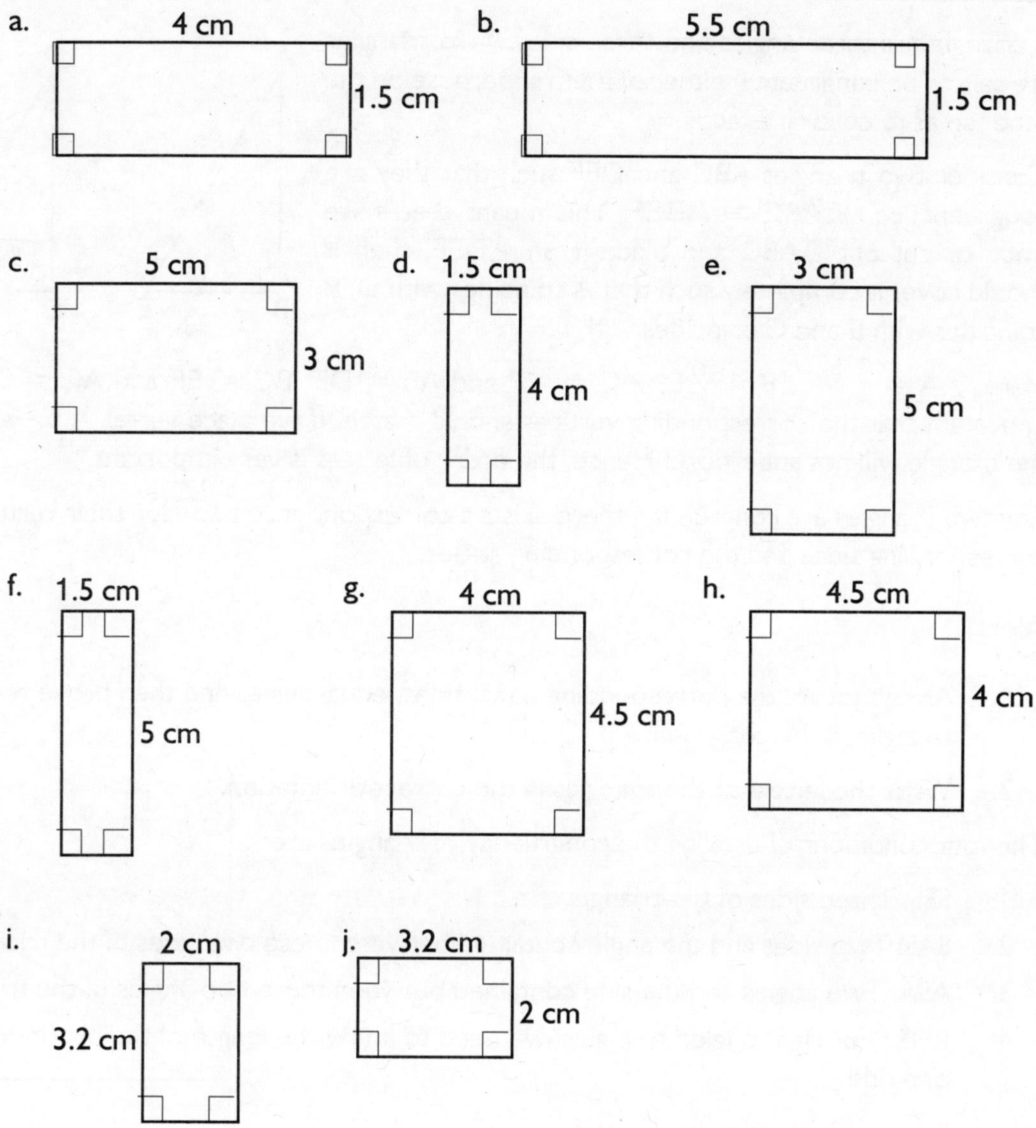

7. Draw two congruent equilateral triangles ABC and PQR using a protractor and ruler.

8. Fill in the blanks.

   a. Two circles are congruent if their __________ is the same.

   b. If the length of a side is same, then two __________ are congruent.

   c. Two line segments are congruent if __________.

   d. Two angles are congruent if __________.

   e. Two rectangles are congruent if their __________ and __________ are the same.

Congruence of Triangles

A triangle has three angles and three sides. Two triangles are said to be congruent if either of them superpose on the other so as to cover it exactly.

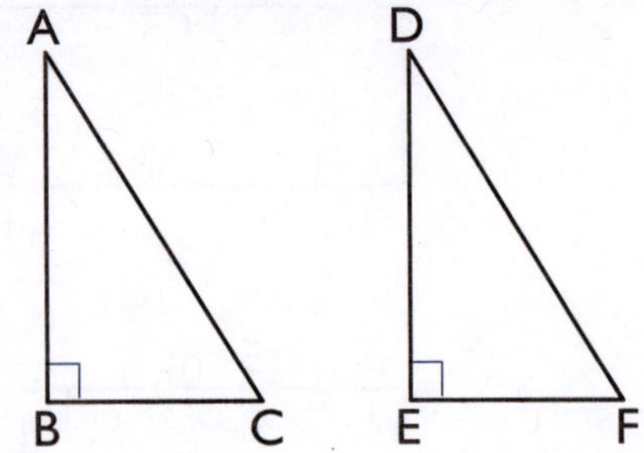

Consider two triangles ABC and DEF such that they are congruent, i.e., $\triangle ABC \cong \triangle DEF$. This means that if we trace or cut out $\triangle ABC$ and place it on $\triangle DEF$, then it should cover it completely such that A coincides with D, B coincides with E and C coincides with F.

Here, $\angle A = \angle D$, $\angle B = \angle E$, $\angle C = \angle F$ and AB = DE, BC = EF and AC = DF. It is important that the corresponding vertices should match. If we place vertex A on vertex E, the triangle will not superpose. Hence, the order of letters is very important.

Any two triangles are congruent if there exists a correspondence between their vertices, the corresponding sides and the corresponding angles.

Alert!

1. Always locate the corresponding equal sides, equal angles and then prove two triangles to be congruent.
2. Write the letters of the triangles in the correct orientation.

The four conditions of proving the congruency of triangles are:

1. SSS: Three sides of the triangle
2. SAS: Two sides and the angle contained between these two sides of the triangle.
3. ASA: Two angles and the side contained between these two angles of the triangle.
4. RHS : For right-angled triangles, we need to know the length of the hypotenuse and one side.

We shall discuss each of them in detail.

The SSS Condition of Congruence

When the length of each of the three sides of a triangle is known, its exact shape and size is also known.

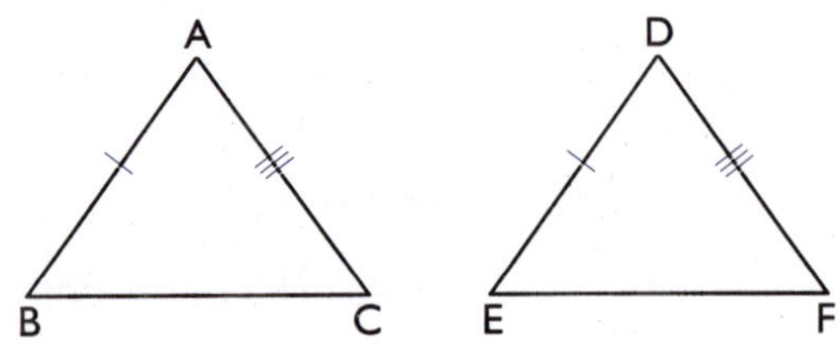

Draw a $\triangle ABC$ with AB = 5 cm, BC = 6.2 cm and CA = 4 cm. Draw another triangle DEF with DE = 5 cm, EF = 6.2 cm, FD = 4 cm.

If we trace $\triangle ABC$ and superpose it on $\triangle DEF$ then A will coincide with D; we write it as $A \leftrightarrow D$, $B \leftrightarrow E$ and $C \leftrightarrow F$. Thus, AB = DE, BC = EF and AC = DF. The two triangles will cover each other exactly.

Thus, if three sides of a triangle are equal to the three corresponding sides of another triangle, the two triangles are congruent.

Example 1: Two triangles, ABC and XYZ are given. Check whether the two triangles are congruent. State the congruence condition. Is $\angle Z = \angle C$?

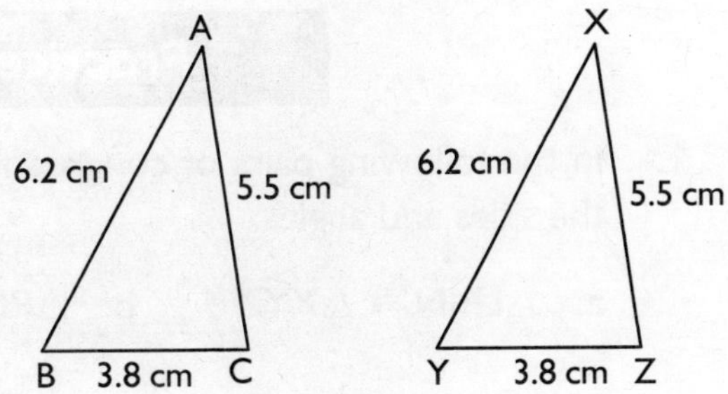

Here, AB = XY = 6.2 cm

BC = YZ = 3.8 cm

AC = XZ = 5.5 cm

Three sides of a triangle are equal to three sides of another triangle.

Hence, $\triangle ABC \cong \triangle XYZ$ (by SSS condition)

$\angle Z = \angle C$ (they are corresponding parts of congruent triangle)

Alert!

"Corresponding parts of congruent triangles" is written in short as CPCT. After proving that the triangles are congruent, we can apply and write this condition to show corresponding sides or angles to be equal.

Example 2: In the given figure, PQR and PQS are two triangles with QR = PS and PR = QS. Name the two congruent triangles.

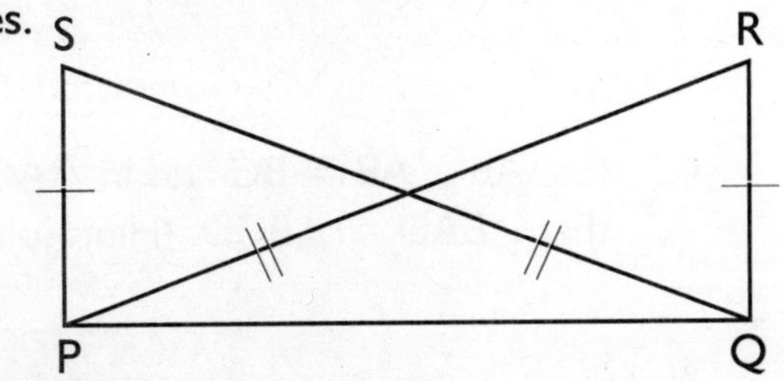

In $\triangle PQR$ and $\triangle PQS$,

QR = PS (given)

PR = QS (given)

PQ = PQ (common side)

We can see that $P \leftrightarrow Q$, $Q \leftrightarrow P$ and $R \leftrightarrow S$.

$\therefore$ $\triangle PQR \cong \triangle QPS$ (by SSS condition)

Example 3: In the given figure, ABC and DAC are two triangles, where AB = AD and BC = DC.

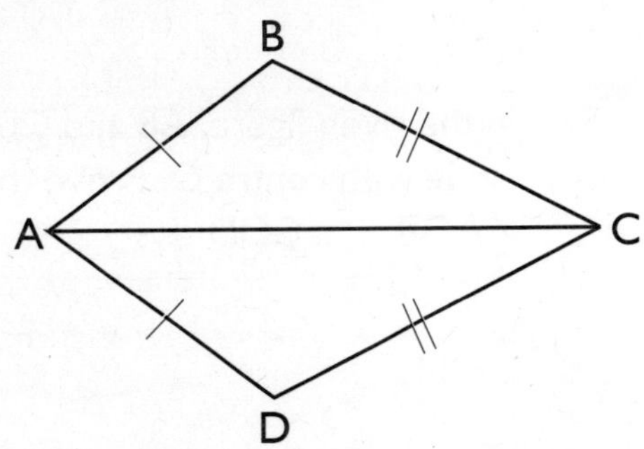

Show that

a. $\triangle ABC \cong \triangle ADC$.

b. $\overline{AC}$ bisects $\angle BAD$.

In $\triangle ABC$ and $\triangle ADC$,

AB = AD (given)

BC = DC (given)

AC = AC (common side)

So $\triangle ABC \cong \triangle ADC$ (by SSS condition)

Since the triangles are congruent,

$\angle BAC = \angle DAC$ (CPCT)

So, $\overline{AC}$ bisects $\angle BAD$.

Practice Exercise 11.2

1. In the following pairs of congruent triangles, state the correspondence between the sides and angles.

   a. $\triangle LMN \cong \triangle XYZ$ b. $\triangle PQR \cong \triangle DEF$ c. $\triangle GHI \cong \triangle MNO$

2. In the given figure, AB = AD and BC = DC. Show that $\triangle ABC \cong \triangle ADC$. Write the condition applied. Show that $\angle B = \angle D$.

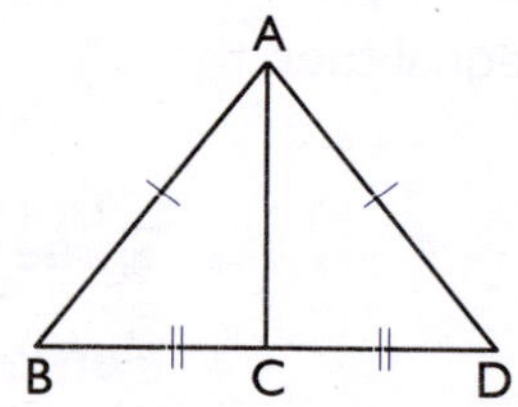

3. ABCD is a rectangle and AC is a diagonal of the rectangle. Show that the diagonal divides the rectangle into two congruent triangles. Name the triangles and conditions applied to prove that they are congruent.

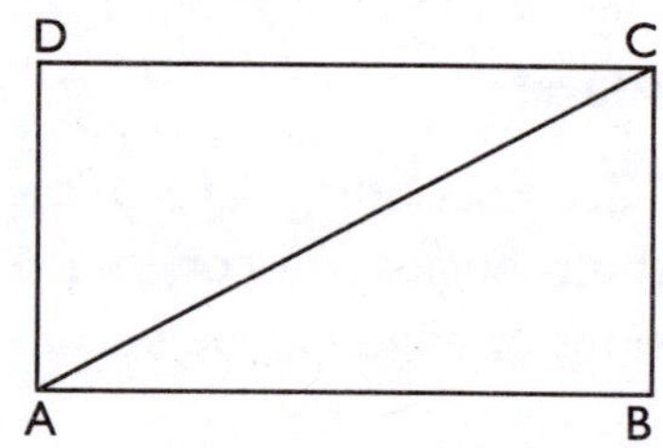

4. In $\triangle ABC$, AB = BC and in $\triangle ACD$, AD = CD. Prove that $\angle BAD = \angle BCD$. (Hint: Join BD.)

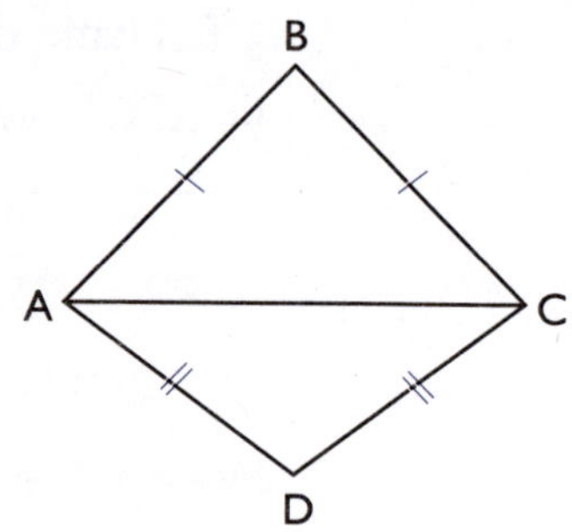

5. In the given figure, AB and CD are equal chords of a circle with centre O. Prove that $\triangle AOB \cong \triangle COD$ and $\angle AOB = \angle COD$.

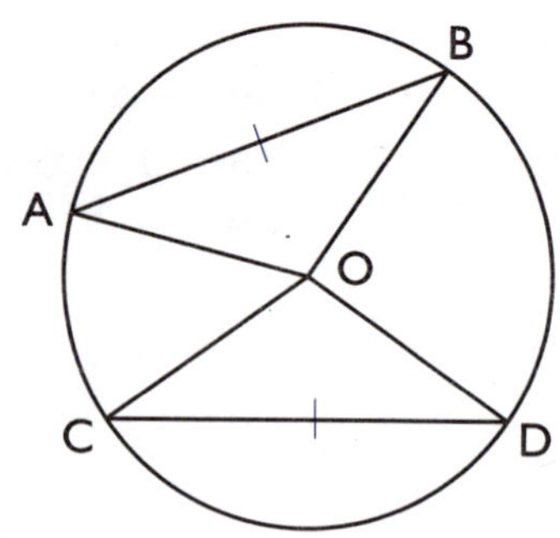

The SAS Condition of Congruence

If two sides and the angle contained by them are known, we know the exact shape and size of a triangle.

Draw a triangle ABC with AB = 5 cm, $\angle A = 50°$ and AC = 4 cm. Draw another triangle PQR with PQ = 5 cm, $\angle P = 50°$ and PR = 4 cm.

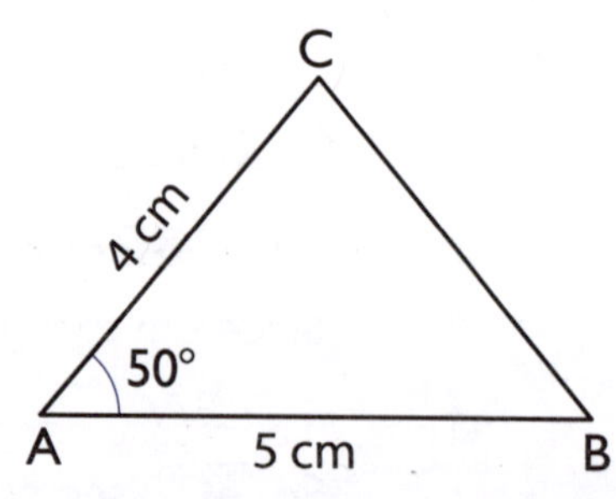

If we trace $\triangle ABC$ and superpose it on $\triangle PQR$, then A will coincide with P, that is $A \leftrightarrow P$, $B \leftrightarrow Q$ and $C \leftrightarrow R$. Also, $AB = PQ$, $BC = QR$ and $AC = PR$.

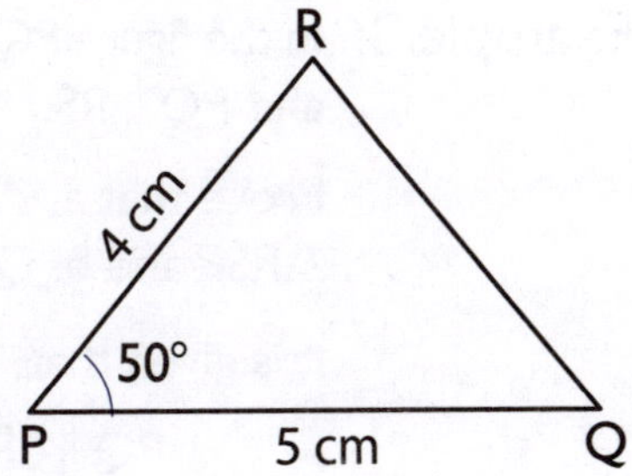

Thus, the two triangles will cover each other exactly.

Hence, if two triangles have two corresponding sides that are equal and the angle contained by the two sides is also equal then the two triangles are congruent.

Example 1: Two triangles ABC and DEF are given. Are they congruent? State the property for congruence. List the other sides and angles that are equal.

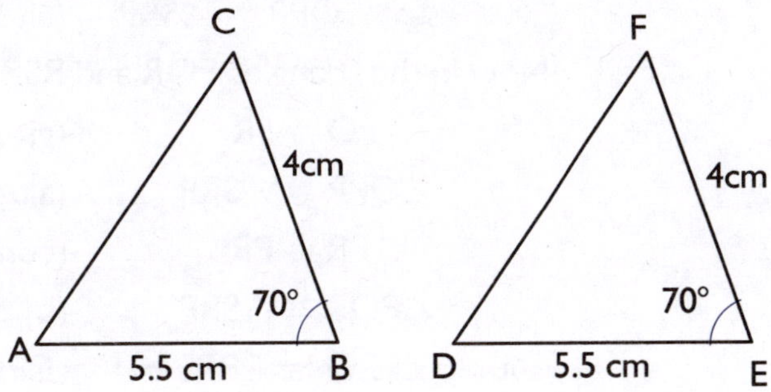

Here, $AB = DE = 5.5$ cm

$BC = EF = 4$ cm

$\angle ABC = \angle DEF = 70°$

So, $\triangle ABC \cong \triangle DEF$ (by SAS condition)

Hence, $\left.\begin{array}{l}\angle A = \angle D \\ \angle C = \angle F \\ AC = DF\end{array}\right\}$ (CPCT)

Example 2: In an isosceles triangle, show that the angles opposite to equal sides are equal.

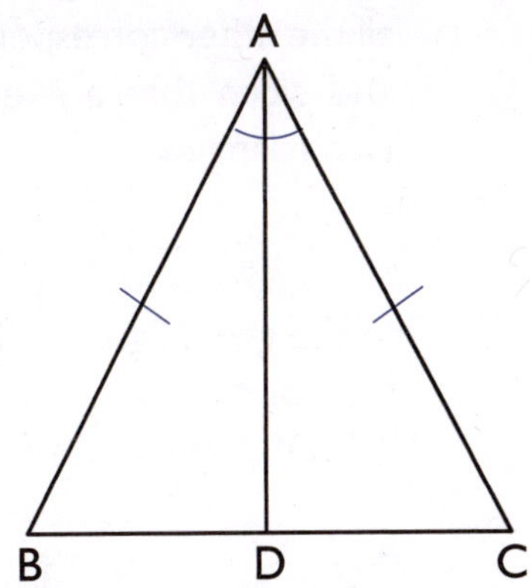

The triangle ABC is an isosceles triangle with $AB = AC$.

We have to prove that $\angle B = \angle C$.

We draw AD as the angular bisector of $\angle A$, that begins from A to meet base BC at point D.

In the triangles ABD and ACD,

$AB = AC$ (given)

$\angle BAD = \angle CAD$ (AD is the angular bisector by construction)

$AD = AD$ (common side)

Therefore $\triangle ABD \cong \triangle ACD$ (by SAS condition)

Hence, $\left.\begin{array}{l}BD = CD \\ \angle B = \angle C\end{array}\right\}$ (CPCT)

Thus, in an isosceles triangle, the angles opposite to equal sides are equal.

Example 3: In the figure PQRS, PQ = RS and PQ || RS.

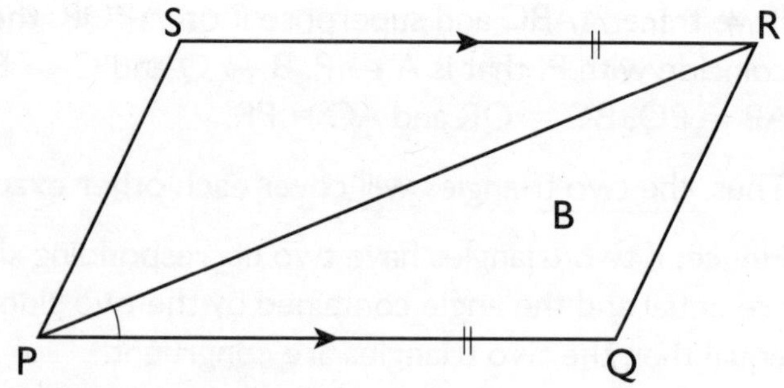

Prove that a. $\triangle PQR \cong \triangle RSP$ and b. QR || PS

It is given that,

PQ || SR and PR is the transversal

So, $\angle QPR = \angle SRP$ (alternate angles)

Now in the triangles PQR and RSP,

PQ = SR	(given)
$\angle QPR = \angle SRP$	(alternate angles)
PR = PR	(common side)
$\therefore$ $\triangle PQR \cong \triangle SRP$	(by SAS condition)
$\angle PRQ = \angle RPS$	(CPCT)

But these are alternate angles for QR and PS with PR as transversal,

Therefore, QR || PS.

Practice Exercise 11.3

1. Are the two given triangles congruent? If they are, state the condition for congruency. Name all the other corresponding angles and sides that are equal in the two triangles.

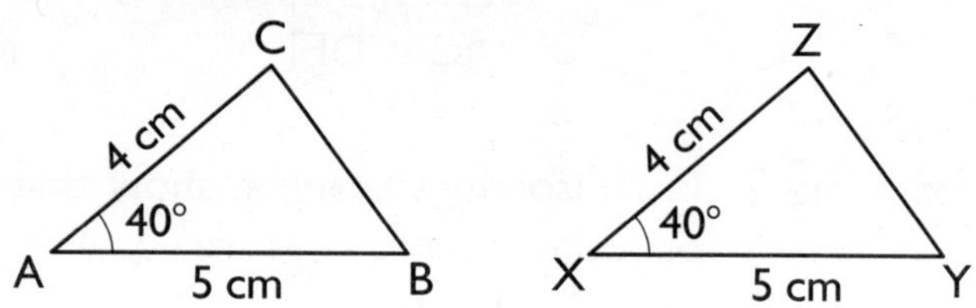

2. In the given figure, MN and RS are two line segments that bisect each other at O. Show that $\triangle MOR \cong \triangle NOS$. Also name the angles that are equal.

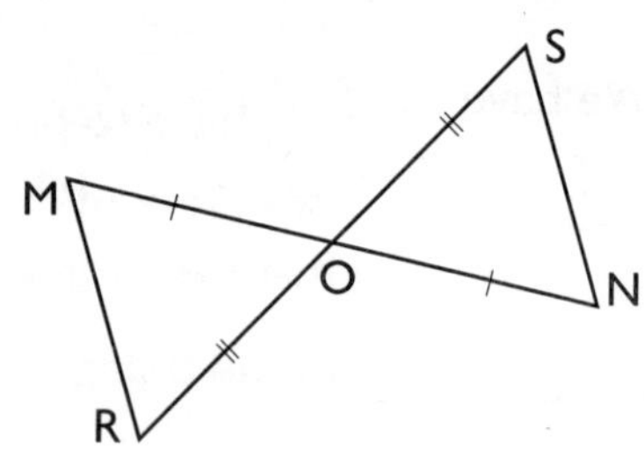

3. In the given figure, show that $\triangle EFG \cong \triangle EHG$. Also is EF = EH? Give reasons for your answer.

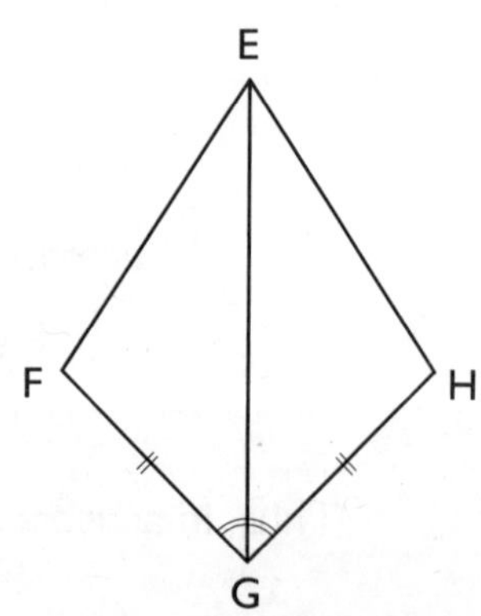

4. In the given figure, BD = CF, EF = AB and $\angle EFD = \angle ABC$. Prove that $\triangle DEF \cong \triangle CAB$.

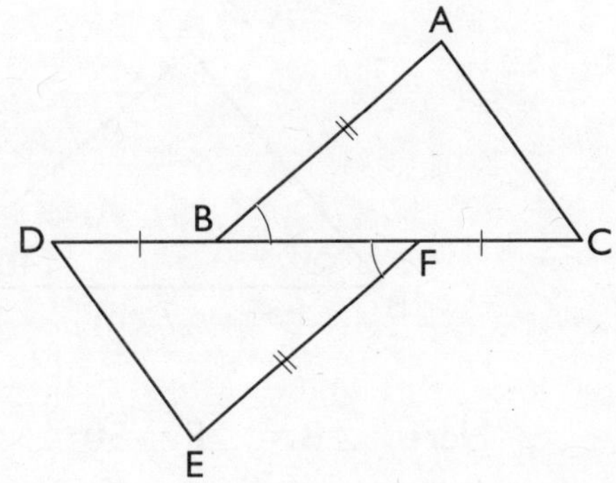

5. In an isosceles triangle ABC, AB = AC. If D and E are the mid points of AB and AC respectively, prove that CD = BE.

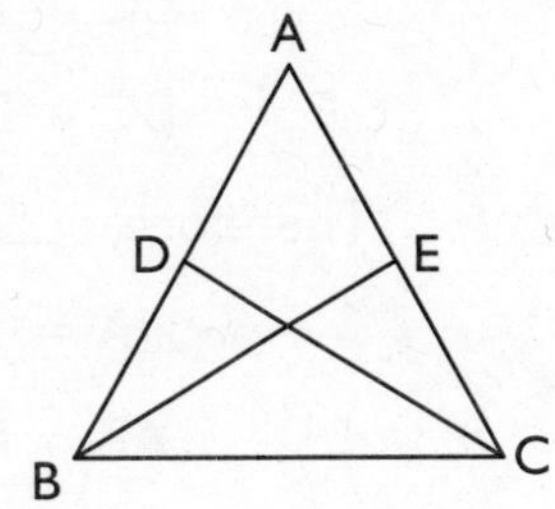

The ASA Condition of Congruence

The measures of two angles of a triangle and the included side help us to construct a unique triangle.

Look at the two triangles given below.

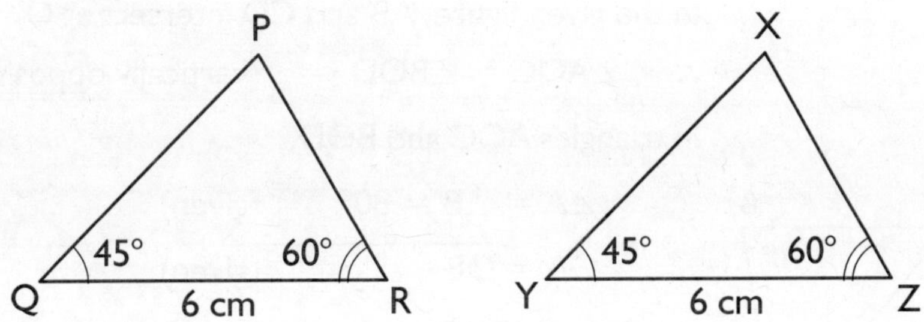

We have $\angle Q = \angle Y = 45°$

$\angle R = \angle Z = 60°$

QR = YZ = 6 cm

If we trace $\triangle PQR$ and superpose it on $\triangle XYZ$ then it will completely cover it, such that $P \leftrightarrow X$, $Q \leftrightarrow Y$, $R \leftrightarrow Z$, $\angle Q = \angle Y$ and $\angle R = \angle Z$.

Any two triangles are congruent if two angles and the included side of one triangle are equal to the corresponding two angles and the included side of the other triangle.

Example 1: In the given triangles, the measures of certain elements are given. Are the triangles congruent? State the condition of congruency. Also write down the remaining sides and angles which are equal.

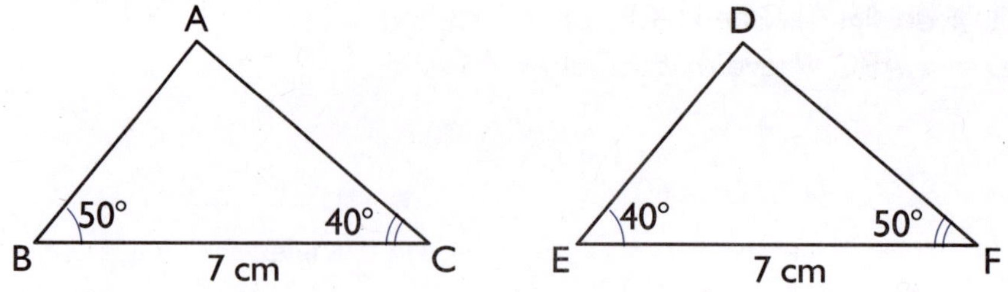

Here $\angle B = \angle F = 50^\circ$

$\angle C = \angle E = 40^\circ$

$BC = EF = 7$ cm

Therefore, $\triangle ABC \cong \triangle DFE$ (by ASA condition)

$\left.\begin{array}{l}\angle A = \angle D \\ AB = DF \\ AC = DE\end{array}\right\}$ (CPCT)

Example 2: In the given figure, $\overline{AB}$ and $\overline{CD}$ intersect at O such that OA = OB and $\angle A = \angle B = 80^\circ$. Show that the triangles AOC and BOD are congruent and OC = OD.

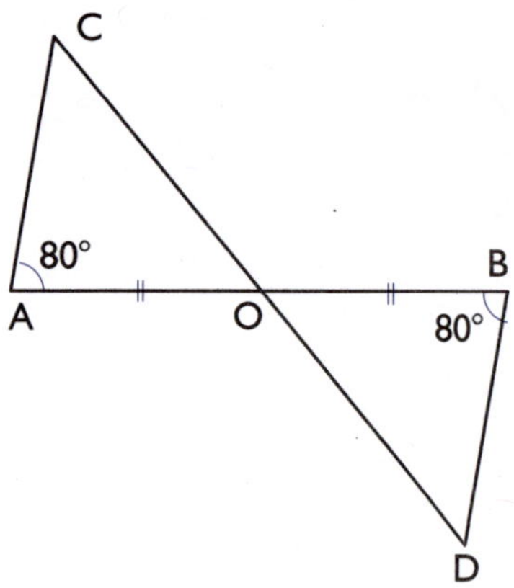

In the given figure, $\overline{AB}$ and $\overline{CD}$ intersect at O,

$\therefore$ $\angle AOC = \angle BOD$ (vertically opposite angles)

In triangles AOC and BOD,

$\angle A = \angle B = 80^\circ$ (given)

$OA = OB$ (given)

$\angle AOC = \angle BOD$ (vertically opposite angles)

$\therefore$ $\triangle AOC \cong \triangle BOD$ (by ASA condition)

Hence, OC = OD (CPCT)

Example 3: The two triangles ABC and DEF are such that AC = DF = 4 cm, $\angle A = 30^\circ$, $\angle B = 90^\circ$, $\angle F = 60^\circ$ and $\angle E = 90^\circ$.

Is $\triangle ABC \cong \triangle DEF$? If yes, give the condition of congruency. Also is AB = DE?

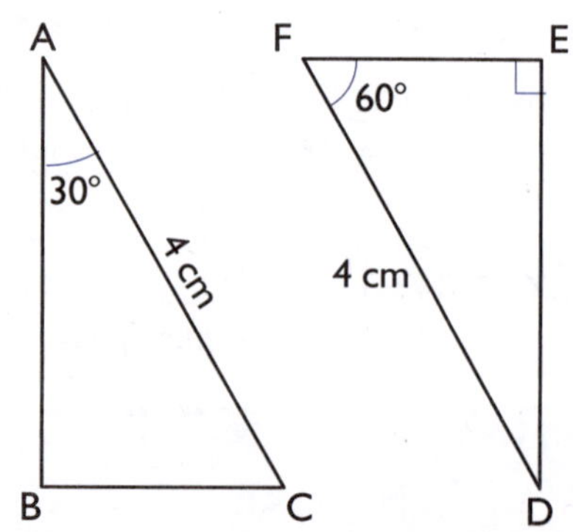

In the triangles ABC and DEF,

$\angle B = \angle E = 90^\circ$

$\angle BAC = 30^\circ$ $\therefore$ $\angle BCA = 60^\circ$

$\angle EFD = 60^\circ$ $\therefore$ $\angle FDE = 30^\circ$

(sum of the angles of a triangle is 180°)

$\therefore$ In triangles ABC and DEF,

$\angle BAC = \angle EDF = 30°$

AC = FD = 4 cm (given)

$\angle BCA = \angle EFD = 60°$

$\therefore$ By ASA the triangles are congruent.

Hence, AB = DE (CPCT)

Practice Exercise 11.4

1. The line segment $\overline{AB}$ intersects $\overline{CD}$ at O, such that CO = OD and AC || BD. Show that $\triangle AOC \cong \triangle BOD$ and write the condition of congruency.

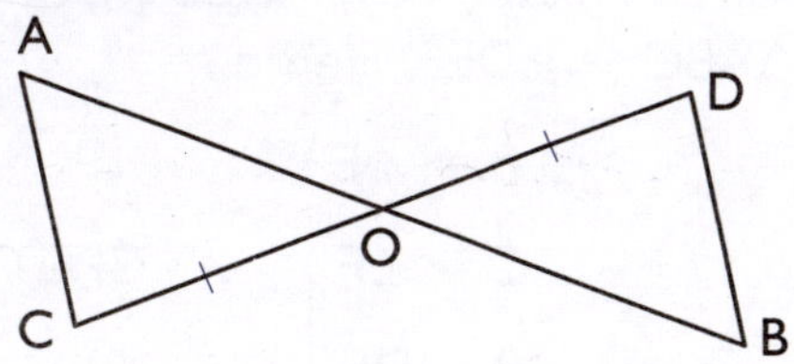

2. In the given figure, $\angle A = \angle B = 90°$. If AC = BD, prove that AO = OB.

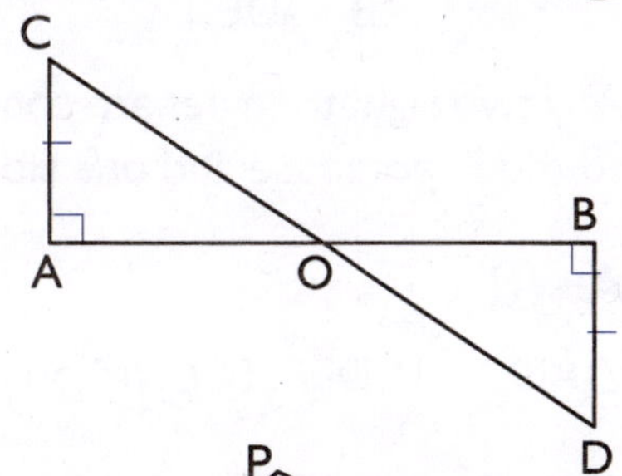

3. In the given figure, PQRS is a quadrilateral. If $\overline{QS}$ is the angle bisector of $\angle PQR$ and $\angle PSR$, show that $\triangle PQS \cong \triangle RQS$. Also prove that PS = RS.

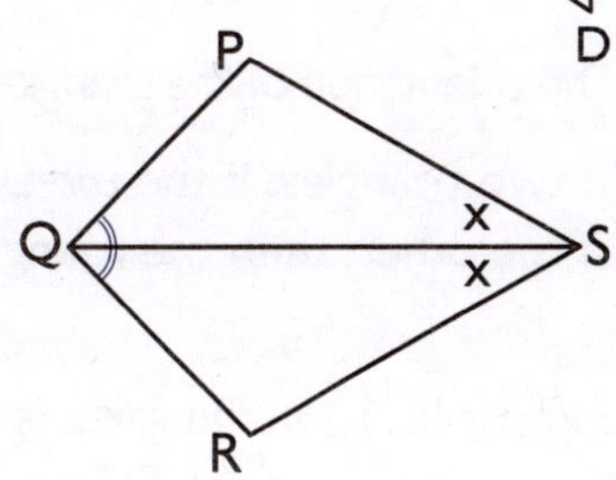

4. In the given figure, $\triangle LMN$ is an isosceles triangle with ML = NL. Also OL is the angular bisector of $\angle MLN$.

   Use the ASA condition to prove that $\triangle MLO \cong \triangle NLO$. Also show that O is the mid point of MN.

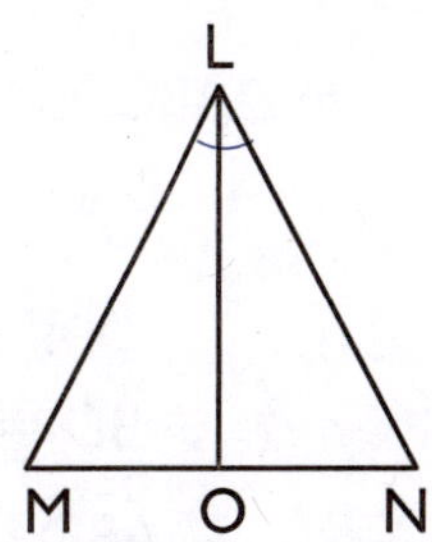

5. The figure ABCD is a quadrilateral in which AB || DC and AD || BC. The segment AC is the diagonal. Use the ASA condition of congruency to prove that AB = CD.

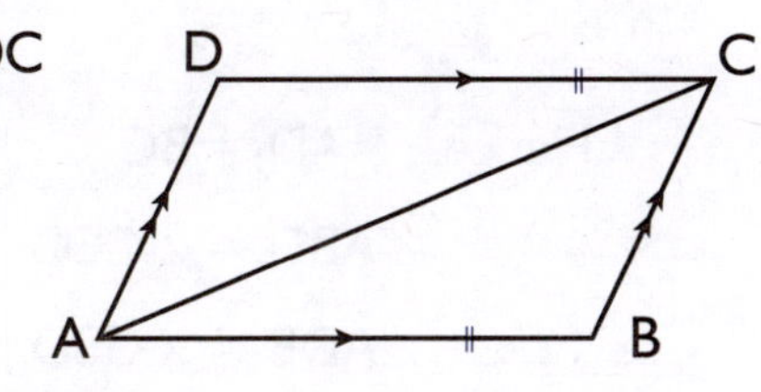

The RHS Condition of Congruence

The size and shape of a right triangle are fixed if the length of the hypotenuse and one side of the triangle are known.

Consider the two right triangles ABC and DEF.

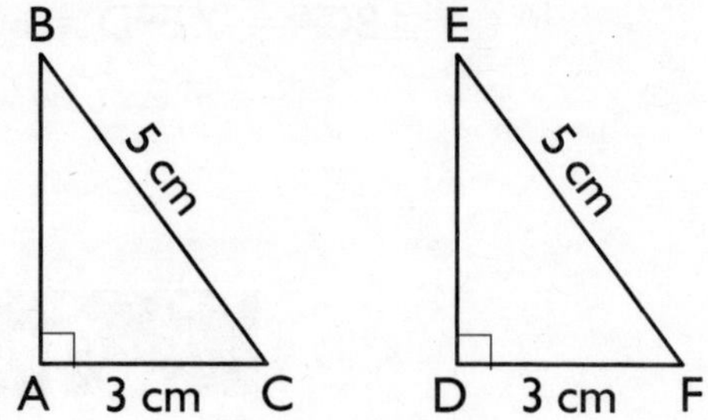

Here, $\angle A = \angle D = 90°$

$AC = DF = 3$ cm

$BC = EF = 5$ cm

If we trace $\triangle ABC$ and place it on $\triangle DEF$, it will completely cover it. So we can say that $\triangle ABC \cong \triangle DEF$. Hence,

$$\left.\begin{aligned} \angle B &= \angle E \\ \angle C &= \angle F \\ AB &= DE \end{aligned}\right\} \quad \text{(CPCT)}$$

Any two right triangles are congruent if the hypotenuse and one side of one triangle are equal to the hypotenuse and one side of the other triangle.

Alert!

$\triangle ABC \cong \triangle DEF$. But we cannot write $\triangle ABC \cong \triangle EFD$.

The orientation of the triangles should be correct and according to the condition of congruency.

In two triangles, if the *three angles* of one triangle are respectively equal to the three angles of the other, then the triangles are *not* necessarily congruent.

Example 1: In the given figure, $\angle A$ and $\angle C$ are right angles and $AB = CD$. Show that $\triangle ABD \cong \triangle CDB$ by the RHS condition. Show that the other elements are also equal.

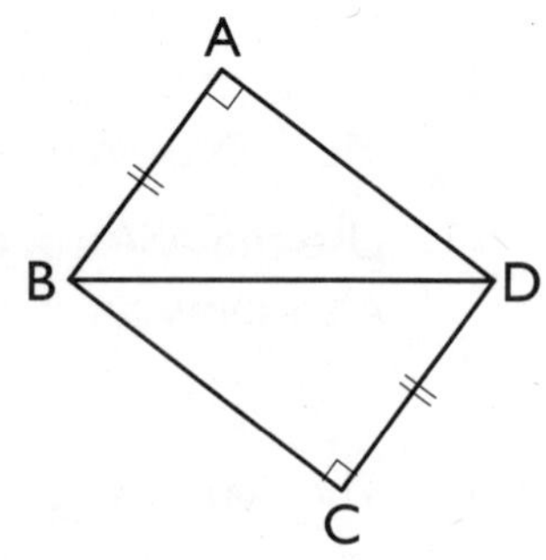

In $\triangle ABD$ and $\triangle CDB$,

$\angle A = \angle C = 90°$	(given)
$AB = CD$	(given)
$BD = DB$	(common hypotenuse)
$\therefore \quad \triangle ABD = \triangle CDB$	(by RHS condition of congruency)

Hence, $$\left.\begin{aligned} AD &= BC \\ \angle ABD &= \angle CDB \\ \angle ADB &= \angle CBD \end{aligned}\right\} \quad \text{(CPCT)}$$

Example 2: In the given figure $\triangle ABC$ is an isosceles triangle with $AB = AC$. The segment AD is perpendicular to BC. Show that $\triangle ABD \cong \triangle ACD$, by the RHS condition. Also show that $BD = CD$.

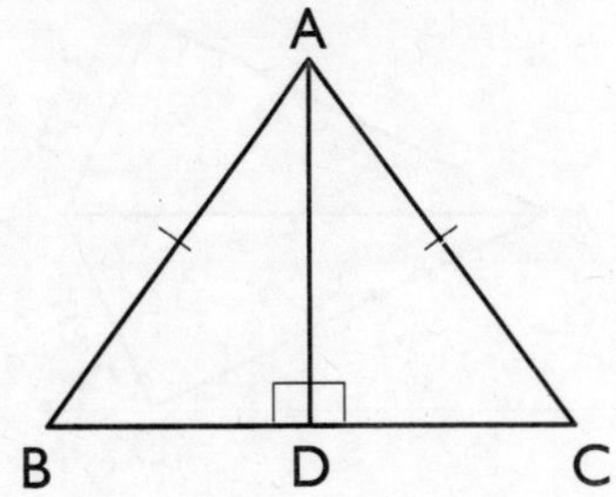

In $\triangle ABD$ and $\triangle ACD$,

	$AB = AC$	(given)
	$\angle ADB = \angle ADC = 90^\circ$	(given)
	$AD = AD$	(common side)
$\therefore$	$\triangle ABD \cong \triangle ACD$	(by RHS condition of congruency)

Hence, $BD = CD$ (CPCT)

Example 3: In the given figure, $PL \perp OA$ and $PM \perp OB$ such that $PL = PM$. Prove that OP bisects $\angle AOB$.

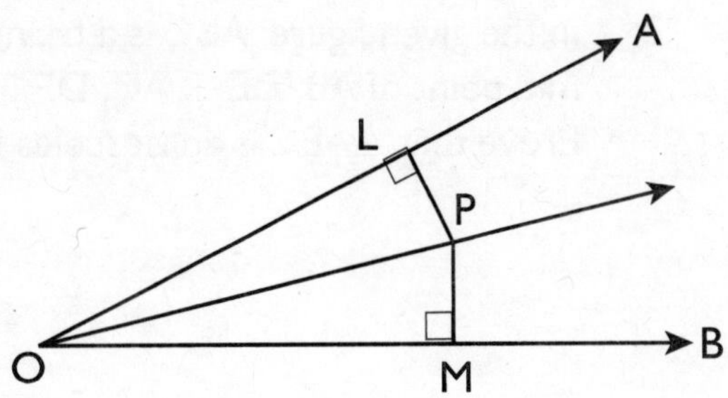

Let us consider the triangles POL and POM.

	$PL = PM$	(given)
	$\angle PLO = \angle PMO = 90^\circ$	
	$OP = OP$	(common side)
$\therefore$	$\triangle POL \cong \triangle POM$	(by the RHS condition of congruency)
$\therefore$	$\angle POL = \angle POM$	(CPCT)

Hence, OA bisects $\angle AOB$.

Practice Exercise 11.5

1. In the following pairs of right triangles, state in symbolic form which pair of triangles is congruent.

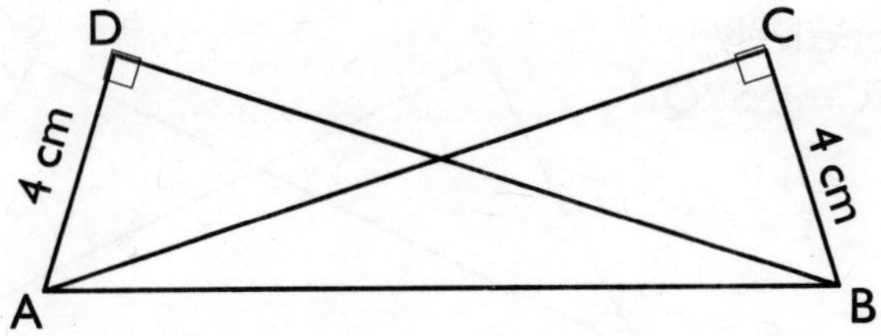

a.

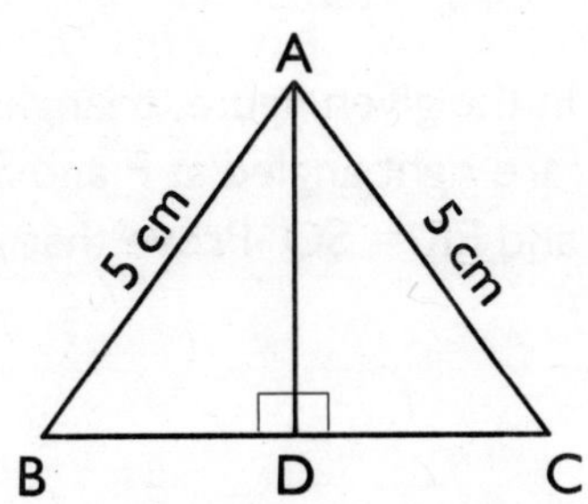

b.

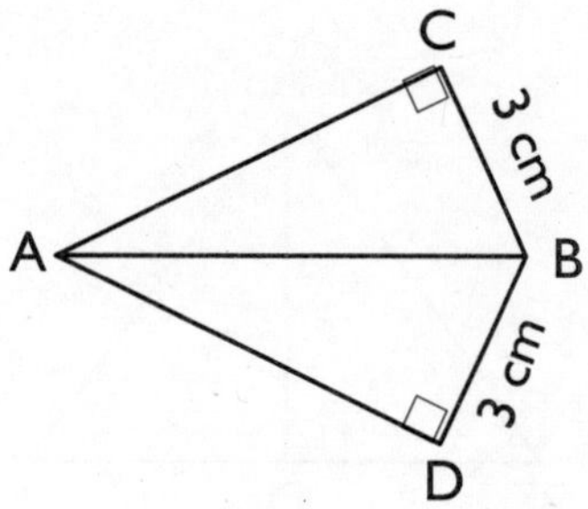

c.

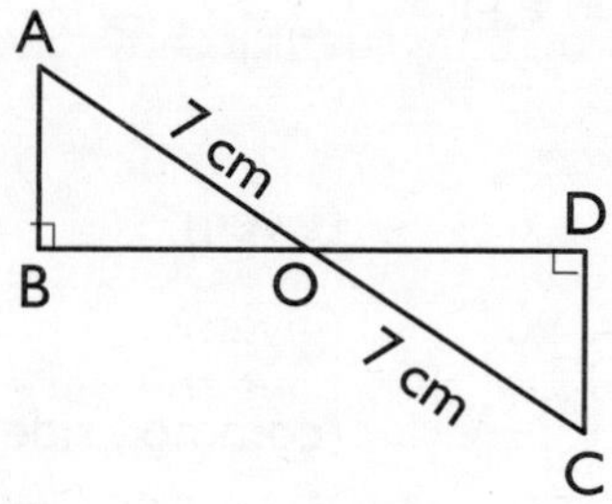

d.

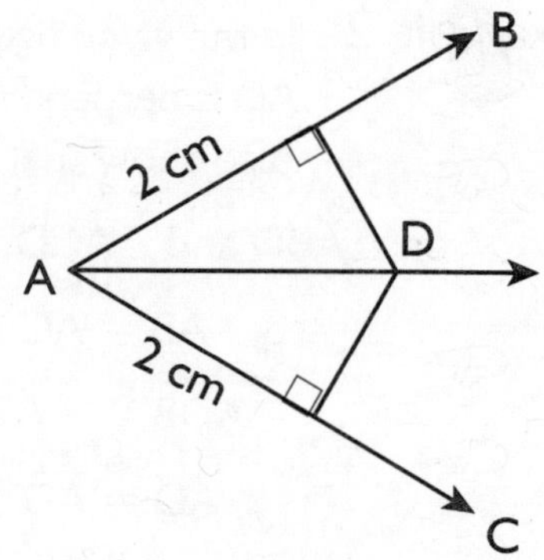

e.

2. In the given figure, ABC is a triangle with D as the mid point of AB, DE $\perp$ AC, DF $\perp$ BC. Also DE = DF. Prove that $\triangle$ABC is an isosceles triangle.

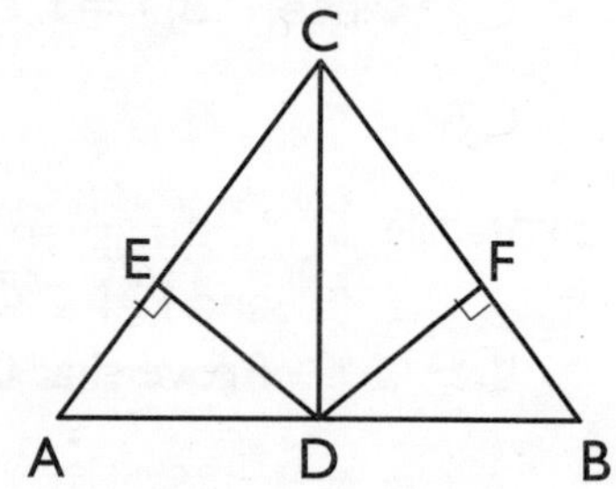

3. In the given figure, $\angle$A and $\angle$D are right angles and BE = CE. If E is the mi dpoint of AD, show that $\triangle ABE \cong \triangle DCE$ and prove that AB = DC.

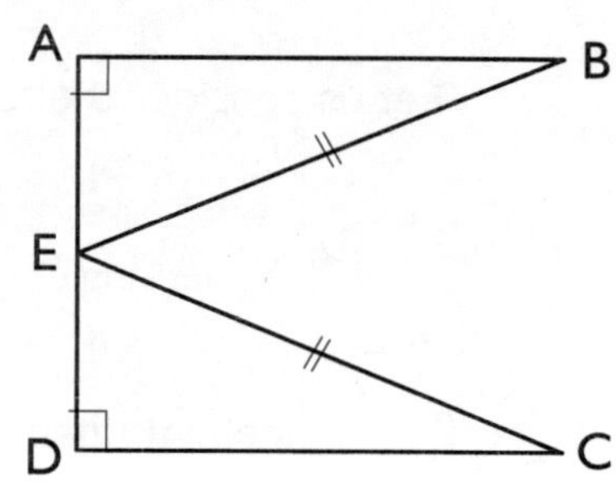

4. In the given figure, AP $\perp$ CB and AB = DC. If P is the mid point of BC, show that $\triangle ABP \cong \triangle DCP$. List all the other equal elements in the two triangles.

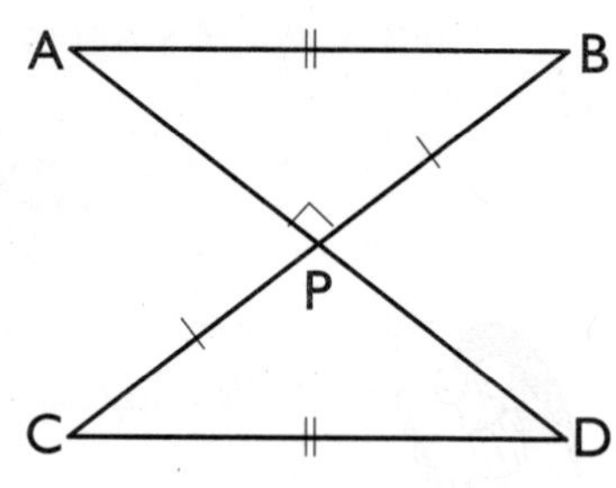

5. In the given figure, triangles PQR and SRQ are right angled at P and S, respectively, and PR = SQ. Prove that $\triangle PQR \cong \triangle SRQ$.

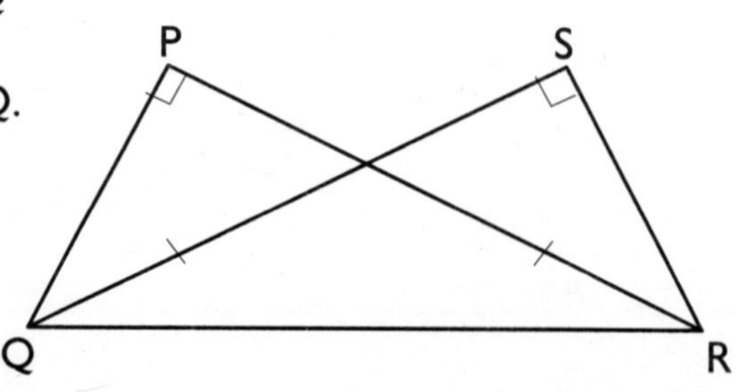

Highlights

- Two figures are said to be congruent if they have the same shape and size.
- Two line segments are congruent if they have the same length.
- Two angles are congruent if they have the same measure.
- Two circles are congruent if they have the same radius.
- Two squares are congruent if the measures of their sides are equal.
- Two rectangles are congruent if they have the same length and breadth.
- Two equilateral triangles are congruent if the measure of their sides are equal.
- Two triangles are congruent if the three sides and three angles (called the elements of the triangle) of one triangle are respectively equal to the corresponding parts of the other triangle.
- Two triangles are congruent if:
  - Three sides of one triangle are correspondingly equal to three sides of the other triangle. (SSS condition).
  - Two sides and the included angle of one triangle are correspondingly equal to two sides and the included angle of the other triangle. (SAS condition.)
  - Two angles and the included side of one triangle are correspondingly equal to two angles and the included side of the other triangle. (ASA condition.)
  - The hypotenuse and one side of one triangle are correspondingly equal to the hypotenuse and one side of the other triangle. (RHS condition.)

How many squares are there in all?

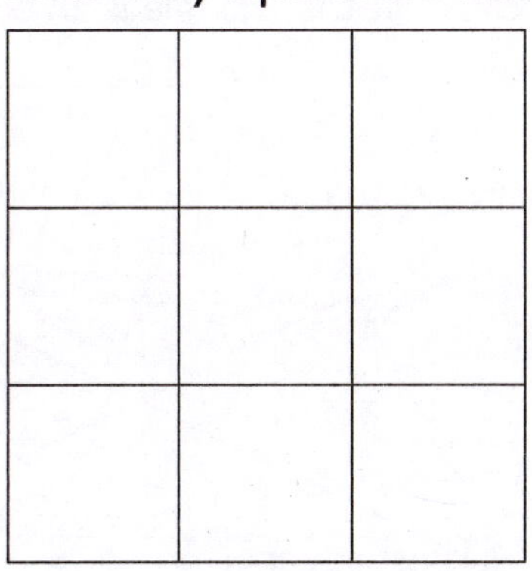

Answer for Brainteaser on page 192

Are We Congruent??

Objective: To understand the concept of congruency of triangles.

Material required: coloured glaze paper, a pair of scissors, geometry box

Method:

Step 1 Each student draws 5 triangles on the white side of the glazed paper.

Step 2 Each pair of students has a different coloured glaze paper.

Step 3 Once the construction of triangles is done, the students cut out the triangles.

Step 4 Students fit the congruent triangles in pairs.

Step 5 One triangle will not be congruents, hence its pair cannot be found. Find out which one.

The student pair that matches all the pairs of congruent triangles first is the winner.

Higher Order Thinking Skills

HOTS

1. If three altitudes of a triangle are equal, prove that the triangle is an equilateral triangle.

2. In $\triangle ABC$, AD is the altitude from A on BC. Prove that $AB^2 - AC^2 = BD^2 - DC^2$.

Answer for Brainteaser from page 191

14 squares (9 small squares, 4 larger square and 1 largest square)

Practical Geometry: Constructions

CHAPTER 12

We have learnt how to construct line segments, angles, circles and perpendicular lines. We shall now learn about the construction of parallel lines and triangles.

Construction of a Line Parallel to a Given Line

The following steps are involved in the construction of a line parallel to a given line from a point outside:

Step 1: Draw a line AB and mark a point P anywhere in the plane outside the line AB.

Step 2: Mark any point Q on the line AB.

Step 3: Join the points P and Q.

Step 4: With Q as the centre and any radius, draw an arc intersecting AB at point E and PQ at point F.

Step 5: Again with P as the centre and the same radius as in Step 4, draw an arc intersecting PQ at point G.

Step 6: With G as the centre and radius equal to EF, draw an arc to intersect the arc in Step 5 at point H.

Step 7: Join PH and extend on both sides to form line CD. The line CD will be parallel to line AB.

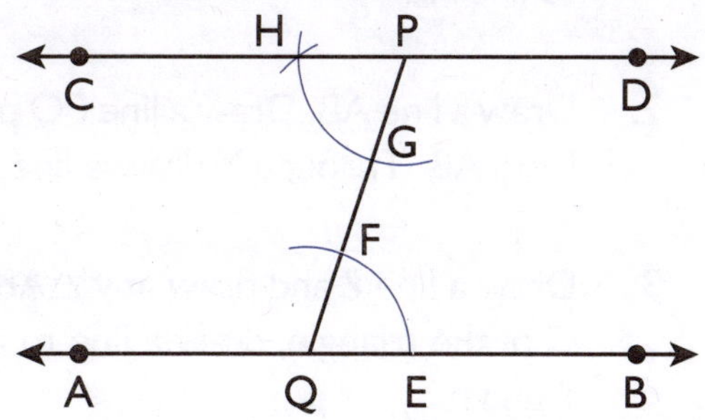

Since the line CD is parallel to line AB,

$\angle BQP = \angle CPQ$ (alternate angles)

Alert!

1. It is always useful to draw a rough diagram before the actual construction. It helps to know the shape of the required construction and the steps of construction involved.
2. Always use a fine tipped pencil for constructions.

Example 1: Construct a line parallel to AB at a distance of 4 cm from AB.

Step 1: Draw a line AB and mark any point P on it.

Step 2: Using a compass and using points A and B one-by-one form arcs just above P in such a way that the arcs cross each other. Extend the line from point P to the point of intersection of the arcs to get a $\perp$ on AB.

Step 3: Cut off PQ = 4 cm.

Step 4: Make an angle of 90° at point P so that $\angle APQ = 90°$.

Step 5: Using a compass, make an angle of 90° at point Q so that $\angle PQD = 90°$.

Step 6: The line CD is the required line parallel to AB at a distance of 4 cm from it.

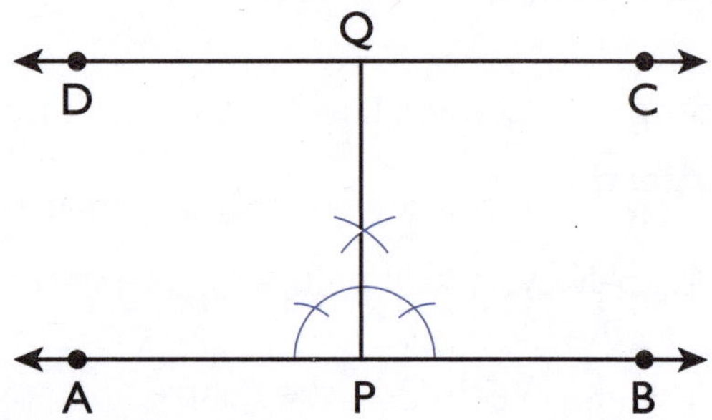

Practice Exercise 12.1

1. Draw a line AB. Mark a point X outside the line. Through X draw a line CD parallel to line AB.

2. Draw a line AB. Draw a line PQ perpendicular to it. Mark a point Y on PQ that is 5 cm from AB. Through Y draw a line parallel to AB.

3. Draw a line ℓ and draw any $\triangle ABC$ such that $\overline{AB}$ is a part of line ℓ. Through the vertex C of the triangle, draw a line m that is parallel to ℓ. Name two transversals for lines ℓ and m.

Construction of Triangles

We can construct triangles with specific measurements in the following ways:

SSS Triangle Construction

(SSS $\Rightarrow$ Side-Side-Side)

When the length of the three sides of a triangle are given, we can construct a specific triangle.

Example: To construct a triangle PQR, where , PQ = 5 cm, QR = 6 cm and PR = 7 cm.

Steps involved in the construction

Step 1: Draw a line segment PR = 7 cm using a ruler.

Step 2: With P as the centre and radius of 5 cm, cut off an arc on one side of the line PR.

Step 3: With R as centre and radius of 6 cm, cut off the previous arc on the same side of PR at a point Q.

Step 4: Join PQ and QR to get the required triangle PQR.

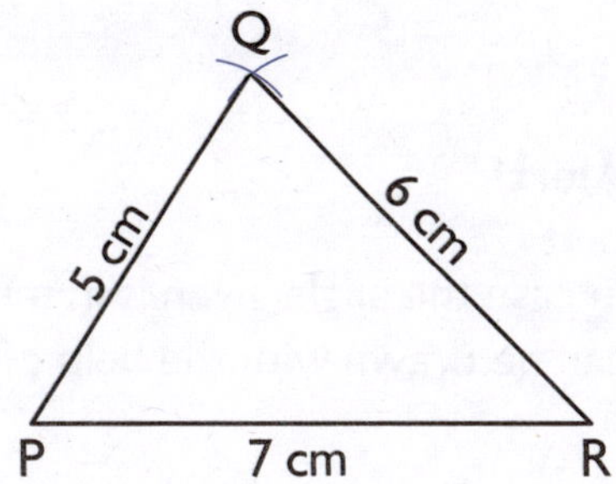

Alert!

1. Always check before construction that the sum of any two sides is always greater than the third side.
2. Draw a rough diagram of the required triangle.

Practice Exercise 12.2

Construct the following triangles the lengths of whose sides are given.

1. $\triangle$ABC, where AB = 4.8 cm, BC = 10 cm and AC = 6.5 cm.
2. $\triangle$XYZ, where XY = 8.1 cm, YZ = 5.7 cm and XZ = 4.2 cm.
3. $\triangle$UVW, where UV = 6.3 cm, VW = 7.8 cm and UW = 5.4 cm.

SAS Triangle Construction

(SAS $\Rightarrow$ Side-Angle-Side)

When the length of two sides of a triangle and the angle contained between the two sides are given, we can construct a specific triangle.

Example: To construct a $\triangle$ABC, where BC = 6 cm, $\angle$B = 60° and AB = 4.5 cm.

Steps involved in the construction

Step 1: Draw a line segment BC equal to 6 cm using a ruler.

Step 2: At point B, construct an angle of 60° using a protractor.

Step 3: Along $\overline{BX}$, cut off BA = 4.5 cm using a compass.

Step 4: Join the points A and C. The required triangle is ABC.

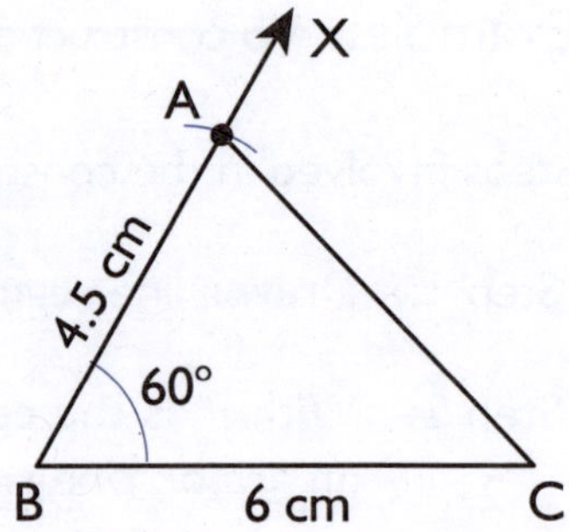

Alert!

In case the angle given is in multiples of 15°, then construct it with a compass. Other angles can be drawn with the help of a protractor.

Practice Exercise 12.3

1. Construct a triangle MNO where MN = 7.5 cm, NO = 8.0 cm and ∠N = 35°.

2. Construct a triangle DEF where DE = 4.8 cm, DF = 6 cm and ∠D = 120°.

3. Construct a triangle PQR where QR = 6.5 cm, PR = 7.8 cm and ∠R = 45°.

ASA Triangle Construction

(ASA ⇒ Angle-Side-Angle)

When the measure of two angles and the side contained between the two angles are given, we can construct a specific triangle.

Example:

To construct a triangle ABC where AB = 5.2 cm, ∠A = 70° and ∠B = 55°.

Steps involved in the construction

Step 1: Draw a line segment AB equal to 5.2 cm using a ruler.

Step 2: At point A construct an angle of measure 70°, that is, ∠XAB = 70°.

Step 3: At point B construct an angle of measure 55°, that is, ∠YBA = 55°.

Step 4: Extend lines X and Y. The point where X and Y intersect is the vertex C.

△ABC is the required triangle.

Practice Exercise 12.4

1. Construct a triangle LMN, where MN = 5.5 cm, ∠M = 65° and ∠N = 80°.

2. Construct a △DEF where ∠D = 30°, ∠E = 100° and DE = 5 cm.

3. Construct a △XYZ where ∠X = 60°, ∠Y = 45° and XY = 6 cm.

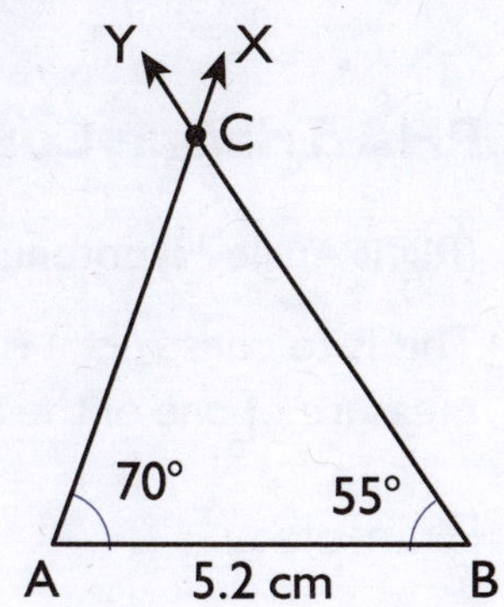

RHS Triangle Construction

(RHS ⇒ Right Angle-Hypotenuse-Side)

This is to construct a right-angled triangle only. If we know the length of the hypotenuse and the length of a side, we can construct a specific triangle.

Example:

To construct a right-angled triangle PQR in which QR = 5 cm, ∠Q = 90° and the hypotenuse PR = 6.5 cm.

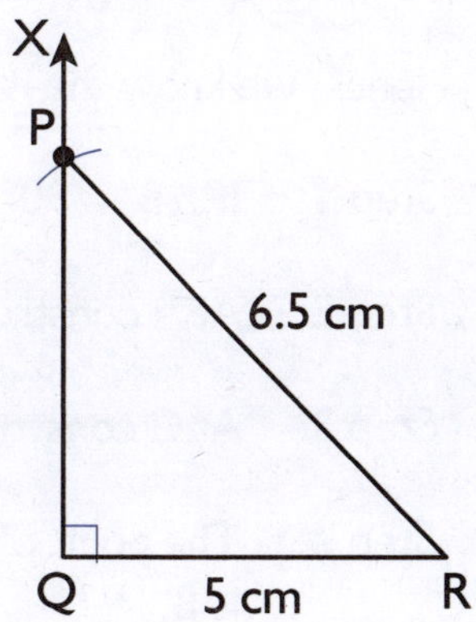

Steps involved in the construction

Step 1: Draw a line segment QR = 5 cm.

Step 2: At point Q construct an angle ∠RQX of measure 90° using a protractor.

Step 3: With point R as the centre and radius of 6.5 cm, draw an arc to intersect QX at point P.

Step 4: Join the points P and R.

△PQR is the required triangle.

Practice Exercise 12.5

1. Construct △XYZ where ∠X = 90°, YZ = 5 cm and XZ = 3 cm. Measure the length XY using a ruler.

2. Construct $\triangle MNO$ where $\angle O = 90°$, MN = 7.5 cm and NO = 4.8 cm.

3. Construct $\triangle PQR$ where $\angle P = 90°$, QR = 8.1 cm and PQ = 5.6 cm.

RHA Triangle Construction

(Right Angle-Hypotenuse-Angle)

This is to construct a right-angled triangle. If we know the length of the hypotenuse and the measure of one of the acute angles, we can draw the required triangle.

Example:

To construct a triangle ABC where $\angle B = 90°$, $\angle C = 30°$ and hypotenuse AC is 5.6 cm.

Steps involved in the construction

$$\angle A + \angle B + \angle C = 180°$$
$$\angle A + 90° + 30° = 180°$$
$$\angle A = 180° - 120° = 60°$$

Hence, we know the measure of all the angles of the triangle and the length of the hypotenuse.

Step 1: If $\angle B = 90°$, AC is the hypotenuse. Draw AC = 5.6 cm.

Step 2: At A construct an angle of 60° using a protractor.

Step 3: At C construct an angle of 30° using a protractor.

Step 4: The point of intersection of the arms of the two angles is B.

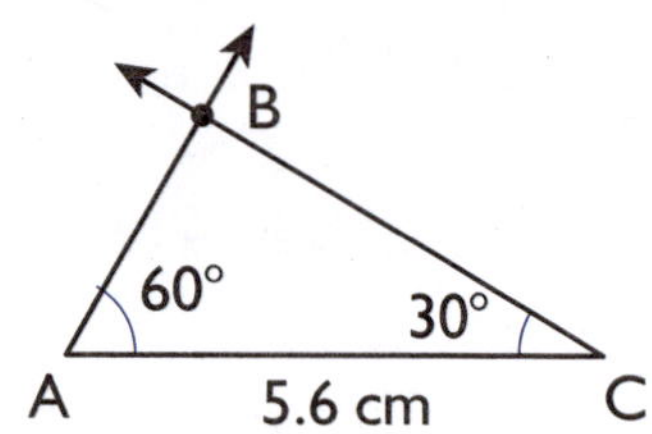

Step 5: Measure $\angle B$ to check whether it is 90°.

Practice Exercise 12.6

1. Construct a $\triangle LMN$ where $\angle M = 90°$, LN = 8.7 cm and $\angle N = 50°$.

2. Construct a $\triangle XYZ$ where $\angle Z = 90°$, XY = 10 cm and $\angle X = 45°$. Measure the length of XZ and YZ.

3. Construct a $\triangle ABC$ where $\angle A = 90°$, BC = 7.1 cm and $\angle C = 75°$.

Highlights

- If a line and a point outside the line are given, we can construct a line parallel to the given line passing through the given point.
- Triangles can be constructed: if three sides of the triangle are given (SSS); if two sides and the angle included between them is given (SAS); if two angles and the side contained between them is given (ASA); if the hypotenuse and a side of a right-angled triangle are given (RHS); and if the hypotenuse and an angle of a right-angled triangle are given (RHA).

Higher Order Thinking Skills

HOTS

Construct a $\triangle ABC$ in which AB = 4 cm, AC = 5 cm and $\angle ABC = 90°$. Construct the perpendicular bisectors of AB and AC and let them meet at O. With O as the centre and OA or OB as radius, draw a circle. Does it pass through the three vertices of the $\triangle ABC$? Find out the special name of the circle constructed.

Brainteaser

What has three feet and one leg?

Answer for Brainteaser on page 200

Two Equilateral Triangles in Two Circles!

Objective: To construct an equilateral triangle.

Material required: plain sheet of paper, a geometry set, a few coloured sketch pens

Method:

Take a compass and measure a radius of 4 cm. Now draw a circle. Mark its centre as O.

On any point on the circumference of this circle and with the same radius 4 cm, draw another circle. Mark its centre O′.

Now you have a common region between the two circles. Join the two centres O and O′. Also join O to the two points where the circles intersect. Join O′ also to the two points where the circles intersect. Name these points as A and B. Now measure the sides OA, O′A and OO′. Are they equal? Also, measure OB, O′B and OO′. Are they equal? Which type of triangles are these? Write the answer.

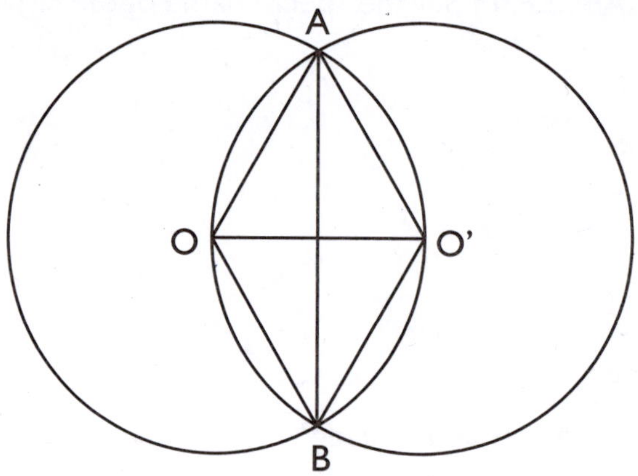

Answer for Brainteaser from page 199

A yardstick!

1. Given below are pairs of congruent triangles. Using the SSS rule of congruency, name the congruent triangles in each case

a.

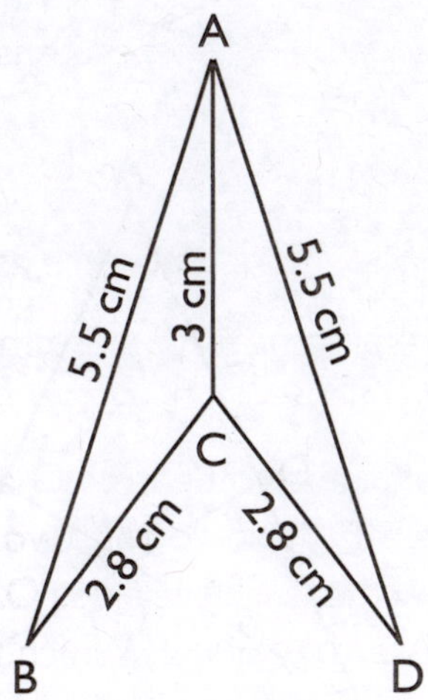

b.

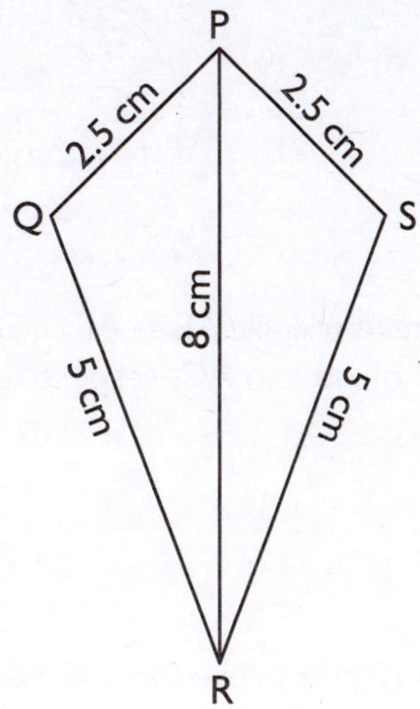

c.

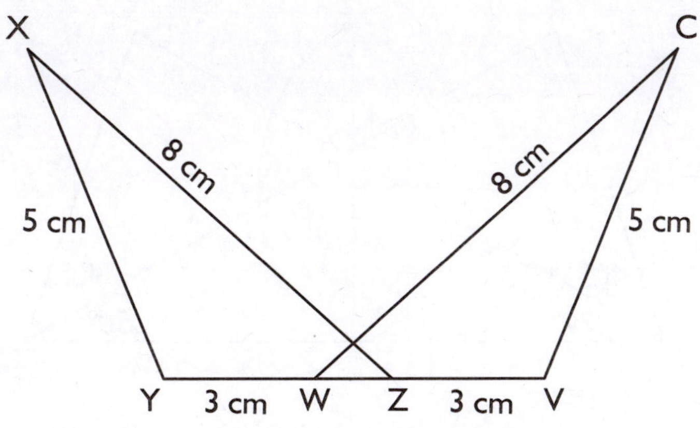

2. In the given figure, AB and CD are two equal chords of a circle with centre O. Prove that $\triangle AOB \cong \triangle COD$.

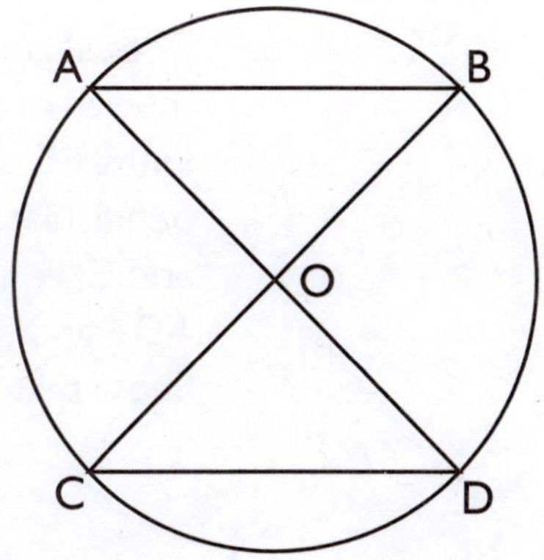

Rewind

3. The two lines segments AB and CD bisect each other at point O. Prove that $\triangle AOD \cong \triangle BOC$. Also show that AD = BC and AD || BC

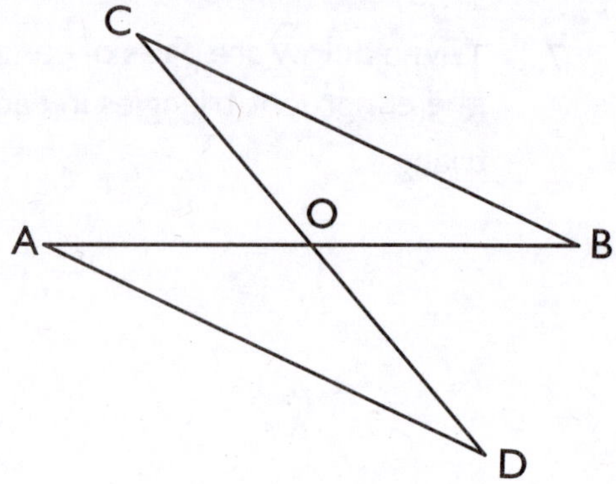

4. In an isosceles triangle AB = AC. If D and E are the midpoints of AB and AC, respectively, prove that CD = BE.

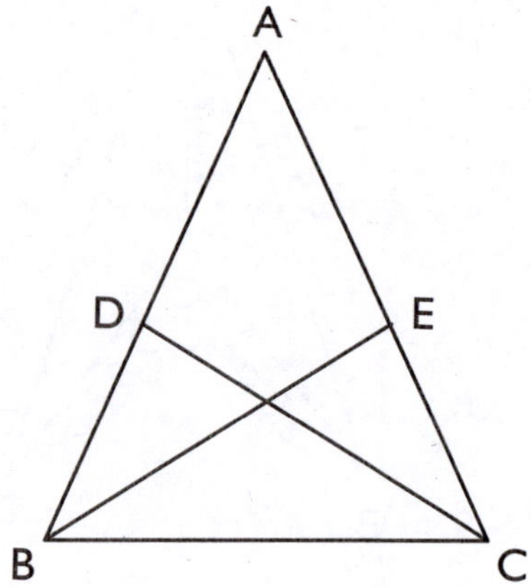

5. In the given figure, prove that the triangles PQR and PQS are congruent. Which condition of congruency has been applied?

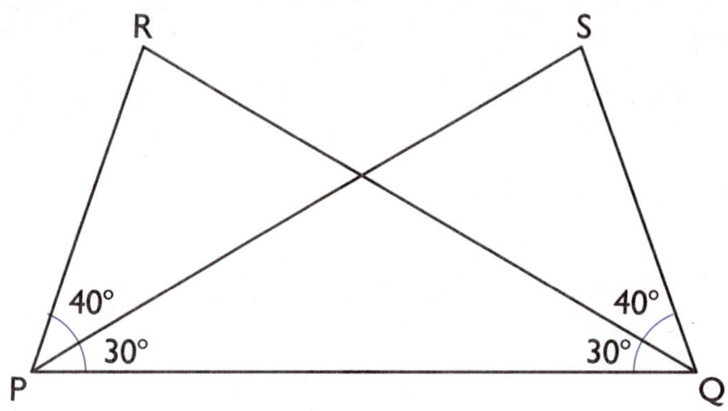

6. The segment AD is the median of the triangle ABC. Lines BE and CF are perpendicular from points B and C, respectively, on line AD and AD produced. Show that BE = CF.

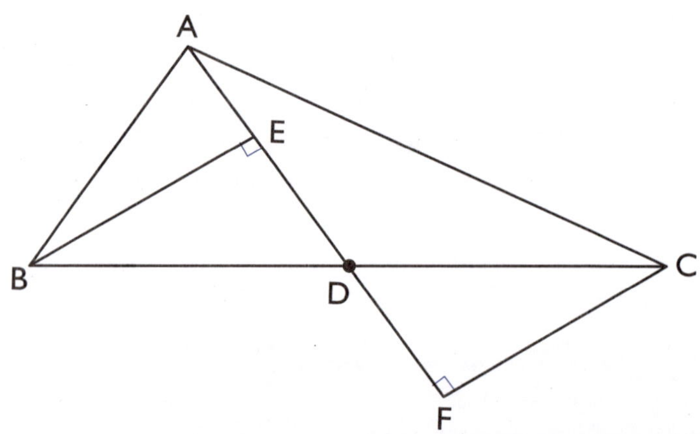

7. Triangle XYZ has O as the mid point of XY. Segments OM and ON are perpendicular to sides XZ and YZ, respectively. Also OM = ON. Prove that △XYZ is an isosceles triangle.

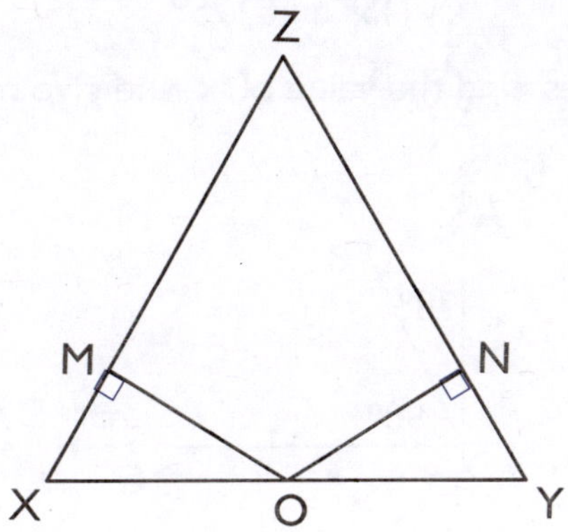

8. Draw a line parallel to a given line ℓ at a distance of 5.5 cm from it.

9. Construct a △ABC such that CB = 6.5 cm, CA = 4.2 cm and BA = 5.1 cm.

10. Construct a △ABC such that AB = 3.2 cm, BC = 3.9 cm and ∠ABC = 120°.

11. Construct △PQR such that PQ = 6 cm, ∠P = 60° and ∠Q = 45°. Measure ∠R.

12. Construct an isosceles △ABC, such that BC = 6.4 cm and the base angles are 40° each.

13. Construct a right-angled triangle △ABC in which ∠B = 90°, BC = 4.5 cm and hypotenuse CA = 5.5 cm.

14. Construct an equilateral triangle △ABC each of whose sides is 5.2 cm.

15. Construct a △PQR given that PQ = 5 cm, ∠P = 45° and ∠Q = 60°. Measure ∠R. From point R draw a perpendicular on PQ and measure the distance.

Test Yourself

Unit III

1. What type of angles are the following pairs—complementary or supplementary?

   a. 63° and 27° b. 110° and 70° c. 58° and 122°

   d. 58° and 32° e. 45° and 125°

2. In the following figures, find the value of 'x' and give reasons for your answer.

a.

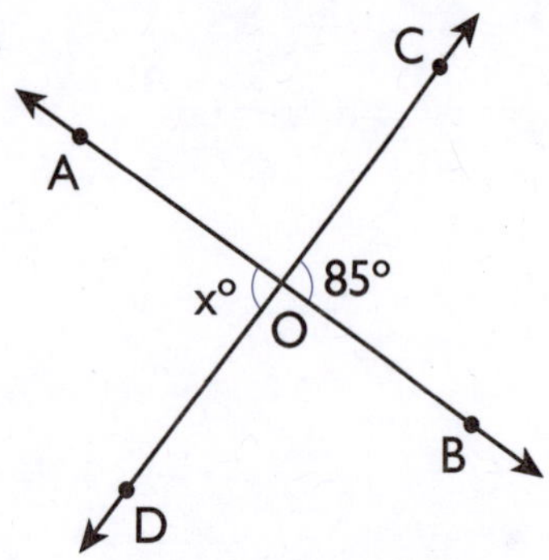

b.

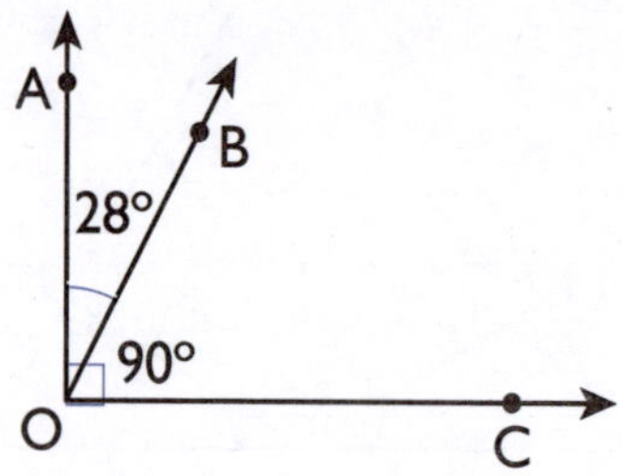

c.

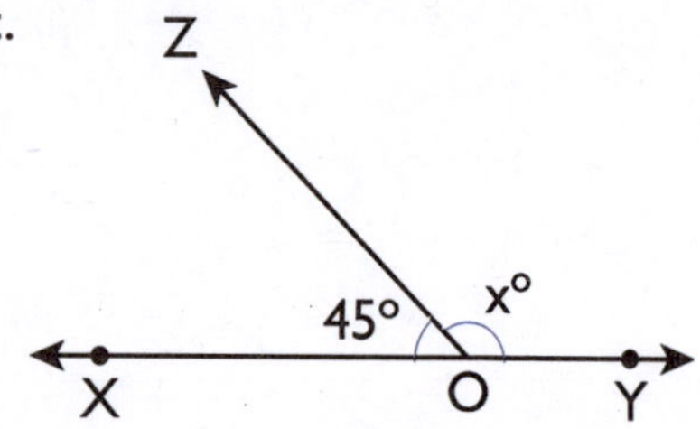

3. In the given figure, find the values of x, y and z.

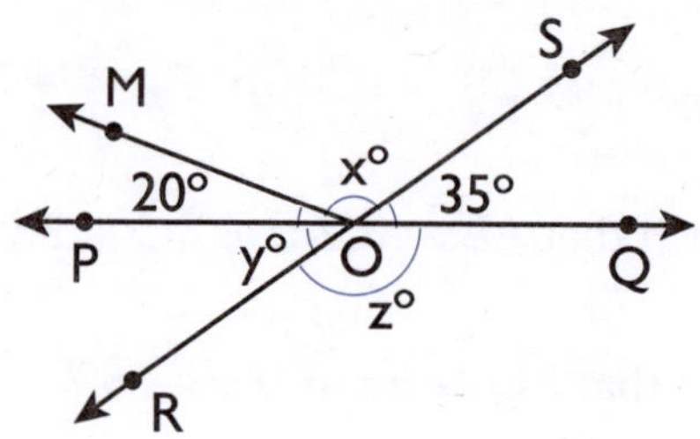

4. In the given figure, lines ℓ and m are parallel to each other. Two transversals 't' and 's' intersect the lines at A, B, C and D. Find the values of x, y and z.

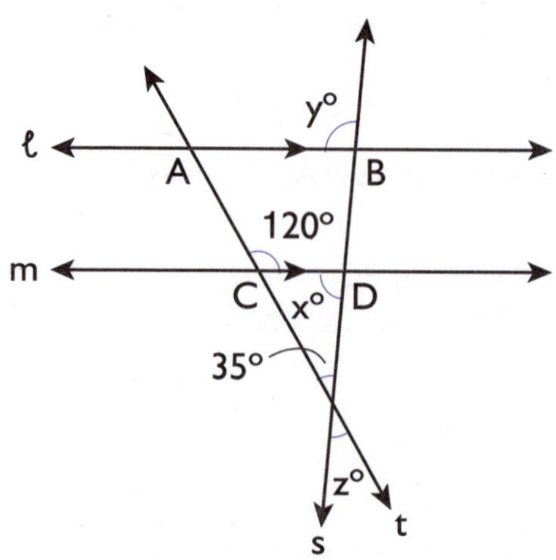

5. In the given figures, lines ℓ and m are parallel to each other. Find the value of x in each figure.

a.

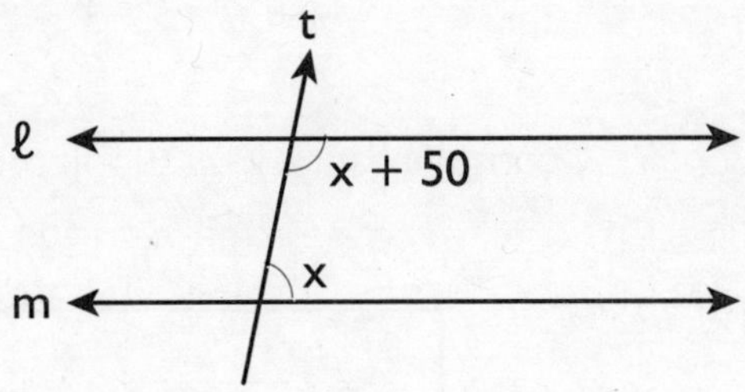

b.

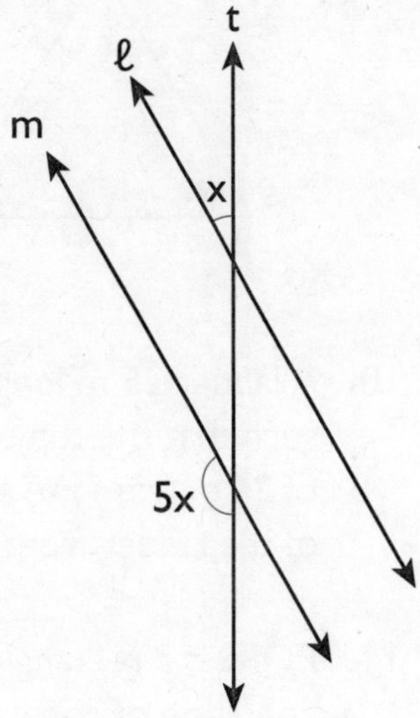

c.

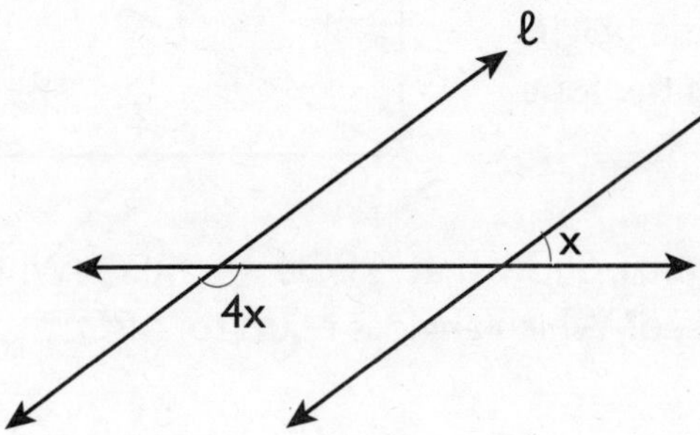

6. The measures of the three angles of a triangle are given. Find the measure of the third angle and name the type of angle.

a. 60°, 40° b. 90°, 40° c. 120°, 40° d. 39°, 65° e. 100°, 27°

7. The three angles of a triangle are in the ratio 4:5:9. Find their measures.

8. In the given figures, find the value of y and the measure of each angle.

a.

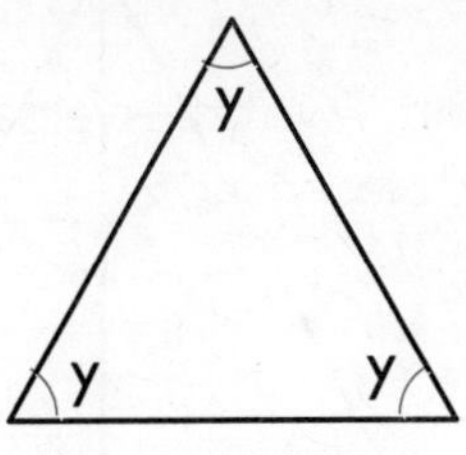

b.

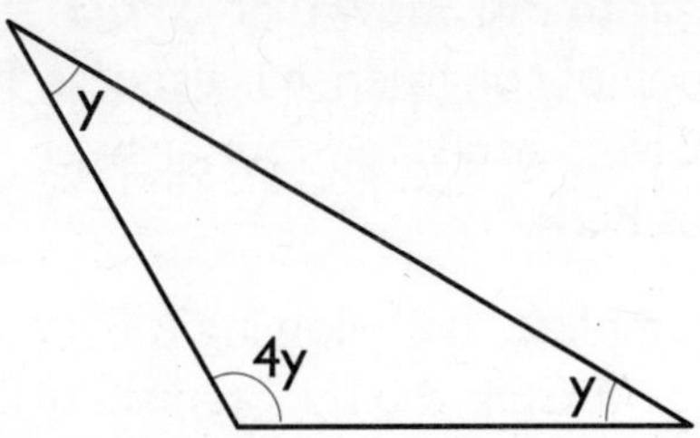

c.

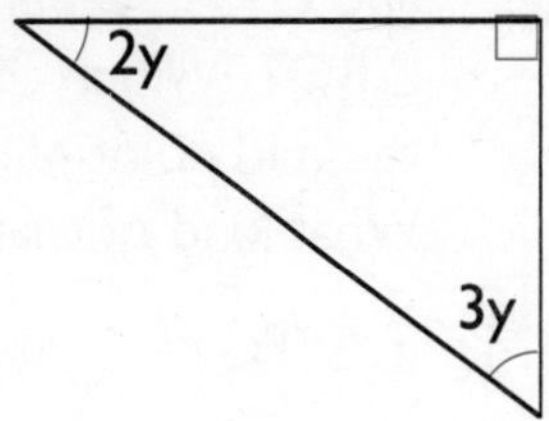

9. Find the value of w in each of the given figures.

a.

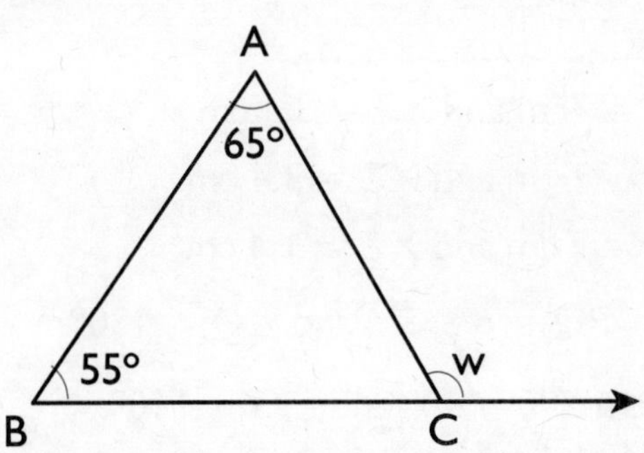

b.

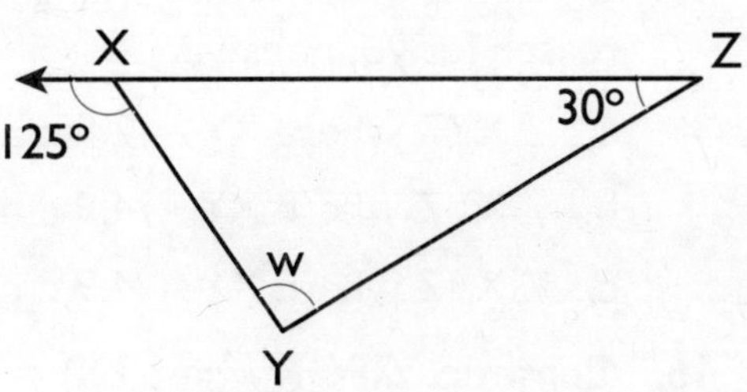

c.

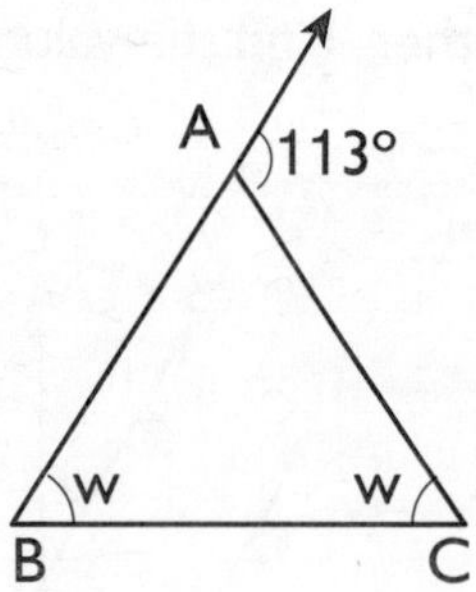

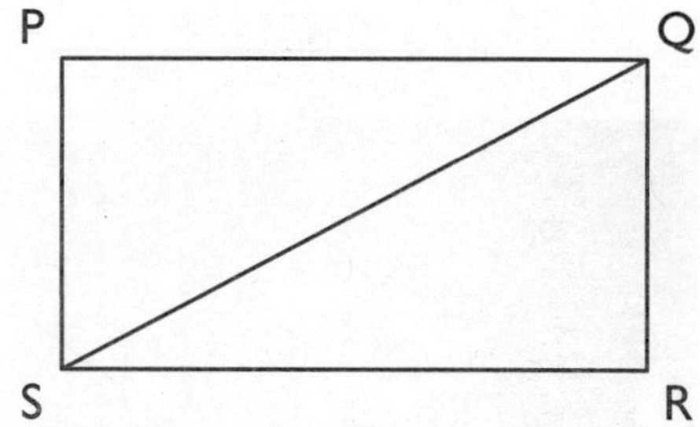

10. A ladder 25 m long was rested along a wall such that the top touched the wall at a height of 24 m from the ground. How far is the foot of the ladder from the wall?

11. PQRS is a rectangle and QS is a diagonal. Show that $\triangle PQS \cong \triangle RSQ$. Which condition of congruence has been used? Which angle is equal to $\angle PQS$?

12. Prove the $\triangle ABC$ and $\triangle XYZ$ are congruent. Write down the pairs of equal sides and angles.

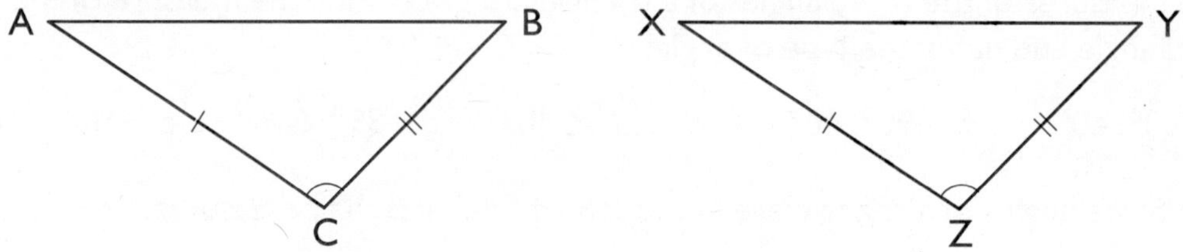

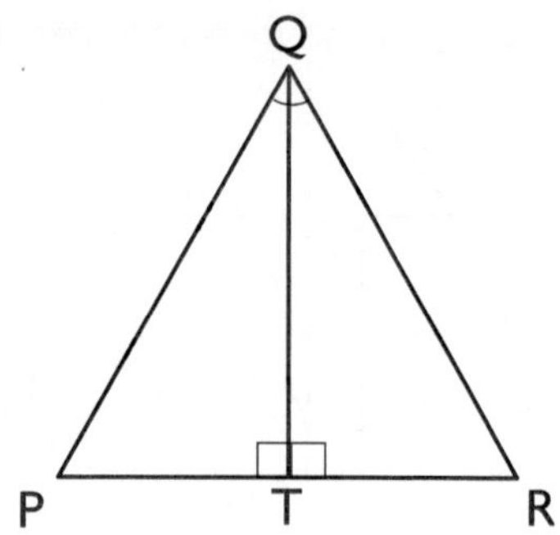

13. In the triangle PQR given here, QT bisects the $\triangle PQR$ and QT is perpendicular to PR. Show that $\triangle PQT = \triangle RQT$. Which condition of congruence is used? Is T the mid point of PR? Give reasons for your answer. What kind of triangle is PQR.

14. If $\triangle EFG \cong \triangle MNP$, complete the following $\angle E =$ ______; $\angle G =$ ______. If GE is the hypotenuse of $\triangle EFG$ then _____ is the hypotenuse in $\triangle MNP$.

15. Construct the following triangles. (In case these cannot be constructed, give reason for your answer)

    a. $\triangle XYZ$ where XY = 2.9 cm, YZ = 7cm and XZ = 3.4 cm

    b. $\triangle XYZ$ where XY = 4.9 cm, YZ = 7 cm and XZ = 3.4 cm

    c. $\triangle XYZ$ where XY = 4.9 cm, YZ = 7 cm and XZ = 1.4 cm

16. Construct $\triangle PQR$ where QR = 8 cm, PQ = 6.3 CM and $\angle Q = 150°$.

17. Construct $\triangle LKG$, where KG = 7.2 cm $\angle K = 40°$ and $\angle G = 110°$.

18. Construct $\triangle PQR$, where $\angle P = 90°$ QR = 8.1 cm and PQ = 5.6 cm.

Symmetry

CHAPTER 13

Symmetry, as discussed earlier, is the quality of being made up of exactly similar parts facing each other or around an axis. Leaves, shells, flowers and animals display symmetry in nature. We also see symmetry in man-made structures like buildings, arches, bridges, etc.

Taj Mahal

Gateway of India

If there exists a line about which a figure can be folded so that its two parts thus created coincide, then the figure is symmetrical. The line is called the **axis of symmetry**.

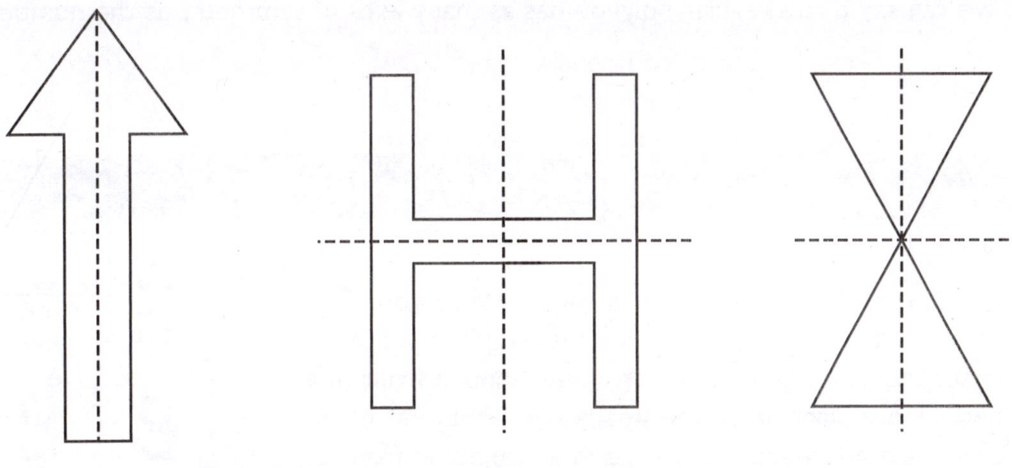

If the figures are folded about their axes (the dotted line), the two halves will coincide. We can say that the two halves are congruent as they have the same shape and size. There are some figures that have more than one axis of symmetry.

Axes of Symmetry of Regular Polygons

Polygons are plane figures made up of line segments. Regular polygons are those where all the line segments are equal. These polygons thus have equal sides and equal angles.

We are familiar with some of the regular polygons. We also know that the axis of symmetry of a regular polygon depends on its sides. Some ploygons along with their axes of symmetry are tabulated below.

Table 13.1

Name of Polygon	Number of Sides	Number of Axes of Symmetry
Equilateral triangle	3	3
Square	4	4
Pentagon	5	5
Hexagon	6	6
Septagon	7	7
Octagon	8	8
Nonagon	9	9
Decagon	10	10

Hence, we can say that a regular polygon has as many axes of symmetry as the number of sides.

Line Symmetry and Mirror Reflection

Line symmetry is closely related to a mirror reflection. The important point in a mirror reflection is the left-right discrepancy in the object and its image in a mirror. If we stand in front of a mirror and lift our right hand, the image will lift its left hand. This is called lateral inversion. If we keep an object in front of a mirror, the object and its reflection are symmetrical and the mirror line is the axis of symmetry.

Here are few figures and their mirror images.

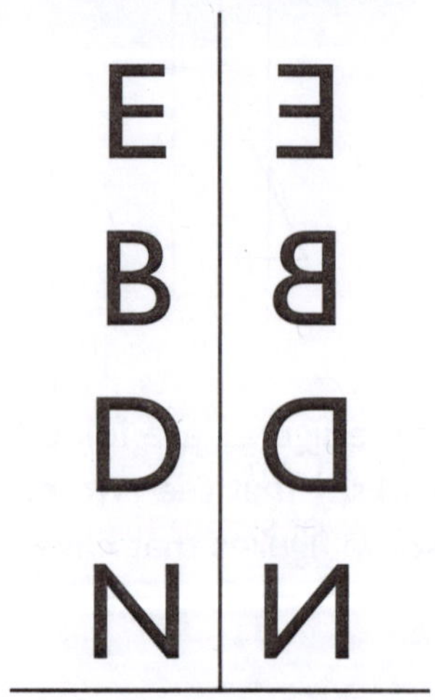

Practice Exercise 13.1

1. Draw the axes of symmetry of the following figures.

a. b. c. d. e.

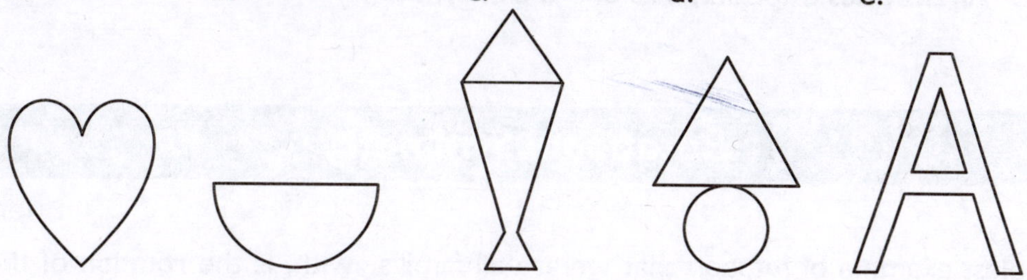

2. Draw the axes of symmetry of the following figures.

a. b. c. d. e.

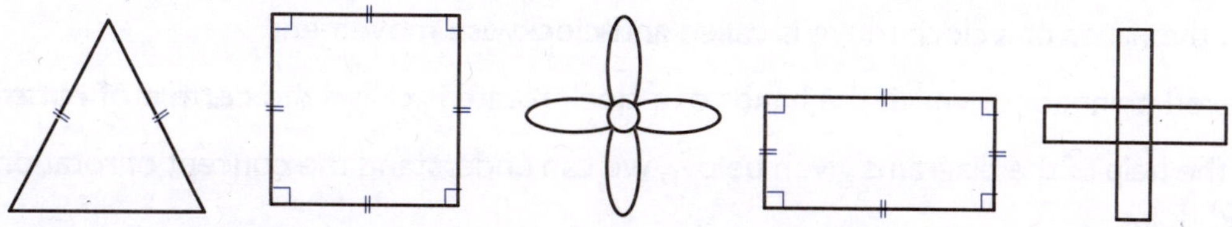

3. Use the dotted line as a mirror line and complete the figures by drawing the image on the other side.

a. b. c. d. e.

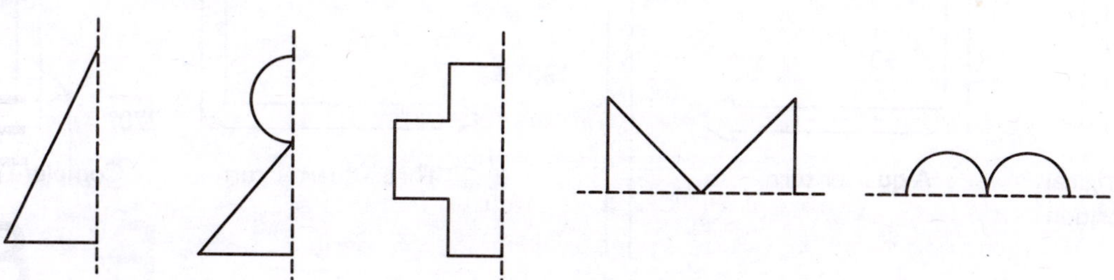

4. Construct a $\triangle UVW$ with $UV = 6$ cm, $\angle U = \angle V = 50°$. Draw its line (or lines) of symmetry.

5. Indicate whether the following statements are true (T) or false (F).

   a. A parallelogram has two lines of symmetry.
   b. An angle has two lines of symmetry.
   c. A semicircle has an infinite number of lines of symmetry.
   d. A regular hexagon has six lines of symmetry.
   e. An isosceles trapezium has one line of symmetry.

Rotational Symmetry

The simplest example of *rotation* that we are all familiar with, is the rotation of the earth around its axis causing day and night.

The hands of a clock rotate about a point. The minute hand moves through an angle of 360° at the end of one hour and the hour hand moves through the same angle in twelve hours. A circular movement corresponding in direction to the movements of the hands of a clock is called clock-wise movment. A circular movement in the opposite direction to the way in which the hands of a clock move is called anti-clockwise movement.

The fixed point about which the hands of a clock rotate is called the **centre of rotation.**

With the help of the diagrams given below, we can understand the concept of rotation about a fixed point.

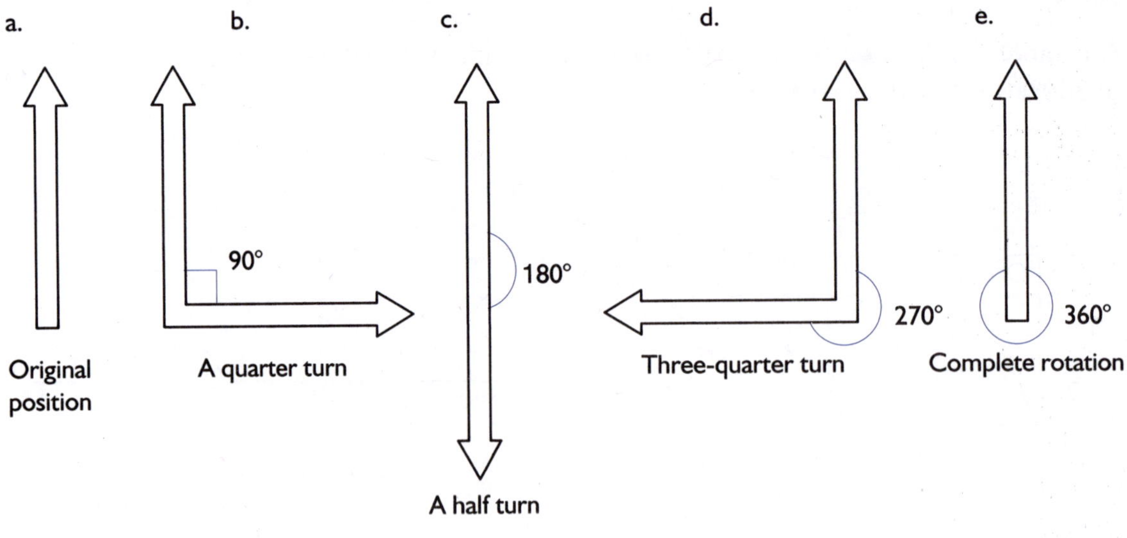

All figures when rotated through 360° come back to their original positions.

Table 13.2

Original position	90° turn	180° turn	270° turn	360° turn
	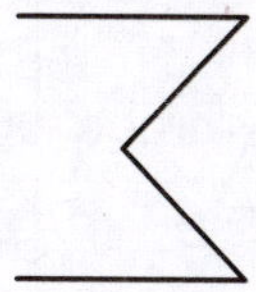	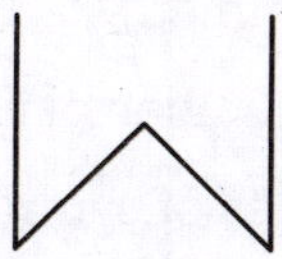	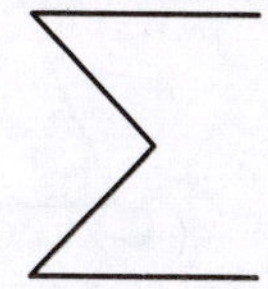	

	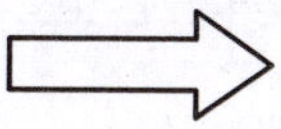		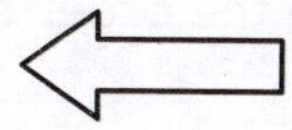	

When a figure is rotated through an angle ($\leq 180°$) and the figure looks the same, it is said to have rotational symmetry.

The number of times a figure fits onto itself in one complete rotation is called the order of the rotational symmetry.

If a figure looks the same after a rotation through an angle θ (where $\theta \leq 180°$) then $\frac{360}{\theta}$ gives the rotational order of the figure.

Alert!

A rotational symmetry of order 1 (i.e., if it looks the same after one complete rotation of 360°) is considered insignificant.

Rotational symmetry of Order 2, 3 and 4

Table 13.3

	Original position	90° turn	180° turn	270° turn	360° turn
a.	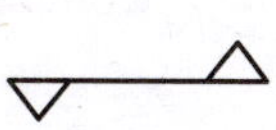		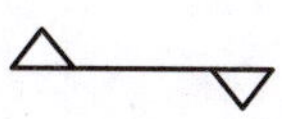		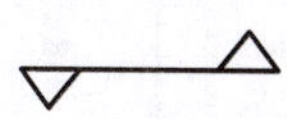
b.	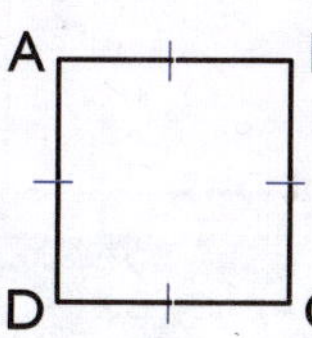	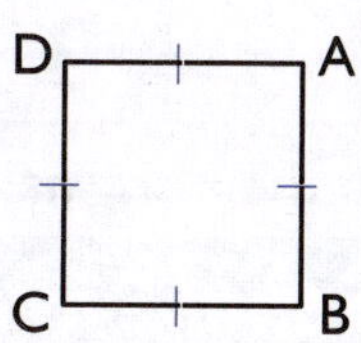	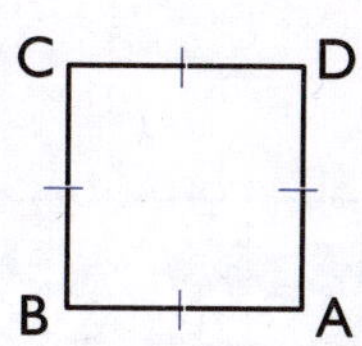	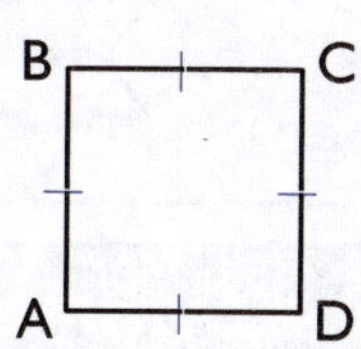	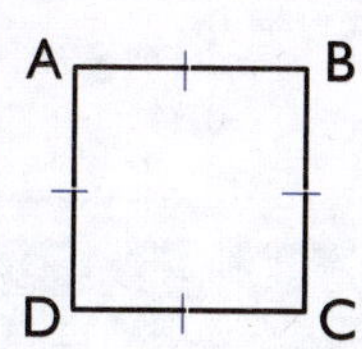

c.

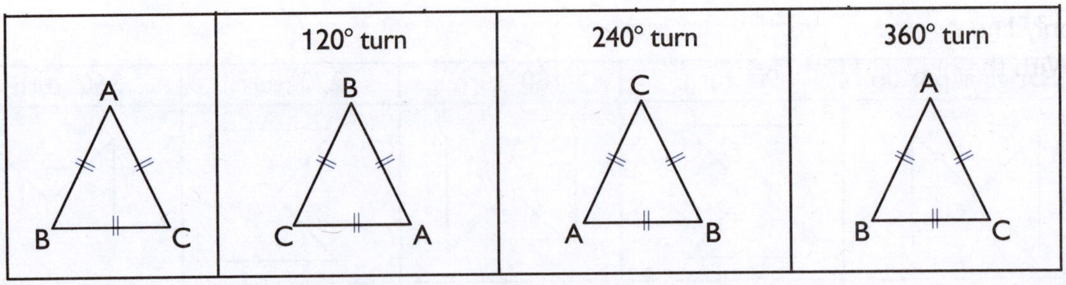

In figures a, b and c we can see the rotational symmetry of order 2, 3 and 4 in figures (a), (b) and (c) respectively.

Practice Exercise 13.2

1. Draw the following figures on rotation through the angles 90°, 180°, 270° and 360° and write the order of rotational symmetry in each one.

a. b. c. d. e.

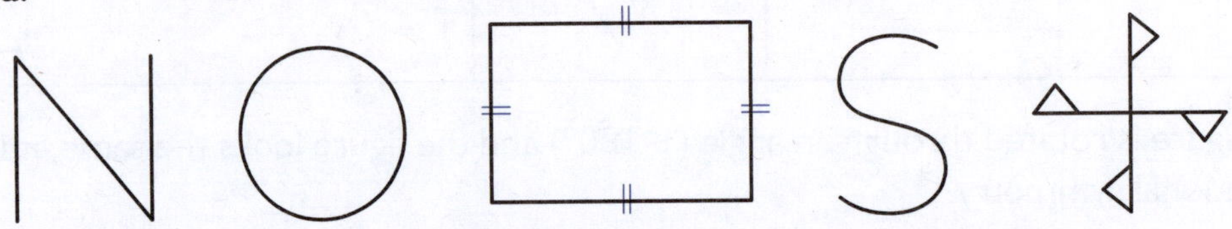

2. Match the following figures with their order of rotational symmetry.

	Figure	Order of Rotational Symmetry
a.	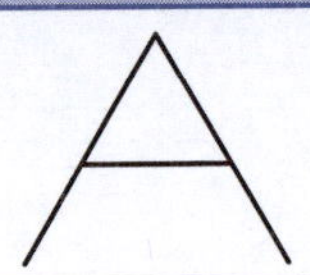	4
b.	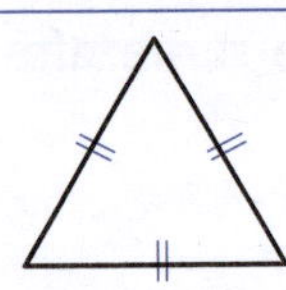	5
c.	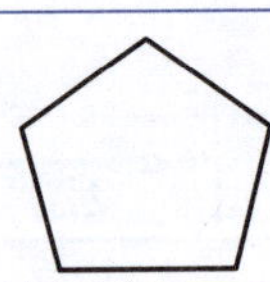	1
d.	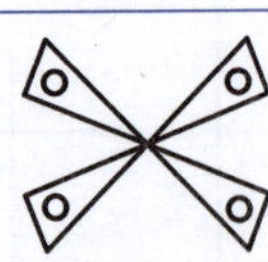	6
e.		3

Line Symmetry and Rotational Symmetry

After studying line symmetry and rotational symmetry (of order greater than 1) we can conclude that some figures have line symmetry as well as rotational symmetry, some have only line symmetry or only rotational symmetry and some others have neither. With the help of examples we shall study each case.

Figures with Both Line Symmetry and Rotational Symmetry

a. 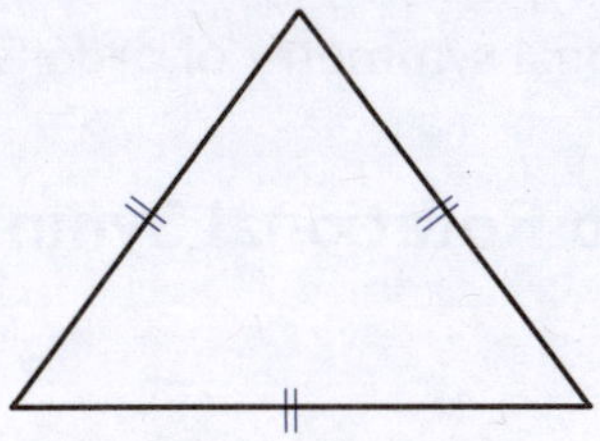

Equilateral triangle

Three axes of symmetry
Rotational symmetry of order 3

b. 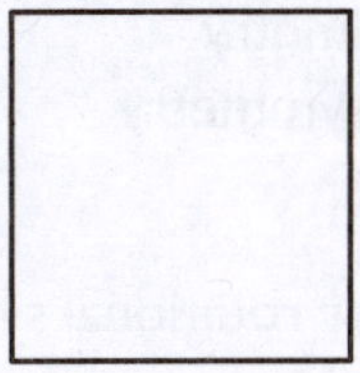

Square

Four axes of symmetry
Rotational symmetry of order 4

c. 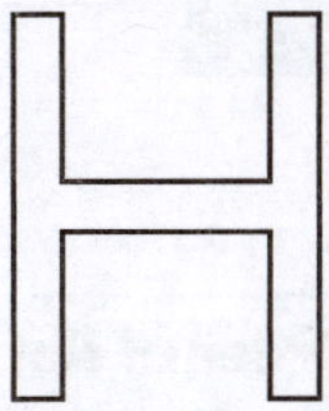

The letter H

Two axes of symmetry
Rotational symmetry of order 2

Figures with Only Line Symmetry

(Rotational symmetry of order 1 is not considered.)

a. 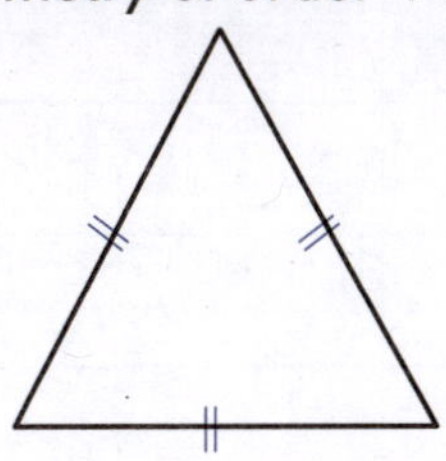

Isosceles triangle

One axis of symmetry
No rotational symmetry

b. 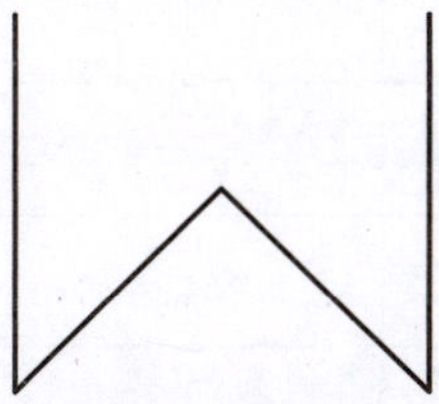

The letter W

One axis of symmetry
No rotational symmetry

c. 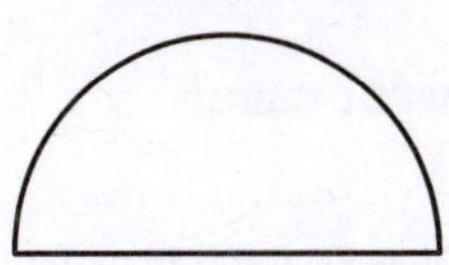

A semicircle

One axis of symmetry
No rotational symmetry

Figure with Only Rotational Symmetry

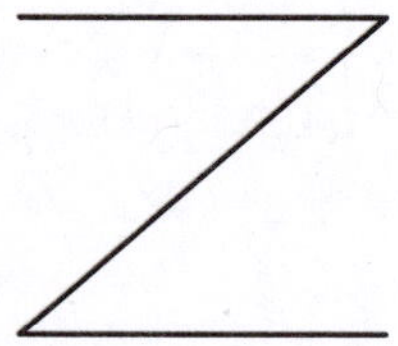

No line symmetry
Rotational symmetry of order 2

Figures with No Line of Symmetry and No Rotational Symmetry

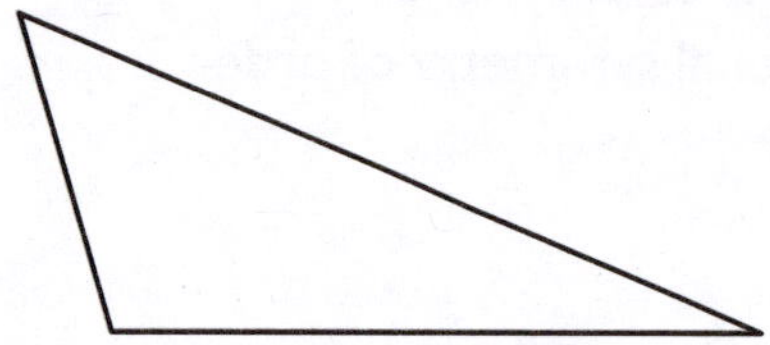

No axis of symmetry
No rotational symmetry

A scalene triangle

Any irregular polygon will have neither an axis of symmetry nor rotational symmetry.

Practice Exercise 13.3

Complete the following table.

S. No.	Letter / Figure	Number of Axes of Symmetry	Order of Rotational Symmetry
a.	E		
b.	S		
c.	I		
d.	X		
e.	M		
f.	Square		
g.	Rectangle		
h.	Scalene triangle		
i.	Isosceles triangle		
j.	Regular hexagon		

What do you say when you see an empty parrot cage?

Answer for Brainteaser on page 216

Highlights

- A figure is symmetrical about the line that divides the figure in two identical parts. The line is called the axis of symmetry or simply line of symmetry.
- A figure may have no axis of symmetry or can have more than one axes of symmetry.
- Regular polygons have as many axes of symmetry as the number of sides.
- Mirror reflection leads to symmetry but with lateral inversion (or change in orientation.
- Rotation turns an object about a fixed point known as the centre of rotation.
- Rotation by 90° is a quarter rotation, by 180° is a half rotation, by 270° is a three-quarter rotation and by 360° is one complete rotation.
- If during a rotation an object looks exactly the same, we say it possesses rotational symmetry.
- In a complete rotation (360°) the number of times an object looks exactly the same is called the order of rotational symmetry.
- The order of rotational symmetry can be calculated by the quotient $\frac{360}{\theta}$, where $\theta \leq 180°$.
- Every object has a rotational symmetry of order 1, as it looks the same after a complete rotation.
- Some figures have a line of symmetry as well as rotational symmetry and some figures have neither.

Higher Order Thinking Skills

HOTS

1. Draw an isosceles triangle OAB in which AO = AB. With O as a fixed point, rotate the triangle through (i) 90° (ii) 180° and (iii) 270°. Draw a diagram to represent the above rotations.

2. What is the order of rotational symmetry of a ceiling fan with (i) 3 blades (ii) 4 blades.

Symmetrical Figures

Objective: To observe symmetry in the environment.

Material required: sheet of paper, sketch pens, a pair of scissors

Procedure:

Step 1 Take a sheet of paper and fold it into two equal halves.

Step 2 Cut it off along the edges as shown in the figure below.

Step 3 Unfold the paper.

Step 4 You will observe that the figure is divided into two equal parts, which are identical in size and shape along the fold.

Step 5 You can colour the two parts with different colours.

Step 6 If we take the sheet of paper and fold it into four equals parts, we will get a pattern on cutting along the edges. How many lines of symmetry will it have?

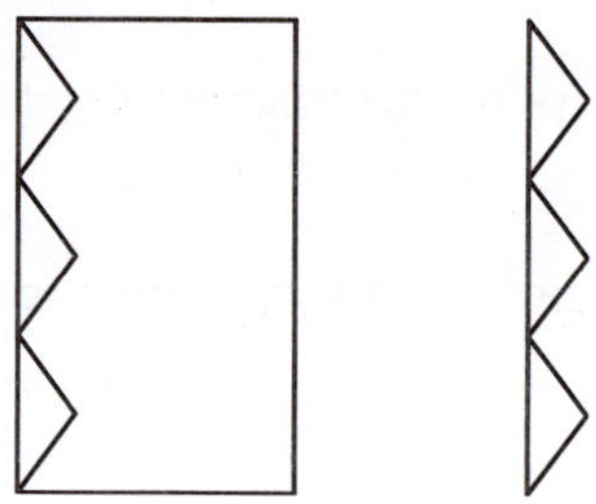

Answer for Brainteaser from page 214

Polygon

Solid Shapes or 3-D Shapes

CHAPTER 14

We see solid shapes all around us at home, in school and in the market place. Any object that has length, breadth and thickness is a solid figure. Since a solid shape has three dimensions, it is called a three-dimensional or 3-D figure.

All 3-D shapes occupy space and hence have volume.

We know that plane figures have only length and breadth and are known as two-dimensional or 2-D figures.

All closed 2-D shapes enclose a region, which is the area of the figure.

Alert!

For 2-D shapes, we calculate the area.

For 3-D shapes, we calculate the volume.

A few 2-D and 3-D shapes are tabulated below.

S. No.	2-D Shapes	3-D Shapes
1.	Square	Cube
2.	Rectangle	Cuboid
3.	Circle	Sphere
4.	Triangle	Cone
5.	Polygons	Cylinder

3-D Shapes

Objects that have a definite shape and size are called solids. A solid occupies a fixed amount of space.

All solid shapes have **faces**, which are plane figures. Two faces meet at an **edge** and edges meet at a **vertex**.

A **net** is an arrangement of figures connected at their edges, all lying in the same plane, which can be folded to make a solid three-dimensional shape.

Let us observe the following solids and identify the number of faces, edges and vertices in each.

Cube

A cube has **six** faces, **twelve** edges and **eight** vertices.

Each edge of a cube has the same length and each face has the same area.

Faces – 6
Edges – 12
Vertices – 8

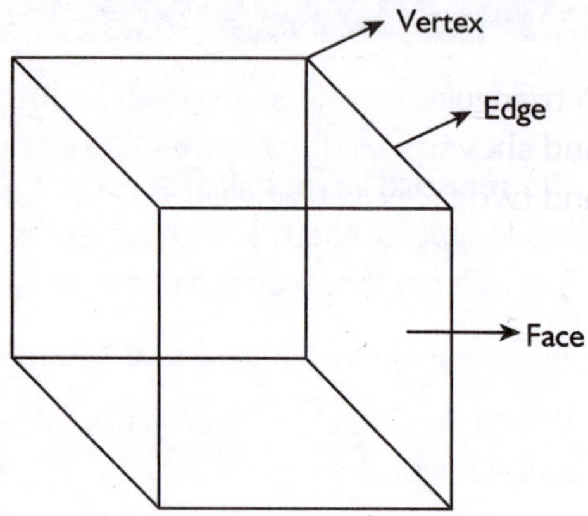

Cuboid

A cuboid has **six** faces, **twelve** edges and **eight** vertices.

The opposite faces of a cuboid are equal in area.

The side faces of a cuboid are called lateral faces. The twelve edges are according to the length, breadth and height of the cuboid.

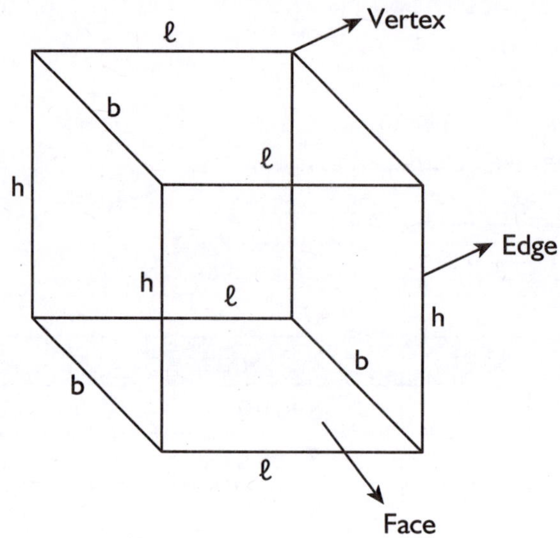

ℓ = length
b = breadth
h = height

Faces – 6
Edges – 12
Vertices – 8

Square Pyramid

A square pyramid has **five** faces, **eight** edges and **five** vertices. The base is a square and the other faces of the pyramid are triangles.

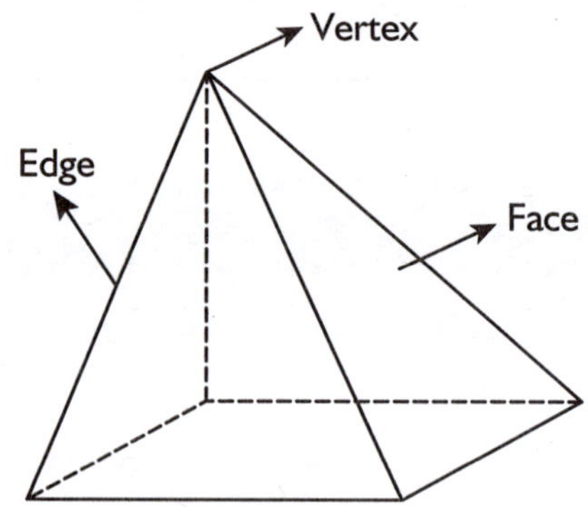

Faces – 5
Edges – 8
Vertices – 5

Triangular Pyramid

A triangular pyramid has **four** faces, **six** edges and **four** vertices. The base is a triangle and the other three faces are also triangles.

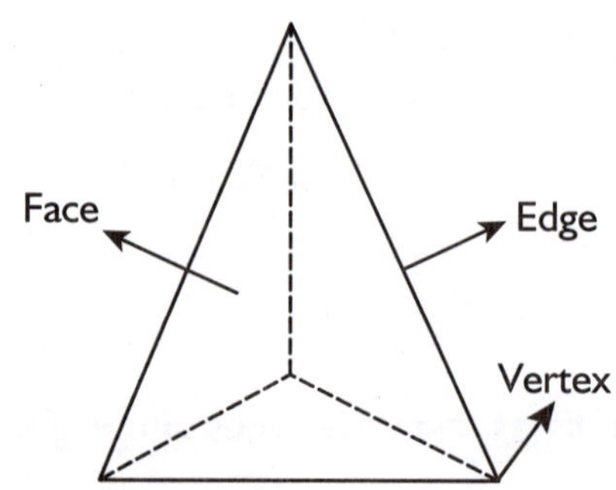

Faces – 4
Edges – 6
Vertices – 4

Triangular Prism

A triangular prism has **five** faces, **nine** edges and **six** vertices. It has three faces as rectangles and two faces as triangles.

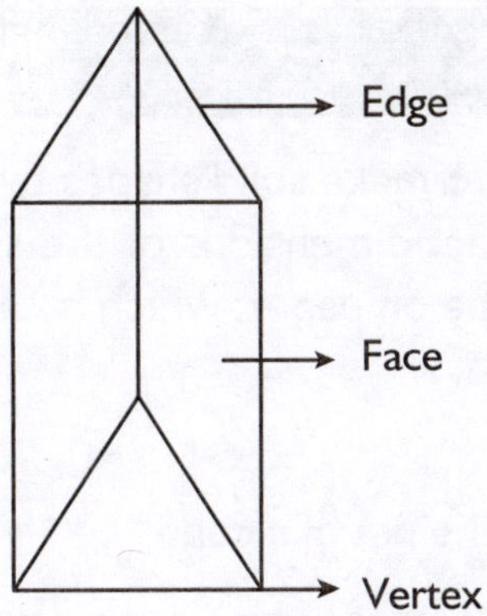

Faces – 5
Edges – 9
Vertices – 6

Cylinder

A cylinder has no straight edges. It has **three** faces, **two** of which are circular and one is a curved face.

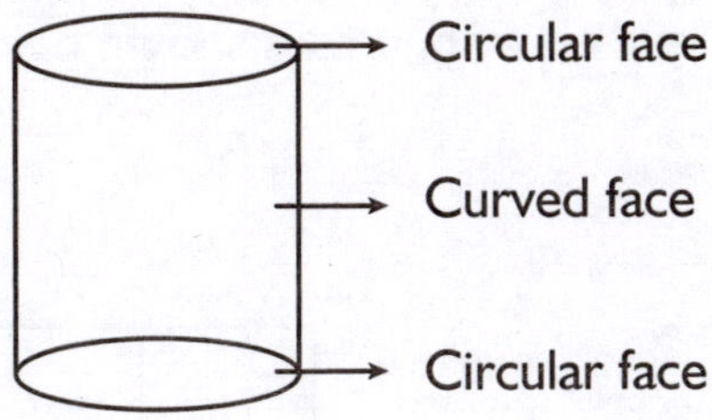

Faces – 3
Edges – 2

Cone

A cone has no straight edges. It has **two** faces, out of which one is circular and one is curved.

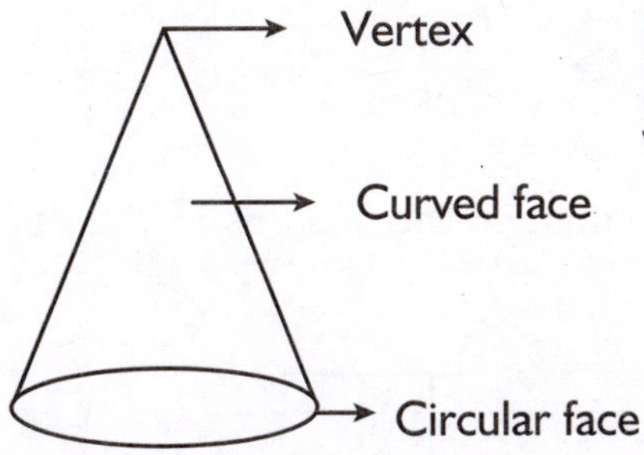

Faces – 2
Edges – 1
Vertex – 1

Sphere

The sphere has no flat surface. It has only **one** face.

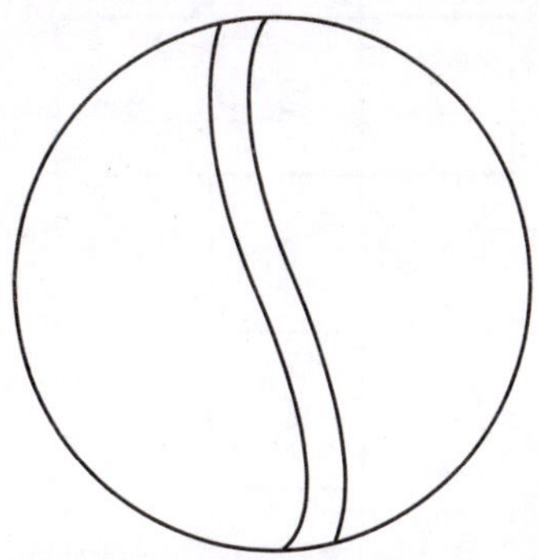

Faces – 1

Solids	Cube	Cuboid	Square pyramid	Triangular pyramid	Triangular prism	Cylinder	Cone
Faces	6	6	5	4	5	3	2
Edges	12	12	8	6	9	2	1
Vertices	8	8	5	4	6	—	1

Nets of Solids

It is possible to make solid shapes by cutting out and folding a piece of paper. We need to know the exact dimensions of the shape to be cut out. First, we make a drawing of the unfolded shape on paper, which is called the **net** of the solid shape and then cut it to form the solid.

Example:

Let us make the net of a cube.

A cube has six faces, which are squares. The net will consist of six congruent squares. The arrangement of the six squares is shown below.

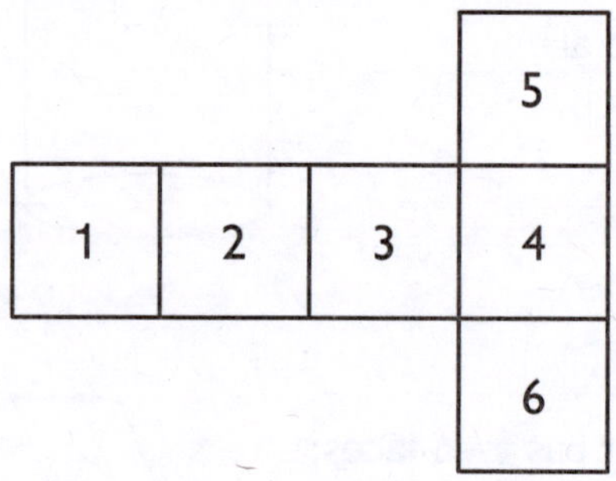

The arrangement of the squares in the net of the cube can also have two other possible options.

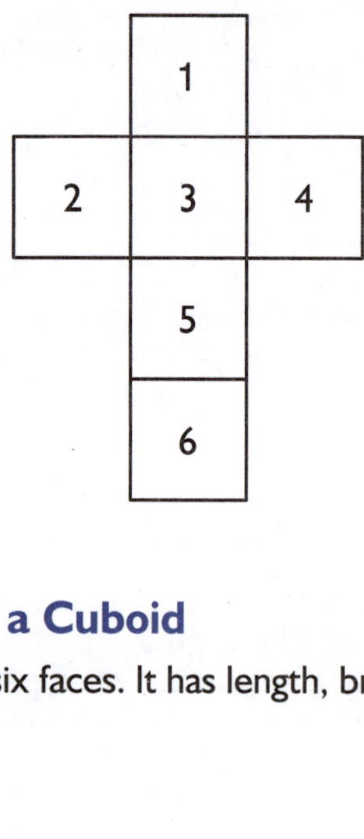

or

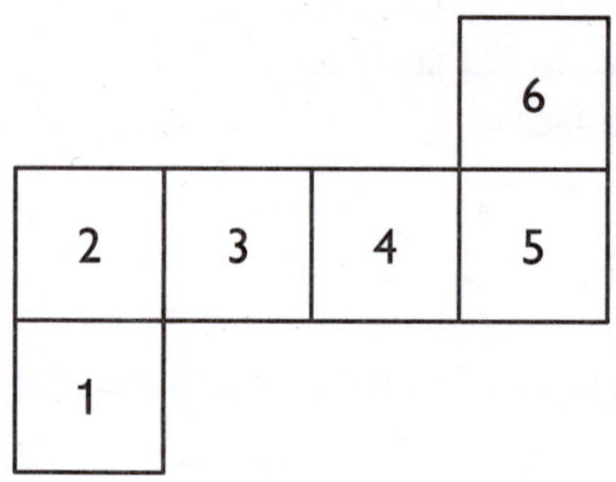

The Net of a Cuboid

A cuboid has six faces. It has length, breadth and height. The net will be as follows.

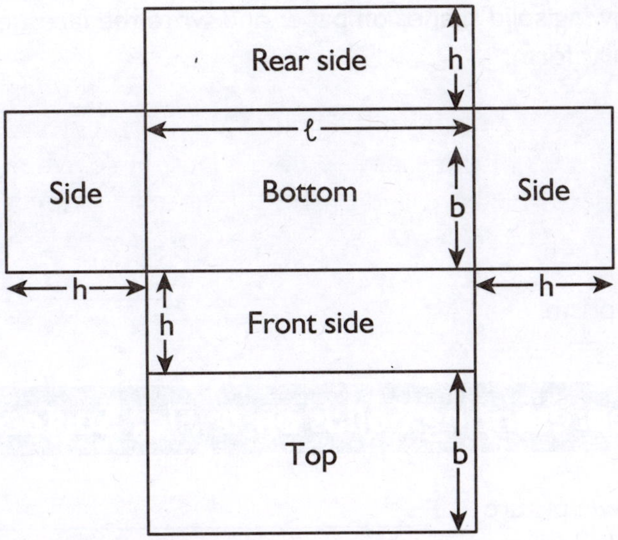

The Net of Square Base Pyramid

A square base pyramind has five faces. The base is a square and the other four faces are triangles of the same shape and size. The net will be as follows.

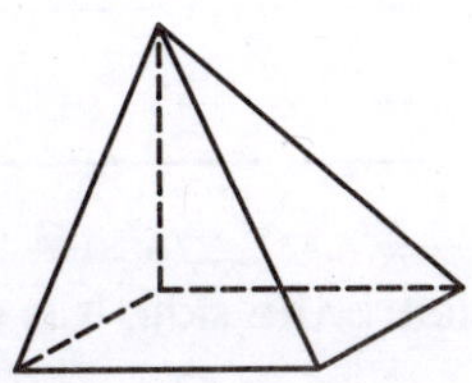

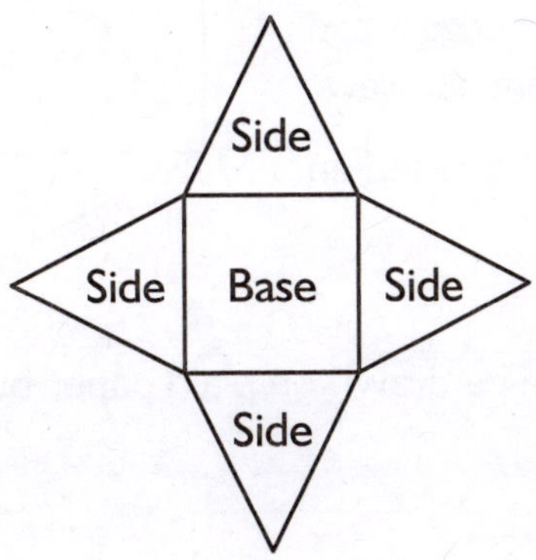

Alert!

When we cut out the net for a solid shape, we must have only one piece of paper in the end, which when folded will form the required solid figure.

Practice Exercise 14.1

1. Make a net of a cube with one 6 cm edge on a chart paper. Fold it to form a cube.
2. Abir bought a birthday cake for his mother in a box. He opened the box to check whether it was a cube or a cuboid. He found it to be a cuboidal shape. Can you help Abir make a net of the box with the following dimensions: length 18 cm, breadth 12 cm and height 10 cm?
3. Make the net of a cylinder whose height is 'h' cm and radius 'r' cm.
4. Draw the net of a triangular prism.

5. Draw the following solid shapes on paper and write the faces, edges and vertices of each in tabular form.

   a. Cube
   b. Cylinder
   c. Cuboid
   d. Sphere
   e. Triangular prism

Representing Solids on a Flat Surface

When we need to draw a picture of a solid shape on a flat surface, for example, on paper or on a blackboard, we need to represent the three dimensions in a two dimensional form. In such a case, some of the faces, edges and vertices are hidden from our view.

This sketch of a solid is called an oblique sketch.

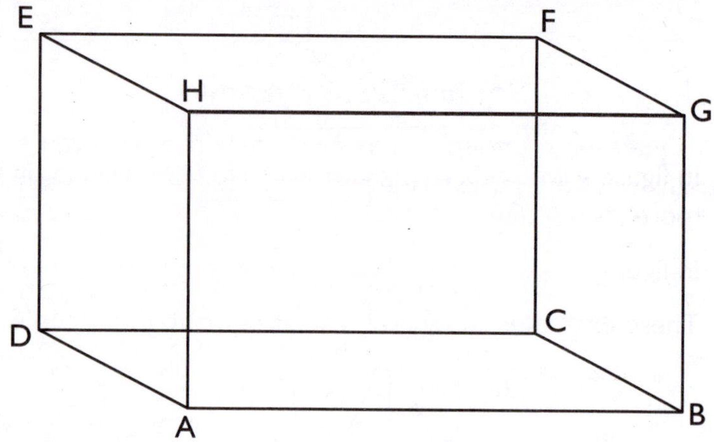

Oblique sketches can be drawn on plain paper but to learn the skill, it is useful to do so on a square lined paper.

Visual Estimation

Imagine you have a cardboard box in the shape of a cuboid. You have several chalk boxes, which are cubical in shape and need to be packed in the cardboard box. How many chalk boxes will fit in the cardboard box?

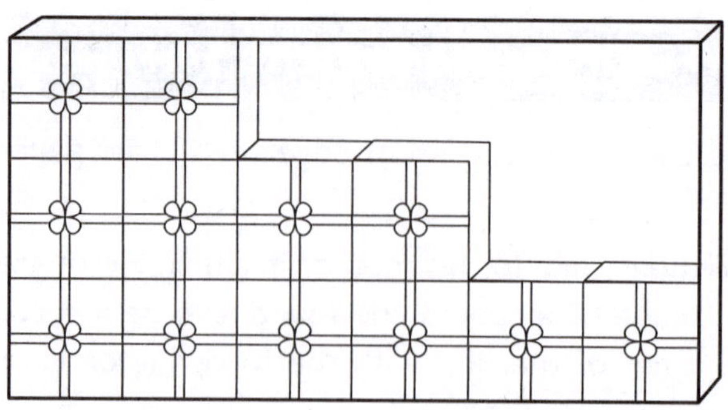

By looking at the size of boxes, we can estimate the number of chalk boxes that can fit in the cardboard box.

As many as three rows of six boxes each can be fitted in the cardboard box. Thus, eighteen chalk boxes can be fitted in one big box.

We have, thus, made a guess about the space available without actually measuring it. This process is said to be **visual** estimation of space. The estimates are an approximation of finding the area or volume by visual outputs. We come across such estimations in our daily life.

Look at the shelves containing some boxes or cartons as shown in figures a and b below.

a.

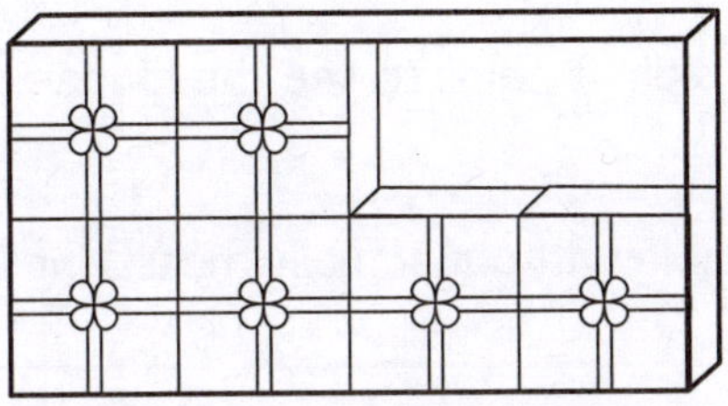

b.

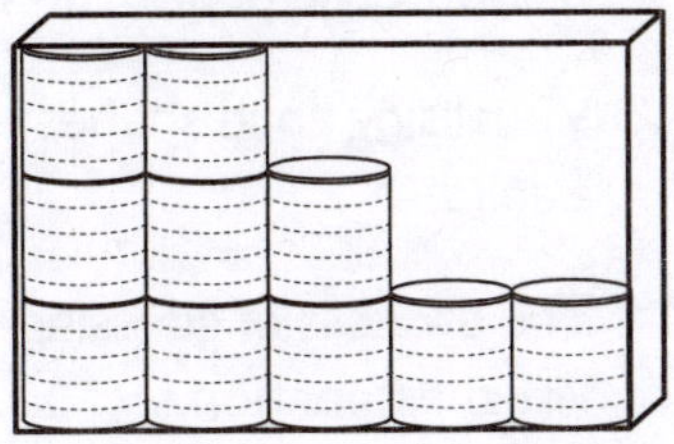

In figure a we see that six cartons have been placed on the shelf. We can estimate that two more cartons can fit on the shelf.

In figure b, ten tins have been kept on the shelf. We can find space for five more tins.

These examples show how visual estimation of space is possible.

Practice Exercise 14.2

1. Indicate the shape of the following articles.

   a. Book
   b. Battery cell
   c. Tennis ball
   d. Ice cream cone
   e. Candle
   f. Powder tin
   g. Geometry box
   h. Lunch box
   i. Dice
   j. A cardboard carton

2. Estimate how many more boxes and tins can fit into the shelf in each of the figures shown below.

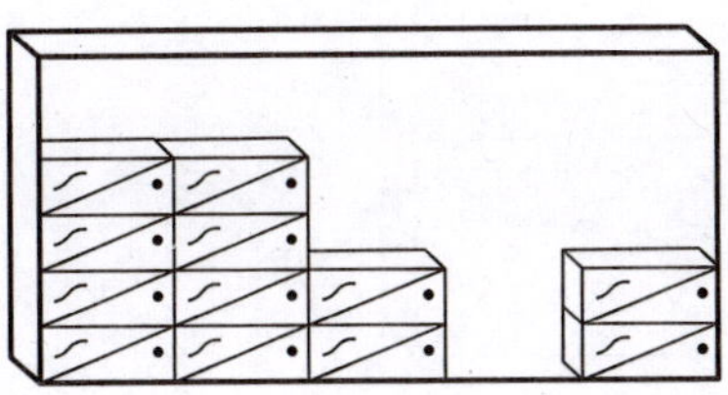

a.

b.

Highlights

- Plane figures have two dimensions and solid shapes have three dimensions.
- Most solids have faces, edges and vertices.
- A net is an arrangement of plane figures connected at their edges, that can be folded up to make a solid.
- Representation of 3-D figures in 2-D can be done by oblique sketches. Squared or isometric paper can be used for this purpose.
- Visualising solid shapes is a very useful skill. It helps to see the hidden parts of a solid.
- The process of guessing the space available without actually measuring is called visual estimation.

Look at the circular cake. How can you cut it into eight equal pieces using only three cuts?

Answer for Brainteaser on page 227

Make a Box

Objective: To make a net of a cuboid and then fold it into a box.

Material required: a thick chart paper, a pair of scissors, adhesive tape and coloured pens.

Procedure:

Step 1 Draw the net of a cuboid as shown in the figure below. You can choose the length (ℓ), breadth (b) and height (h) of the cuboid.

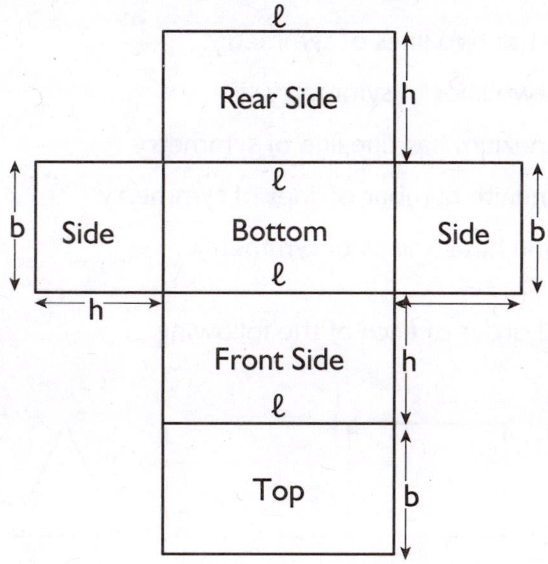

Step 2 After drawing the net on the chart paper, cut it out in one piece.

Step 3 Fold at the edges to make a box.

Step 4 Colour and draw on the box to make it more attractive.

Rewind

1. Draw the lines of symmetry for each of the following.

   a. Line segment b. Isosceles triangle c. Square

   d. Rectangle e. Regular pentagon

2. Draw the lines of symmetry for the following letters of the English alphabet.

3. Indicate whether the following statements are true (T) or false (F).

   a. A parallelogram has two lines of symmetry.

   b. A rhombus has two lines of symmetry.

   c. An isosceles trapezium has one line of symmetry .

   d. A circle has an infinite number of lines of symmetry.

   e. A regular hexagon has six lines of symmetry.

4. Write the rotational order of each of the following.

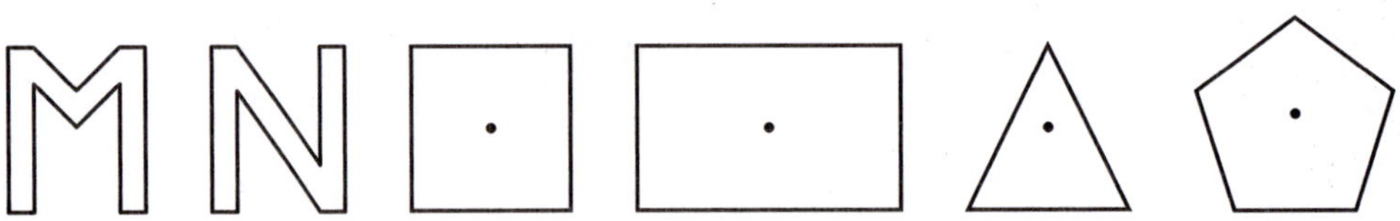

5. Write the letter S and rotate it through 90°, 180°, 270° and 360° about a point.

6. State which of the following are reflections and which are rotations.

   a.

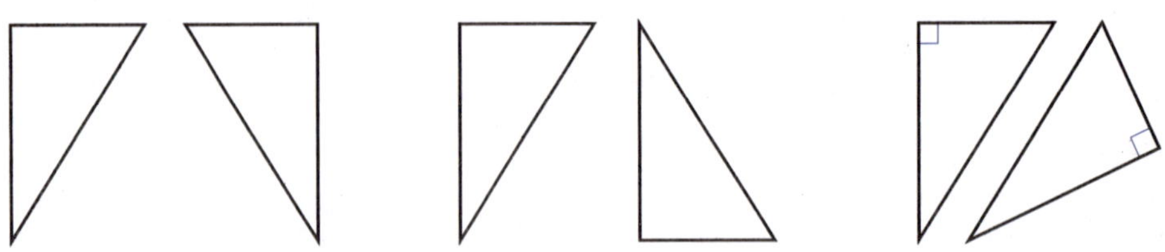

   i. ______ ii. ______ iii. ______

b. 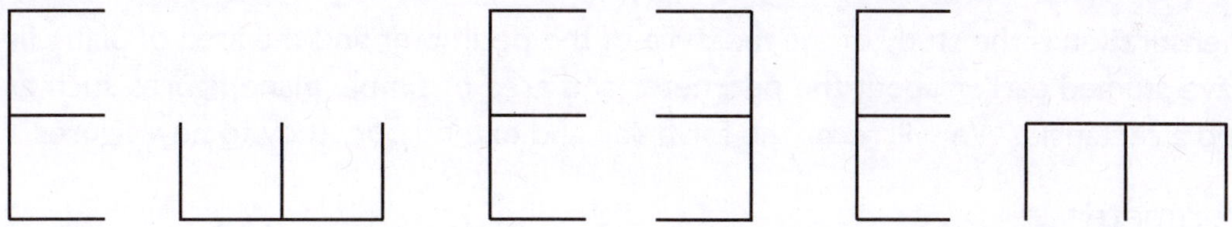

i. ______ ii. ______ iii. ______

c. 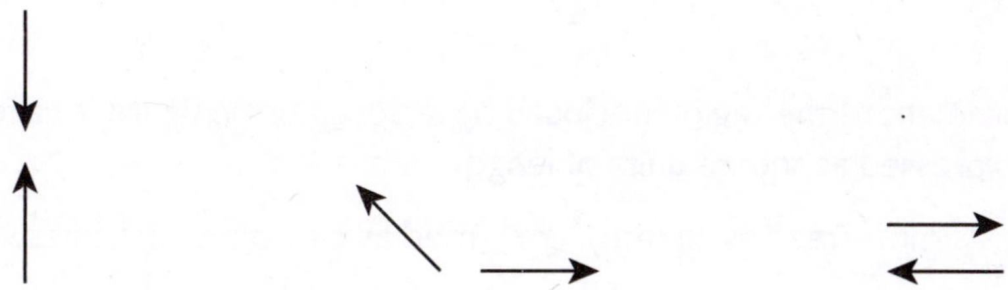

i. ______ ii. ______ iii. ______

7. Complete the following table.

Solid Shapes	Cube	Cuboids	Cylinder	Cone	Triangular prism
Number of faces					
Number of edges					
Number of vertices					

8. Make a net of a cube with one of the edges as 6 cm.

Answer for Brainteaser from page 224

First use two cuts and make the cake into four pieces. Now slice the cake horizontally from the centre to get eight equal pieces.

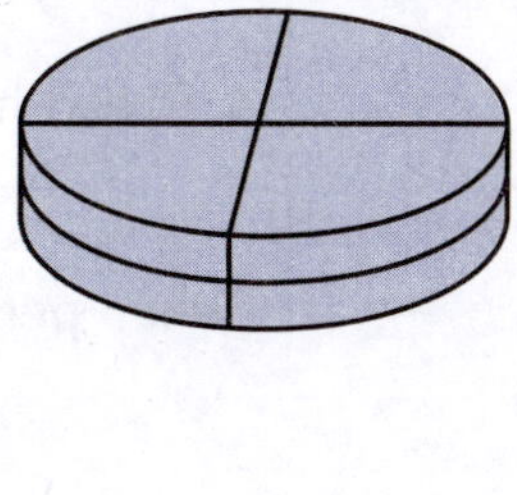

CHAPTER 15 Mensuration

Mensuration is the study of the measure of the perimeter and the area of plane figures. We have studied earlier about the perimeter and area of simple plane figures such as a square and a rectangle. We will recall the formulae and extend our study to new figures.

Perimeter

The perimeter of a closed plane figure is the length of its boundary. The unit of perimeter is the unit of length. It is measured in mm, cm, m, km etc.

Area

The measurement of the region enclosed by a closed plane figure is called its area. The unit of area is expressed as square units of length.

It is written as mm^2 (read as sq mm), cm^2 (read as sq cm), m^2 (read as sq m), etc.

Let us recall the formulae for the perimeter and area of a square and a rectangle.

Square

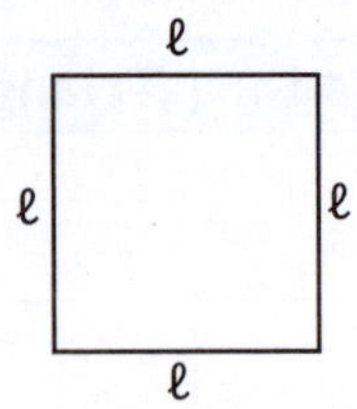

Formulae

1. Perimeter of a square $= \ell + \ell + \ell + \ell$
$= 4\ell$
$= 4 \times$ side
2. Area of a square $= \ell \times \ell = \ell^2 = \text{Side}^2$
3. Side of a square $= \dfrac{\text{Perimeter}}{4}$ (when perimeter is given)
4. Side of a square $= \sqrt{\text{Area of square}}$ (when area is given)

Rectangle

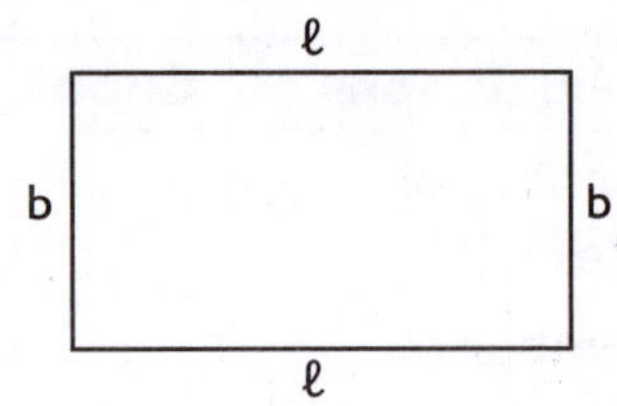

Formulae

1. Perimeter of a rectangle $= \ell + b + \ell + b$
$= 2\ell + 2b$
$= 2(\text{length} + \text{breadth})$
2. Area of rectangle $= \ell \times b =$ length $\times$ breadth
3. Length of a rectangle $= \dfrac{\text{Perimeter}}{2} - \text{Breadth}$ (when perimeter and breadth are given)
4. Breadth of a rectangle $= \dfrac{\text{Perimeter}}{2} - \text{Length}$

(when perimeter and length are given)

5. Length of a rectangle $= \frac{\text{Area}}{\text{Breadth}}$

(when area and breadth are given)

6. Breadth of a rectangle $= \frac{\text{Area}}{\text{Length}}$

(when area and length are given)

Conversion of Units of Perimeter and Area

Perimeter or Length Units	Area or Square Units
1 cm = 10 mm	$1\ cm^2 = 1\ cm \times 1\ cm = 10\ mm \times 10\ mm = 100\ mm^2$
1 dm = 10 cm	$1\ dm^2 = 1\ dm \times 1\ dm = 10\ cm \times 10\ cm = 100\ cm^2$
1 m = 10 dm	$1\ m^2 = 1\ dm \times 1\ dm = 10\ dm \times 10\ dm = 100\ dm^2$
1 m = 100 cm	$1\ m^2 = 1\ m \times 1\ m = 100\ cm \times 100\ cm = 10000\ cm^2$
1 dam = 10 m	$1\ dam^2 = 1\ dam \times 1\ dam = 10\ m \times 10\ m = 100\ m^2$
1 hm = 100 m	$1\ hm^2 = 1\ hm \times 1\ hm = 100\ m \times 100\ m = 10000\ m^2$
1 km = 1,000 m	$1\ km^2 = 1\ km \times 1\ km = 1{,}000\ m \times 1{,}000\ m = 1{,}000{,}000\ m^2$
	$1\ are = 100\ m^2$
	$1\ hectare = 10{,}000\ m^2$

Alert!

1. When we convert a bigger unit into smaller unit, we multiply.
2. When we convert a smaller unit into a bigger unit, we divide.
3. The units of length and breadth should be the same. If they are different, convert them to the same unit.
4. Proper units must be written with the answer.

Example 1: The area of a rectangular field is $3456\ m^2$. If the breadth of the field is 48 m, find its length and perimeter.

We know that area = length × breadth

$$\text{length} = \frac{\text{area}}{\text{breadth}}$$

$$\text{length} = \frac{3456\ m^2}{48\ m}$$

length = 72 m.

$$\text{Perimeter} = 2(\ell + b)$$

$$= 2(72 + 48)$$

$$= 2(120) = 240\ m$$

Example 2: The cost of mowing grass is ₹2.50 per sq m. Mr Mathur has a square lawn having length 25 m and Mr Mehta has a rectangular lawn of length 22 m and breadth 26 m. Who will pay more to get his lawn mowed and by how much?

Area of a square = $(\ell)^2$

∴ Area of Mr Mathur's lawn = 25 m × 25 m

= 625 m^2

Area of a rectangle = length × breadth

∴ Area of Mr Mehta's lawn = 22 m × 26 m

= 572 m^2

Mr Mathur will pay 625 × 2.50 to set his lawn mowed

Mr Mehta will pay 572 × 2.50 to set his lawn mowed

∴ Mr Mathur pays more to set his lawn mowed.

Difference amount = 2.5 (625 − 572)

= 2.5 × 53

= ₹132.50

Mr Mathur will pay ₹132.50 more to get the lawn grass mowed.

Example 3: Find the area of the shaded portion in the following figures.

a.

Area of the shaded portion = Area of the outer rectangle − Area of the inner rectangle

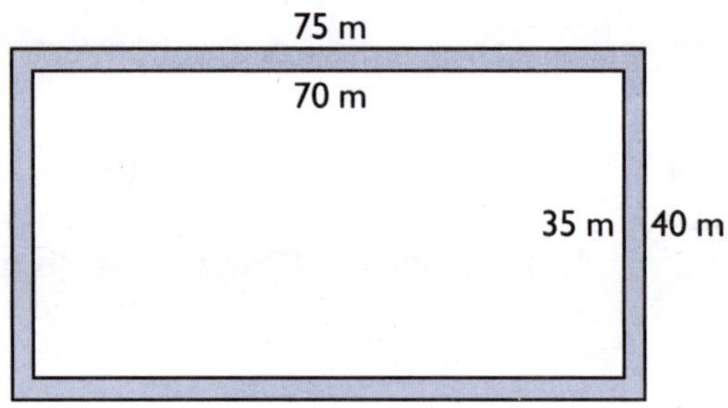

= 75 m × 40 m − 70 m × 35 m

= 3000 m^2 − 2450 m^2

= 550 m^2

b.

Area of the shaded region = Area of the outer rectangle − Area of the inner rectangle

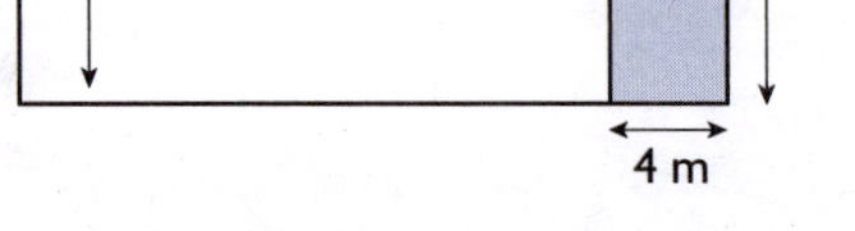

= 24 m × 19 m − 20 m × 16.5 m

= 456 m^2 − 330 m^2

= 126 m^2

c.

Area of the rectangle = $40 \text{ m} \times 30 \text{ m} = 1200 \text{ m}^2$

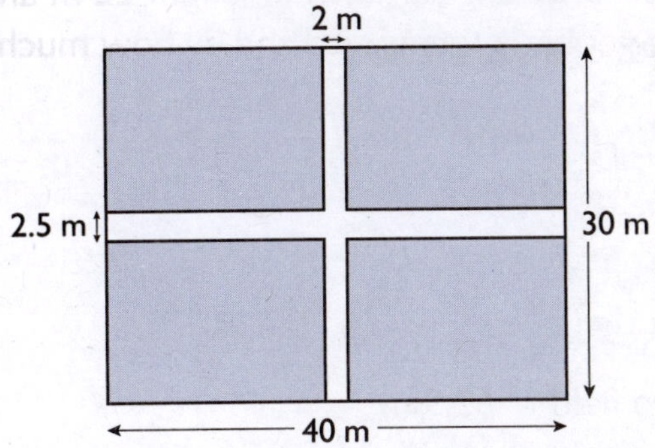

Area of the horizontal white strip = $40 \text{ m} \times 2.5 \text{ m} = 100 \text{ m}^2$

Area of the vertical white strip = $30 \text{ m} \times 2 \text{ m} = 60 \text{ m}^2$

Area of the small rectangle at the centre = $2.5 \text{ m} \times 2 \text{ m} = 5 \text{ m}^2$

Area of the shaded portion = Area of the rectangle − Area of the horizontal strip − Area of the vertical strip + Area of the small rectangle at the centre = $1200 \text{ m}^2 - 100 \text{ m}^2 - 60 \text{ m}^2 + 5 \text{ m}^2 = 1045 \text{ m}^2$

Answer: Area of the shaded portion is 1045 m^2.

Example 4: A roll of chart paper is 15 m 20 cm long and 8 m 30 cm wide. A square chart paper of size 5 m 50 cm is to be cut from the roll to make four posters. How much paper will be left?

Area of a roll of chart paper = 15 m 20 cm × 8 m 30 cm

= (1500 cm + 20 cm) × (800 cm + 30 cm)

= 1520 cm × 830 cm

= $1{,}261{,}600 \text{ cm}^2$

Area of paper for poster = 5 m 50 cm × 5 m 50 cm

= (500 cm + 50 cm) × (500 cm + 50 cm)

= 550 cm × 550 cm

= $302{,}500 \text{ cm}^2$

Area of paper for 4 posters = 302,500 × 4

= $1{,}210{,}000 \text{ cm}^2$

Area of paper left = $1{,}261{,}600 \text{ cm}^2 - 1{,}210{,}000 \text{ cm}^2$

= $51{,}600 \text{ cm}^2$

Example 5: A rectangular field is 75 m in length and 50 m in breadth. A fence has to be put around the field. The cost of wire is ₹45 per m. Find the total cost of fencing. If a square field has to be fenced at the same cost, what should be its maximum length?

Perimeter of the rectangular field = $2[\ell + b]$

= 2[75m + 50 m] = 2[125m]

= 250 m

Cost of fencing = 250 × 45

= ₹11,250

The cost of fencing the square field is also ₹11,250.

1 m of fencing cost ₹45.

Perimeter of square field = 4 × length of a square field

Cost of 4ℓ m = ₹11,250.

$$\text{Length of the square field} = \frac{11250}{4 \times 45}$$

$$= \frac{11250}{180}$$

So, the maximum length of the square field = 62.5 m

Practice Exercise 15.1

1. Which will have a greater area—a rectangle with length and breadth 40 m and 28 m, respectively, or a square of side 35 m? Also compare their perimeters.
2. The perimeter of a rectangle of sides 35 cm and 24 cm is equal to the perimeter of a square. Find the side and area of the square.
3. The sum of the perimeters of two squares of sides 18 cm and 12 cm, respectively, is equal to the perimeter of a rectangle. If the length of the rectangle is 36 cm, what should be the breadth of the rectangle? Which is greater—the sum of the areas of the two squares or the area of the rectangle and how much?
4. A square field of side 78 m is to be fenced with barbed wire that has to go around the boundary four times. How much wire will be required? What will be the cost of fencing if the wire costs ₹55 per metre and labour charges are ₹2,150?
5. A square courtyard of side 45 m has to be tiled. If the size of a tile is 15 cm by 15 cm, how many tiles will be required for the courtyard. If the cost of a tile is ₹30, find the total cost incurred?
6. A rectangular park is 50 m long and 35 m broad. A 3.5 m broad pavement runs along the boundary of the park. Find the cost of cementing this pavement at the rate of ₹400 per 8 m^2.
7. Find the area of the shaded portion in the figures given below.

a.

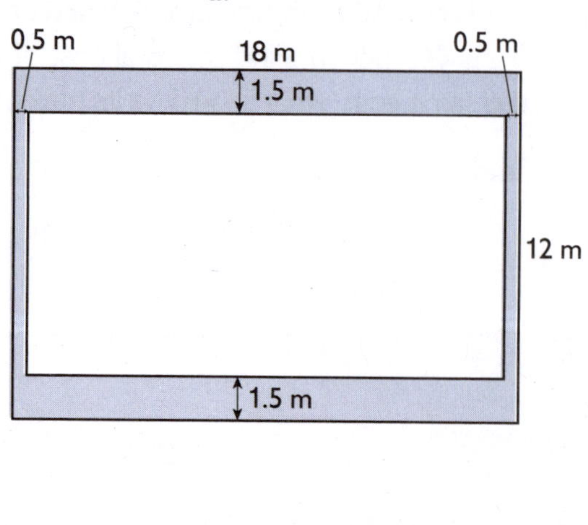

b.

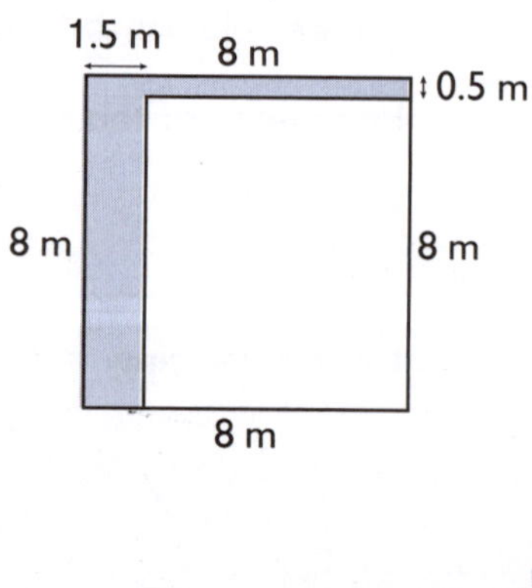

c.

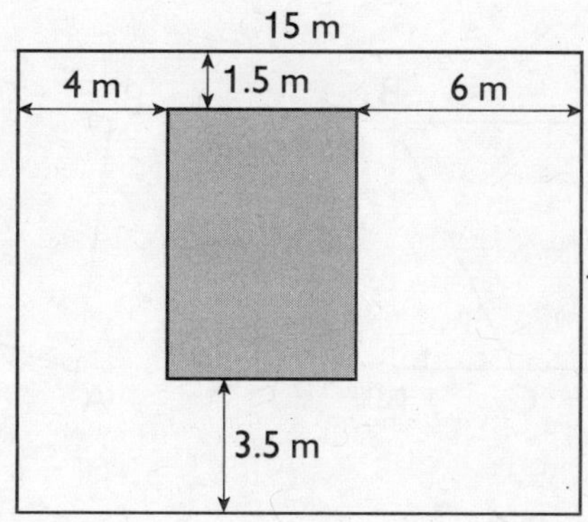

8. A rectangular park has two pathways that are 5 m wide built in the manner as shown in the figure. If the length and breadth of the park are 32 m and 18 m, respectively, find the area of the pathways and the area of the remaining park.

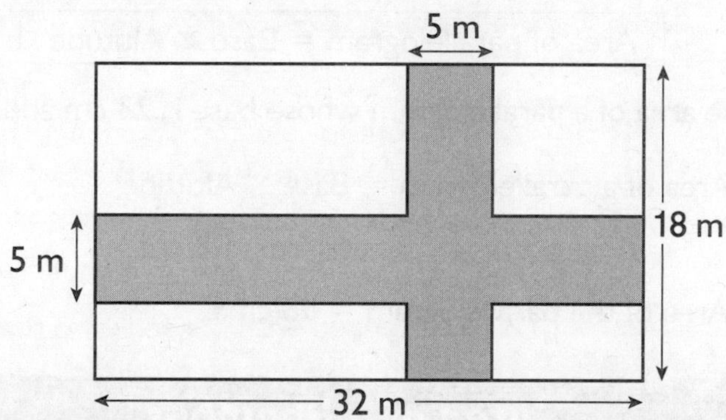

Area of a Parallelogram

A parallelogram is a quadrilateral in which the opposite sides are equal and parallel.

The area of a parallelogram is the product of its base and perpendicular. The perpendicular is called the altitude. The base is the side opposite to the vertex through which the perpendicular is dropped.

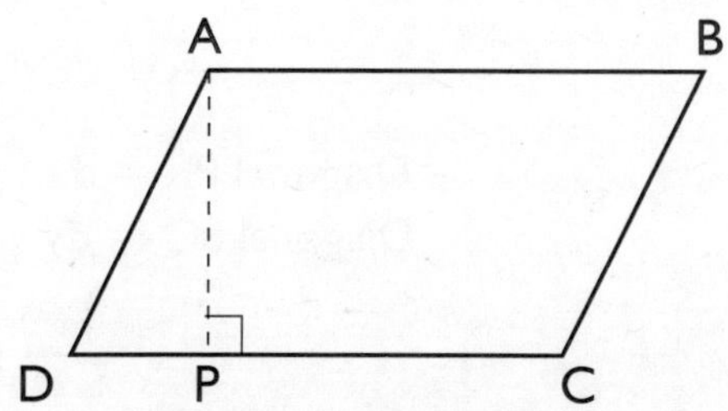

In this figure, the base is CD while the altitude or the perpendicular is AP.

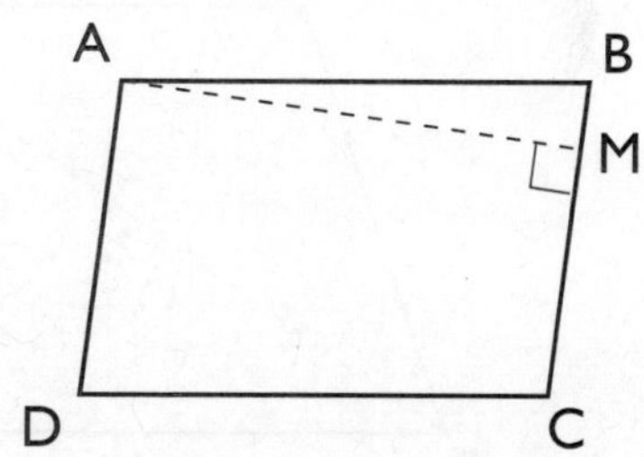

In this figure, the base is BC while the perpendicular or altitude is AM.

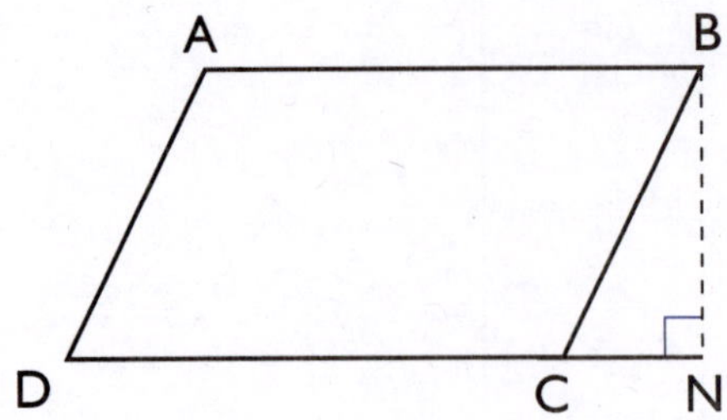

In this figure, the base is DC while the altitude or perpendicular is BN.

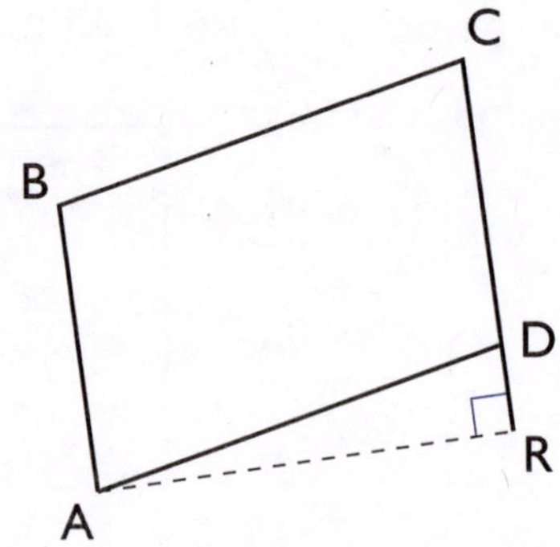

In this figure, the base is CD while the altitude is AR.

Thus, we see from the figures discussed here that the altitude is the perpendicular dropped from the vertex opposite the base.

Area of parallelogram = Base × Altitude

Example: Find the area of a parallelogram whose base is 23 cm and altitude is 8 cm.

Area of a parallelogram = Base × Altitude

= 12 cm × 8 cm

∴ Area of the parallelogram = 96 cm^2.

Area of a Rhombus

A rhombus is a special type of parallelogram in which all sides are equal and the opposite sides are parallel. Thus, we can use the formula of calculating area of a parallelogram to find the area of a rhombus.

Since the diagonals of a rhombus bisect each other at right angles, there is another formula to find its area.

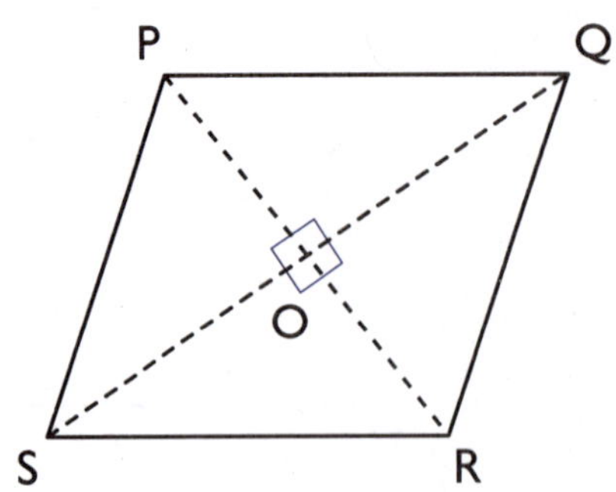

Diagonal PR = d_1
Diagonal SQ = d_2

Area of the rhombus $= \frac{1}{2}$(product of its diagonals)

$= \frac{1}{2}(d_1 \times d_2)$ or

Area of a rhombus = Base × Altitude

Either formula can be used to determine the area of a rhombus.

Example: Find the area of a rhombus with diagonals 18 cm and 20 cm.

$$\text{Area of rhombus} = \frac{1}{2}(\text{product of the diagonals})$$

$$= \frac{1}{2}(d_1 \times d_2)$$

$$= \frac{1}{\cancel{2}} \times \overset{10}{\cancel{20}}\text{ cm} \times 18\text{ cm}$$

$$= 180\text{ cm}^2$$

Area of a Triangle

The diagonal of any parallelogram divide it into two triangles. Hence, we can say that the area of a triangle is half the area of a parallelogram.

$$\text{Area of the triangle} = \frac{1}{2}(\text{Area of the parallelogram})$$

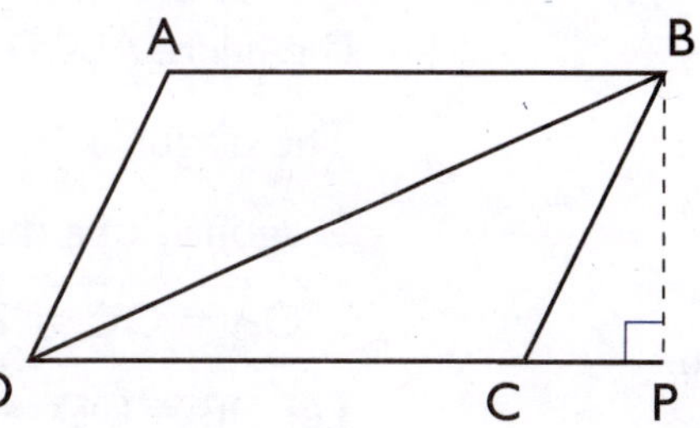

$\triangle ABD \cong \triangle BCD$ (SSS congruency condition)

Hence, a diagonal divides the parallelogram into two congruent triangles, and their areas are equal.

$$\text{Area of the triangle} = \frac{1}{2}(\text{Area of the parallelogram})$$

$$\text{Area of the triangle} = \frac{1}{2}(\text{Base} \times \text{Altitude})$$

$$\text{Area of } \triangle ABD = \text{Area of } \triangle BCD$$

$$= \frac{1}{2} \times DC \times BP$$

Alert!

Altitude is the perpendicular dropped from the opposite vertex to the base. It is also called the height of a figure.

Example 1: Find the altitude of a triangle whose area is 24 cm^2 and the base is 6 cm.

$$\text{Area of triangle} = \frac{1}{2} \times \text{base} \times \text{altitude}$$

$$\text{Altitude} = \frac{2 \times \text{area of triangle}}{\text{base}}$$

$$\text{Altitude} = \frac{2 \times \overset{10}{\cancel{24}}}{\underset{1}{\cancel{6}}} = 8\text{ cm}$$

$\therefore$ Altitude of the triangle = 8 cm

Example 2: The area of a rhombus is 252 cm^2 and its perimeter is 56 cm. Find its altitude. All four sides of a rhombus are equal, hence,

Perimeter of a rhombus = 4 × side

$$\text{Side of a rhombus} = \frac{\text{Perimeter}}{4}$$

$$= \frac{56}{4} = 14 \text{ cm}$$

Area of a rhombus = area of a parallelogram

Area of a rhombus = base × altitude

$$\text{Altitude} = \frac{\text{area of a rhombus}}{\text{base}}$$

$$\text{Altitude} = \frac{252 \text{ cm}^2}{14 \text{ cm}} = 18 \text{ cm}$$

Alert

Since all four sides of a rhombus are equal, any side can be taken as the base

Example 3: Find the area of a rhombus in which each side is 15 cm long and one of whose diagonals is 24 cm.

The figure ABCD is a rhombus whose side is 15 cm.

The diagonal AC is 24 cm.

Diagonals of a rhombus bisect each other at right angles.

∴ OA = OC = 12 cm

Let OB = OD = x cm

Using the Pythagoras theorem:

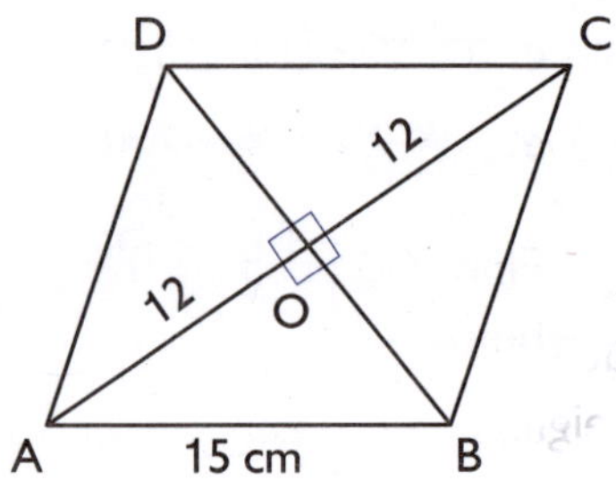

$$AB^2 = OA^2 + OB^2$$

$$15^2 = 12^2 + x^2$$

$$15^2 - 12^2 = x^2$$

$$225 - 144 = x^2$$

$$x^2 = 81 \text{ cm}^2$$

$$x = \sqrt{81}$$

$$x = 9 \text{ cm}$$

$$BD = 2 \times OB = 2 \times 9 = 18 \text{ cm}$$

$$\text{Area of a rhombus} = \frac{1}{2} \times d_1 \times d_2$$

$$= \frac{1}{\cancel{2}_1} \times 24 \times \cancel{18}^{9}$$

Area of a rhombus = 216 cm^2

Example 4: Find the area of the quadrilateral PQRS whose diagonal PR is 30 cm in length and the lengths of the perpendiculars to it from the opposite vertices are 8.6 cm and 6.8 cm, respectively.

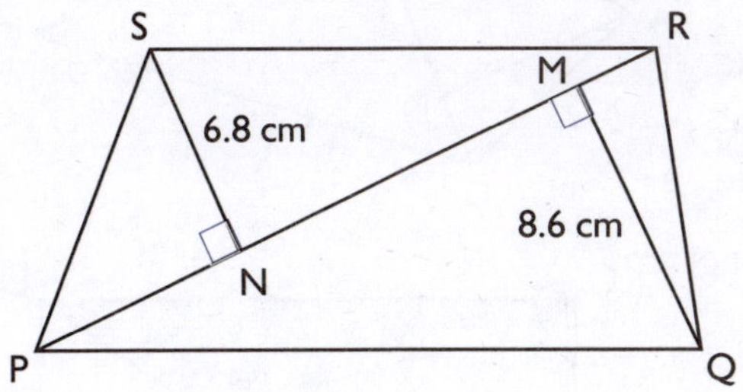

Here, PQRS is the given quadrilateral in which PR is the given diagonal.

SN is $\perp$ to PR and QM is $\perp$ to PR.

PR = 30 cm, SN = 6.8 cm and QM = 8.6 cm

Area of quadrilateral PQRS = area of $\triangle$PSR + area of $\triangle$QPR

Area of quadrilateral PQRS $= \frac{1}{2} \times PR \times SN + \frac{1}{2} \times PR \times QM$

$= \frac{1}{2} \times 30 \times 6.8 + \frac{1}{2} \times 30 \times 8.6$

$= \frac{1}{2} \times 30 \times [6.8 + 8.6]$

$= \frac{1}{2} \times 30 \times [15.4] = 231 \text{ cm}^2$

Practice Exercise 15.2

1. Find the area of the parallelograms whose base and altitudes are given below.
   a. 5.5 cm and 6.4 cm
   b. 10.8 cm and 2.5 cm
   c. 14.9 cm and 7.8 cm
   d. 1 m 60 cm and 75 cm
   e. 14 cm and 6.5 cm
2. Find the area of the following rhombi the lengths of whose diagonals are given below.
   a. 15 cm and 24 cm
   b. 7.8 cm and 10.2 cm
   c. 13.5 cm and 9.6 cm
   d. 6.85 cm and 3.2 cm
   e. 16.54 cm and 14.22 cm
3. Find the height of a parallelogram whose area is 428.04 cm^2 and base is 24.6 cm.
4. Find the area of a rhombus given that its side measures 13 cm and one of diagonals measures 10 cm.
5. The area of a rhombus is 441 cm^2 and its perimeter is 84 cm. Find its altitude.
6. The base of a triangular park is 420 m and its altitude is 325 m. Find the cost of levelling the park at the rate of ₹5 per 1000 m^2.

7. Find the area of the quadrilateral ABCD, if BD is 16.8 cm, AM = 8.6 cm and CN = 10.2 cm. Here AM and CN are perpendicular to BD.

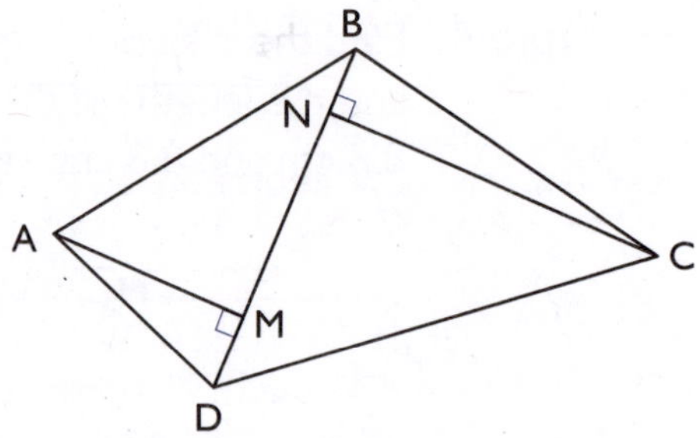

8. The area of a parallelogram with base 24.8 cm and altitude 16.5 cm is equal to the area of a rhombus whose diagonal is 22 cm. Find the length of the other diagonal of the rhombus.

9. In the given figure, ABCD is a rectangle with length 36 m and breadth 24 m. In $\triangle ADE$, EF is $\perp$ to AD and EF = 15 m. Calculate the area of the shaded region.

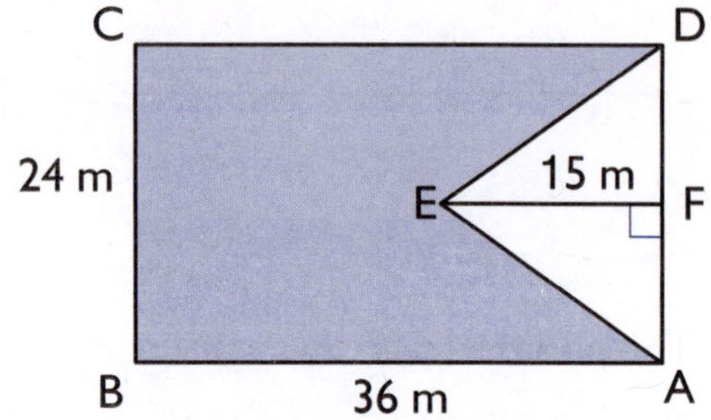

10. In the given figure, PQRS is a rectangle in which PQ = 40 cm and QR = 25 cm. If W, X, Y, Z are the mid points of PQ, QR, RS, and SP, respectively, find the area of the shaded region.

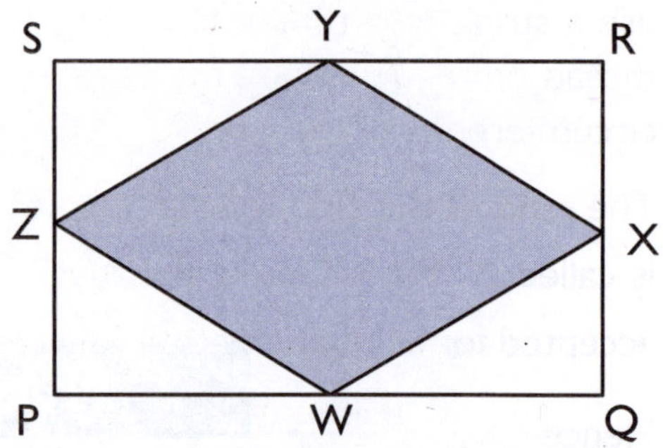

Circle

The circle is known by its radius and the centre. Every point on the circle is equidistant from the centre. This distance is called the radius of the circle. Let us recall the following basic elements of a circle.

Centre The fixed point about which the circle is drawn.

Radius The distance between the centre of the circle and any point on the circle. A circle has infinite radii that are all equal.

Chord A line segment joining any two points on the circle.

Diameter It is the longest chord and it passes through the centre of the circle. The diameter (d) is twice the radius (r) of the circle. (d = 2r).

Segment The area of the circle enclosed by a chord is known as a segment.

Sector The area of the circle that lies between two radii is known as a sector.

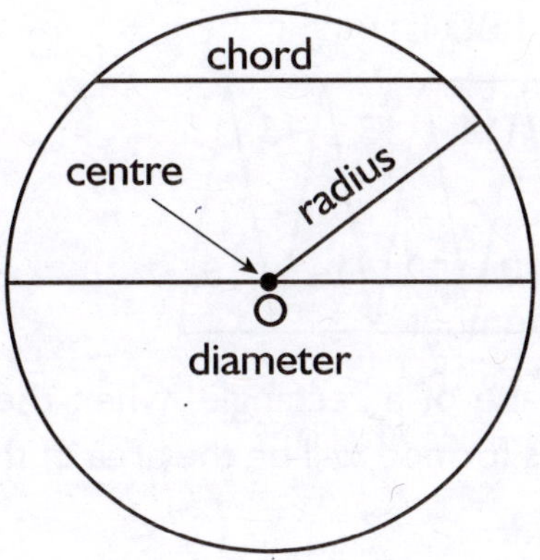

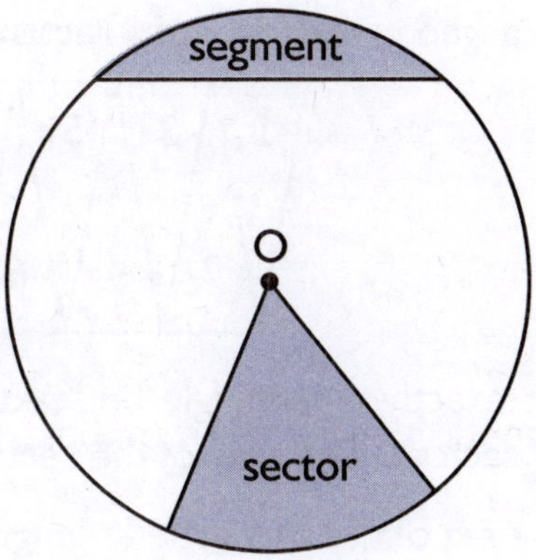

Circumference of a Circle

The perimeter or boundary of a circle is called its circumference.

Since the boundary is a curved line, we cannot measure it with the help of a ruler. We can use a string or a thread and place it along the boundary. We can then place the string or thread on the ruler and measure its length. This will give the measure of the perimeter or circumference of the circle.

The ratio of the circumference to the diameter of a circle is a constant. This constant ratio is called π (Pi), a Greek alphabet. Its approximate value is $\frac{22}{7}$ or 3.14. This value of π is accepted for all mathematical calculations. π is not a rational number.

Hence $\quad \frac{\text{Circumference (C)}}{\text{Diameter (D)}} = \pi$

or $\quad \frac{C}{D} = \pi$

but $\quad$ Diameter = 2 × Radius

$\therefore \quad \frac{C}{2r} = \pi$

or $\quad C = 2\pi r$

The circumference of the circle = $2\pi r$

Area of a Circle

Draw a circle with a radius r cm on a chart paper. With the help of a pair of scissors, cut the chart paper along the circumference, which gives us a circular disc having radius r cm. Divide the circular region into 16 equal parts by folding the disc along the diameters. Cut out the 16 parts, which are 16 sectors and arrange them as shown on the next page.

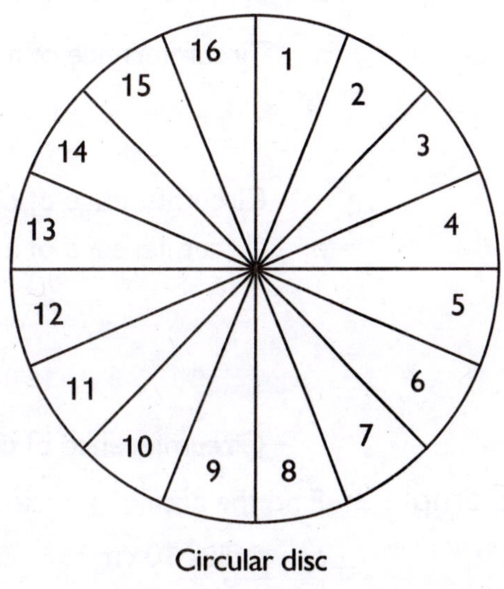

Circular disc

Sectors arranged in the form of a rectangle.

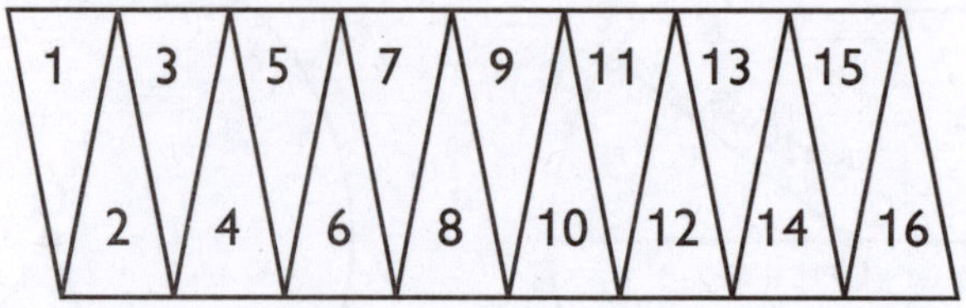

This is not exactly a rectangle but takes the shape of a rectangle, when there are more number of sectors. The area of the rectangle thus formed will be the area of the circle.

However, Area of the rectangle = length × breadth

Comparing we see that the length of the rectangle will be half the circumference of the circle and the breadth will be the radius.

$\therefore \quad \ell \times b = \frac{1}{2} \times$ circumference of the circle × radius

$$\ell \times b = \frac{1}{\cancel{2}} \times \cancel{2}\pi r \times r^2 = \pi r^2$$

But, the area of the rectangle is equal to the area of the circle

$\therefore \quad$ Area of the circle $= \pi r^2$

Hence, if we know the radius of the circle, we can draw a circle and know its circumference and area.

Alert

Diameter of the circle (d) = 2r

Circumference of the circle (C) = $2\pi r$

Area of the circle (A) = πr^2

Example 1: Find the circumference of a circle with

a. radius = 14 cm

b. diameter = 21 cm $\left(\text{use } \pi = \frac{22}{7}\right)$

a. Circumference of a circle = $2\pi r$

$$= 2 \times \frac{22}{\cancel{7}_1} \times \cancel{14}^2$$

Circumference of circle = 88 cm

b. Circumference of a circle = $2\pi r$

$= \pi d$ (since 2r = d)

$$= \frac{22}{\cancel{7}_1} \times \cancel{21}^3$$

Circumference of circle = 66 cm

Example 2: Find the area of a circle with

a. radius 10 cm (use $\pi = 3.14$)

b. radius 7 cm $\left(\text{use } \pi = \frac{22}{7}\right)$

a. Area of a circle $= \pi r^2$

Area of the circle $= 3.14 \times 10 \times 10$

$= 314 \text{ cm}^2$

b. Area of a circle $= \pi r^2$

Area of the circle $= \frac{22}{7} \times 7 \times 7$

$= 154 \text{ cm}^2$

Example 3: Find the area of circle if the circumference is 440 m. Use $\pi = \frac{22}{7}$.

We know that the circumference of a circle $= 2\pi r$

or $2\pi r = C$

$$2 \times \frac{22}{7} \times r = 440$$

$$\frac{44}{7} r = 440$$

$$r = \frac{\overset{10}{\cancel{440}} \times 7}{\cancel{44}_1} = 70 \text{ m}$$

Now, since the radius is known, we can find the area.

Area of the circle $= \pi r^2$

$$= \frac{22}{\cancel{7}_1} \times 70 \times \cancel{70}^{10}$$

$$= 22 \times 700$$

Area of the circle $= 15{,}400 \text{ m}^2$

Example 4: The area of a circular plot of land is 616 m^2. Find the circumference of the plot.

Area of a circle $= \pi r^2$

$$\frac{22}{7} \times r^2 = 616$$

$$r^2 = \frac{\overset{308\ 28}{\cancel{616}} \times 7}{\cancel{22}_{\cancel{11}_1}} = 28 \times 7 = 4 \times 7 \times 7$$

$$r^2 = 2 \times 7 \times 2 \times 7 = 14 \times 14$$

$$r = 14 \text{ cm}$$

Circumference of the circle $= 2\pi r$

$$= 2 \times \frac{22}{7} \times 14 = 88 \text{ cm}$$

Example 5: Find the area of the shaded region between the two concentric circles in the figure given here, where the circumference of the outer circle is 176 cm and the circumference of the inner circle is 132 cm. $\left(\text{Use } \pi = \frac{22}{7}\right)$

Let the radius of the outer circle be R cm and the radius of the inner circle be r cm.

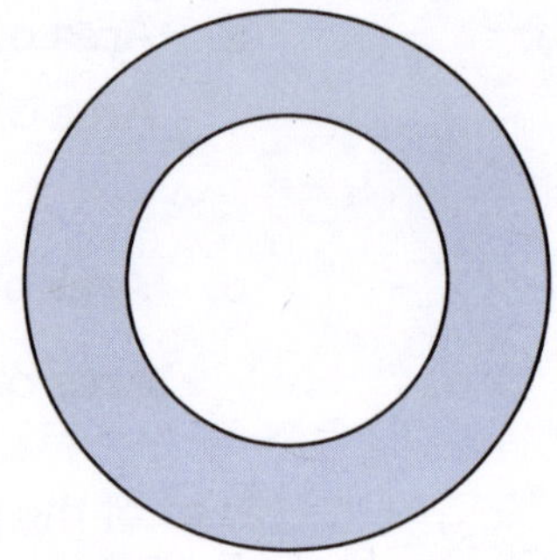

$2\pi r =$ Circumference of the outer circle

$$2 \times \frac{22}{7} \times R = 176$$

$$R = \frac{176 \times 7}{2 \times 22} = 28 \text{ cm}$$

$2\pi r =$ Circumference of the inner circle

$$2 \times \frac{22}{7} \times r = 132$$

$$r = \frac{132 \times 7}{2 \times 22} = 21 \text{ cm}$$

Area of the outer circle $= \pi R^2$

$$= \frac{22}{7} \times 28 \times 28$$

$$= 88 \times 28 = 2464 \text{ cm}^2$$

Area of the inner circle $= \pi r^2$

$$= \frac{22}{7} \times 21 \times 21$$

$$= 66 \times 21 = 1386 \text{ cm}^2$$

Area of the shaded region = Area of outer circle − Area of inner circle

Area of the shaded region $= 2464 \text{ cm}^2 - 1386 \text{ cm}^2 = 1078 \text{ cm}^2$.

Example 6: The diameter of the wheel of a car is 77 cm. How many revolutions will it make to cover a distance of 72.6 m?

Distance covered by the wheel in one revolution is the circumference of the wheel.

$$C = 2\pi r = \pi d$$

$$\therefore \quad C = \frac{22}{7} \times 77 = 22 \times 11 = 242 \text{ cm}$$

Total distance is 72.6 m = 7260 cm

$$\text{Number of revolutions} = \frac{\text{Total distance}}{\text{Circumference}}$$

$$= \frac{7{,}260 \text{ cm}}{242 \text{ cm}} = 30$$

$\therefore$ Number of revolutions = 30

Example 7: Find the area of the given figure where ABCD is a rectangle with length AB = 21 cm and BC = 14 cm.

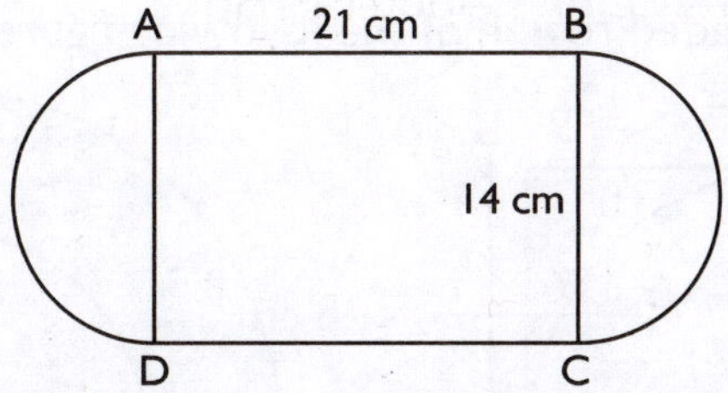

Area of the given figure = Area of the rectangle ABCD + Area of semicircle with diameter AD + Area of semicircle with diameter BC.

Area of the rectangle $= \ell \times b$

$= 21 \times 14 = 294 \text{ cm}^2$

Area of the semicircle $= \frac{\pi r^2}{2}$

Area of the two semicircles $= \frac{\pi r^2}{2} \times 2 = \pi r^2$. (Area of both the semicircles are equal as the diameter is the same)

$= \frac{22}{7} \times 7 \text{ cm} \times 7 \text{ cm}$ $\left(\begin{array}{l} d = 14 \text{ cm} \\ \therefore r = 7 \text{ cm} \end{array} \right)$

$= 154 \text{ cm}^2$

Total area of the figure $= 294 \text{ cm}^2 + 154 \text{ cm}^2$

$= 448 \text{ cm}^2$

Practice Exercise 15.3

1. Find the circumference and area of the circles with the following radii, using $\pi = \frac{22}{7}$.

   a. 35 mm b. 21 cm c. 70 cm d 21 m e 0.7 km

2. Find the radius, diameter and area of a circle with circumference 43.96 m using $\pi = 3.14$.

3. The area of a circular plate is 38.5 cm. Find its circumference using $\pi = \frac{22}{7}$.

4. The diameter of a wheel is 56 cm. Find the distance travelled by it in 500 revolutions. Write the distance in cm, m and km.

5. Find the cost of planting grass in a circular lawn of radius 21 m at the rate of ₹15 per sq m. Also find the cost of fencing the lawn at the rate of ₹5 per m.

6. A rectangular plywood measures 2.1 m by 70 cm. Circular discs are to be cut out from the plywood of diameter 14 cm. How many discs can be cut and how much plywood will be left?

7. A wire 44 cm long is bent to form a square. A ribbon 44 cm long is made to form a circular ring. Which encloses more area and by how much?

8. Find the area of the shaded region of the following figures.

a.

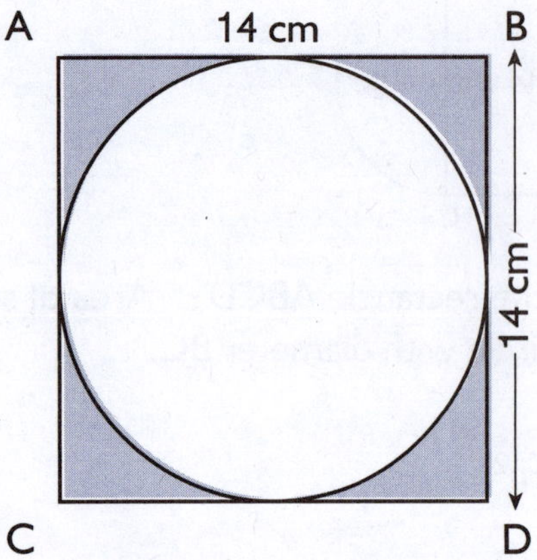

Square ABCD with side = 14 cm

b.

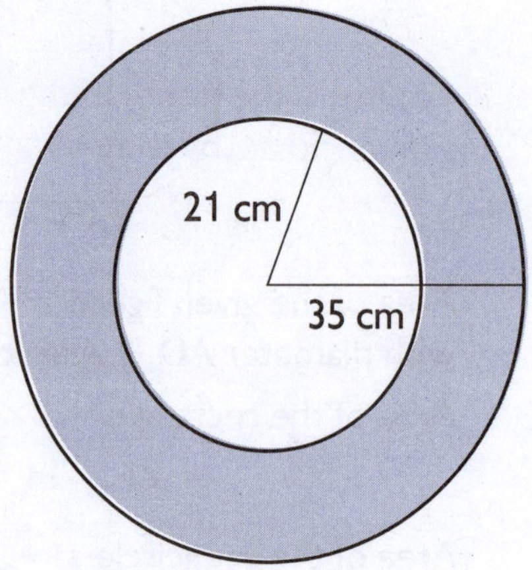

Concentric circles with radii 35 cm and 21 cm

c.

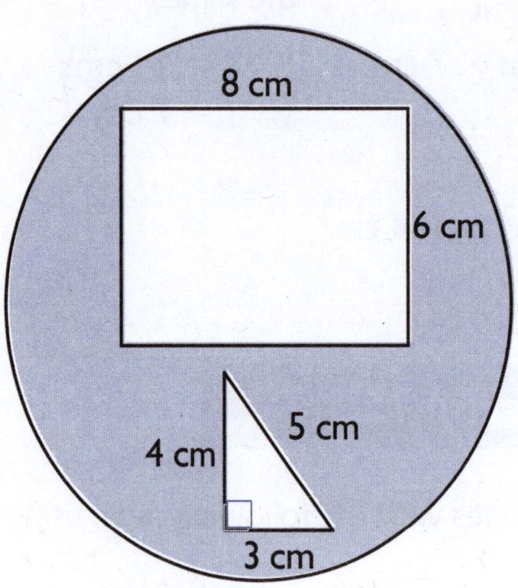

Circle with radius 7 cm

d.

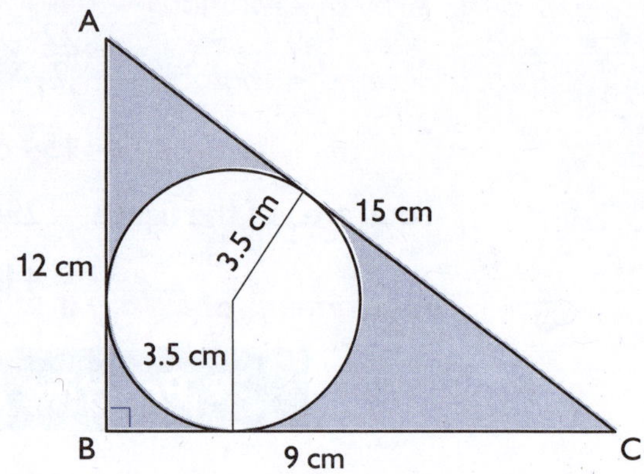

Higher Order Thinking Skills

HOTS

1. The length of a rectangle is 12 m and the length of its diagonal is 15 m. Find the area of the rectangle.
2. The radius of a wheel is 7 cm. How many revolutions will it make in covering 44 km?
3. One side of a rhombus is 20 cm and one of its diagonal measures 24 cm. Find the area of the rhombus.
4. The inner and outer radii of a cylindrical pipe are 5 cm and 5.5 cm, respectively. Find the area of the cross-section of the pipe.

Highlights

- Perimeter is the length of the boundary of a plane closed figure and area is the region enclosed by the boundary.

- Perimeter is expressed in units of length—mm, cm, m, km, etc. Area is expressed in sq units of length—mm^2, cm^2, m^2, km^2, etc.

- a. Perimeter of a square = 4 × length of side

  b. Perimeter of a rectangle = 2 (length + breadth)

  c. Area of a square = $(\text{side})^2$

  d. Area of a rectangle = length × breadth

  e. Area of a parallelogram = base × height

  f. Area of a rhombus = base × height

  g. Area of a rhombus = $\frac{1}{2} \times d_1 \times d_2$

  (when the lengths of the diagonals d_1 and d_2 are given)

  h. Area of triangle = $\frac{1}{2}$ × base × height

- The perimeter of a circle is called its circumference.

  $C = 2\pi r$ (r is the radius) or $C = \pi d$ (d is the diameter)

  π is a constant value. It is approximately equal to $\frac{22}{7}$ or 3.14.

  $\pi = \frac{C}{2r}$ or $\pi = \frac{C}{d}$

- Area of a circle (A) = πr^2, where r is the radius of the circle.

Is it possible to add eight 8's to get the number 1,000 using only addition?

Answer for Brainteaser on page 246

A Colourful Disc!

Objective: To find the area of a circle.

Material required: a large sheet of glazed paper with one coloured side and one white side, a pair of scissors

Procedure: Draw a large circle. The diameter of the circle should be the largest that can fit on the sheet of paper. Fold the sheet into two. Then refold into four and then again into eight and so on. Cut alongs the folds and arrange them alternatively sectorwise. If you have cut out 16 sectors then place one colourful sector, one white and so on. The figure formed will look like a parallelogram. If you can cut 64 sectors, the figure will look like a rectangle.

Arrange the sectors alternately as such.

The area of the rectangle will be the area of the circle.

Area of rectangle $= \ell \times b$

The breadth of the rectangle is the radius of the circle and the length is half the circumference of the circle.

$$l \times b = \frac{1}{2} \times \text{circumference} \times \text{radius}$$

$$= \frac{1}{2} \times 2\pi r \times r = \pi r^2$$

Answer for Brainteaser from page 245

888 + 88 + 8 + 8 + 8 = 1,000

Data Handling

CHAPTER 16

The branch of mathematics that deals with the collection, organisation, presentation, analysis and interpretation of data is called statistics.

Statistics is a very important branch of mathematics. Data is collected in several activities. Any branch of science, sports, politics, school results, market surveys, commerce, finance, births and deaths—just everything depends on statistics.

Let us learn about some common terms used in statistics.

Data A collection of numerical figures giving some particular type of information is called data.

Example: The marks obtained by ten students in a class test are:

7, 12, 15, 18, 19, 20, 11, 5, 16, 15

Raw data Data obtained in the original form is called raw data. The example given above shows raw data.

Array Arranging the numerical figures of a data in ascending or descending order is called an array.

Tabulation of data Arranging data in a systematic form in a table is called tabulation of data.

Observation Each numerical figure included in the data is called an observation.

Frequency of an observation The number of times a particular observation occurs is called its frequency.

Range of the data It is the difference between the highest numerical value and the lowest numerical value in the data.

We shall now study the analysis of data. The analysis of data is done by a single numerical value that can represent the entire data in the best possible way. This number gives the central value of the data and it is called the measure of the central tendency.

Measures of Central Tendency

There are three measures that represent the data as the most commonly used value or around which the values are mostly clustered. They are: mean, median and mode.

Mean

The mean is also called the arithmetic mean and is the sum of all the observations or scores divided by the number of observations or scores.

$$\text{Mean} = \frac{\text{Sum of all observations}}{\text{Number of observations}}$$

Example 1: The marks of 10 students in mathematics in a class test are as follows.

Rohit	Sana	Gaurav	Anurag	Vidushi
8	18	20	14	18
Radhika	Sarthak	Maria	Ishan	Bhuvan
20	8	10	8	14

What is the mean score of the class?

$$\text{Mean} = \frac{\text{Sum of all the marks}}{\text{Number of students}}$$

$$\text{Mean} = \frac{8 + 18 + 20 + 14 + 18 + 20 + 8 + 10 + 8 + 14}{10}$$

$$= \frac{138}{10} = 13.8$$

The mean score of the class is 13.8.

Example 2: The runs scored by Sachin Tendulkar in 7 one-day international matches are 99, 66, 102, 72, 48, 89 and 62, respectively. Find his mean score.

$$\text{Mean} = \frac{\text{Sum of runs scored}}{\text{Number of matches played}}$$

$$\text{Mean} = \frac{99 + 66 + 102 + 72 + 48 + 89 + 63}{7}$$

$$= \frac{539}{7} = 77$$

Mean runs scored by Sachin are 77.

Example 3: The temperatures recorded in Delhi during a fortnight in May were:

37°C, 38.3°C, 35°C, 35.6°C, 40.2°C, 38.7°C, 39.4°C, 40.1°C, 42.2°C, 44.4°C, 42.5°C, 41.3°C, 40.3°C, 40.7°C, 39.8°C

Find the mean temperature.

$$\text{Mean} = \frac{\text{Sum of temperatures}}{\text{Number of days}}$$

$$= 37 + 38.3 + 35 + 35.6 + 40.2 + 38.7 + 39.4 + 40.1 + 42.2 + 44.4 + 42.5 + 41.3 + 40.3 + 40.7 + 39.8 = 595.5$$

$$\text{Mean temperature} = \frac{595.5}{15} = 39.7°\text{C}$$

Example 4: Calculate the mean weight of 20 students from the following data.

Weight (in kg) for each student	45	46	47	48	49	50
Number of students	3	4	2	6	3	2

Weight "x" (in kg)	Number of students "f"	Total weight x × f
45	3	$45 \times 3 = 135$
46	4	$46 \times 4 = 184$
47	2	$47 \times 2 = 94$
48	6	$48 \times 6 = 288$
49	3	$49 \times 3 = 147$
50	2	$50 \times 2 = 100$
Total	20	948

$$\text{Mean} = \frac{\text{Total weight}}{\text{Number of students}}$$

$$= \frac{948}{20} = 47.4 \text{ kg}$$

Hence, the mean weight = 47.4 kg.

Median

When the data is arranged in ascending or descending order of magnitude, the value of the middle observation is called the median. The observations can be either even or odd in number.

If the number of observations are an odd number, we can easily locate the middle value and hence the median. If the number of observations are an even number, there will be two middle values and we take their mean.

If n is odd, the median is the value of $\left(\frac{n+1}{2}\right)$th observation.

If n is even, take the mean of the middle values, i.e., $\left(\frac{n}{2}\right)$th and $\left(\frac{n}{2}+1\right)$th observation.

If median is given in the form of a frequency table, we arrange the observations in ascending or descending order. We add the frequencies from which we find the position of the median by the formula $\left(\frac{n+1}{2}\right)$ for an odd number of observations and mean of $\left(\frac{n}{2}\right)$ and $\left(n+\frac{1}{2}\right)$ if there are an even number of observations.

Example 1: Find the median of the following data: 4, 9, 7, 5, 12, 3, 8, 10, 8

We first arrange the values in ascending order.

3, 4, 5, 7, 8, 8, 9, 10, 12

There are 9 observations given. It is an odd number, therefore, the median will be given by $\left(\frac{9+1}{2}\right)$th term or the 5th term, which is 8.

$\therefore$ the median value is '8'.

Example 2: Find the median of the following data: 18, 37, 24, 59, 41, 26, 63, 45, 57, 29

First, we arrange the numbers in ascending order.

18, 24, 26, 29, 37, 41, 45, 57, 59, 63

The position of the median is $\frac{10 + 1}{2} = 5.5$

This means that the median lies between the fifth and sixth positions. So the median is the average of the fifth and sixth terms, which is

$$\frac{37 + 41}{2} = \frac{78}{2} = 39$$

Example 3: The maximum daily temperatures (in °C) for the first week of a month in Delhi are 37, 35, 38, 34, 39, 33 and 33. Calculate the median temperature of the week.

Arranging the temperature in descending order we get,

39, 38, 37, 35, 34, 33, 33

There are seven observations, therefore, the median will be the $\frac{n + 1}{2}$ th term $= \frac{7 + 1}{2} = 4^{th}$ term.

Therefore, the median is the value of the fourth term, which is 35°C.

Example 4: The heights (in cm) of 50 students in a class are given below.

Height (in cm)	156	154	155	151	157	152	153
Number of students	8	4	10	6	7	3	12

Find the median.

We will arrange the height in ascending order.

Height (in cm)	Number of students 'f'	Cummulative Frequency 'cf'
151	6	6
152	3	6 + 3 = 9
153	12	9 + 12 = 21
154	4	21 + 4 = 25
155	10	25 + 10 = 35
156	8	35 + 8 = 43
157	7	43 + 7 = 50

Now, the number of observations are 50, which is an even number. So, the median will be the average of the $\frac{50}{2}$th and $\frac{50}{2} + 1^{th}$, i.e., $25^{th} + 26^{th}$ values, which are 154 and 155, respectively. So the median is $\frac{154 + 155}{2}$

$= 154.5$ cm

Mode

The most frequently occurring value in a group of observations is called the mode of that data. Thus, mode is defined as the observation that occurs maximum number of times in a given data.

Example 1: Find the mode in the following data: 3. 3, 5, 5, 5, 5, 6, 8, 9, 10

In these 10 observations, the number 5 occurs the maximum number of times. The frequency is 4. Hence, the mode of the data is 5.

Example 2: The sale of school uniform shoes in a footwear shop is given as follows:

Size (in number): 4, 5, 7, 7, 8, 8, 6, 6, 5, 4, 6, 6, 4, 9, 6

Arrange the data in ascending order.

4, 4, 4, 5, 5, 6, 6, 6, 6, 6, 7, 7, 8, 8, 9

Size 6 is sold the maximum.

$\therefore$ The mode of the data is Size 6.

Example 3: The marks obtained by 50 students in a class are given in the table below.

Find the modal marks.

Marks	0	5	10	15	20
Number of students	4	8	19	12	7

Here, 19 students got 10 marks, which is the maximum number of observations of the data given.

Alert!

1. Mean and median of a given data may not be the same.
2. Always arrange the data in ascending or descending order while finding the median or mode.
3. If in a data there is more than one observation that occurs the maximum number of times, then the data is called bimodal. Bimodal means that there are two observations with the same frequency.
4. A data is said to be multimodal if it has more than two modes.
5. The mean, median and mode always lie within the range of the data.

Relationship Between the Measures of Central Tendency

Mode = 3 Median − 2 Mean

Practice Exercise 16.1

1. Find the range and mean of the following.

   a. 75, 52, 41, 68, 67, 33
   b. 92, 94, 97, 98, 99, 91, 95
   c. 300, 350, 325, 225, 250, 300, 375, 350
   d. 37, 35, 38, 34, 39, 36, 33, 34, 36
   e. 9, 28, 42, 76, 34, 59, 68, 12, 85, 99

2. Find the median of the following data.

   a. 3, 12, 6, 9, 7, 8, 10, 11, 8, 9, 15
   b. 25, 31, 27, 29, 32, 25, 28, 25
   c. 4, 10, 8, 5, 12, 18, 13, 17, 7, 10
   d. 55, 60, 35, 51, 29, 63, 72, 91, 85, 82
   e. 34, 28, 115, 16, 0, 92, 45, 110, 78, 5, 45, 58, 45, 20, 105

3. Find the mode of the following data.

   a. 6, 10, 8, 10, 6, 8, 7, 8, 4, 8
   b. 3, 7, 8, 5, 6, 9, 6, 4, 6
   c. 23, 2, 15, 38, 21, 19, 23, 23, 26, 34, 23
   d. 10, 8, 4, 7, 8, 8, 11, 15, 8, 6, 8
   e. 28, 34, 32, 41, 36, 32, 32, 38, 32, 40, 41

4. A survey was done in Class VII to find the amount of pocket money each student got during a week. The data is given below. Find the mean amount of pocket money students in Class VII get during a week.

Pocket money (in ₹)	10	20	30	40	50
Number of students	3	12	15	8	2

5. The heights (in cm) of 20 children selected for a competition are given below.
   96, 90, 98, 105, 90, 96, 120, 115, 96, 98, 112, 90, 88, 110, 90, 96, 90, 110, 92, 90
   Make a frequency table for the data using tally marks and then find the mean height.

6. Calculate the median for the following data.

Marks	17	20	22	15	30	25
Number of students	5	9	4	3	10	6

7. Find the median weight for the following data.

Weight (in kg)	45	46	48	50	52	54	56
Number of students	8	5	6	9	7	4	2

8. Data for the number of cars by colour sold by a company is given below.

Colour	White	Black	Silver	Grey	Red	Beige	Blue
Numbers of cars	15	10	22	18	25	20	13

Which colour car is preferred by most of the customers?
Which measure of central tendency did you use to find it?

9. The demand for different shirt sizes in a supermarket is given below.

Size (in cm)	37	38	39	40	41	42	43	44
Number of shirts	6	8	10	20	15	9	7	5

Find the mode.

10. The marks of 20 students who scored 45 and above marks in a unit test are given below. Find the mean, median and mode of the data.

Marks	45	46	47	48	49	50
Number of students	3	4	2	6	1	4

Bar Graph

With the help of bar graphs, we can derive conclusions about the data at a glance.

Bar graphs should be drawn on a graph paper for accurate results.

A horizontal line called the x-axis and a vertical line called the y-axis is drawn.

The point of intersection of the two lines, marked 'O', is called the origin.

On the x-axis, we write the variable and on the y-axis the corresponding frequency.

The bars drawn are of equal width. The distance between two bars remains the same.

A suitable scale is determined according to the data. The bars can be coloured or shaded to make them more attractive and prominent.

The construction of bar graphs is shown with the help of examples.

Example 1: The following table shows the favourite sports of 250 students of a school. Represent the data in a bar graph.

Sports	Cricket	Football	Tennis	Badminton	Swimming
Number of students	75	35	50	25	65

Steps Involved in the Construction

Step 1: Draw the horizontal axis (x-axis) and the vertical axis (y-axis) on a graph paper. The point of intersection of the two axes is, or the origin, marked as 0.

Step 2: On the x-axis, write the names of the sports and on the y-axis the number of students.

Step 3: Look at the range of observations. The minimum value is 25 and the maximum 75. So mark the divisions up to 80.

Step 4: Let 10 divisions represent 10 students, i.e., one small division represents 1 student (on a cm graph 10 divisions = 1 cm).

Step 5: Five bars are required to represent the five sports. They should be of equal width and the spaces between them should be uniform.

Each bar is 1 cm wide and the space between two bars is also 1 cm.

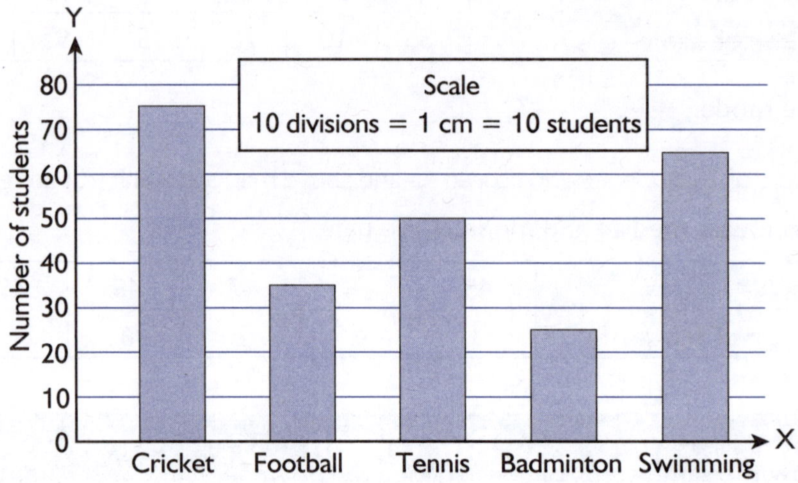

Example 2: The average rainfall recorded in the months of June to November in Allahabad is given in the table below. Represent the information on a bar graph.

Months	June	July	August	September	October	November
Average rainfall (cm)	20	30	45	25	15	5

Steps Involved in the Construction

Step 1: Draw the x-axis and y-axis and mark their point of intersection as O.

Step 2: On the x-axis, write the months and on the y-axis the average rainfall.

Step 3: The minimum rainfall is 5 cm and the maximum is 45 cm. So mark the divisions till 50.

Step 4: Let 10 divisions represent 5 cm of rainfall.

Step 5: Six bars will represent the 6 months.

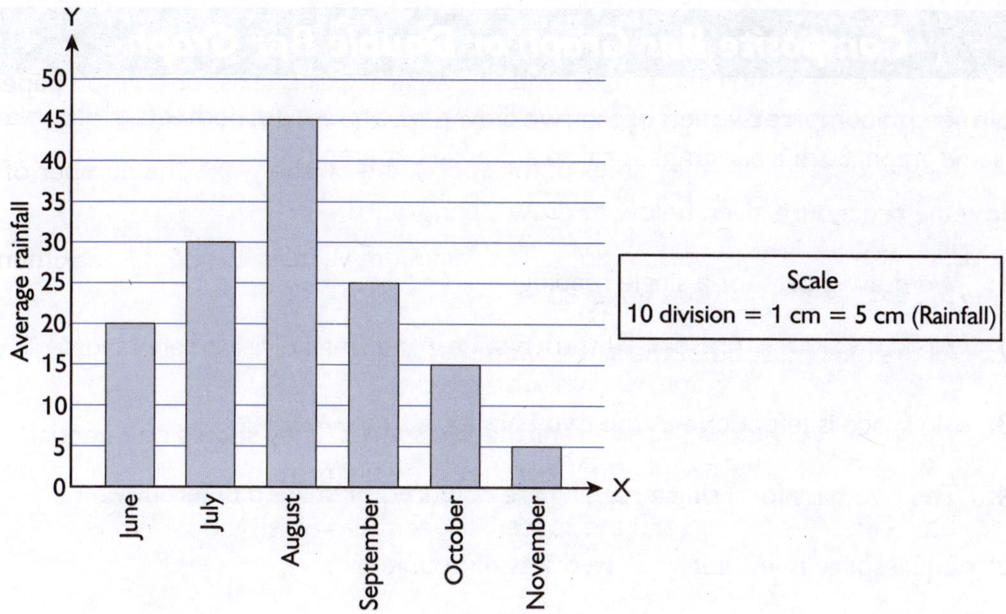

Example 3: Draw a bar graph to represent the following data that gives the favourite car colours of a particular brand of car. Write the favourite car colour and also the total number of people on whom the survey was done.

Colour of the car	Black	White	Grey	Red	Silver	Blue	Yellow
Number of buyers	45	75	25	55	60	15	10

We follow the same steps of construction as shown earlier and draw the graph.

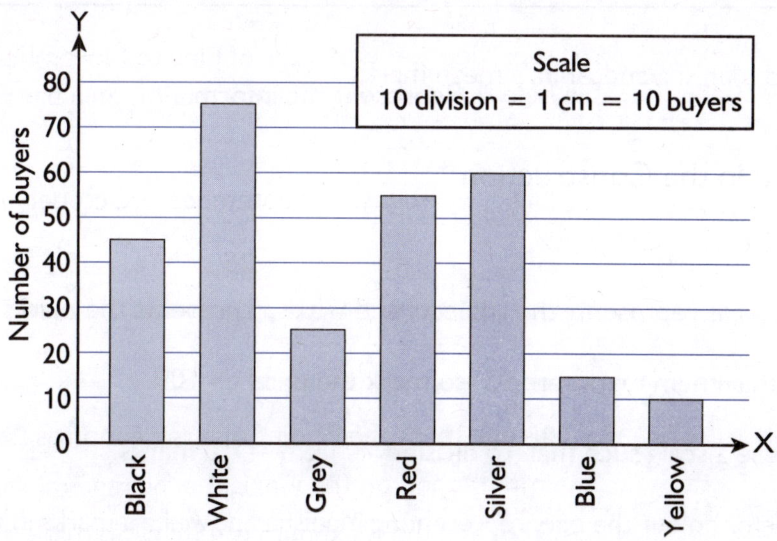

The favourite car colour is white.

The total number of people on whom the survey was done = 285

Composite Bar Graph or Double Bar Graph

When we need to compare two sets of data, we draw the bar graphs of both sets of observations on the same graph. Such a bar graph is called a double bar graph.

We follow the procedure given below to draw a bar graph.

Step 1: We draw 2 bars for a single reading.

Step 2: All the bars must be of the same width.

Step 3: No space is left between the two bars for a single reading.

Step 4: The two bars for a single reading are coloured or shaded differently.

Step 5: Equal space is left between two sets of double bars.

Step 6: On the graph, we mention the scale and what the double bars stand for. In case they are coloured, we can say Colour A for one set of data and Colour B for the other set.

Example 1: Compare the marks obtained by Manisha and Anita in a mid-term examination in various subjects with the help of a bar graph.

Subject	English	Hindi	Maths	Science	Social Science
Manisha	68	60	95	90	58
Anita	80	75	65	72	70

Also find Manisha and Anita's mean marks.

Steps Involved in the Construction

Step 1: Draw x-axis and y-axis.

Step 2: The x-axis represents the subjects and y-axis represents the marks.

Step 3: The maximum marks are 95, so mark the units till 100.

Step 4: Choose a scale such that 10 division = 1 cm = 10 marks.

Step 5: Shade or colour the bars representing Manisha and Anita's marks in different ways.

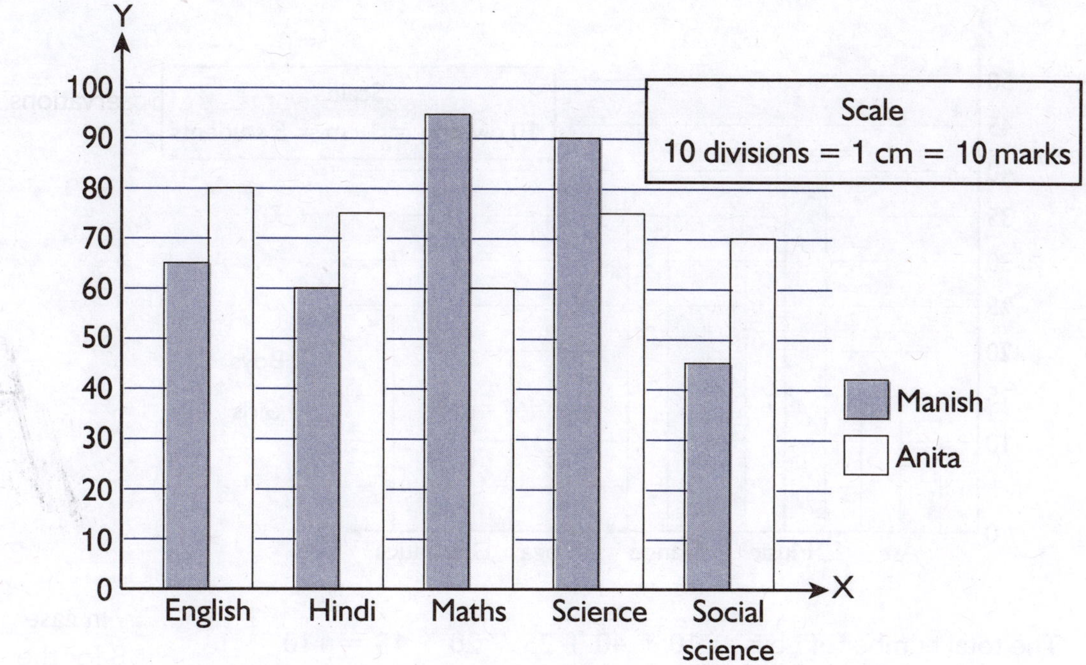

We observe that Anita is good in English, Hindi and social science, whereas Manisha has an aptitude for mathematics and science.

$$\text{Manisha's mean marks} = \frac{68 + 60 + 95 + 90 + 58}{5} = \frac{371}{5} = 74.2$$

$$\text{Amita's mean marks} = \frac{80 + 75 + 65 + 72 + 70}{5} = \frac{362}{5} = 72.4$$

Example 2: Draw a bar graph to compare the various activities taken up by boys and girls of Class VII in school.

Activities	Art	Music	Dance	Yoga	Dramatics
Boys	10	40	25	20	15
Girls	15	30	35	20	25

How many boys are there in all the activities? How many girls are there in all the activities?

Who exceeds in participation of activities—boys or girls?

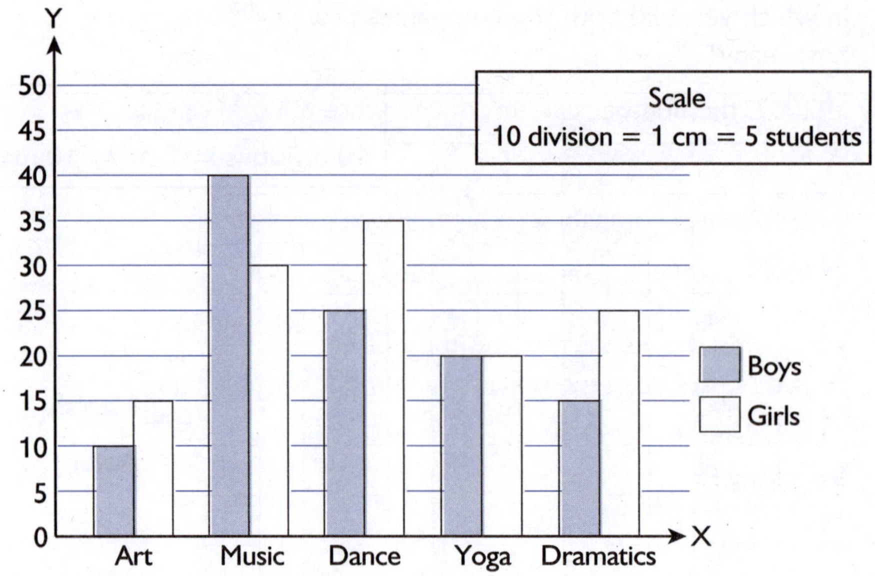

The total number of boys = 10 + 40 + 25 + 20 + 15 = 110

The total number of girls = 15 + 30 + 35 + 20 + 25 = 125

The participation of girls is more than that of boys.

Example 3: The following bar graph shows the production of cars by two companies, A and B, from 2000–2004.

Answer the questions related to the bar graph.

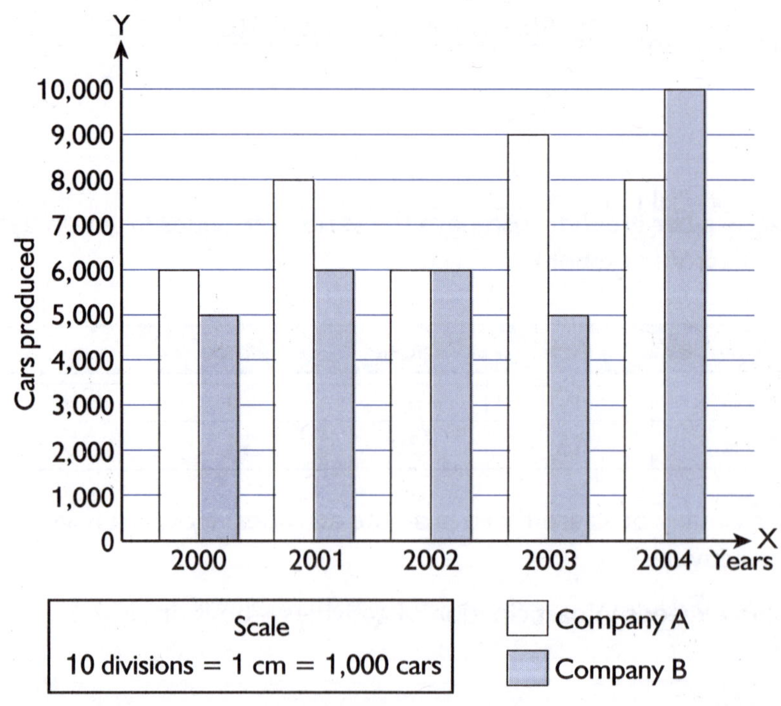

a. In which year did both the companies produce the same number of cars and how many?

In 2002, the number cars produced were 6000, which was the same number by both the companies.

b. In 2000 which company produced more cars and what was the difference?

In 2000, Company A produced 1,000 cars more than Company B.

c. What was the maximum number of cars produced during a year? Which company produced the maximum number of cars during a year and when?

The maximum number of cars produced was 10,000 in the year 2004 by Company B.

Practice Exercise 16.2

1. The following table gives the birthdays of 50 students in a class. Illustrate the data by a bar graph.

Days	Sun	Mon	Tue	Wed	Thur	Fri	Sat
Number of students	3	8	9	6	11	6	7

2. The marks obtained by Darshan in his annual examination are given in the table below. Illustrate the data by a bar graph.

Subject	English	Hindi	Maths	Science	Social science
Marks	75	60	90	85	55

3. The profit (in ₹lakh) of six supermarkets are tabulated below. Illustrate the data by a bar graph.

Supermarkets	A	B	C	D	E	F
Profit (in ₹lakh)	48	52	75	60	30	25

4. The bar graph that follows shows the number of air conditioners sold in a shop during a week in May. Read and interpret the graph. Answer the following questions.

   a. On which day of the week were the sale minimum?

   b. On which day of the week were the sale maximum?

   c. What was the total sale during the week?

   d. Which day was the shop closed as the weekly off?

   e. What is the scale used to draw the graph?

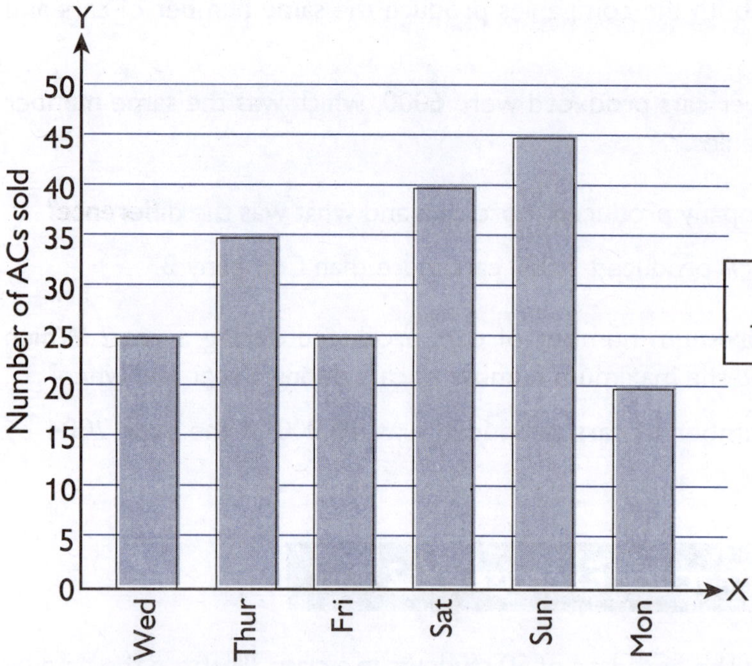

Scale
10 divisions = 1 cm = 5 ACs

5. The expenditure of a family during a month is represented by the bar graph given below. Interpret the graph and answer the questions that follow.

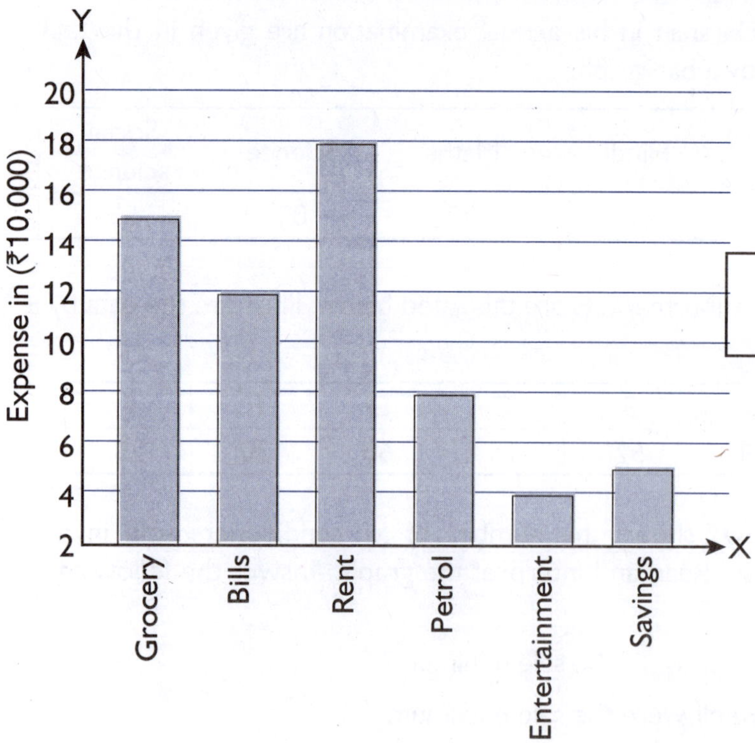

Scale
10 divisions = 1 cm = ₹2,000

a. What is the maximum expenditure of the family?

b. What is the minimum expenditure of the family?

c. What are the monthly savings of the family?

d. What is the total income of the family in a month?

e. Write the ratio of the savings to the money spent on petrol.

6. Compare the maximum and minimum temperatures of five cities on a particular day by a double bar graph.

City	J	K	L	M	N	O
Max. temp	25°	44°	43°	36°	45°	22°
Min. temp	15°	28°	29°	23°	30°	10°

Use an appropriate scale to represent the bar graph.

a. Which city has the largest difference in the maximum and minimum temperatures?

b. Which city has the least variation in temperatures?

7. The following table gives the earnings of an import–export company during a period of five years. Depict the data by a double bar graph.

Year	2001–2002	2002–2003	2003–2004	2004–2005	2005–2006
Export (in ₹crore)	20	25	15	30	45
Import (in ₹crore)	10	15	25	40	35

8. A survey was done in five schools of Gurgaon to know the number of girls and boys studying there. The following table gives the data collected. Draw a double bar graph to show the comparison.

School	A	D	H	R	S
Boys	800	900	400	700	600
Girls	700	110	300	500	400

a. Which school has the maximum strength of students?

b. Which school has the least number of girl students?

c. Find the difference of the total number of boys and total number of girls.

9. The following double graph shows Payal's marks in two mid-term examinations. Read the graph and answer the questions.

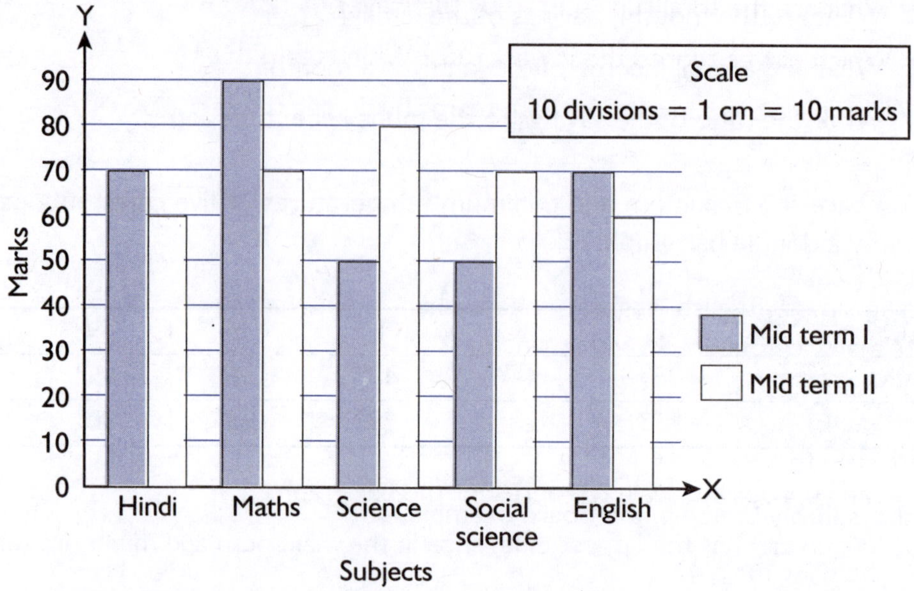

a. What are Payal's mean marks in the two term examinations?

b. In which subjects did Payal do better in the first mid-term exam?

c. In which subjects did Payal improve upon in the second mid-term exam?

d. In which subject did she score the highest in the first mid-term exam?

e. In which two subjects did she score the same marks in the second mid-term exam?

10. The following graph shows the runs scored by four batsmen of two teams, A and B, in a cricket match. Study the graph and answer the questions.

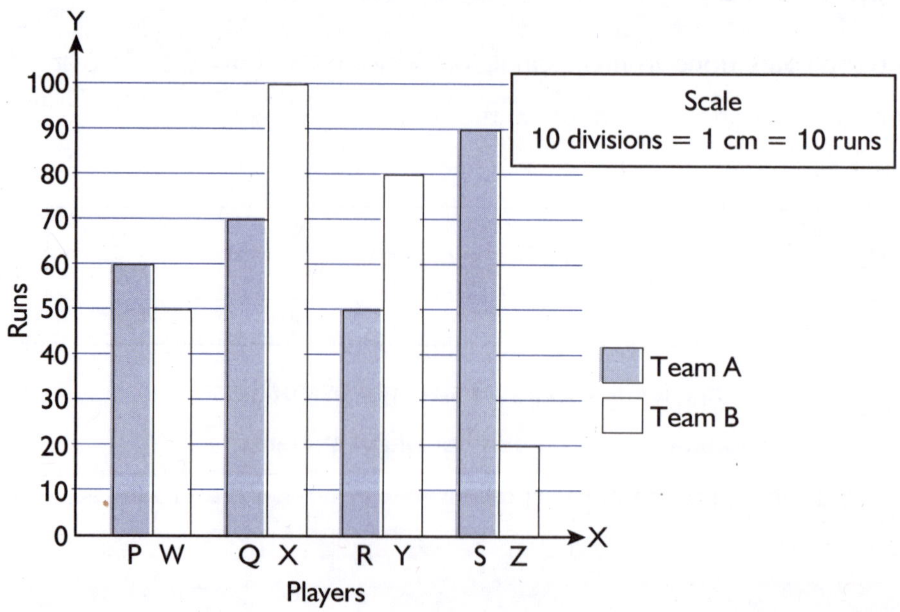

a. Which player scored the highest runs? Which team does he belong to?

b. What are the total runs scored by the players of Team A?

c. What are the total runs scored by the player of Team B?

d. Which player scored the lowest runs? Which team does he belong to?

e. Compare the run rates of both teams by finding the mean.

Probability

Probability in simple English language means chance. Knowingly or unknowingly, we make statements that are concerned with chance.

Example:

a. It **may** rain today.

b. Varsha is **likely** to top in the board examination.

c. The train **may** be late.

d. India **may** win the World Cup this year.

e. It **may** be a holiday tomorrow.

All these statements are based on chance. They may or may not happen. Mathematicians have derived formulae to calculate this uncertainty. It is studied under the heading called probability.

Let us consider a few examples to illustrate the concept of probability.

1. A coin is tossed and we know it will land on its **head** or **tail**. Both heads and tails have an equal chance to come up. Hence, in a cricket match, when a coin is tossed, both the captains have a 50–50 chance to get a head and make the decision to bat or field.

   The total outcomes when a coin is tossed are either heads (H) or tails (T), that is 2

   Only one can occur at a time, so the probability of heads is $\frac{1}{2}$ and the probability of tails is $\frac{1}{2}$.

   > **Probability** is the measure of the chance of the happening of an event.

2. We have all played Ludo or Snakes and Ladders. We use a die to play the game.

   A die is a cube which has six faces. Each face is marked with dots from 1 to 6.

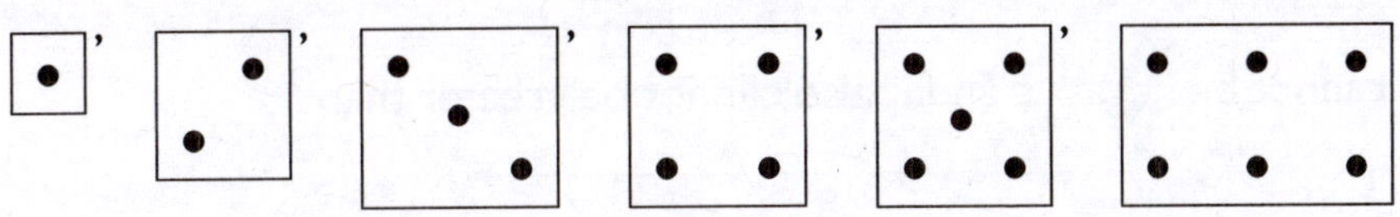

The die is cast and any face can come up. There are six possible outcomes and each is equally likely or has the same chance of coming up. The probability of any number coming up is $\frac{1}{6}$.

3. If we have four coloured cards lying face downwards and any one card is turned, we can get any of the four coloured cards.

Red	Blue	Green	Yellow

There are four possible outcomes and the probability of drawing each coloured card is $\frac{1}{4}$.

Let us understand the terms used in the examples given earlier.

1. **Experiment:** This is an activity that is performed and the result obtained is called an outcome. For example, tossing a coin is an experiment and to get heads or tails is an outcome.
2. **Random experiment:** This is an experiment where the outcome cannot be predicted in advance. For example, when we toss a coin we cannot predict in advance whether we will get heads or tails.
3. **Event:** It is the outcome that we want in a particular experiment. For example, tossing a coin is an experiment where the two possible outcomes are heads or tails. If we **desire** to get heads then the correct outcome is called an event.
4. **Sample space:** All possible outcomes of an experiment are called a sample space. For example, when we throw a dice, the possible outcomes are

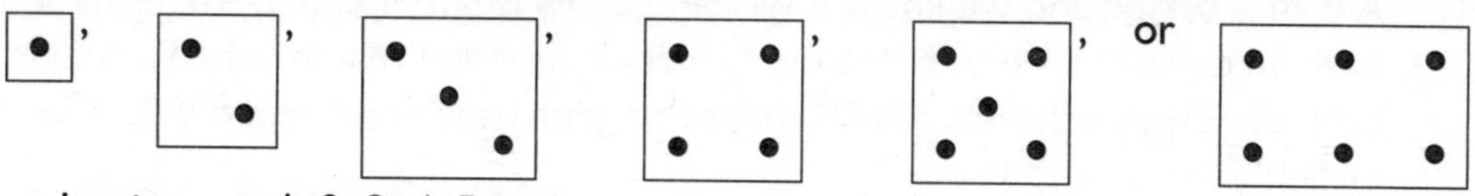

and written as 1, 2, 3, 4, 5 or 6.
5. **Sure event:** It is an event that is definitely going to happen and has a probability of 1.
6. **Impossible event:** It is an event that will not happen and has a probability of 0.

The probability of any event lies between 0 and 1.

If the probability that an event will occur is p then the probability that it will not occur is 1−p.

$$\text{Probability of an event} = \frac{\text{Number of favourable outcomes}}{\text{Total possible outcomes of the experiment}}$$

Alert!

Probability cannot be negative and it also cannot be greater than 1.

Example 1: What is the probability of getting the number 4 when a dice is thrown?

The possible outcomes are 1, 2, 3, 4, 5 or 6.

The event is to get the number 4.

So the probability of getting a 4 is $\frac{1}{6}$.

There is only **one** face marked as 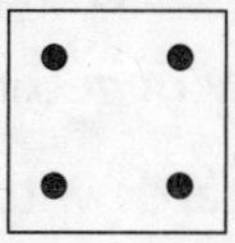 4

Example 2: There are four flash cards—one red, one green and two blue. What is the probability of drawing a blue card?

R	G	B	B

The total number of cards are four. There are two three cards so the probability of getting a blue card is $\frac{2}{4} = \frac{1}{2}$.

Example 3: A pack of playing cards consists of 52 cards. There are 4 suits—Spades (♠), Diamonds (♦), Hearts (♥) and Clubs (♣)—of 13 cards each. The 13 cards are numbered 1, 2, 3, 4, 5, 6, 7, 8, 9, 10, J (Jack), Q (Queen) and K (King). The number 1 is called an Ace. The Spades and Clubs are black in colour while Diamonds and Hearts are red.

From a pack of playing cards, a card is drawn.

a. What is the probability of getting an Ace of Hearts?

b. What is the probability of drawing a red Queen?

c. What is the probability of drawing a King from any suit?

a. The probability of getting an ace of heart is $\frac{1}{52}$ because there is only one Ace of Heart.

b. The probability of a red Queen is $\frac{2}{52} = \frac{1}{26}$ because there are two red queens—one of Hearts and the other of Diamonds.

c. The probability of getting a king from any suit is $\frac{4}{52} = \frac{1}{13}$ as there are four kings—one in each suit.

Example 4: In a bag, there are seven cards numbered 1 to 7.

1	2	3	4	5	6	7

A card is picked at random. What is the probability of picking:

a. 5? b. an odd number? c. an even number?

d. a prime number? e. 0?

The total number of cards is 7.

a. There is only one card with the number 5.

$\therefore$ probability of getting a 5 $= \frac{1}{7}$

b. There are four cards with odd numbers—1, 3, 5 and 7.

$\therefore$ the probability of getting an odd number is $\frac{4}{7}$.

c. There are three cards that bear an even number—2, 4 and 6.

$\therefore$ the probability of getting an even number is $\frac{3}{7}$.

d. There are four cards with prime numbers—2, 3, 5 and 7.

$\therefore$ the probability of getting a prime number is $\frac{4}{7}$.

e. There is no card marked 0.

$\therefore$ the probability of getting a 0 is $\frac{0}{7}$.

To get a 0 in this experiment is an impossible event.

Example 5: A box contains 3 red, 2 blue and 5 green marbles. A marble is drawn at random. What is the probability of getting

a. a red marble? b. a blue marble? c. a green marble?

There are 3 red + 2 blue + 5 green marbles = 10 marbles in a box.

The probability of getting a red marble $= \frac{3}{10}$, since there are 3 red marbles in the box.

The probability of getting a blue marble $= \frac{2}{10} = \frac{1}{5}$, because there are 2 blue marbles in the box.

The probability of getting a green marble $= \frac{5}{10} = \frac{1}{2}$, since there are 5 green marbles in the box.

Practice Exercise 16.3

1. A cricket match is to happen between teams A and B. A coin is tossed once and the captain who gets heads will decide the course of play. What is the probability that the captain of Team B will be the deciding captain?

2. Arnav and Ambar start to play Ludo. The game begins when one of them throws a six. What is the probability of getting a six?

3. Arun, Tarun and Varun are contesting for the selection of games captain. All three are equally good, however, only one is to be selected. What is the probability of Varun being selected?

4. A wheel with 8 equal parts has 2 parts that are painted red, 1 is blue, 3 are green and 2 are yellow. What is the probability that on spinning the wheel, it will come to rest on

   a. red? b. blue? c. green? d. yellow?

5. Write the probability of picking a shaded card from the following:

a. 

b. 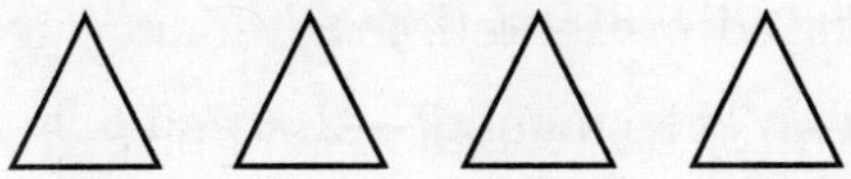

c. 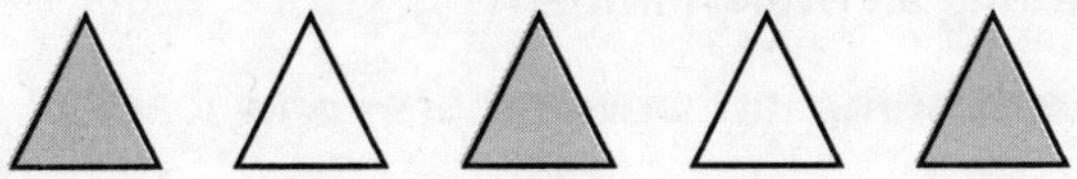

d. 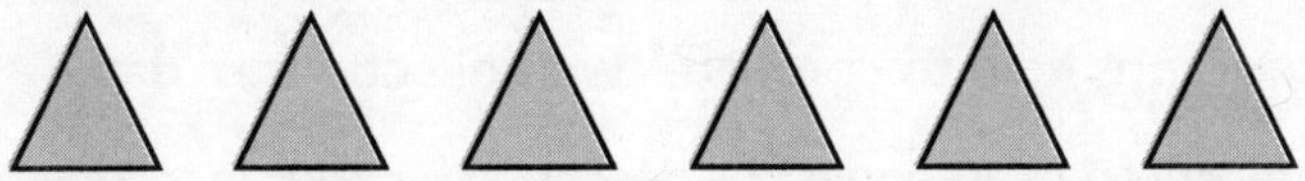

e. 

Which of these is a sure event and which is an impossible event?

6. There are five identical white envelopes kept on a table turned upside down. Only one of them has the address and postage stamp on it and has to be posted. Ravi has to identify the correct envelope to post it. What is the probability that he will be able to identify it? What is the probability he will be unable to do so?

7. From a pack of 52 cards, one card is drawn. Write the probability of picking up the following:

a. an Ace. b. a red card. c. a black card.

d. a King of Spades. e. a card from the Heart suit.

8. A raffle was held for which 500 tickets were sold, each with a unique number on it. Devyani bought 20 tickets, Bhairvi bought 25 tickets, Aarti bought 10 tickets and Shristi bought 5 tickets. What is the probability of each of the girls winning the raffle?

9. A box contains numbers marked from 1–20. Arpit draws out a number from the box and notes it down. What is the probability that he draws:

a. a number between 1 to 5? b. a number between 11 to 20?

c. an even number? d. an odd number?

e. a prime number?

10. The letters of the word FAITH are placed in a box. One letter is taken out at random. What is the probability that it is an A? What is the probability that it is not on A?

Highlights

- Information collected regarding any survey is called data.
- After collecting data, it is organised, presented, analysed and interpreted.
- Data is presented in the form of bar diagrams and pictographs that helps in interpretation at a glance.
- A bar graph is a representation of numbers using bars of uniform width.
- Double bar graphs help to compare two collections of data.
- The data presented in ascending or descending order is called an array.
- There are three measures of central tendency—mean, median and mode.
- $\text{Mean} = \dfrac{\text{Sum of all observations}}{\text{Number of observations}}$
- Median is the value that lies in the centre, when the data is arranged in an array.
- Mode is the observation that occurs the maximum number of times.
- Probability is the measure of the chance of an event happening.
- The probability of an event lies between 0 and 1.
- The probability of an impossible event is 0.
- The probability of a sure event is 1.
- If the probability of the happening of an event is p, then the probability of its not happening is (1 − p).

The number 8,549,176,320 is unique since it is only one of its kind. Can you find out what is so special about it?

Answer for Brainteaser on page 271

How Tall Am I?

Objective: To learn comparisons at a glance.

Material required: a measuring tape, pencil and paper

Procedure:

Step 1 Form groups of students house-wise. Form four teams.

Step 2 The students are to stand in alphabetic order of their names.

Step 3 Measure their heights with the measuring tape.

Step 4 The team leader notes down the data.

Step 5 Each house has to make a bar graph to depict the heights of students in their group.

Higher Order Thinking Skills

HOTS

1. A survey of 150 people showed that 63 like tea and the others dislike it. Out of these, one person is chosen at random. What is the probability that the chosen person

   a. likes tea? b. dislikes tea?

2. Two coins are tossed simultaneously 200 times and we get:

   two heads: 58 times
   one heads: 83 times
   no heads: 59 times

   When two coins are tossed at random what is the probability of getting

   a. 2 heads? b. 1 head? c. 0 head?

3. A pair of dice is rolled once. What is the probability that both the dice show the same numbers?

CHAPTERS 15–16 Rewind

1. Find the diameter of a circle when the circumference is 43.96 m (use $\pi = 3.14$).

2. A piece of wire is 44 cm long. It is shaped into a rectangle. Find the length of the rectangle if the breadth is 8 cm. The same wire is reshaped to form a circle, find the radius of the circle.

3. A rectangular courtyard of dimensions 30 m × 20 m has a 3 m wide verandah all around it. Find the area of the verandah.

4. The circumference of a circular park is 440 m. Find its area $\left(\pi = \frac{22}{7}\right)$.

5. The area of a circular lawn is 616 m^2. Find its circumference. Find the cost of fencing it at the rate of ₹50 per m.

6. The diameters of two circles are 6 cm and 12 cm. Find the ratio of the larger area to the smaller area.

7. A wire 88 cm long is bent to form a square and the same wire is bent to form a circle. Find the difference between their areas. Which has a larger area—the square or the circle?

8. Two concentric rings have a circumference of 132 cm and 176 cm. Find the width between the rings $\left(\text{use } \pi = \frac{22}{7}\right)$.

9. The length of the minute hand of a wall clock is 4.2 cm. Find the area swept by it in:

   a. 60 minutes. b. 2 hours. c. 15 minutes.

10. The diameter of the wheel of a car is 77 cm. How many revolutions will it make to travel 121 km?

11. Find the area of a parallelogram whose base is 16 cm and altitude 8 cm.

12. Find the mean, median and mode of the data given below.

Pocket money (in ₹)	100	200	300	400	500
Number of children	5	10	20	9	6

Rewind

CHAPTERS 15–16

13. The heights (in metres) above sea level of 7 cities of India are given below. Construct a bar diagram to illustrate the data.

City	Allahabad	Delhi	Agra	Patna	Ajmer	Jaipur	Udaipur
Height	190	220	170	40	700	580	580

14. Find the probability of each of the following:
    a. To get a head when a coin is tossed.
    b. To get a 5 when a dice is rolled.
    c. To get a red card from a pack of 52 cards.
    d. To get a black bead from a bag containing 10 red beads.
    e. To get a bottle of cola from a crate containing 24 cola bottles.

15. The data collected from a group of 30 students of Class VII to know the average height (in cm) of the class is given below.

Height (in cm)					
145	150	142	144	147	150
148	147	149	151	140	150
147	146	151	149	144	150
146	148	150	149	144	151
148	147	146	151	149	150

    a. What is this data called?
    b. Write the data in an array.
    c. Write the range of the data.
    d. Write the data in a frequency distribution table.
    e. Find the mean, median and mode of the distribution.

Answer for Brainteaser from page 268

It is the only number that has all of the digits placed in alphabetical order.

Test Yourself

Unit IV

1. Name the solid that has:

   a. six plane faces, which are congruent squares.

   b. no flat (or plane) surface.

   c. one square face and four triangular faces.

   d. two circular faces and one curved face.

   e. one circular and one curved face.

2. Name the letter and geometrical figure:

   a. that has both a line of symmetry and rotational symmetry (of order more than 1).

   b. that has line of symmetry but no rotational symmetry (of order more than 1).

   c. that has no line of symmetry and no rotational symmetry (of order more than 1).

3. The perimeter of a rectangle of sides 26 cm and 14 cm is equal to the perimeter of a square. Find the side and area of the square.

4. The length and breadth of a playground are 40 m 50 cm and 32 m 25 cm. Find the cost of turfing the playground at the rate of ₹10 per square meter.

5. A wall 16.5 m by 8.2 m is to be painted excluding a glass window that measures 1.5 m by 1m. Find the cost of painting the wall at the rate of ₹250 per square meter.

6. The area of a triangle is 87.96 cm^2. If its altitude is 14.66 cm, find its base.

7. $\triangle XYZ$ is a right-angled triangle, right angled at Y and YO is perpendicular to XYZ. Find the area of $\triangle XYZ$ and the length of YO if $XY = 8$ cm and $YZ = 6$ cm.

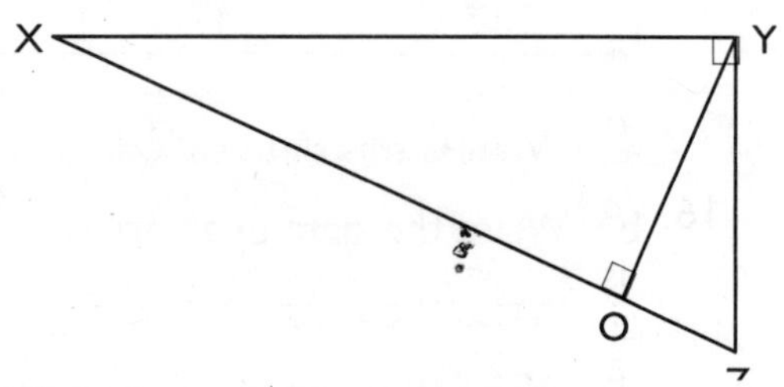

8. The diagonals of a rhombus are 10.8 cm and 12.6 cm. If the area of the rhombus is the same as the area of a parallelogram with base 10 cm, find the altitiude of the parallelogram.

9. Find the perimeter of the figure (quarter circle) that is given. Also find its area (Use $\pi = 3.14$).

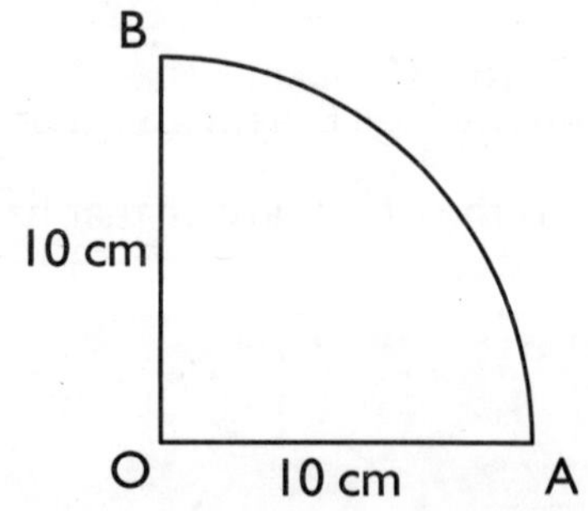

10. Find the area of the given figure, if ABCD is a rectangle with sides 30 cm and 10 cm. Semicircles are drawn on the four sides of the rectangle (use $\pi = 3.14$).

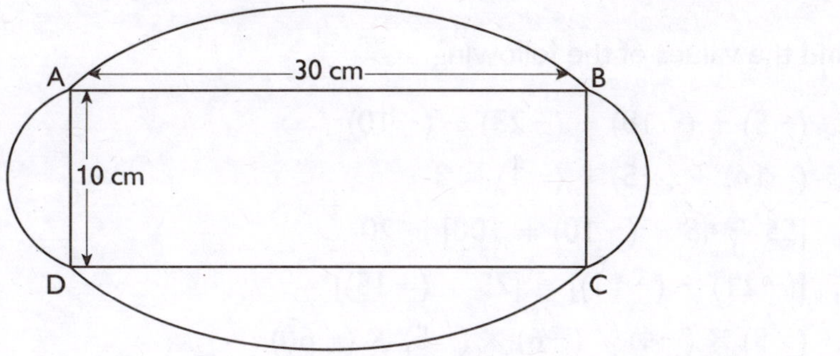

11. Find the length of lace to be to put around the edge of 15 round table cloths with diameter 140 cm each. Find the cost of the lace required if the rate is ₹20 per meter.

12. The hour hand of a clock is 14 cm long. Find the distance its tip will cover in 24 hours. $\left(\text{use } \pi = \frac{22}{7}\right)$.

13. Three table tops in the shape of a circle, a square and a rectangle are to be polished at the rate of ₹300 per m^2. If the radius of the circle is 35 cm, the side of the square is 35 cm and the dimensions of the rectangle are 35 cm × 25 cm, find the ratio of their areas and also the cost of polishing their tops.

14. The following is the data for the height in cm of people in a group. Arrange the data in an ascending order and find the range of the data

110, 115, 98, 88, 121, 116, 130, 105, 111, 112, 123, 118, 106, 99, 100, 89, 125 and 108.

15. A dice is rolled. Find the chance of getting:

a. a 6. b. a multiple of 3. c. a multiple of 2.

d. a 7. e. a number less than 7.

16. A bag contains 3 red, 4 blue and 5 green balls. A ball is picked up at random. What is the probability that the ball is

a. red? b. black? c. green? d. yellow? e. blue?

17. The maximum daily temperatures (in °C) during the peak of summer in north India during a week are 41°, 44°, 42°, 39.5°, 40°, 43.5°, 44°. Find the mean temperature.

18. Calculate the mean marks of 45 students in a class test (out of 10) in mathematics.

Marks	0	1	2	3	4	5	6	7	8	9	10
Numbers of students	1	2	3	4	5	7	8	6	4	3	2

Model Sample Test Paper

Time: ____________

1. Find the values of the following.

   a. $(-5) + (-18) - (-23) - (-10)$
   b. $(-14) + (-5) \div (-1) \times 3$
   c. $[55 - 45 + (-10) + 100] \div 20$
   d. $[(-21) \div (-11)] - [75 \div (-15)]$
   e. $(-5) \times (-4) \times (-6) \times (-5) \times (-60)$

2. a. The sum of two integers is (-15). If one of them is 20, find the other.
   b. The sum of two integers is 98. If one of them is -89, find the other.
   c. What must be subtracted from -13 to get -19?
   d. The product of two numbers is (-112). If one of them is (-7) find the others.
   e. Divide (-120) by (-12) and add to the quotient, the product of (-25) and 4.

3. Multiply the number 23.456 by each of the following and write the product.

   a. 10 b. 1,000 c. 100 d. 0.01 e. 0.001

4. Divide the number 248.97 by each of the following and write the result.

   a. 10 b. 1,000 c. 100 d. 0.03 e. 0.003

5. The cost of $6\frac{1}{2}$ kg of mangoes is ₹149.50. Find the cost of 1 kg mangoes.

6. Find 7 rational numbers between $\left(-\frac{1}{3}\right)$ and $\frac{2}{3}$.

7. Find the values of the following.

   a. $\frac{3}{7} + \frac{5}{12}$ b. $\frac{7}{15} - \frac{1}{4}$ c. $\frac{6}{11} \times \frac{4}{18}$

   d. $\frac{5}{18} \div \frac{8}{9}$ e. $\left[\frac{3}{4} + \frac{2}{3} - \frac{7}{12} \times \frac{1}{14}\right] \div 11$

8. Find the values of the following.

   a. $7^0 \times 8^0 \times 9^0$ b. $(-3)^2 \times (-1)^{10} \times (-2)^3$ c. $[3^2]^2 \times [2^3]^2$

9. Write the following in scientific notation.

   a. 2470000000 b. 367942178 c. 123000000000.

10. If $a = 1$, $b = (-2)$ and $c = 3$, find the value of the following.

    a. a^2bc^3 b. $abc - a^2bc$ c. $a^2b^3c - a^3 + b^3 - c^3$

11. Add and subtract the following algebraic expressions as indicated.

a. $\begin{array}{r} 11a^2 - 3b^2 \\ 5a^2 + 7b^2 \\ + (-2a^2) + 4b^2 \\ \hline \end{array}$

b. $\begin{array}{r} 9p^3 - 2p^2 + 11p \\ - \; 3p^3 + 5p^2 - 7p \\ \hline \end{array}$

c. $\begin{array}{r} 3x^2 + 7xy - 9y^2 \\ + \; (-7x^2) - 3xy + 18y^2 \\ \hline \end{array}$

12. Solve the following equations.

a. $4(2x + 1) = 36$ b. $\frac{8x}{3} + 4 = 12$ c. $\frac{7x}{5} - 4 = 3$

13. The sum of the digits of a two-digit number is 9. If 27 is added to the number, the digits are interchanged. Find the number.

14. The cost of two dozen oranges is ₹248. Find the cost of 18 oranges.

15. Find the value of x if:

a. 25% of x is ₹900. b. 48% of x is 25 books.

c. $33\frac{1}{3}$% of x is 500 chocolates.

16. Radha bought a refrigerator and then sold it at a loss of 9% for ₹45,500. At what price did she purchase it?

17. Study the given figure and answer the questions that follow.

a. Write down the two pairs of adjacent angles.

b. Indicate which is the straight angle.

c. Find the value of x.

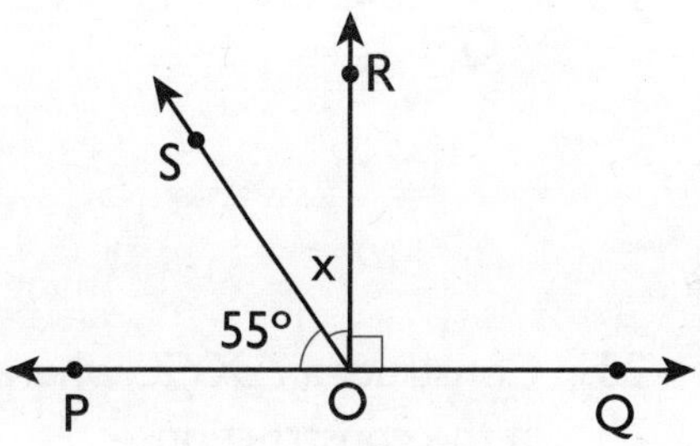

18. In the given figure, the lines ℓ and m are parallel and s and t are the transversals. Find the values of x, y, z and w.

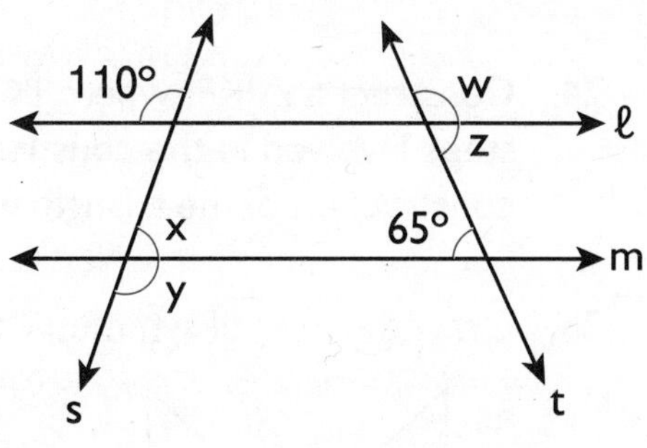

19. In the given figure, if ∠SQR = 55° and ∠TPR = 140°, find the measures of the three angles of △PQR.

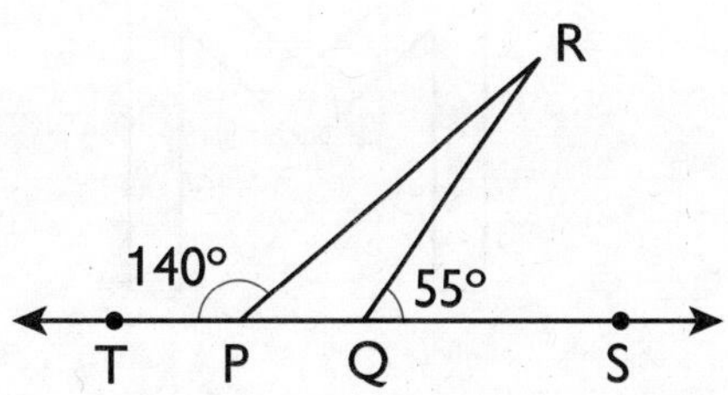

20. Consider the length of a triangular park as in the figure shown below. AC is 24 m. The joint D is the middle point of length AC and the length of DB is 9 m. Vikram jogs from point A to point B and then from point B to point C. What is the total distance he covers while jogging? If he returns to the starting point A from C, what is the total distance covered by him?

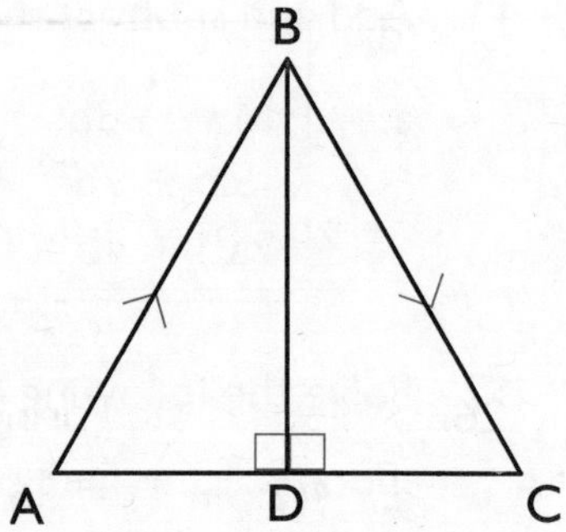

21. In the given figures, two line segments MN and RS bisect each other at O. Show that $\triangle MOR \cong \triangle NOS$. Write the condition of congruency applied. Complete the following.

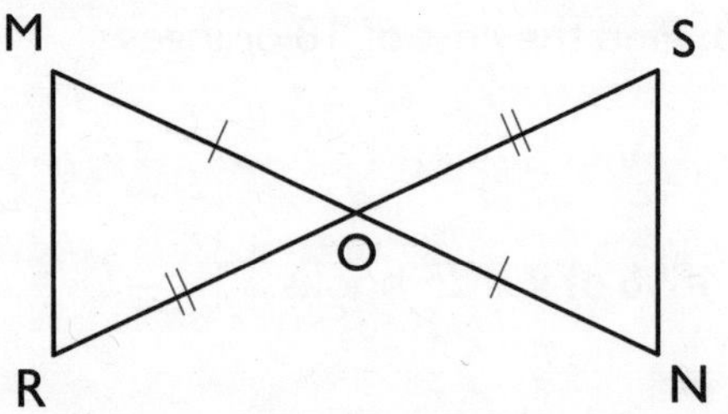

a. $\angle RMO = \angle ?$
b. $\angle MRO = \angle ?$

22. In the given figure, $PS \perp RT$ and $PQ \perp RM$ also $PS = PQ$. Prove that RP is the angular bisector of $\angle QRS$.

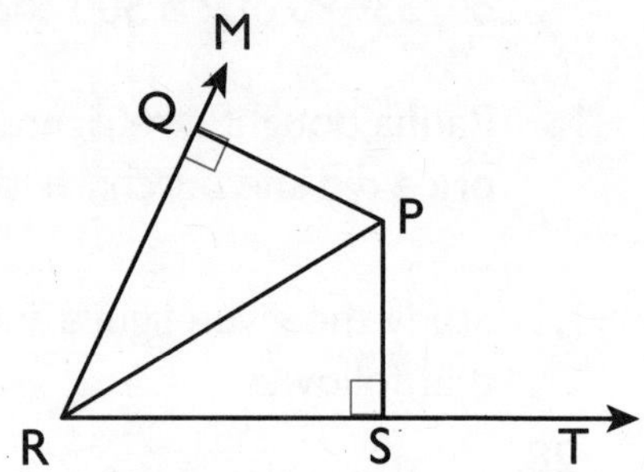

23. Construct a $\triangle XYZ$, where $YZ = 6.2$ cm, and $\angle Y = 75°$. Write the steps involved in the construction.

24. Construct a $\triangle JKP$, where $JK = 9.2$ cm, $KP = 6.1$ cm and $JP = 5.5$ cm. Write the steps involved in the construction. Which condition did you apply to check if the construction of the triangle was possible?

25. Draw the axes of symmetry for the following figures.

a. 

b. 

c. 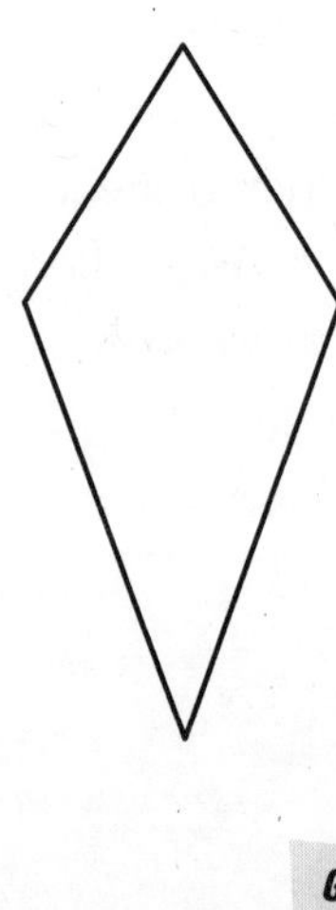

d. 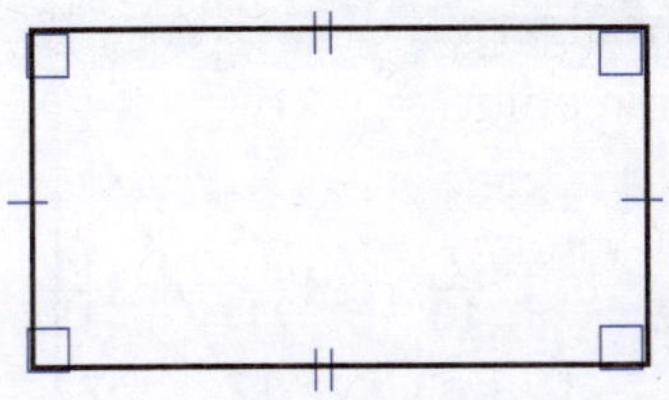 e. 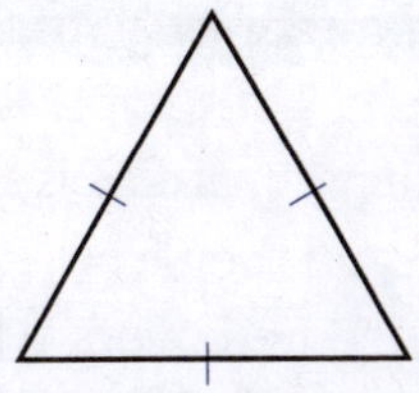

26. A floor is tiled using 1,800 tiles of size 25 cm × 20 cm each. If the length of the floor is 15m, find its breadth.

27. Find the area of the shaded portion in the figure.

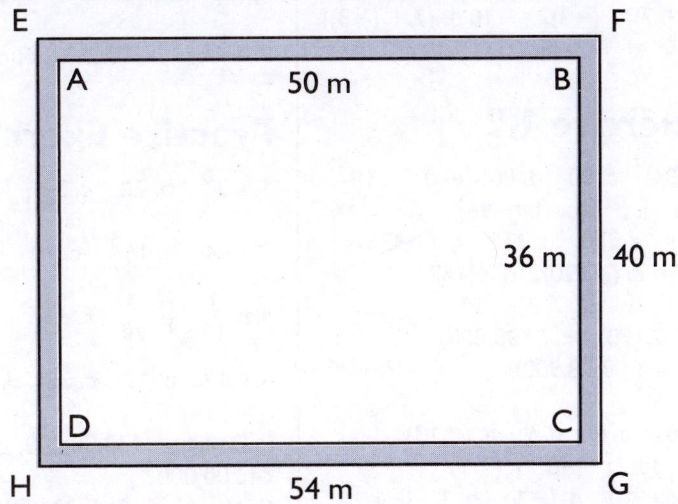

28. The circumference of a circle is 440 cm. Find its area.

29. Draw a bar graph to compare the strength of students in 7 schools during a period of 5 years.

School	A	B	C	D	E	F	G
2000–2001	1,500	1,200	900	1,800	1,100	500	800
2005–2006	1,600	1,300	1,100	2,000	1,400	600	600

30. The following table shows the aggregate marks of 40 children in Class VII. Find the mean, median and mode.

Marks	50	60	70	80	90
Number of students	4	10	14	9	3

Are the three measures of central tendency equal? Which is the most accurate and why?

Answers

Practice Exercise 1.1

1.a. +87   b. (−253)   c. 0   d. 2010   e. (−18)
2.a. 8   b. (−9)   c. (−32)   d. (−51)   e. (−77)
3.a. (−51)   b. 726   c.(−2,089)   d.(−1,170)   e. 0
4.a. (−74)   b. 106   c. (−219)   d. (−10)   e. 28
5. (−80)   6. (−21)   7. (−71) 8. 82
9. Commutative $(-10) + 7 = 7 - 10$, $7 + (-3) = (-3) + 7$, $(-10) + (-3) = (-3) + (-10)$
Associative, $(-10 + 7) + (-3) = -10 + (7 + (-3))$
10.a. F   b. F   c. T   d. T   e.F

Practice Exercise 1.2

1.a. (−84)   b. (−84)   c. 80   d. 80   e. 0   f. 18
g. (−17)   h. 100   i. (−56)   j. (−96)
2.a. 30   b. (−770)   c. 280   d. 315   e. (−336)
3.a. (−27)   b. 256   c. (−120)   d. 1,152
e. (−1,440)
4.a. (−380)   b. (−5,170)   c. (−35,000)
d. (−2,47,800)   e. (−3,98,900)
5. (−2,079) · 196
6.a. (−13)   b. (−6)   c. 6   d. 9   e. (−13)
f. (−6)   g. 5   h. 38   i. −48   j. (−1)
7. a. 2   b. (−2)   c.(−6)   d. (−1)   e. 1   8. 1
9. 2   10. 85

Practice Exercise 1.3

1.a. (−57)   b. 14   c. (−14)   d. 74   e. 84
2.a. (−54) b. (−56)   c. (−126)   d. 0   e. (−100)
3.a. 8   b. 7   c. 9   d. (−4)   e. 0
4.a. (−6)   b. 142   c. 1   d. 10   e.135
5.a. 22   b. (−6)   c. 10   d. (−1)   e. 201
6.a. (−42)   b. (−28)   c. 81   d. 10   e.819
7.a. (−10,500)   b. (−2,600)   c. (−63,500)
d. 5,000   e. (−990)
8.a. (−4)   b. (−25)   c 4   d. 25   e. 35
9.a. $>$ b. $>$ c. $>$ d. $<$ e. $<$
10.a. F   b. F   c. T   d. T   e. F

HOTS

1. 5   2. (−1)   3. 0

Practice Exercise 2.1

1. Any three equivalent fractions to be written for all the parts.
2.a. 1   b. $\frac{11}{13}$ c. $1\frac{8}{15}$ d. $\frac{31}{44}$ e. $\frac{7}{8}$
3.a. $5\frac{7}{12}$ b. $11\frac{7}{10}$ c. $4\frac{1}{21}$ d. $3\frac{14}{15}$ e. $3\frac{78}{125}$
4. a. $\frac{3}{7}$ b. $\frac{1}{9}$ c. $\frac{3}{10}$ d. $\frac{17}{35}$ e. $\frac{7}{12}$
5.a. $4\frac{3}{14}$ b. $\frac{2}{3}$ c. $1\frac{33}{50}$ d. $4\frac{2}{9}$ e. $4\frac{1}{10}$
6. a. $4\frac{2}{3}$ b. $3\frac{3}{10}$ c. $5\frac{7}{30}$ d. $1\frac{1}{6}$ e. $1\frac{17}{30}$
7. $7\frac{1}{2}$ 8. The sum of $2\frac{1}{4}$ and $5\frac{1}{2}$, $1\frac{3}{4}$
9. $4\frac{1}{4}$ kg   10 $2\frac{1}{12}$ hours

Practice Exercise 2.2

1.a. $2\frac{6}{7}$ b. $2\frac{2}{7}$ c. $3\frac{3}{10}$ d. $5\frac{1}{5}$ e. $\frac{12}{17}$
2.a. 44   b. $16\frac{3}{7}$ c. 70   d. $77\frac{2}{5}$ e. $11\frac{5}{11}$
3.a. $\frac{3}{16}$ b. $\frac{7}{20}$ c. $\frac{25}{72}$ d. $8\frac{1}{8}$ e. $10\frac{11}{16}$
4.a. 12   b. 17   c. 72   d. 1   e. $\frac{5}{18}$
5. Daughter ₹30,00,000, grandson ₹18,00 000 sister ₹42,00,000
6. 4 m   7. Pink 324, Purple 432 and Yellow 324
8. ₹4,000; ₹48,000   9. 775 sqm.   10. 91, $\frac{1}{8}$

Practice Exercise 2.3

1.a. $\frac{9}{7}$ b. $\frac{1}{18}$ c. $\frac{4}{11}$ d. $\frac{8}{15}$ e. $\frac{1}{101}$
2.a. $\frac{15}{16}$ b. $\frac{1}{26}$ c. $2\frac{21}{52}$ d. $3\frac{3}{13}$ e. $142\frac{6}{7}$
3. $\frac{2}{3}$ litres   4. $\frac{8}{9}$ kg   5. ₹$18\frac{3}{4}$ 6. ₹32
7. $\frac{3}{8}$ kg   8. 24   9. $15\frac{1}{2}$ m   10. 95

Practice Exercise 2.4

1.a. $7 \times 10 + 2 \times 1 + \frac{3}{10} + \frac{0}{100} + \frac{2}{1000}$
b. $2 \times 100 + 9 \times 10 + 3 \times 1 + \frac{0}{10} + \frac{0}{100} + \frac{7}{1000}$
c. $9 \times 10 + 9 \times 1 + \frac{9}{10} + \frac{9}{100} + \frac{9}{1000}$
d. $5 \times 100 + 0 \times 10 + 0 \times 1 + \frac{0}{10} + \frac{0}{100} + \frac{5}{1000}$
e. $6 \times 10 + 8 \times 1 + \frac{3}{10} + \frac{2}{100}$

Answers

2.a. 455.508 b. 990.707 c. 76.498
d. 1920.89 e. 530.755
3.a. 12.55 b. 81.63 c. 58.713 d. 4.831 d. 1.13
4. 52.61 km 5. ₹155.52 6. Mony; ₹25.50
7. 1050.95 litres 8. 50 m 9.a. 27.43 b. 47.43
10. 6.05 kg.

Practice Exercise 2.5

1.a. 68.9 b. 563.8 c. 53 d. 7,418 e. 9,860
f. 3,290 g. 457.3 h. 368.5 i. 9,005 j. 9,680
2.a. 787.52 b. 86.4 c. 0.9782 d. 0.40750
e. 7804.50 f. 1083.0 g. 68823.3 h. 199.896
i. 1760.044 j. 5719.56
3.a. 3.84 b. 53.742 c. 761.8050 d. 2679.285
e. 0.46725 f. 0.4907 g. 0.009261
h. 16941.375 i. 16.632 j. 95.920
4. ₹492.375 5. ₹988.20 6.a. 4.28 b. 8.3768
c. 0.35426 d. 0.078 e. 0.004 f. 0.00493
g. 0.08005 h. 9.1919 i. 0.3923 j. 0.68515
7.a. 5.6 b. 1.03 c. 21.03 d. 0.1208
e. 0.042 f. 143.2 g. 17.25 h. 12.08
i. 50.4 j. 0.0715
8.a. 4.1 b. 11.38 c. 134 d. 0.32 e. 6
f. 16.93 g. 7.56 h. 384.4 i. 88 j. 0.47
9. ₹25.5, ₹765.00 10. 98.5 kg

HOTS

1. $\frac{63}{256}$ 2. 0.008 3. $3\frac{1}{3}$

Rewind (Chapters 1–2)

1.a. F b. F c. F d. T e. F
2.a. (−900) b. 1,200 c. 31,7000 d. 500 e. 3,900
3.a. 16 m 4. 22 Sec
5.a. 1st b. 1st c. 2nd d. 1st e. 2nd
6.a. (−16) b. 5 c. 4 d. 0 e. 1

7.a. 2 b. $\frac{1}{64}$ c. $\frac{2}{7}$ d. 45 e. $\frac{2}{9}$

8.a. $4\frac{2}{3}$ b. $4\frac{12}{25}$ c. 140 d. $3\frac{3}{4}$ e. $15\frac{3}{4}$

9.a. $\frac{7}{9}$ b. 6 c. $\frac{5}{6}$ d. $\frac{2}{3}$ e. 2
10.a. ₹5,300
11. Black 1000, White 800
12. $\frac{2}{3}$ litres 13. $7\frac{1}{12}$ kg

14. $\frac{1}{4}$ kg, 25 kg 15. 150 m

Practice Exercise 3.1

1.a. $\frac{15}{1}$ b. $\frac{27}{10}$ c. $-\frac{18}{1}$ d. $\frac{67}{100}$ e. $\frac{0}{1}$

2. Positive rational numbers b, c, e, g, h
Negative rational numbers a, d, f, i, j

3.a. $\frac{4}{5}$ b. $-\frac{1}{3}$ c. $-\frac{1}{5}$ d. $\frac{1}{11}$ e. $\frac{1}{2}$

4. Write three equivalent rational numbers for each part.

5. Draw a number line and mark the rational numbers on it

6.a. $\frac{7}{8}$ b. $-\frac{1}{7}$ c. $\frac{9}{17}$ d. $-\frac{12}{25}$ e. $\frac{12}{13}$

7.a. $-\frac{3}{4}, -\frac{1}{5}, \frac{1}{2}$ b. $-\frac{1}{4}, -\frac{11}{55}, \frac{2}{7}$ c. $-\frac{2}{7}, -\frac{3}{21}, \frac{0}{5}, \frac{1}{3}$ d. $-\frac{1}{3}, -\frac{2}{9}, \frac{4}{9}$ e. $-\frac{6}{7}, \frac{3}{14}, \frac{1}{3}$

8.a. $-\frac{1}{4}, -\frac{3}{8}, -\frac{7}{12}$ b. $\frac{11}{12}, -\frac{3}{4}, -\frac{7}{6}$ c. $\frac{0}{8}, \frac{6}{-16}, -\frac{3}{4}$ d. $\frac{2}{7}, -\frac{8}{21}, -\frac{3}{7}$ e. $\frac{11}{13}, -\frac{1}{3}, -\frac{10}{13}$
9. Find any four rational numbers for each part.
10. Find any ten rational numbers for each part.

Practice Exercise 3.2

1.a. $\frac{5}{8}$ b. $\left(-\frac{4}{7}\right)$ c. $\frac{3}{11}$ d. $\frac{2}{10}$ e. $\left(-\frac{6}{5}\right)$

2.a. $\frac{2}{21}$ b. $\left(-\frac{9}{5}\right)$ c. $\left(-\frac{5}{12}\right)$ d. $\frac{7}{6}$ e. $\frac{47}{60}$

3.a. $\frac{7}{9}$ b. $\left(-\frac{6}{11}\right)$ c. $\left(-\frac{7}{15}\right)$ d. $\frac{21}{100}$ e. $\frac{17}{35}$

4.a. $\left(-\frac{11}{16}\right)$ b. $\left(-\frac{13}{14}\right)$ c. $\frac{21}{19}$ d. $\frac{3}{8}$ e. $\left(-\frac{38}{23}\right)$

5.a. $\frac{37}{30}$ b. $\frac{53}{39}$ c. $\left(-\frac{27}{22}\right)$ d. $\left(-\frac{5}{48}\right)$ e. $\left(-\frac{37}{24}\right)$

6.a. $\frac{9}{7}$ b. $\frac{17}{30}$ c. $\frac{25}{24}$ d. $\left(-\frac{37}{24}\right)$ e. $\frac{7}{3}$

7. $\frac{112}{95}$ 8. $\frac{1}{12}$ 9. $\frac{17}{16}$

10. The sum of $-\frac{3}{10}$ and $\frac{7}{9}$, $\frac{41}{180}$

Practice Exercise 3.3

1.a. $\frac{21}{5}$ b. $\left(-\frac{1}{5}\right)$ c. $\left(-\frac{27}{88}\right)$ d. $\frac{25}{3}$ e. $\frac{10}{3}$

2.a. $\left(-\frac{5}{3}\right)$ b. $\left(-\frac{9}{7}\right)$ c. $\frac{35}{10}$ d. $\frac{27}{15}$ e. $\left(-\frac{19}{17}\right)$

Answers

3.a. $\left(-\frac{18}{5}\right)$ b. $\frac{11}{9}$ c. $\frac{6}{65}$ d. $\left(-\frac{5}{2}\right)$ e. $\frac{65}{2}$
4.a. 3.125 b. (−7.8125) c. (−12.96) d. (−8.328) e. 17.85
5.a. $\frac{14}{3}$ 6. $\left(-\frac{91}{86}\right)$ 7. $\left(-\frac{5}{6}\right)$ 8. $\left(-\frac{6}{595}\right)$
9. (−6) 10.a. $\left(-\frac{5}{36}\right)$ b. $\left(-\frac{8}{6}\right)$ c. $\frac{247}{105}$
d. $\left(-\frac{5}{8}\right)$ e. $\left(-\frac{263}{35}\right)$

HOTS

1. x = (−9) 2. 67.4208 3. $\left(-\frac{1}{8}\right)$ and $\frac{15}{24}, \frac{57}{35}$

Practice Exercise 4.1

1.a. Base 10, Exponent 7 b. a. Base 9, Exponent 4 c. a. Base (−13), Exponent 5 d. Base 8, Exponent 3 e. Base 2, Exponent 10
2.a. 7^5 b. $6^3 \times 5^2$ c. 10^4 d. $4^3 \times 11^2$ e. $(-2)^6$
3.a. 128 b. (−243) c. 625 d. 16,000 e. 10,816
4.a. 2^9 b. 3^6 c. 2^{10} d. 5^6 e. 3^4
5.a. $3^3 \times 5^2$, 675 b. $2^5 \times 7^2$, 1,568
c. $10^4 \times 9^2$, 8,10,000 d. $(-7)^4 \times 6^2$, 86,436
e. $(-4)^3 \times (-3)^3$, 1,728
6.a. 1 b. −1 c. 1 d. −1 e. 1
7.a. $2^4 \times 5^2$ b. $2^4 \times 5^3$ c. $2^6 \times 3^4$ d. 3^8
e. $5^4 \times 3^4$
8.a. Base m, Power 3 b. Base x, Power 10 c. Base p, Power q d. Base (−r), Power 5 e. Base y, Power z
9.a. p^5 b. t^7 c. $m^3 \times n^2$ d. $(-a)^5$ e. $y^3 \times (-z)^4$
10. a. 225 b. 1,000 c. (−54) d. 360 e. 18,000

Practice Exercise 4.2

1.a. 18^{17} b. 15^7 c. 19^6 d. $(-7)^{11}$ e. 4^9
2.a. 17^3 b. $(-10)^5$ c. 4^5 d. $(-13)^4$ e. 8^{m-n}
3.a. 12^2 b. 15^8 c. 9^{10} d. $(-3)^9$ e. 6^0
4.a. 1 b. 3 c. 26 d. 15 e. 91
5. Any 5 different bases
6.a. $(3^2 \times 4^2)$, 16 b. $2^5 \times 3^5$, 4,651 c. $2^{10} \times 2^0$, 924
7.a. 5^{24} b. $(-8)^{12}$ c. 11^{28} d. 9^0 e. 7^0
8.a. 2^{20} b. $(-9)^7g^7$ c. 3^9 d. 11^4f^4 e. $2^0 \times 3^0$
9.a. 14 b. 3^{11} c. 4^{12} d. 5 e. $\frac{3^7}{2^{21}}$
10. They are equal.

Practice Exercise 4.3

1.a. $3 \times 10^5 + 7 \times 10^4 + 0 \times 10^3 + 2 \times 10^2 + 9 \times 10^1 + 5 \times 10^0$
b. $3 \times 10^6 + 6 \times 10^5 + 0 \times 10^4 + 0 \times 10^3 + 2 \times 10^2 + 8 \times 10^1 + 5 \times 10^0$
c. $2 \times 10^6 + 3 \times 10^5 + 8 \times 10^4 + 9 \times 10^3 + 0 \times 10^2 + 6 \times 10^1 + 0 \times 10^0$
d. $7 \times 10^6 + 0 \times 10^5 + 7 \times 10^4 + 8 \times 10^3 + 2 \times 10^2 + 8 \times 10^1 + 2 \times 10^0$
e. $5 \times 10^7 + 4 \times 10^6 + 9 \times 10^5 + 3 \times 10^4 + 6 \times 10^3 + 0 \times 10^2 + 0 \times 10^1 + 7 \times 10^0$
2.a. 75,34,892 b. 9,75,31,864 c. 8,64,02,135
3.a. 7.82×10^{13} b. 6.3×10^{12}
c. 4.875×10^{12}
4.a. 1.496×10^8 b. 2.873×10^6
c. 9.837×10^7
5.a. 24 b. 72 c. 1

HOTS

1. $\frac{1}{81}$ 2. c and e 3. 4

Rewind (Chapters 3–4)

1. Write any three rational numbers for all the parts.
2.a. $\frac{3}{10}, \frac{7}{15}, \frac{4}{5}$ b. $-\frac{5}{2}, \frac{9}{8}, \frac{7}{4}$ c. $-\frac{5}{6}, \frac{2}{3}, \frac{7}{8}, \frac{11}{12}$
d. $-\frac{5}{6}, -\frac{3}{4}, -\frac{2}{3}$ e. $-\frac{8}{3}, -\frac{3}{4}, -\frac{8}{15}, -\frac{7}{15}, -\frac{3}{10}$
3.a. $\frac{9}{10}$ b. $\frac{1}{3}$ c. $-\frac{13}{28}$ d. $-\frac{25}{12}$ e. $-\frac{185}{132}$
4. $\frac{30}{308}$ 5. $\frac{16}{9}$ 6.a. $-\frac{79}{30}$ b. $\frac{151}{576}$
c. $\frac{89}{280}$ d. $-\frac{1}{8}$ e. $\frac{1042}{90}$ 7. $-\frac{43}{280}$ 8. $\frac{4}{3}$
9.a. 6.952 b. 0.0150 c. 2.32 d. 0.5355 e. 114.3
10. 236.190 kg. 11.a. 432 b. 3136 c. 3888
12.a. 289 b. 1 c. $\frac{25}{196}$ d. 625 e. $\frac{169}{289}$
13.a. $\left(\frac{3}{4}\right)^{16}$ b. $\left(\frac{2}{11}\right)^{25}$ c. $\left(\frac{1}{3}\right)^{10}$
d. $\left(-\frac{3}{5}\right)^{42}$ e. $\left(\frac{2}{3}\right)^{20}$
14.a. 6 b. 6 c. 6 d. 2 e. 3
15.a. 2^9 b. $\left(\frac{10}{6}\right)^3$ c. $\left(\frac{1}{3}\right)^6$ d. $(-9)^3$ e. $\left(-\frac{3}{5}\right)^5$

Test Yourself: Unit 1

1. a. 10 b. (−8) c. 22 d. (−40) e. 51
2. a. (−90) b. (−90) c. 99 d. (−400) e. 225
3. a. (−125) b. (−100) c. (−1) d. 1 e. 7891
4. a. (−4) b. (−50) c. 9 d. 19 e. −200

5. a. T b. F c. T d. F e. T
6. The sum of $3\frac{2}{3}$ and $3\frac{1}{2}$, by $\frac{7}{15}$
7. blue: 315, red: 420, green: 315
8. 53 9. Vibha, by 0.32 kg 10. ₹160.88
11. 36.75 kg, 735 kg 12. 13. $\frac{9}{16}$
14. a. $-\frac{3}{8}$ b. 2 c. $-\frac{1}{3}$ d. $-\frac{27}{41}$ e. $\frac{2}{9}$
15. $-1, 0, 1, 2, \frac{5}{2}$
16. a. $2^6 \times 5^2$ b. $3^4 \times 7^2$ c. 3^8 d. $3^3 \times 2^2 \times 5^2$ e. $2^3 \times 11^3$
17. a. 19^7 b. 18^4 c. 13^6 d. 4^5 e. 9^4
18. a. 5^{21} b. 7^8 c. $-10^3 \times 6^{15}$ d. n^{24} e. $(-d^{455})$
19. a. $4 \times 10^5 + 3 \times 10^4 + 2 \times 10^3 + 7 \times 10^2 + 8 \times 10^1 + 3 \times 10^0$
b. $1 \times 10^6 + 8 \times 10^5 + 6 \times 10^4 + 9 \times 10^3 + 5 \times 10^2 + 9 \times 10^1 + 3 \times 10^0$
c. $4 \times 10^6 + 3 \times 10^5 + 5 \times 10^4 + 9 \times 10^3 + 7 \times 10^2 + 6 \times 10^1$
d. $7 \times 10^8 + 6 \times 10^5 + 8 \times 10^3 + 9 \times 10^2 + 4 \times 10^1$
e. $5 \times 10^7 + 4 \times 10^6 + 9 \times 10^5 + 3 \times 10^4 + 6 \times 10^3 + 5 \times 10^0$
20. a. $\frac{3^4 \times 1}{2^4 \times 5^2}$ b. $\frac{2^5 \times 3^2}{3^4 \times 7^3}$ c. $\frac{-(3^2)}{2^2 \times 4^2}$
d. $\left(-\frac{2 \times 7^2}{5^3}\right)$ e. $\frac{23}{25}$

Practice Exercise 5.1

1.a. $11 \times x \times y \times z$ b. $9 \times x \times x \times y$ c. $-10 \times x \times y \times y$ d. $-15 \times y \times z \times z$ e. $20 \times a \times b \times c$ f. $14 \times a \times a \times a \times b \times b \times b$ g. $-7 \times p \times q \times r$ h. $-p \times p \times q \times q$ i. $42 \times a \times x \times p \times m$ j. $-l \times m \times n$
2.a. Monomial b. Trinomial c. Binomial d. Trinomial e. Binomial f. Monomial g. Binomial h. Trinomial i. Monomial j. Monomial
3.a. 4 b. (−10) c. 20 d. (−100) e. (−64) f. (−9) g. 0 h. (−1) i. 0 j. (−10)
4.a. $(-2x^{2)}$ b. xy c. $(-21x^{3)}$ d. $5y^3$ e. (−1) f. (−10) g. $(-25x^2y^{2)}$ h. 7 i. a j. (−1)
5.a. 3ab, 7ab $15ab^2$, $9ab^2$ b. $2ab^2$, $3b^2a$ a^2b, $7a^2b$ c. pqr^2, qr^2p r^2pq d. $-xy$, 10xy, 25xy xy^2, $-3xy^2$ e. 10xyz, 15xyz $25x^2yz$, $-10zx^2y$ f. pqr^2, $10pqr^2$ $-pqr$, 7pqr g. ab, ba bc, −3bc abc, −2abc h. xyz, −3xyz x^2y^2z, $12x^2y^2z$ i. a^3, $-7a^3$ b^3a, $14ab^3$ ab, 10ba j. 81c, −9c, c 81d, 9d, d
6.a. $3ab - 2c + 7b$ b. $x - 2y + z$ c. $x^2 - y^2 + z^2 - 3xyz$ d. $ab + bc + ca - a^2 - b^2 - c^2$
e. $-x^2 + y^2 - 2xy$ f. $40 + x^2 - y^2$ g. $100 - p^2$ h. $m^2 - m - 10$ i. $2x - y^2 + xy$ j. $a^3 - b^3 - 3a^2b + 3ab^2$
7.a. 0 b. 14 c. 15 d. 8 e. 1
8.a. 1 b. 27 c. 2 d. 38 e. 19
9.a. (−3) b. 3 c. 2 d. (−18) e. (−9)
10.a. $-15x^2y^2 + xy^2 + xy + 10$ b. $5a^3b^2 + 15a^3 - 2b^2$ c. $30a^2b^2 - 10ab + 21a$ d. $-64x^3y^3 + 16x^3$ e. $25x^2y$

Practice Exercise 5.2

1.a. $9p + 3q$ b. 13ab c. 2pq d. $3x + 2y + z$ e. $-2ab^2$ f. $6xy^2 + 3x^2y$ g. $-5a - 3b - c$ h. $6ab + 8bc + ac$ i. $x + y + z - xy - yz - zx$ j. $4m^2 + 6n^2$
2.a. 9c b. $9x^2 + 6x$ c. $3x^2 + 3y^2 + 8$ d. $-3p^2 + q^2 - 3r^2 - pqr$ e. $4x + 2y + 6z$ f. $18x^3 - 7x^2 - 7x$ g. $2x^3 - 5x^2 - 6x + 1$ h. $-2ab + 2bc + 4ca$ i. $18a^2b + ab$ j. $6m^3 - 6m^2 - 9m$
3.a. $15 - 6x$ b. $13x - 17x^2 - 21$ c. $2x^3 + 5x^2 + 7$ d. $-7xz - 4xy - 11yz$ e. $z^3 + 4x^3 - 2xyz$ f. $-2a + 4b + 4c - 1$ g. $7r - 11pq$ h. $5m^3 - 7mn + 15$ i. 4ab j. $x^2 - 2y^2 + 6xy$
4. $-5x + 6y - 12z$ 5. $-8x^2 + 8xy$
6. $6x - 2y + z$ 7. $3p^3 + 6q^2$ 8. $8x^2 - 9x - 3$
9. $6m^3 - 3m^2 + 2m$ 10. $2x^3 + 2x^2 - 2x + 3$

HOTS

1. $x^2 - 2x + 3$ 2. $7 + 14a + 2a^2$ 3. $4x - 4y$

Practice Exercise 6.1

1.a. $x + 15 = 35$ b. $9x = 54$ c. $\frac{x}{2} = 19$
d. $3x + 17 = 62$ e. $x - 25 = 50$
f. $10x + 11 = 121$ g. $\frac{x}{5} + 29 = 39$
h. $7x - 15 = 48$
i. $\frac{1}{2}(x-20) = 40$ j. $2x - 10 = 88$
2.a. F b. F c. F d. F e. T f. T g. F h. F i. T j. F
3.a. 8 b. 4 c. $\frac{7}{2}$ d. 6 e. 2
4.a. 4 b. (−18) c. 3 d. 2 e. 5
5.a. 15 b. 18 c. 27 d. 2 e. 5
6.a. 6 b. 20 c. 15 d. 3 e. 17
7.a. (−1) b. 9 c. 7 d. (−1) e. (−1)
8.a. $\frac{8}{45}$ b. 48 c. 30 d. 3 e. 10

Answers

9.a. 3 b. $\frac{11}{8}$ c. 10 d. 5 e. $\frac{19}{5}$
10.a. 6 b. 1 c. 9 d. $-\frac{6}{5}$ e. 5

Practice Exercise 6.2

1.a. 56 b. 160 c. 44, 46, 48 d. 56, 57, 58, 59
e. b = 33, l = 38 f. 18, 27, 27 g. 4, 60 h. 3, 33
i. ₹2 coins are 50, ₹5 coins are100
j. ₹24,000, 8,000 k. $\frac{3}{7}$ l. $\frac{22}{27}$ m. 16
n. 93 o. ₹4,00,000 p. 400 km, 240 km q. 55, 33
r. 200 s. ₹190, ₹340 t. 8

HOTS

1. 24 2. 84 3. 12, 36

Rewind Chapters 5–6

1.a. 0 b. 8 c. 12 d. 1 e. 21
2.a. $9x - 10y + 4$ b. $-x^2 + x + 9$
c. $11a + 4b - 19c + 1$ d. $2x^3 - 5x^2 - 6x + 1$
e. $-3p^2 + q^2 - 3r^2 - pqr$
3.a. $2x - 2y$ b. $-7xz - 4xy - 11yz$
c. $-7x^3 + 17xy - 7y^2$ d. $-2a + 4b + 4c - 1$
e. $5\,m^3 - 7\,mn + 7$
4. $6x - 4y + 3z$ 5. $5xyz^2 + 3cd + 2c$
6. 3 7. 9 8. 15 9. $\frac{7}{9}$ 10. $\frac{32}{3}$
11. 16, 48 12. 15 yrs, 40 yrs 13. 81 cm, 54 cm
14. 35 15. 50°, 60°, 70°

Practice Exercise 7.1

1.a. 3 : 20 b. 3: 8 c. 5: 3 d. 2: 1 e. 3: 4
2.a. 210, 240 3. 320, 240
4.a. 6 b. 17·5 c. 28
5.a. 81 b. 48 c. 28 6.a. 12 b. 0.06 c. 42
7. ₹624 8. 1500 9. 4 hrs 10 minutes 10. 12 days.

Practice Exercise 7.2

1.a. ₹10,625 b. 27 c. 42 days d. 105 men
e. 12 kg f. 20 sheets g. 10 h. 3 hrs

Practice Exercise 7.3

1.a. 20% b. 24% c. 65% d. 775% e. $43\frac{1}{5}$%
2.a. $\frac{27}{100}$ b. $\frac{7}{20}$ c. $\frac{43}{100}$ d. $\frac{13}{25}$ e. $\frac{61}{100}$
3.a. 0·28 b. 0·35 c. 0·12 d. 0·075 e. 0·005
4.a. 62·5% b. 2·5% c. 375% d. 0.8% e. 150%
5.a. ₹72 b. 360 hrs c. 40 km d. 97·5 kg e. 600
6.a. 2000 b. 6000 c. 500 d. 3000 e. 2700
7.a. $65\frac{5}{13}$% : $34\frac{8}{13}$% b. 45% : 55%
c. 52% : 48% d. 70% : 30% e. $58\frac{1}{3}$% : $41\frac{2}{3}$%
8. Rent ₹5,000; Transport ₹7,500; grocery ₹25,000; news paper and magazine ₹2,500; bills ₹4,000; entertainment ₹6,000.
9. 30%, 50%, 20%, 3,000, 5,000, 2,000
10. 30 gm, 100 g, 120 g

HOTS

1. 15:10:6 2. 35 years, 25 years 3. 3

Practice Exercise 8.1

1.a. 5% b. 10% c. 10% d. $13\frac{1}{3}$% e. $112\frac{1}{2}$%
2.a. 10% b. $37\frac{1}{2}$% c. 20% d. 15% e. 25%
3. Mr. A, ₹156 4. ₹800 5. ₹3,750, 34%
6. 13% 7. 9,000 8. 378 9. $16\frac{2}{3}$%
10. 220 days, 11 days

Practice Exercise 8.2

1.a. Profit 20% b. Loss 0.6% c. Profit 25%
d. Loss 5% e. No loss or gain
2.a. SP = ₹1,007 b. ₹11,200 c. ₹722
d. ₹4,104 e. ₹690
3.a. CP = ₹840 b. ₹1,560 c. ₹925
d. ₹1,700 e. ₹12,800
4. Profit 12% 5. ₹27,000 6. ₹9000
7. S.P. of Anubhav ₹22,500, S.P. of Sambhav ₹27,500
8. Loss of 2% 9. ₹5 10. $16\frac{2}{3}$% Profit

Practice Exercise 8.3

1.a. ₹975 b. ₹2,250 c. ₹72
d. ₹315 e. ₹40, 000
2.a. 9% b. 11% c. $7\frac{1}{2}$%
d. 8% e. 9%
3.a. 1 year 4 months b. $2\frac{1}{2}$ years c. 4 years
d. 2 years e. 2 years
4.a. P = ₹3,000, A = ₹3,720
b. P = ₹7,500, A = ₹11,100
c. P = ₹2,765, A = ₹3594.50
d. P = ₹2,500, A = ₹2,875
e. P = ₹4,500, A = ₹4,590
5. Rita; ₹324 more 6. Raghavi 7. ₹7,00,000
8. ₹3656.25; ₹11,156.25 9. ₹1,15,000 10. ₹8,500

HOTS

1. 0 2. $2\frac{1}{2}\%$ 3. 450 4. 8% 5. $16\frac{2}{3}\%$

Rewind Chapter 7–8

1.a. 320:9 b. 11:5 c. 100:9
d. 4:1 e. 10:3
2. ₹24, ₹36, ₹48
3.a. 9:10 b. 1:10 c. 9:1
4. 560 m 5.a. 4 b. 28 c. 3
6.a. $\frac{9}{25}$ b. $\frac{81}{100}$ c. $\frac{19}{20}$
d. $\frac{7}{25}$ e. $\frac{11}{25}$
7. 52% 8. $6\frac{2}{3}\%$ 9. 19%
10. 12% 11. ₹16,000 12. ₹1987.90
13. 6% 14. Profit % is $15\frac{5}{9}\%$
15. ₹1,440

Test Yourself: Unit II

1. a. Monomial b. binomial c. trinomial
d. binomial e. monomial
2. a. $-15p^2q^2 + p^2q + pq + 10$
b. $4a^3b^3 + 16a^3 - 3b^2$
c. $9x^2y^2 + 10xy + 18x$ b. $-13x^2y^3 + 15x^3$
e. $45a^2b$
3. a. $9x^2 + 6x$ b. $3x^3 + 3y^3 - 12$
c. $13p^2q - 3pq - 8$ d. $9a^2 + 3b^2 - 20$
e. $20p + 14p^2 - 6$
4. $6p^3 - 3p^2 + 2p$ 5. $3x^3 + 6y^2$
6. a. 11 b. 1 c. 10
7. 47, 49, 51 8. 126 ₹2 coins, 63 ₹1 coins
9. 63, 64, 65, 66, 67 10. $\frac{5}{9}$ 11. a, b, d
12. a. 90% b. 140% c. $\frac{39}{50}$ d. 0.45 e. 0%
13. a. ₹300 b. 45 c. 100 d. 270 e. 340
14. Raunaq
15. 25% yellow, 33.33% red, 41.67% white
16. a. 3,240 b. 40,590 c. 8,775 d. 7.2 kg
e. 4 hrs 30 minutes
17. ₹39,900 18. ₹15,000, ₹16,500
19. 10 years 20. ₹5,000

Practice Exercise 9.1

1.a. 28° b. 18° c. 42°
d. 46° e. 32° f. 37°
g. 15° h. 78° i. 69°
j. 84°
2.a. 89° b. 160° c. 134°
d. 65° e. 118° f. 80°
g. 48° h. 162° i. 103°
j. 45°
3.a. F b. F c. F
d. T e. T f. F
g. T h. T i. T
j. F
4.a. 36° b. 80° c. 90°
5.a ∠AOB, ∠BOC; ∠BOC, ∠COD; ∠COD, ∠DOE
b. i. adjacent: ∠SPM, ∠SPN; ∠SPN, ∠NPR; ∠NPR, ∠RPM; ∠RPM, ∠MRS
ii. vertically opposite: ∠SPN, ∠MPR; ∠MPS, ∠NPR;
iii. linear pair: ∠MPS, ∠SPN; ∠SPN, ∠NPR; ∠NPR, ∠RPM; ∠MPS
6. ∠WOZ = 40°, ∠YOW = 140°, ∠ZOX = 140°
7.a. 145° b. 20° c. 105°
8.a. 65° b. 50° c. 45°
9. x = 34°, ∠AOC = 82°, ∠BOC = 98°
10.a. x = 30°, y = 150° b. x = 120°, y = 145°
c. x = 30°, y = 40°

Practice Exercise 9.2

1.a. n b. r
c. No transversal d. c e. t
2. To number and then names the angles
3.a. ∠APQ and ∠DQP; ∠BPQ and ∠PQC
b. ∠APE and ∠DQF; ∠BPE and ∠CQF
c. ∠APQ and ∠CQP; ∠BPQ and ∠DQP
4. ∠1 = 70°, ∠3 = 70°, ∠4 = 110°, ∠8 = 110°
5. x = 36°, 72°, 108°, 72°, 108°, 72°, 108°, 72°, 108°
6. x = 150°, y = 125°
7.a. parallel b. not parallel c. parallel
d. parallel e. not parallel
8.a. 70° b. 30° c. 39°
9. 130° 10.a. x = 95°, y = 95°, b. x = 85°, y = 95°

HOTS

1. Vertically opposite angles, interior alternate angles, corresponding angles are equal. Co-interior angles are supplementary.
2. x = 150° 3. 119°

Practice Exercise 10.1

1.a. 70° b. 50° c. 20°
d. 85° e. 53° f. 110°
g. 40° h. 77° i. 120° j. 70°

Answers

2. a, b, c, f, h
3. 55° 4. x = 85°, y = 60°, z = 35°
5. x = 120°, y = 60°, z = 70°
6. x = 20°, y = 70°, z = 50° 7. 75°
8.a. Yes b. Yes c. No
d. Yes e. Yes

Practice Exercise 10.2

1.a. ∠BCD, ∠CBE b. ∠PRS, ∠QRT
c. ∠QNL, ∠NMP d. ∠UYZ, ∠VZY
e. ∠CBD
2.a. 110° b. 50° c. 50° d. 120° e. 45
3. ∠1 = 30°, ∠2 = 30°, ∠3 = 60°, ∠4 = 90°
4. Base angles are 80° each, ∠A = 20°, ∠BCD = 100°
5. ∠ACB = 120° ∠AED = 90°
6. ∠PRS= 80°, ∠PSR = 60°, ∠SPM = 90°
7. ∠XYZ = 130°, ∠XZY = 30°, ∠YXZ = 20°
8. ∠QPR = 90°, ∠PQR = ∠PRQ = 45°,
∠TQP = 135°, ∠PRS = 135°, ∠QPU = 90°
9.a. x = 70°, y = 50° b. x = 65°, y = 115°
c. x = 50°, y = 90° d. x = 30°, y = 70°
e. x = 75°, y = 105°
10.a. Yes b. Yes c. No d. Yes e. No
f. No g. Yes h. No i. Yes j. Yes

Practice Exercise 10.3

1.a. 10 cm b. 5 cm c. 13 cm
2.a. Right triangle b. Right triangle c. Right triangle
f. Right triangle g. Right triangle j. Right triangle
3.a. 9 b. 6 c. 25
4.a. 13 cm b. 17 cm c. 29 cm
5. 12 cm 6. 34 m 7. 25 km
8. 39 m 9. 23 m 10. 25 m

HOTS

2. Isoceles right triangle.

Rewind (Chapters 9–10)

1.a. F b. F c. F d. T e. F
2.a. 85°, 95° b. 20°, 70°
3.a. 36° b. 80° 4. x = 85°, y = 40°, z = 55°
5. a = 60°, b = 60°, c = 60°, d = 60°
6. y = 95° 7. x = 50°, y = 60° 8. x = 20°,
y = 70°, z = 50° 9. x = 95° y = 60°, z = 25°
10.a. hypotenuse b. $26^2 = 24^2 + 10^2$
c. $c^2 = a^2 + b^2$ 11. 40 m 12. 8 cm 13. 34 m
15. 45°, 65°, 70°

Practice Exercise 11.1

3. a and e are congruent; they have the same radii
5. ∠BOD 6. a and d; c and e; i and j; g and h
8.a. radius b. squares c. their length is the same
d. measure of the angle is the same
e. length and breadth

Practice Exercise 11.2

1.a. LM = XY, MN = YZ, LN = XZ, ∠L = ∠X,
∠M = ∠Y, ∠N = ∠Z
b. PQ = DE, QR = EF, PR = DF, ∠P = ∠D,
∠Q = ∠E, ∠R = ∠F
C. GH = MN, HI = NO, GI = MO, ∠G = ∠M,
∠H = ∠N, ∠L = ∠O,
3. △ADC ≅ △ABC, SAS condition

Practice Exercise 11.3

1. Yes. SAS. BC = YZ, ∠B = ∠Y, ∠C = ∠Z
2. ∠MOR = ∠NOS, ∠RMO = ∠SNO,
∠MRO = ∠NSO

Chapter 12

Constructions

Rewind (Chapter 11–12)

1.a. △ABC ≅ △ADC, b. △PQR ≅ △PSR
c. △XYZ ≅ △CVW 5. ASA

Test Yourself: Unit III

1. a. complementary b. supplementary
c. supplementary d. complementary
e. none
2. a. 85° b. 62° c. 135°
3. x = 125°, y = 35°, z = 145°
4. x = 85°, y = 95°, z = 35°
5. a. 65° b. 30° c. 36°
6. a. 80°, acute b. 50°, acute c. 20°, acute
d. 76°, acute e. 53°, acute 7. 40°, 50°, 90°
8. a. y = 60° b. y = 30°, 4y = 120°
c. y = 18°, 2y = 36°, 3y = 54°
9. a. 120° b. 95° c. 56.5° 10. 7 m
11. SSS, ∠RSQ
12. AC = XZ, CB = ZY, AB = XY, ∠ABC =
∠XYZ, ∠BCA = ∠YZX, ∠CAB = ∠Z
13. Isosceles 14. ∠M, ∠P, PM

Answers

Practice Exercise 13.1

5.a. F b. F c. F d. T e. T

Practice Exercise 13.2

2.a. (iii) b. (v) c. (ii) d. (i) e. (iv)

Practice Exercise 13.3

Figure	a	b	c	d	e	f	g	h	i	j
Axes of Sym.	1	0	2	2	1	4	2	0	1	6
Rotational Sym.	1	0	2	2	1	4	2	0	1	6

HOTS

2.i. 3 ii. 4

Practice Exercise 14.2

1.a. Cuboid b. Cylinder c. Sphere d. Cone
e. Cylinder f. Cylinder g. Cuboid
h. Cuboid/cube i. Cube j. Cuboid
2.a. 25 b. 8 3. 400

Rewind (Chapter 13–14)

3.a. F b. F c. T d. T e. T
4.a. 1 b. 2 c. 4 d. 2 e. 6 f. 5
6.a. (i) Reflection (ii) Rotation (iii) Reflection
b. (i) Rotation (ii) Reflection (iii) Rotation
c. (i) Reflection (ii) Rotation (iii) Rotation
7.

Solid Shapes	Cube	Cuboid	Cylinder	Cone	Triangular Prism
No. of faces	6	6	3	2	5
No. of edges	12	12	2	1	9
No of vertices	8	8	–	1	6

Practice Exercise 15.1

1. Square will have a greater area. Perimeter of the square is greater
2. 29.5 cm, 870.25 sq cm 3. 24 cm; area of rectangle, 396 cm^2 4. 1248 m, ₹70,790
5. 90,000 tiles, ₹27,00,000 6. ₹27,300
7. a. 63 m^2 b.1525 m^2 c. 35 m^2
8. 225 m^2, 351 m^2

Practice Exercise 15.2

1.a. 35.2 cm^2 b. 27 cm^2 c. 116.22 cm^2
d. 12,000 cm^2 e. 91 cm^2
2.a. 180 cm^2 b. 39.78 cm^2 c. 64.80 cm^2
d. 10.96 cm^2 e. 117.5994 cm^2
3. 17.4 cm^2 4. 120 cm^2 5. 21 cm
6. ₹341.25 7. 157.92 cm^2 8. 37.2 cm
9. 684 cm^2
10. 500 cm^2

Practice Exercise 15.3

1.a. C = 220 mm A = 3,850 mm^2
b. C = 132 cm A = 1,386 cm^2
c. C = 440 cm A = 15,400 cm^2
d. C = 132 m A = 1,385 m^2
e. C = 4.4 km A = 1.54 km^2
2. r = 7 cm, d = 14 cm, A = 154 cm^2
3. 22 cm 4. 88,000 cm, 880 m, 0.88 km
5. ₹20,790, ₹660
6. 95 discs, 70 cm^2
7. Circular Ring, 33 cm^2 8.a. 42 cm^2 b. 2464 cm^2
c. 100 cm^2 d. 15.5 cm^2

HOTS

1. 108 m^2 2. 1,00,000 3. 384 cm^2
4. 16.5 cm^2

Practice Exercise 16.1

1.a. 42, 56 b. 8, 95.142 c. 150, 309.375
d. 6, 35.778 e. 90, 51.2
2.a. 9 b. 27.5 c. 10 d. 61.5 e. 45
3.a. 8 b. 6 c. 23 d. 8 e. 32 4. ₹28.50
5. 98.6 6. 22 7. 50 8. Red, Mode. 9. 40 cm
10. Mean = 47.5 median = 48, mode = 48

Practice Excerice 16.2

4.a. Monday b. Sunday c. 190 d. Tuesday
e. 10 division = 1 unit = 5A.C.'s
5.a. Rent b. Entertainment c. ₹5,000
d. ₹1,24,000 e. 5:8
6. K, J 8.a. D b. H c. 400
9.a. Mid-term I-66 Mid-term I-68 b. Hindi, Math, English c. Science, Social Science
10.a. X b. 270 c. 250 d. z, Team B e. Team A-Mean 67.5 Team B-Mean 62.5

Answers

Practice Exercise 16.3

1. $\frac{1}{2}$ 2. $\frac{1}{6}$ 3. $\frac{1}{3}$ 4.a. $\frac{1}{4}$ b. $\frac{1}{8}$ c. $\frac{3}{8}$ d. $\frac{1}{4}$
5.a. $\frac{2}{3}$ b. 0 c. $\frac{3}{5}$ d. 1 e. $\frac{4}{7}$ Sure Event d.
Impossible Event b
6. $\frac{1}{5}, \frac{4}{5}$ 7.a. $\frac{1}{13}$ b. $\frac{1}{2}$ c. $\frac{1}{2}$ d. $\frac{1}{52}$ e. $\frac{1}{4}$
8. Devyani $\frac{1}{25}$ Bhairvi $\frac{1}{20}$ Aarti $\frac{1}{50}$,
Shristi $\frac{1}{100}$ 9.a. $\frac{1}{4}$ b. $\frac{1}{2}$ c $\frac{1}{2}$ d. $\frac{1}{2}$ e. $\frac{2}{5}$
10. $\frac{1}{5}, \frac{4}{5}$

HOTS

1.a. $\frac{21}{50}$ b. $\frac{29}{50}$ 2.a. $\frac{29}{100}$ b. $\frac{83}{200}$ c. $\frac{59}{200}$ 3. $\frac{1}{6}$

Rewind (Chapter 15–16)

1. 14 2. 14, 7 3. 336 m^2 4. 15,400 m^2
5. 88 m ₹4,400 6. 4:1 7. 132 m^2, Circle 8. 7 cm
9.a. 26.4 cm b. 52.8 cm c. 6.6 cm 10. 50,000
11. 128 cm^2 12. Mean ₹302, Median ₹300, Mode ₹300 14.a. 1/2 b. 1/6 c. 1/2 d. 0 e. 1
15.a. Raw data b. Array: 140, 142, 144, 144, 145, 146, 146, 146, 147, 147, 147, 147, 148, 148, 148, 149, 149, 149, 149, 150, 150, 150, 150, 150, 150, 151, 151, 151, 151, c. Range 11
d. Frequency Distribution Table

Height	Tally	Frequency
140	𝍷	1
142	𝍷	1
144	𝍷𝍷𝍷	3
145	𝍷	1
146	𝍷	1
147	𝍷𝍷𝍷𝍷	4
148	𝍷𝍷𝍷	3
149	𝍷𝍷𝍷𝍷	4
150	𝍸𝍷	6
151	𝍷𝍷𝍷𝍷	4

e. Mean 147.63
Median 148
Mode 150

Test Yourself: Unit IV

1. a. Cube b. Sphere c. Square pyramid d. Cylinder e. Cone
2. 3. 20 cm, 400 cm^2 4. ₹13061.25
5. ₹33,450 6. 12 cm 7. 24 cm^2, 4.8 cm
8. 13.608 cm 9. 35.7 cm, 78.5 cm^2
10. 1,085 cm^2 11. 440 cm, ₹88 12. 2,112 cm
13. 22:7:5 (cicle:square:rectangle), 3,850 cm^2 (circle), 1,225 cm^2 (square), 875 cm^2 (rectangle)
14. 88, 89, 98, 99, 100, 105, 106, 108, 110, 111, 112, 115, 116, 118, 121, 123, 125, 125, 132, range = 42 cm
15. a. $\frac{1}{6}$ b. $\frac{1}{3}$ c. $\frac{1}{2}$ d. 0 e. 1
16. a. $\frac{1}{4}$ b. 0 c. $\frac{5}{12}$ d. 0 e. $\frac{1}{3}$
17. 42°C
18. 5.42

Model Sample Test Paper

1.a. 10 b. 1 c. 5 d. 16 e. −36,000
2.a. (−35) b. 187 c. 6 d. 16 e. (−90)
3.a. 234.56 b. 23,456 c. 2345.6 d. 0.23456 e. 0.023456
4.a. 24.897 b. 0.24897 c. 2.4897 d. 8,299 e. 82,990 5. ₹231 kg
6. Any seven rational numbers
7.a. $\frac{71}{84}$ b. $\frac{13}{60}$ c. $\frac{4}{33}$ d. $\frac{5}{16}$ e. $\frac{1}{8}$
8.a. 1 b. (−72) c. 5,184 9.a. 2.47×10^9
b. 3.67942178×10^8 c. 1.23×10^{11}
10.a. (−54) b. 0 c. (−60) 11.a. $14a^2 + 8b^2$
b. $12p^3 + 3p^2 + 4p$ c. $-4x^2 + 4xy + 9y^2$
12.a. 4 b. 3 c. 5 13. 36 14. ₹186
15.a. 3,600 b. 625 c. 1,500 d. 50,000
17.a. ∠QOR, ∠ROS and ∠ROS, ∠SOP
b. ∠POQ c. 35°
18. x = 70°, y = 110°, z = 65°, w = 115°
19. ∠RPQ = 40, ∠RMO = ∠SNO, ∠MRD = ∠NSO
24. Sum of two sides 26. 6 m 27. 360 m^2
28. 15,400 cm^2 30. Mean = 69.25, Median = 70
Mode = 70

Assessment of Mathematical Skills				
	Exceptional	**Good**	**Average**	**Needs Improvement**
Notation and Terminology	Uses appropriate mathematical terminology and notation	Uses near correct mathematical terminology and notation	Partial or scattered usage of mathematical terms and notation	Shows incorrect or no understanding of terms and notations of mathematical concepts
Problem Solving/ Strategising	Is able to efficiently analyse a problem and arrive at an efficient solution	Is able to draw on prior knowledge and arrive at an appropriate solution	Shows some evidence of using concepts learnt resulting in only a partially correct solution	Is unable to apply concepts learnt. Faces difficulties in arriving at a solution.
Methodology, Formulation and Steps	Uses clear effective steps and reasonings to demonstrate the solution	Uses appropriate steps to arrive at the solution	Is able to use steps at times but falters at others	Is unable to identify steps and formulae needed for arriving at the solution, and hence arrives at incorrect solutions.
Calculation and Final Result	Is able to calculate and arrive at the final answer with accuracy and precision	Is able to calculate and arrive at the final answer with a fair level of accuracy	Resists advanced computations and tends to perform incomplete or erroneous calculations	Is prone to calculation errors. Limited understanding of units.

Assessment of Mathematical Skills				
	Exceptional	**Good**	**Average**	**Needs Improvement**
Geometry	Has a clear and visual understanding of the relationship between geometrical figures	Has a fairly good understanding of the relationship between various geometrical figures and is able to visualise concepts with minimum assistance	Is able to understand simple geometrical concepts, but falters while visualising concepts or tackling advanced concepts	Has a high level of difficulty in understanding and recalling geometrical concepts and needs assistance at visualising the solution
Mensuration	Has a clear and visual understanding of mensuration concepts and is able to translate real-world problems to math	Has a good understanding of mensuration concepts and is able to visualise and solve problems with minimum errors	Is able to understand simple mensuration concepts but falters while visualising or solving real-world problems.	Has a high level of difficulty in understanding and visualising 3-D-shapes. Needs assistance in attempting a solution
Algebra	Has a clear understanding of algebraic patterns and formulae and is able to formulate approaches to a problem	Has a good understanding of algebraic patterns and formulae and is able to formulate appropriate solution	Is able to solve simple algebraic problems but has trouble identifying complicated patterns	Has a high level of difficulty in identifying and remembering patterns and needs assistance in attempting a solution